## DATE DUE

| | | | |
|---|---|---|---|
| NO 8 '91 | AP 8 '9 | SE 17 '04 | |
| DE 13 '91 | | MY 9 '06 | |
| JA 29 '93 | | | |
| NO 24 '93 | NV 27 '9 | | |
| | OC 13 '98 | | |
| SE 23 '94 | DE 15 '98 | | |
| FE 17 '95 | | | |
| MY 5 '95 | MR 18 '99 | | |
| MY 10 '96 | AP 7 '99 | | |
| DE 13 '96 | | | |
| MR 27 '9 | MY 6 '99 | | |
| MY 1 '97 | MY 27 '99 | | |
| SE 2 4 '97 | DE 19 '01 | | |
| RENEW | MR 10 '02 | | |
| OC 15 '97 | DE 9 '02 | | |
| | JE 9 '0 | | |
| FE 11 '98 | DE 8 '04 | | |

DEMCO 38-296

# SIGN LANGUAGE RESEARCH

## THEORETICAL ISSUES

**CEIL LUCAS**
EDITOR

Gallaudet University Press
Washington, D.C.

Gallaudet University Press, Washington, DC 20002
© 1990 by Gallaudet University. All rights reserved
Published 1990
Printed in the United States of America

*Library of Congress Cataloging-in-Publication Data*

Sign language research : theoretical issues / Ceil Lucas, editor.
    p.    cm.
    Includes bibliographical references.
    ISBN 0-930323-58-0 :  $49.95
    1. Sign language—Congresses.     I. Lucas, Ceil.
HV2474.S57    1990
419—dc20                                 89-28131
                                                         CIP

# Contents

## Part One: Phonology

## Part Two: Morphology

# *Introduction*

This volume contains twenty-four of the thirty-three papers, including William Stokoe's keynote address, originally presented at the international conference, Theoretical Issues in Sign Language Research, II, sponsored by the Department of Linguistics and Interpreting at Gallaudet University. All presenters were invited to submit their papers for publication. The conference took place May 18–21, 1988, at Gallaudet University's Northwest Campus, and was the second in a series begun in Rochester, New York, in 1986. The conference was attended by 180 researchers representing the United States, Italy, Zambia, Denmark, Thailand, the United Kingdom, Sweden, India, Belgium, Finland, the Netherlands, Japan, Canada, and Uganda. Papers were presented in the areas of phonology, morphology, syntax, sociolinguistics, language acquisition, and psycholinguistics. The papers in this volume are the products of current research on various aspects of sign language structure, and represent the state of the art in sign language research. It was our goal to make the volume available to researchers, university faculty, and other interested parties as soon after the conference as possible, as the papers herein may contribute to current and future research on sign language structure.

In order to achieve some consistency throughout the volume, the following transcription conventions have been adopted: glosses for signs appear in uppercase letters, as do symbols for handshapes; English words appear in italics; phonemic transcriptions are enclosed in back slashes; spoken-language phonetic transcriptions and features of signs are enclosed in brackets; fingerspelling is denoted by the symbol followed by an uppercase gloss; and nonmanual signals appear on a line above sign glosses. Some individual papers adopt special conventions that are explained in the papers in question.

The preparation of this volume proceeded very smoothly and for that I would like to acknowledge Elaine Costello (director), Ivey Pittle (managing editor), Deborah Weiner (production manager), and Nancy Margolis (copyeditor) of Gallaudet University Press, and Bob Johnson and Scott Liddell, my colleagues in the Department of Linguistics and Interpreting at Gallaudet University. I would also like to thank all of the contributors for their exceptional cooperation.

Ceil Lucas
Washington, D.C.
March 1989

# Contributors

Jennifer Ackerman
Centre for Deaf Studies
University of Bristol
Bristol, England

Sung-Ho Ahn
Department of Linguistics
University of Connecticut
Storrs, Connecticut

Diane Brentari
Department of Linguistics
University of Chicago
Chicago, Illinois

Marianne Collins-Ahlgren
University of Wellington
Wellington, New Zealand

Serena Corazza
Istituto di Psicologia del C.N.R.
Rome, Italy

David P. Corina
Salk Institute for Biological Studies
La Jolla, California

Jeffrey Davis
Department of Linguistics
   and Interpreting
Gallaudet University
Washington, D.C.

Mark Ezra
Centre for Deaf Studies
University of Bristol
Bristol, England

Josep M. Fontana
Department of Linguistics
University of Pennsylvania
Philadelphia, Pennsylvania

Giuseppe Gambino
Istituto di Psicologia del C.N.R.
Rome, Italy

Barbara Gerner de Garcia
Applied Psycholinguistics Program
Boston University
Boston, Massachusetts

Enza Giuranna
Istituto di Psicologia del C.N.R.
Rome, Italy

Judy Kegl
Cognitive Science Laboratory
Princeton University
Princeton, New Jersey

Jim Kyle
Centre for Deaf Studies
University of Bristol
Bristol, England

Scott K. Liddell
Department of Linguistics
   and Interpreting
Gallaudet University
Washington, D.C.

Diane Lillo-Martin
Department of Linguistics
University of Connecticut
Storrs, Connecticut

Ceil Lucas
Department of Linguistics
   and Interpreting
Gallaudet University
Washington, D.C.

Barbara Luetke-Stahlman
Department of Educational Psychology
Northern Illinois University
Dekalb, Illinois

Mackenzie Mbewe
Zambia National Association of the Deaf
Lusaka, Zambia

Dana Miller
Department of Linguistics
University of Pennsylvania
Philadelphia, Pennsylvania

Margaret G. Moser
Department of Linguistics
University of Pennsylvania
Philadelphia, Pennsylvania

Anthony Moy
Department of Linguistics
University of California
Berkeley, California

Carol A. Padden
Department of Communication
University of California
San Diego, California

Cynthia Patschke
Preparatory Studies
Gallaudet University
Washington, D.C.

Elena Pizzuto
Istituto di Psicologia del C.N.R.
Rome, Italy

Brenda S. Schick
Boys Town National Institute
   for Communication Disorders in Children
Omaha, Nebraska

Robert Serpell
Department of Psychology
University of Zambia
Lusaka, Zambia

William C. Stokoe
Silver Spring, Maryland

Clayton Valli
Department of Linguistics and Interpreting
Gallaudet University
Washington, D.C.

Lars Wallin
Institute of Linguistics
University of Stockholm
Stockholm, Sweden

Bencie Woll
Centre for Deaf Studies
University of Bristol
Bristol, England

June Zimmer
Department of Linguistics
Georgetown University
Washington, D.C.

# SIGN LANGUAGE RESEARCH

## THEORETICAL ISSUES

# An Historical Perspective on Sign Language Research: A Personal View

William C. Stokoe

It is good to be back together with so many of you at this time and in this place. To the best of my historical knowledge this is only the second sign language research conference to be held on the Gallaudet campus. The only other one I can recall was organized by Robbin Battison back in the early seventies, and it brought together a dozen or so people in the E.M. Gallaudet Memorial Library basement. You see, to get a true historical perspective you must have an omniscient historian, which I am not; and you would need to put absolute trust in the historian's statements. But at meetings like this, presentations are given to elicit questions, objections, and gentle disagreement. I can do no other.

What I propose to do in this paper is first to estimate the number and the size of the major stages in sign language research and then to reflect very briefly on its direction and significance.

To begin with, there was no sign language research in the year 1955. Bernard Tervoort, it is true, began before that to look carefully at the signs of deaf Dutch schoolgirls; but it was only much later that he gave up his (or his superior's) belief that signs serve merely to get children started on "real language"—Dutch or English—and that signs later fade out when the deaf child becomes fully literate and merges smoothly into hearing society.

Thus, when I started learning to make signs and to use them as substitutes for the words that my new students couldn't hear, I found in print little to help. Writers had been compiling sign vocabularies since about 1776, but all of them listed words of French or English followed by descriptions or drawings of signs they alleged would translate those words. Lou Fant, sitting here in the front row, took an interest in the new research and was the first to present signs according to the way they are formed instead of as glosses for a word list.

1

## THE FIRST STAGE

What started me on sign language research in 1955 was a certain mind-set, the kind of thing Ulrich Neisser calls a mental template. In Neisser's view, we all learn new things by fitting them into knowledge we already possess. When I had to begin learning signs I had already made the acquaintance, through books, with the work of Trager and Smith and others of their school.

That school of thought came from a World War II gathering of scientists working in Washington. Coming from several different disciplines, but brought together by the fortunes of war, they were interested in looking at all kinds of systems as complete interconnected wholes. The beginnings of their thinking are not widely known, although Gregory Bateson's *Mind and Nature* explains it long after the fact, but this body of thought constitutes an important step in the evolution of modern science. These scientists greatly stimulated the growth of the ideas that led to very well known developments: cybernetics, computers, space travel, and ecology in its broadest interpretation.

Applying the manual signs deaf people use to this idea, that systems should be studied as systems and not in splendid isolation, made signs look to me like something more than pieces of a code to stand for words. I wondered, might they possibly be integral parts of a system?

What is more, when I met them in 1957, Trager and Smith pointed out that words (which I took to mean signs as well)—where everyone starts when looking at a new language—come somewhere about the middle of the complex system. Words come in the middle, because the system of language as a whole extends from the systematic use of physical material to build words at the one end, to the systematic combinations of words to express thought at the other, the social-cultural end.

Fortunately or unfortunately—depending on where you stand to get the perspective—the Trager and Smith method of dealing with whole systems, their special method that treated language as just one part of the whole system called culture, their strict consideration of language and linguistics as part of cultural anthropology—that whole method got swept aside in the linguistic revolution of 1957. In that year Noam Chomsky said that language as it is performed—the stuff people actually speak or write—is full of error and accident and hardly worth serious attention. Chomsky suggested that the real task of the linguist is finding out about linguistic competence: Why are human beings able to use language at all? From Chomsky's time onward most linguists stopped asking questions about the language people actually use in their interactions with one another and focused instead on trying to find out how every human brain is biologically programmed to "have language." Every normal infant develops in a few years the competence to use an internal, universal, generative grammar, and since Chomsky, linguists have been trying to describe that grammar with more and more precision and to examine language not for what it is and what it does, but for what its outside might tell them about its inside and the inner workings of the human brain.

The first stage of sign language research, which entailed looking at signing as a system and signs as part of that system, lasted about ten years, roughly 1955 to 1965, the year *A Dictionary of American Sign Language* was published. Sign language research at this stage was a small and lonely operation, even at times an uncomfortable one. In 1960, when *Sign Language Structure* and *The Calculus of Structure* were published, the whole Gallaudet faculty in a special meeting denounced my sign language research. They charged me, in effect, with misappropriating funds; I was paid to teach English, they said, not to do research on sign language. They argued that paying attention to sign language could only interfere with the students' proper education. And in this city of Washington, descendants of the founder of the A.G. Bell Association, the National Geographic Society, and other foundations on whose boards they still sit, publicly criticized the National Science Foundation for granting money to me and to Gallaudet College for sign language research and the publication of a dictionary of sign language. They pointed out that Grandfather Bell had shown once and for all that signing retarded the deaf in their struggle to enter the world of the hearing.

I was lonely and reviled at times, but I was not alone. As in any research, the work of many hands and heads was needed. People who helped mightily in the first stage of the research include Leon Auerbach, Tom Berg, Dot Casterline, Allen Crammatte, Carl Croneberg, Jack Gannon, Vilas Johnson, Rex Lowman, Bobby and Don Padden, Bob Panara, Don Peterson, Dick Phillips, T. J. O'Rourke, Roy Stewart, and Eleanor Wetzel. I apologize because I am sure to have left out some names, but many of you will be able to spot what all of these had or have in common.

## TRANSITION AND THE SECOND STAGE

I would locate the next stage of sign language research at about 1971. In the five or six years before that it seemed that the whole thing might die and be forgotten. Uncounted copies of my 1960 monograph, *Sign Language Structure*, and the *Dictionary* published in 1965 grew mold in damp cartons in the basement of Fowler Hall. I kept trying to find out more about the syntax of signing, but by doing so I also kept increasing the resentment of most of my colleagues in the English department—not so much because they didn't want sign language to be explored but because they doubted my claim that systematic knowledge about American Sign Language could help all of us teach English to our students. I kept telling them that we might try teaching English as a second or foreign language to students whose first language was ASL. Of course that meant radically changing our teaching and our thinking. In response to this threat, the second stage of sign language research on the Gallaudet campus began with my complete split from the English department. I devoted full time to the Linguistics Research Laboratory (which had hitherto been a name to put at the top of grant applications so that I could be paid during summer vacations). I was given one low-ceilinged room in an old building, funds for a half-time secretary, and one-quarter released from the teaching time of three assistants (James Woodward, Bob Lombrano, and the late Judy Williams, who were paid from grant funds). As this is a historical perspective, I note for statistically minded historians that sign language research at this stage was costing the college less that $30,000 a year and that the administration was spending more than ten times that amount on cued speech (and $50,000 a year per pupil to run the Model Secondary School for the Deaf, where signing had always to be in English word order).

But I must not too much distort the perspective by focusing on the Gallaudet campus alone. In the five or six years between the first two stages of sign language research, much was happening off campus. In Washington, linguists in the Center for Applied Linguistics (CAL), the Georgetown University School of Language and Linguistics, and the Washington Linguistics Club were hearing from me regularly (or annoyingly) how several aspects of sign language grammar paralleled aspects of the languages they were studying. In Reno, the Gardners were beginning a bold new experiment using sign language. They not only learned more about sign language, but they hired deaf native signers as associates. In San Diego, Ursula Bellugi, impressed, as she has written, with the Gardners' work, was beginning to follow the language development of a deaf child of deaf parents, and using deaf persons as informants. Meanwhile graduate students of linguistics and psychology in the University of California at San Diego studied the parameters of sign language. Farther north in California, Wallace Chafe (who had learned about signers and their culture when Carl Croneberg was his student at Catholic University) was encouraging linguistics graduate students in at Berkeley to go all out with their analyses of ASL grammar.

Although the CAL has headquarters in Washington, it is in fact the center of a national and international network of linguists. Through its good offices, linguists at several major universities became interested in sign languages as unusual examples of the class, languages. Gallaudet and the Center collaborated on a comparative linguistics project funded by the National Institutes of Health. Thomas Sebeok, a center director, proposed an international journal in 1970, and with his help, *Sign Language Studies* first appeared in 1972.

With these and other developments, it is difficult to estimate the size and extent of sign language research in this second stage, the decade of the seventies. In its first two or three years the new journal carried descriptions of sign languages on a Pacific Island, in southern France, and in Denmark, in addition to articles about American Sign Language. National Symposia on Sign Language Research and Teaching and earlier Special Study Institutes organized by T. J. O'Rourke, working through the National Association of the Deaf, stimulated research and its relation to teaching and interpreting immeasurably. And the fever spread: by the end of the decade, an international symposium in Sweden organized by Brita Bergman had brought together practitioners of sign language research from several countries. More nations were heard from at the second International Symposium on Sign Language Research (ISSLR) in 1981 in Bristol. And at the third ISSLR in Rome in 1983, there were almost a score of national delegations, with signed interpretation being provided in ten national sign languages for deaf researchers. But there is no clear count of the numbers of individual researchers actively investigating sign languages.

There is no difficulty, however, in recognizing the intensity and vigor of sign language research in the seventies. To take one measure: the University Microfilm Catalogue lists fifteen Ph.D. dissertations on sign language (or manual communication; the catalog does not distinguish) in the years 1983, 1984, 1985, and 1986, at fourteen major universities. At least one of four dissertations listed in those years for the doctor of education degree breaks new ground in research method.

But this is supposed to be a perspective, not a statistical survey. What impresses me is that in this second stage important new knowledge was being found. Ted Supalla's discussion of the highly visible distinction between noun and verb in ASL is a discovery of the kind that makes every worker in sign language syntax exclaim, "Why didn't I notice that?" Charlotte Baker-Shenk's use of the Ekman and Friesen Facial Action Coding System to describe nonmanual behavior puts knowledge about sign language syntax a long step ahead of the impressionistic notions that usually pass for description. Robbin Battison's dissertation in 1974 (*Lexical Borrowing in ASL*, 1978) seems to have settled the question whether a language without sound can have a phonology; the presenters of papers on ASL phonology today have no need to justify using the term.

## THE THIRD STAGE

I find it convenient to take the interest in sign language phonology as marking the third stage of sign language research. In this stage, linguistics of sign language comes of age; instead of working to "break the code," researchers are engaged in finding the latest way to microanalyze its smaller and smaller fractions. Here we see not pioneering efforts to describe an unknown language but competing theories to describe what is now commonplace. How many parameters of a sign are there, and which of various counts is correct? Do signs have parameters in the strict sense of that term at all? Are signs to be considered the result of rules operating on bundles of simultaneous features contained in HOLD and MOVE segments as described by Scott Liddell and Bob Johnson? Are signs, rather, composed in syllabic form with morae of movement and position, as proposed by David Perlmutter? Is there something called "autosegmentation" going on in tiers, as suggested by Scott Liddell and Bob Johnson, and Wendy Sandler? Are facial expressions and other nonmanual actions part of sign phonology, also described by Scott Liddell and Bob Johnson? More generally, is a sign language like ASL more interesting because of its similarity to spoken languages or because of its differences?

In this uncertainty about final causes, which might seem to be a disadvantage, we have one excellent result of sign language research: some of the knowledge it has gleaned has become part of the intellectual equipment of our time. When increasing numbers of researchers argue about signs, some of the attention that was turned off from signs in 1880 is at least being refocused. The knowledge that sign language can be argued about trickles down to the informed public and changes general intellectual notions of which systems can in truth be called languages and which systems cannot.

But deciding which particular set of rules best defines the phonology of ASL is something to be left to a future stage of sign language research. It is time now to try for a different perspective.

## SIGN LANGUAGE RESEARCH AND LINGUISTIC DETERMINISM

What I see as a scramble to find exactly the right set of universal rules for describing natural languages prompts me to take a more personal perspective. Looking not just at sign language research but at linguistic research generally, I see what looks like a mistake in direction, a tendency to treat grammar as an end in itself, a hermetically sealed set of rules—rigorous as mathematics. Of course more rigorous methods of investigation are fine things in themselves, but language, like any natural system, can never be contained in an abstract, well-ordered set of laws. Trying to find *the* rules of language all laid out in order like a book of propositions may be an absorbing pastime, but when the data to fit the rules have to be made up or selected from a nearly infinite set of data not chosen, the result can miss the target widely.

Copernicus made a beautiful model of the solar system, but he left out too much. Astronomers later found that the planets do not move in perfect circles. Before Copernicus, however, when the earth was though to be the center of the universe, there was no way to discover how things really were. Just so, before there was sign language research, when speech and language, and sometimes even thinking itself, were believed to be inseparable, no one could conceive of signing as language. Such a belief prevented sign language research from happening at all.

We now have had a Copernican revolution in sign language research, but it is important that we do not get hung up on perfect circles—or perfect grammars. If we take our perspective from a point far enough away from the arguments about theories of phonological structure, we may well wonder what difference they will make a hundred years, or fifty years, or thirty years from now. My own historical perspective, based on the position of Trager and Smith, who viewed linguistics as a branch of the science of humanity and human culture, that is, of anthropology, prompts me to reflect that we have no certain evidence either that language is all inside the brain or that language is entirely outside, in the give-and-take of human interaction. Lacking evidence for either extreme theory, we will do well to consider language an effect of combined causes, an evolved system with both physiological and social origins.

I hope it is clear to all of you that I am not putting down sign language linguistics nor linguistics in general. But linguists must keep firmly in mind that no matter how far they go into the fascinating and remote nooks and crannies of linguistic structure, the stuff they work with is the stuff of life of real live human beings. The linguistic and paralinguistic analyses made by Smith and Trager a generation ago have been criticized for being too orderly, too neat to be true, but I never met a scientist with a livelier interest in people and their behavior, individually and socially, than Henry Lee Smith. And knowing so many of you as I do, I know too that your interest in the details of sign language never dims your humane interest in the people who use it.

In a recent issue of *Cognition* (vol. 27, no. 1), Laura Petitto reports on a piece of sign language research that exemplifies this way of proceeding. It makes a neat distinction between gesture and sign language, and leaves the question open whether language is born in us, or comes from interacting with others, or both. The human gesture of pointing to oneself to mean 'me' and pointing at the one addressed to mean 'you' is natural, though not universal. (In some cultures the chin is used for pointing; in others the lips point, etc.) The same pair of inward and outward pointings are also the forms of the pronouns ME and YOUR in American Sign Language. It would seem likely that the deaf child begins using, as all children do, these ''natural'' gestures and then smoothly makes them part of his or her sign language vocabulary and grammar.

In fact, however, as Petitto discovered in a careful longitudinal study, it does not happen that way. The child she observed used the ''self'' and ''other'' pointings at the usual early stage, stopped using them for a time, and then at the age when most children learn pronouns of their spoken language, ''reinvented'' them, but making the kind of mistakes typical of learners. Her study is one clear indication that language and gesture are separate systems; one does not develop smoothly into the other. But whether the child's use of sign pronouns is driven by an internal language-generating device or by interaction with others who are competent in the language, we do not yet know. The likeliest guess is that both forces, internal and external, operate. In any case, we sign language researchers had better not prejudge the matter nor exclude inconvenient data. Language research must look not just at what it is in people's brains that makes language possible but also at what people say to each other and what they believe and expect, what they think about the world and themselves. Data of these kinds must be added to ideas about more and more phonological segments, features, and other constructs to keep sign language research from sterility. Perhaps in the fourth stage it will become clear that language competence and language as it is performed are parts of one system, a system that disappears when parts of it are unhooked from the system and examined separately.

## BRINGING IT UP TO DATE

This view, that equal attention must be given to language, to the people who use it, and to what they use it for and about, has not impressed those who want to find in language a perfect, abstract system. It is a view that recent events have vindicated, however. Consider this: if sign language research in America had been directed solely at the internal structure of ASL, and if a "standard model" grammar of all that linguists know were now in print, very few persons other than linguists would even know it existed. What has happened, however, as everyone in reach of print and electronic media now knows, is that, in passionate defense of their own language and culture, deaf people turned Gallaudet University around. What people fight for is their right to have their culture and their language respected, not the details of that language in the abstract.

The kind of sign language research that makes a real difference is further exemplified by one study of pairs of people, communicating in their preferred mode and language. Because the information passed from one partner to the other in the experiment could be measured precisely, the investigator who designed and conducted the experiment found that pairs of deaf signers communicated as fast and as accurately as pairs of hearing speakers—and that certain deaf pairs even surpassed the hearing control group. In my view it is no coincidence that this research for a doctoral dissertation was done by I. King Jordan, the scholar and teacher who is now the president of Gallaudet University.

## REFERENCES

Baker-Shenk, C. (1983). A microanalysis of the nonmanual components of questions in ASL. Ph.D. diss., University of California, Berkeley.

Bateson, G. (1979). *Mind and nature*. New York: E. P. Dutton.

Battison, R. (1978). *Lexical borrowing in American Sign Language*. Silver Spring, MD: Linstok Press.

Chomsky, N. (1957). *Syntactic structures*. The Hague: Mouton.

Johnson, R., and Liddel, S. K. (1984). Structural diversity in the American Sign Language lexicon. In *Papers from the parasession on lexical semantics*, ed. D. Tosten, V. Mishra, and J. Drogo, 173–86. Chicago: Chicago Linguistic Society.

Liddell, S. K. (1984). THINK and BELIEVE: Sequentiality in American Sign Language signs. *Language* 60:327–99.

———, and Johnson, R. (1985). American Sign Language: The phonological base. Department of Linguistics and Interpreting, Gallaudet University. Unpublished manuscript.

———, and Johnson R. (1986). American Sign Language compound formation processes, lexicalization, and phonological remnants. *Natural Language and Linguistic Theory*. 4:445–514.

Padden, C., and Perlmutter, D. (1987). American Sign Language and the architecture of phonological theory. *Natural Language and Linguistic Theory* 5:335–76.

Perlmutter, D. (1988). A moraic theory of ASL syllable structure. Paper presented at the conference, Theoretical Issues in Sign Language Research, II, 18–21 May, at Gallaudet University, Washington, DC.

Petitto, L. (1987). On the autonomy of language and gesture: Evidence from the acquisition of personal pronouns in ASL. *Cognition* 27:1–52.

Sandler, W. (1986). The spreading hand autosegment of ASL. *Sign Language Studies* 50:1–28.

Stokoe, W. C. (1960). *The calculus of structure*. Washington, DC: Gallaudet College Press.

———. (1978). *Sign language structure*. Rev. ed. Silver Spring, MD: Linstok Press.

———, Casterline, D., and Croneberg, C. (1965). *A dictionary of American Sign Language on linguistic principles*. Washington, DC: Gallaudet College Press.

Supalla, T., and Newport, E. (1978). How many seats in a chair? The derivation of nouns and verbs in American Sign Language. In *Understanding sign language through sign language research*, edited by P. Siple, 91–132. New York: Academic Press.

Trager, G. L., and Smith, H. L. (1951). *An outline of English structure: Studies in linguistics*. Occasional Papers 5, reissued by the American Council of Learned Societies.

# PART

# I

# PHONOLOGY

# A Structured-Tiers Model
# for ASL Phonology

Sung-Ho Ahn

In the tradition of generative phonology since Chomsky and Halle (1968), a segment such as a vowel or a consonant has been represented as a set of phonological features. This view began to be seriously challenged by Goldsmith (1976). Goldsmith argues that there are subsets of features that behave independently from the remaining segmental features. He calls the independent subsets of features "autosegments." The theory of phonology adopting this viewpoint has been called autosegmental phonology. In autosegmental phonology, a sequence of segments or of autosegments is called a segmental or autosegmental tier. An important issue has been determining how such tiers are structured. Among many works addressing the issue, Clements (1985) proposes one plausible model of the phonological structure of segments where a segment is represented as a hierarchical structure of tiers. In this paper, I apply Clements's model to American Sign Language.

Sign language researchers have only recently begun to adopt the approach of autosegmental phonology. Liddell and Johnson (1986), for example, group phonological features of a one-handed sign into two bundles of features, namely segmental and articulatory. The two bundles of features are connected to each other by means of association lines. This article and its predecessor by Liddell (1984) have given rise to interesting debates on the autosegmental representation of ASL signs. Sandler (1986), for example, convincingly argues that features characterizing handshapes constitute an autosegmental tier. Corina (1986) and Wilbur (1986) argue that not only handshapes but also locations constitute separate tiers. On the other hand, Padden and Perlmutter (1987) criticize Liddell and Johnson's model, where weak-hand features are represented independently of strong-hand features and attached to them by means of arrow notations for not being able to capture some phonological aspects, which, they claim, can be probably captured in terms of global features.

In brief, what has been at issue in building autosegmental models for ASL seems to boil down to five questions:

1. How many tiers are needed and sufficient to describe ASL phonology?
2. What aspects of a sign does a tier characterize?

3. How should those tiers be organized?
4. How are global properties of signs such as [alternating] represented in a model?
5. What properties does ASL phonology share with the phonology of spoken languages?

Within the theoretical framework of autosegmental phonology, I will give partial answers to these questions, arguing that sequential segments of an ASL sign are composed of several tiers, which are organized in a hierarchical fashion, following Clements (1985), who provides a model of phonological structure for spoken languages in the same vein. This paper is organized as follows. First, I will present relevant data. Next, 1 will modify Liddell and Johnson's (1985, 1986) model to cope with the data presented in the previous section. In the course of the modification, I will propose a convention on phonological representation utilizing a syntactic notion C-command. Finally, I will analyze some data in the proposed framework and draw conclusions.

## RELEVANT DATA

### Weak Hand as a Single Unit

Liddell and Johnson (1986) bring up interesting compound examples such as NAME^SHINE ('to have a good reputation') and BLACK^NAME ('bad reputation'). They observe that in the first case, the weak hand of NAME perseveres throughout the whole sign of the compound, NAME^SHINE, and in the second case, the weak hand of NAME appears at the beginning of the compound, BLACK^NAME. They proposed that these processes can be captured in autosegmental approaches by autosegmental spreading, which may occur either leftwardly or rightwardly.[1] Whatever framework we work in, this process shows that features specifying the weak hand sometimes undergo a phonological change simultaneously as a group.

Two more interesting properties of the weak hand of signs are observed by Padden and Perlmutter (1987). One property is shown in the "weak-drop" phenomenon: the weak-hand sign may be dropped when, in a two-handed sign, the movements of the two hands are not alternating (for example, in the case of HAPPEN). The other property is displayed in the "weak-freeze" phenomenon: when a two-handed sign is trilled, the weak hand may lose its movement and preserve its initial position (for example, in the case of RAPPING). These two phenomena of weak hands make the same point as the compound case. That is, features specifying the weak hand may undergo some phonological processes simultaneously as a group.

### Temporal Correspondence Between the Strong Hand and the Weak Hand

The examples BAWL-OUT and MILK, which are also discussed by Padden and Perlmutter (1987), show that there are certain temporal correspondences between the strong-hand movement and the weak-hand movement in two-handed signs. In the sign BAWL-OUT, both hands move in the same direction at the same time; in the sign MILK, however, both hands move downward, not at the same time, but alternately. Padden and Perlmutter observe that the alternating movement is preserved even after a sign undergoes a process of trilling. The pair of examples RAP and RAPPING demonstrates this clearly. A crucial generalization extractable from these examples is that there are certain temporal correspondences between the strong-hand movement and the weak-hand movement. Further, the temporal correspondence must be represented phonologically if the process of trilling is phonological.

### Nonmanual Signals as Single Units

Liddell (1978) observes that nonmanual signals may have lexical (for example, in RECENTLY), phrasal (for example, in RECENTLY LAST-YEAR), and clausal (for example, in relative clauses) scope. In other words, a certain nonmanual signal is produced along with certain lexical items if it has them in its scope, even though the nonmanual signal is not necessarily specified in the lexicon as a part of the lexical items. This fact clearly shows that nonmanual signals may sometimes behave as a single unit.[2] That is, in such a case, the features characterizing nonmanual signals spread over a certain number of phonological segments. Further, among the classifiers in ASL, the existence of some body classifiers may be related to the phonological fact in question. (See Supalla, 1986 for detailed discussion.) Supalla imposes a constraint on the use of body classifiers, namely that "the reference scale must be consistent when body classifiers and classifier hand shapes are combined" (1986, 194). This constraint seems to imply that a body classifier may involve a (whole, sometimes) body excluding manual parts. If my surmise is correct, then we may contend that nonmanual signals behave as a group to form a body classifier and to combine the classifier with manual signals.

### Temporal Correspondence Between Manual and Nonmanual Signals

Examples such as BITE illustrate that there are temporal correspondences between manual and nonmanual signals in ASL, most clearly when they are inflected, for example, when they take a MULTIPLE suffix. That is, the sign BITE's manual movement may be accompanied by a biting action using teeth. If the verb takes plural entities as its object, the biting action occurring in the mouth is made multiply at the same time as the hand's signals are replicated.

### Nonmanual Adverbs

The adverbial morphemes *th* ('carelessly') and *mm* ('regularly'), for example, may be accompanied by optional manual signs, CARELESS(LY) and REGULAR(LY), respectively. A striking fact in these adverbial morphemes is that when they attach to verbs consisting only of manual signals, their own manual signals never appear in the combination. This observation must be considered in parallel to some facts relevant to weak-hand signals: first, weak-hand signals cannot constitute lexical items by themselves, but strong-hand signals or nonmanual signals can; second, there is no combination of only weak-hand signals and nonmanual ones constituting lexical items, but there are exclusive combinations of strong-hand signals and weak-hand ones or of strong-hand signals and nonmanual ones. In other words, for their existence in lexical items, weak-hand signals are entirely dependent upon strong-hand signals.

Even though indirect, the facts considered in the preceding paragraph lead us to conclude that features characterizing manual (one-handed or two-handed) signals do sometimes behave as a single unit.

### Descriptive Generalizations

To recapitulate, we can gather the following descriptive generalizations from the data in the preceding discussion.

1. Features characterizing the weak hand may behave as a group in terms of phonological processes, independently of those characterizing the strong hand, which also may behave as a group.
2. Features characterizing the nonmanual signals may behave as a group in terms of phonological processes, independently of those characterizing manual signals.
3. Features characterizing strong-hand and weak-hand signals may behave as a group.
4. There are certain temporal correspondences between weak-hand signals, strong-hand signals, and nonmanual signals.

Given that these are correct facts in ASL, any model must be able to capture the facts in some way. The model that I develop in the following section captures these facts by adopting a hierarchical organization of phonological features.

## AUTOSEGMENTAL PHONOLOGY IN ASL

In Liddell and Johnson's (1985) model, weak-hand signals are represented as a separate string of segmental units, and the segments on the weak-hand segmental string are attached to the co-occurrent segments of the strong-hand segmental string. Their intuition is quite clear. As they note, by such a separation, they attempt to capture the phonetic independence of one hand from the other and the temporal correspondence of the two hands. But how? They use two vertically stacked strings of segments for two-handed signs: the top string represents the strong hand and the bottom one, the weak hand. They view the strong-hand segments, on the top string, as central organizing elements for the timing of co-occurrent segments on the bottom string. This is shown in figure 1a. Liddell and Johnson connect segments on the weak-hand string to those on the strong-hand one by means of arrow notations. They do not give any specification of the arrow notations except that the arrows represent temporal correspondence between the two segmental strings, and that the weak-hand string is dependent on the strong-hand string in terms of timing.

But how would Liddell and Johnson represent signs that include not only manual signals but also nonmanual signals? In their description of the sign KNOW, which is a one-handed sign, they divide all the features into three bundles including the segmental bundle, the articulatory bundle, and the nonmanual bundle, the last of which is left unspecified. Since they assume that the strong hand and weak hand are

a. Strong Hand     s′1   s′2   s′3
                     ↑    ↑    ↑
   Weak Hand      s″1   s″2   s″3

b. Nonmanual      s1   s1   s3
                   ↓    ↓    ↓
   Strong Hand     s′1   s′2   s′3
                   ↑    ↑    ↑
   Weak Hand      s″1   s″2   s″3

*Key:* Notations such as s1, s′1, and s″1 stand for segments on each string.

**Figure 1. Liddell and Johnson's (1985) model for temporal correspondence between strong-hand signs and weak-hand ones (a), and our extended version of it (b).**

independent with respect to their articulations we may imagine that nonmanual bundles are connected to the articulatory bundles of the strong hand by means of association lines. This model predicts that the strong-hand signals and the nonmanual signals behave as a group with respect to weak-hand signals. However, there is no compelling evidence for this model in ASL. Further, this model is inconsistent with Liddell and Johnson's motivation for separating the strong-hand signals and the weak-hand signals on separate strings of segments.

Recall that one of Liddell and Johnson's important motivations for separating strong-hand signals and weak-hand signals is the phonetic independence of the two hands. Nonmanual signals seem to be much more independent of strong-hand signals than are weak-hand signals. Following their logic, the nonmanual signals have to be separated from both of the manual strings. Further, since the temporal correspondence between the strong-hand string and the weak-hand string is represented by means of arrows, the null hypothesis demands that the temporal correspondence between manual and nonmanual signals be represented by means of the same device, that is, arrow notations.[3] Then one more string, to represent the nonmanual signals, has to be added, for example, on the top of the strong-hand string, and the segments on the newly added nonmanual string must be connected to the elements on the strong-hand string by means of arrow notation, as shown in figure 1b. Let us label this model the "extended Liddell and Johnson model" for easy reference. The extended Liddell and Johnson model gives a simple explanation for generalizations 1, 2, and 4, since in the extended Liddell and Johnson model the strong-hand, the weak-hand, and the nonmanual signals are each represented on a separate string of segments, and at the same time the weak-hand segments and the nonmanual segments are connected to the strong-hand segments by means of arrows for the purpose of timing.

The extended Liddell and Johnson model, however, does not provide a satisfactory account for generalization 3. The reason for this will vary depending on the interpretation of arrows in the extended Liddell and Johnson model. First, if we regard an arrow as an association line possessing directionality, the extended Liddell and Johnson model encounters at least one problem: namely that the model incorrectly predicts that in a sign involving both hands and nonmanual signals, the combination of a nonmanual segment and a strong-hand segment can behave as a group in terms of phonological processes with a similar freedom to that enjoyed by the combination of the strong-hand segment and the weak-hand segment. This prediction, which is clearly incorrect, comes because we use the same kind of notation, that is, arrows, to connect the nonmanual segment to the strong-hand segment as we used to connect the weak-hand segments to the strong-hand ones. Second, if we consider an arrow a notation representing only a temporal co-occurrence, then there is no simple way to provide the model with a capability to account for generalization 3, unless we permit two neighboring segmental strings to behave as a group. In that case, however, the extended Liddell and Johnson model encounters the same problem we considered in the first case. That is, the extended Liddell and Johnson model produces the same wrong prediction. We need a way to distinguish the relationship between the strong-hand string and the nonmanual string on the one hand from the strong-hand string and the weak-hand string on the other. Generalization 3 says that the former relationship is stronger than the latter.

We might attain the goal in question by using bracketing notations, as shown in figure 2. However, rather than adding bracketing notation, since the notions of tier and association line are already available in autosegmental phonology, we may proceed to revise the extended Liddell and Johnson model in the following way, in which we follow Clements (1985).

We assume three class tiers for strong-hand, weak-hand, and nonmanual signals in order to capture their independence from one another.[4] Further, we posit two more class tiers labeled the "Manual Tier" and the "Root Tier," the latter of which is associated with the Skeletal Tier, consisting of timing units (= x's).[5] These class tiers are composed of nodes. The Manual Tier dominates at least the Strong-Hand Tier and the Weak-Hand Tier, the Root Tier dominates at least the Manual Tier and Nonmanual Tier. Elements on a tier are connected to elements on another tier by means of association lines. Since a tier may be composed of multiple tiers, association lines represent constituency and temporal correspondence among multiple bundles of features. Further, all tiers are assumed to be parallel to the Root Tier, and a tier and the tier that immediately dominates it form a "plane" (Clements's term). Figure 3 may be a picture of the model we are pursuing.

The plane aa 'c 'c, for example, is called the "Manual Plane," and the cc 'd 'd, the "Weak-Hand Plane." Since the model inevitably comes to be three-dimensional under the current assumptions, it is not easy to discuss specific points in the model. Just for expository purposes, let us distinguish the end view and the side view. The end view is a view where temporal aspects are discarded. In this view, every tier becomes a point, and every plane looks like a line. For example, the root tier is a point labeled aa ', and the strong-hand plane, cc 'e 'e, is a line between the two labels cc ' and ee '. The end view of the model is shown in figure 4.

Since the current system has to allow a class tier to consist of class tiers and feature tiers, this may be the right time to state a geometric convention concerning the end view of the model.

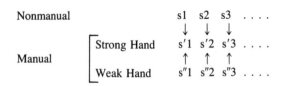

*Figure 2*. **Our revised extended version of Liddell and Johnson's (1985) model.**

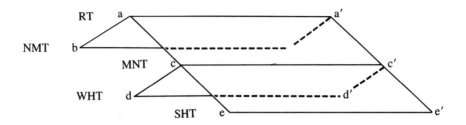

Key:
RT  = Root Tier
NMT = Nonmanual Tier
MNT = Manual Tier
WHT = Weak-Hand Tier
SHT = Strong-Hand Tier

*Figure 3.* **A structured-tiers model for ASL.**

*Figure 4.* **End view of the model in figure 3.**

1. A feature may represent a property of tier constituents that it C-commands (in the end view of the model).
2. A C-commands B (in the end view of the model) if neither A nor B dominates the other and the first branching node that dominates A dominates B (from Reinhart, 1976, 32).

Using the notion C-command, which is widely used in syntactic discussions, this convention opens a way to represent a global feature of a sign such as [alternating], which Padden and Perlmutter (1987) believe deteriorates the Liddell and Johnson-style model considerably. We turn to this issue in the next section.

On the other hand, the side view is a view that discards spatial aspects. The side view of the model is not easy to draw in a single picture. So we have to dismantle the model depending on our focus of discussion. Figure 5, for example, contains some of the pictures showing parts of the side view.

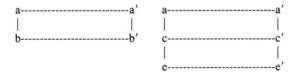

Key:
aa′b′b: Nonmanual Plane
aa′c′c: Manual Plane
cc′e′e: Strong-Hand Plane

*Figure 5.* **Side view of three planes of the model in figure 3.**

In terms of internal structure of the three tiers, i.e., the Strong-Hand Tier, the Weak-Hand Tier, and the Nonmanual Tier, not many points are available to be made. (See Corina [1988] for a model dealing with handshapes from a similar perspective.) Generally following Sandler (1986), Corina (1986), and Wilbur (1986), we simply assume that hand configuration, location, and hand orientation are represented on separate "articulatory" tiers. These three articulatory tiers may form a flat or hierarchical structure in an end view, in relation to the Strong-Hand Tier. These are shown in figure 6.

Another logical possibility includes a case where the three articulatory tiers form a constituent, the Articulatory Tier ($=$ ii ' in figure 7). These are illustrated in figure 7. Which one is the right picture of the phonological structure of ASL is an empirical question. As Wilbur (1986) notes, there is also a possibility that properties not represented by the three articulatory tiers, for example, manners of movement (jj ' in figure 8), may be represented on one or more tiers. If we want to capture Liddell and Johnson's original insight on the dichotomy of the segmental bundle and the articulatory bundle, the model in figure 8 may be appropriate as a working hypothesis to start the discussion. Also, the Nonmanual Tier may have more than one subtier, whose relational structure can be determined only empirically.

The last point is that the Weak-Hand Tier is underspecified in many ways (see Archangeli, 1984). In deciding which features are to be underspecified, constraints such as Battison's (1978) Morpheme Structure Constraints are probably at work. It is not easy to determine whether such constraints are linguistically universal or ASL-specific constraints. In either case, these conditions, coupled with the structured-tiers phonological feature system, simplify lexical entries. This implies that ASL learners have much less burden in acquiring signs. As a first approximation, we assume that every redundant feature between the two manual tiers is unspecified on the Weak-Hand Tier. The binary values ($+$ or $-$) of such features are provided by the Strong-Hand Tier by copying feature values along the association lines. In the case of HAPPEN, for example, every feature value on the Weak-Hand Tier is unspecified in the lexicon, but provided by the Strong-Hand Tier, which results in the total mirror relationship of the two hands. Considering the symmetry shown in human organs, we may claim that the features of the two hands of the sign HAPPEN have exactly

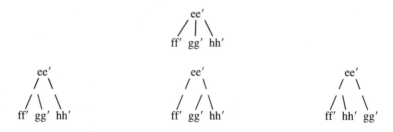

*Key:*
ee': Strong-Hand Tier
ff' : Hand-Configuration Tier
gg': Location Tier
hh': Hand-Orientation Tier

*Figure 6.* **Possible internal structures of manual tiers (from the end view).**

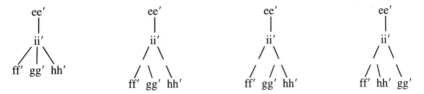

*Figure 7.* **Alternative possible internal structures of manual tiers (from the end view).**

the same values in some level of phonological representation.[6] (See Battison [1978].) A derivation of such a process copying feature values will look like figure 9.

Figure 9a contains phonological feature specifications of HAPPEN in the lexicon. Actual feature names, which are not relevant to our discussion, are deliberately avoided. In the lexicon, HAPPEN has specified features only for the strong hand. $MM_1$ is the cluster of features specifying the manner of movement of the strong hand; $L_1$ and $L_2$ are clusters of features specifying the two locations between which the strong hand travels; in the same way, $HS_1$ is the cluster of features specifying the hand configuration of the strong hand. Since the handshape does not change during the movement of the strong hand, there is only one cluster of features specifying the handshape. Likewise, $HO_1$ and $HO_2$ specify the first and the last orientations of the strong hand. But the features on the weak-hand side do not have subscripts, which means that the features of the Weak-Hand Tier do not contain specified values. Figure 9b shows the phonological representation of the sign HAPPEN when the process of copying feature values applies.[7]

## SOME ANALYSES

The model accounts for generalizations 1 through 4 in a straightforward way. Instead of talking about the generalizations, therefore, we will discuss the Weak-Drop phenomenon, the Weak-Freeze phenomenon, and global features such as [alternating].

As mentioned earlier, in Padden and Perlmutter (1987) the Weak-Drop phenomenon is described as follows: nonalternating two-handed signs optionally change into one-handed signs. This phenomenon frequently appears in rapid and relaxed

*Key:*
ee′: Strong-Hand Tier
jj′ : Manner-of-Movement Tier
ii′ : Articulatory Tier
ff′ : Hand-Configuration Tier
gg′: Location Tier
hh′: Hand-Orientation Tier

*Figure 8.* **The internal structure of manual tiers assumed in the present system (from the end view).**

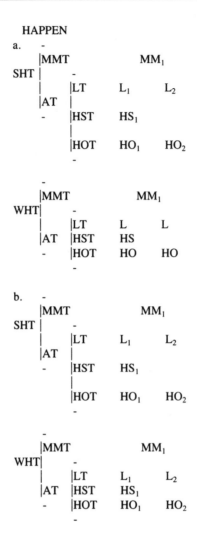

Key:
SHT   = Strong-Hand Tier
MMT = Manner-of-Movement Tier
AT     = Articulatory Tier
LT     = Location Tier
HST   = Handshape Tier
HOT   = Hand-Orientation Tier
WHT   = Weak-Hand Tier

*Figure 9.* **A process copying feature values. Underlying representation of HAPPEN (a); intermediate representation of it (b).**

signing. We assume Perlmutter's very convincing argument that Weak Drop is the right formulation of the phenomenon rather than a rule making two-handed signs out of one-handed signs, and we incorporate their rule into our system. The Weak-Drop rule proposed by Padden and Perlmutter is stated in our system as in figure 10.

This rule uses only the end view. On this view, the global feature [-alternating] is attached to the Manual Tier, thereby C-commanding the two manual tiers, namely

Weak Drop (optional)

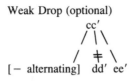

[− alternating]   dd′ ee′

*Key:*
cc′ = Manual Tier
dd′ = Weak-Hand Tier
ee′ = Strong-Hand Tier

**Figure 10. The Weak-Drop rule in our system (from the end view).**

the Strong-Hand Tier (ee ′)and the Weak-Hand Tier (dd ′). By convention 5, this indicates that the two hands do not move alternatingly. In stating a rule in autosegmental phonology, the association line marked '' = '' means that the rule disconnects the two entities that are connected to each other through the association line. Thus, the rule states that under the condition that a two-handed sign is not alternating, the Weak-Hand Tier is disconnected optionally. The effect this has for the signs in question is that the Weak-Hand Plane is cut off optionally. This model does not account for why such a rule exists in ASL, but at least it might explain why dropping of segments occurs in the Weak-Hand Tier: namely, the Weak-Hand Tier is greatly underspecified in many cases.

Alternatively, instead of using convention 5 and global features, we may use the structure itself to represent such global features as [αalternating].[8] In this alternative, the Weak-Drop rule is stated as in figure 11. In the rule, the structural description requiring that the movement be alternating is expressed in terms of the phonological structure. The rule states that in such a structure the Weak-Hand Tier (or the segment on the Weak-Hand Tier, more correctly) is optionally disconnected. We will not pursue this alternative here, however, without implying that the alternative is disadvantaged.

Padden and Perlmutter (1987) state the Weak-Freeze rule as follows: If a two-handed sign has a property of [ + trilled], then the Weak-Hand optionally loses its (trilled) movement. In the present model, the same rule may be stated as in figure 12. In figure 12, the Weak-Hand Tier is viewed from the side, but the Manual Tier is viewed from the end. The feature [ + trilled] is attached to the Manual Tier, C-commanding the Weak-Hand Tier as well as the Strong-Hand Tier. This indicates

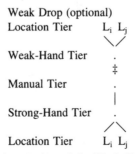

**Figure 11. An alternative version of the Weak-Drop rule in our system (from the side view).**

Weak Freeze (Optional)

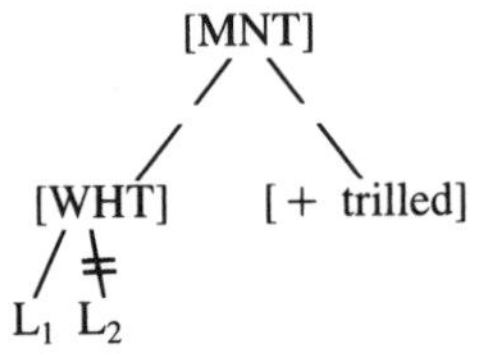

```
              [MNT]
             /  \
            /    \
       [WHT]    [+ trilled]
         / ‡
       L₁ L₂
```

*Key:*
MNT = Manual Tier
WHT = Weak-Hand Tier

***Figure 12.* The Weak-Freeze rule in our system (from the end view).**

that the manual signs show a trilled movement. $L_1$ and $L_2$ stand for the two locations between which the movement of the weak hand, if not trilled, might travel. In the structural change, the association line marked " = " indicates that the second location of the weak-hand movement is delinked. Consequently, the Weak-Freeze rule states that when a two-handed sign is [ + trilled], the second articulatory segment in the Weak-Hand Tier is optionally disconnected. Consequently, the weak hand stays at its first location all through the sign.

We now move on to the "facial" adverbs. As mentioned in the previous section, such adverbs as *th* ('carelessly') and *mm* ('regularly') optionally involve the manual signs CARELESSLY and REGULARLY, respectively.[9] Whether this optionality is to be captured in the lexicon or in the form of a rule, it must be the case that the manual tiers, namely the Strong-Hand Tier and the Weak-Hand Tier, are referred to together as a group. In the present model, we refer to the Manual Tier, which is shown as cc ' in figure 4, repeated as figure 13.

That is, the Manual Tier ( = cc ') is optionally disconnected in such adverbs. When such an adverb combines with a verb involving only manual signals, the optional Manual Tier of the adverb is replaced by that of the verb. Alternatively, we may say that the Nonmanual Tier of the adverb(s) is substituted for the verb's vacant Non-manual Tier. In the former case, what is replaced is the Manual Tier (cc ') of the adverb. In the latter case, however, what is replaced is the Nonmanual Tier of the verb. In either case, this model correctly predicts that the Weak-Hand signing of the

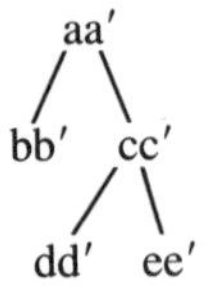

```
            aa'
           /  \
          /    \
       bb'     cc'
        /  \
      dd'   ee'
```

*Key:*
aa' = Root Tier
bb' = Nonmanual Tier
cc' = Manual Tier
dd' = Weak-Hand Tier
ee' = Strong-Hand Tier

***Figure 13.* The end view of the model in figure 3. (cf. figure 4.)**

a. *th* ('carelessly')
   Nonmanual Tier       NM$_1$
   Strong-Hand Tier     SH$_1$
   Weak-Hand Tier       WH$_1$
b. WRITE
   Nonmanual Tier
   Strong-Hand Tier     SH$_2$
   Weak-Hand Tier       WH$_2$
c. _____*th*
   WRITE ('to write carelessly')
   Nonmanual Tier       NM$_1$
   Strong-Hand Tier     SH$_2$
   Weak-Hand Tier       WH$_2$
d.*_____*th*
   WRITE
   Nonmanual Tier       NM$_1$
   Strong-Hand Tier     SH$_2$
   Weak-Hand Tier       WH$_1$

*Figure 14.* **Combination of *th* and WRITE.**

sign corresponding to the facial adverb never appears mixed with the Strong-Hand signing of a verb, even in the combination of the adverb with a one-handed verb.[10]

Let us consider an example. If *th* ('carelessly') combines with WRITE, the combined form might be represented as in figure 14. In figure 14, irrelevant details are deliberately avoided again. NM$_1$ in figure 14a is the cluster of features that specifies that the head is tilted back, the tongue is extruded, and the gaze is upward. Likewise, SH$_1$ and WH$_1$ are clusters of features characterizing the movements and other features of the strong hand and the weak hand of CARELESSLY; SH$_2$ and WH$_2$ in figure 14b stand for the clusters of features characterizing the movements and other features of the strong hand and the weak hand of WRITE. The combined form of the two signs is shown in figure 14c, where NM$_1$ is put in the Nonmanual Tier of the sign WRITE, which had contained only the segments on the manual tiers, namely, SH$_2$ and WH$_2$. Sign combinations like those in figure 14d cannot arise in our system because the Manual Tier or the Nonmanual Tier may be referred to, but the combination of the Nonmanual Tier and the Weak-Hand Tier cannot.

## CONCLUSION

By revising Liddell and Johnson's (1985, 1986) model, we show that generalizations 1 through 4 are accounted for by means of geometrical properties of phonological representations in ASL, and that there is a way to reconcile their insights with Padden and Perlmutter's (1987) legitimate objections to the model. Further, underspecifying the Weak-Hand Tier might partly explain how children can learn ASL, and it might also explain why the Weak-Drop and the Weak-Freeze phenomena occur on the Weak Hand. To determine the detailed and minute internal structure of each tier, we have to wait for more extensive studies on phonological processes of ASL.

Throughout the discussion, we repeatedly address the questions collected in the first section. Partial answers to them within the present model are as follows. First, at least five class tiers are necessary for an appropriate explanation of ASL phonological phenomena. The five tiers are the Manual Tier, the Strong-Hand Tier, the Weak-Hand Tier, the Nonmanual Tier, and the Root Tier. Second, in ASL the five class tiers characterize constituency of phonological features. For example, the Manual Tier states that the features characterizing the strong-hand signals and the weak-hand signals occasionally behave as a group. Third, the tiers are organized according to the structure in figure 3. That is, the Strong-Hand Tier and the Weak-Hand Tier form one constituent, namely the Manual Tier. The Manual Tier and the Nonmanual Tier make the highest tier, namely the Root Tier. Fourth, global properties of signs can be represented in a model by regarding C-command as a geometrical property of phonological representations. Finally, the phonologies of ASL and spoken languages share the property of hierarchically structured tiers in phonological representations.

# NOTES

I have been immeasurably indebted to Diane Lillo-Martin, who taught me the structure of ASL and has been very kind to help me in every respect of my sign language research. Thanks go to Robert Johnson, Charles Ulrich, and Ronnie Wilbur for the discussions I have had with them.

1. Liddell and Johnson (1985) also contend that each hand must be represented as a separate string of segmental notations noting one hand's phonetic independence from the other.
2. In drawing out the generalization here, however, I do not include features characterizing body shifting into the features characterizing nonmanual signals in question. The features of body shifting might constitute a separate, floating, segment, which might be inserted in syntax. In this respect, the features might be viewed as constituting a morpheme that has a unique function.
3. If a new device has to be introduced to represent the temporal correspondence between manual and nonmanual signals, the model will lose much of its attraction.
4. I follow Clements's II (1985) line in revising the extended Liddell and Johnson model here to assume that each feature constitutes a tier, which is labeled a "feature tier," and that multiple tiers may be immediately dominated by a tier, which is labeled a "class tier." A class tier consists of nodes each of which may dominate multiple elements in feature tiers. The highest class tier dominating every tier is called the root tier. (Readers are referred to Clements [1985] and references cited there for detailed discussion.) In Clements's terms, the discussion here is concerned with class tiers. Even though terminology such as "Right-Hand Tier," "Left-Hand Tier," and "Central Skeletial Tier" were used when this material was presented at the conference, here the terms the "Strong-Hand Tier," "Weak-Hand Tier," and "Root Tier" are adopted, following Padden and Perlmutter (1987) and Clements (1985). Thanks go to Robert Johnson and Charles Ulrich for reminding me of these.
5. There are a few different ideas on the identity of such timing units. Corina (1986), for example, imports two categories C and V as timing units for ASL phonological representations from CV phonology. Roughly, movement corresponds to V and nonmovement corresponds to C. Two-handed signs, however, demonstrate that in many cases the strong-hand-movement period corresponds to the weak-hand-nonmovement period. For Corina, such temporal correspondence is captured phonetically. If the two hands must be presented together phonologically, however, the two categories C and V have to be neutralized in some way.
6. As Diane Lillo-Martin pointed out to me in a personal communication, ASL has two-handed signs such as BAPTIZE that involve totally symmetric movements. Such signs presumably have to be more specified in the lexicon than the signs that involve mirror-image movements.
7. The details of underspecification of features have to be worked out in more detail if Archangeli's (1984) system is going to be adopted in some way in sign language research. The reason for

this is that in Archangeli's system, a feature, say, $[F_1]$ is specified only when it has a positive value. Then the feature is unspecified in the lexicon in a case where it has to have a negative value. In such a case, a general phonological rule states that an unspecified value "slot" of a feature is filled with the opposite value specifying the feature in the lexicon. Thus, if $[F_1]$ is unspecified in some lexical element, the lexical item comes to have $[-F_1]$ by the operation of the rule.

As shown, in our system copying feature values through association lines provides the unspecified features under the Weak-Hand Tier with exactly the same values of the features under the Strong-Hand-Tier. It doesn't seem to be difficult to find a way to harmonize the two systems in terms of technical mechanisms. Before such a work is attempted, however, it should be determined what relevance Archangeli's proposal may have to ASL. This line of research is outside of the scope of the present paper.

8. This alternative was pursued when this paper was presented at the conference.

9. As Charles Urlich correctly points out in a personal communication, the manual signs concerning such adverbial morphemes may not constitute evidence motivating the Manual Tier. This is so because even in a model that assumes that the Nonmanual Tier, the Strong-Hand Tier, and the Weak-Hand Tier are immediately dominated by the Root Tier, it is possible to represent facial adverbs such as *th* ('carelessly') as affixes in the Nonmanual Tier of either manual adverbs such as CARELESSLY or verbs such as WRITE. But it is controversial whether the signs such as CARELESSLY may appear without their facial signal counterparts. Charles Ulrich also suggests that the fact that there are no signs involving an alternating movement of the strong hand and a nonmanual organ, for example, the head seems to be a case motivating the Manual Tier.

10. In a personal communication R. Wilbur points out that such a restriction might be explained by Battison's (1978) constraints on two-handed signs, or the other way around. Battison proposes two morpheme structure constraints, one of which is the "Symmetry Condition." This condition states that if both hands of a sign move independently during its articulation, then both hands must be specified for the same location, the same handshape, the same movement, and the specifications for orientation must be either symmetrical or identical. Currently there seems to be no way to test whether Battison's account or our account is the real explanation for of the lack of signs violating these conditions. What is quite plausible is that Battison's constraints may be in effect in the lexicon when phonological features characterizing the weak hand are underspecified, thereby alleviating the ASL learner's burden to a significant extent.

# REFERENCES

Archangeli, D. (1984). Underspecification in Yawelmani phonology and morphology. Ph.D. diss., MIT.

Battison, R. (1978). *Lexical borrowing in American Sign Language*. Silver Spring, MD: Linstok Press.

Chomsky, N., and Halle, M. (1968). *The sound pattern of English*. New York: Harper and Row.

Clements, G. N. (1985). The geometry of phonological features. *Phonology Yearbook 2*:225–53.

Corina, D. (1986). ASL phonology: a CV perspective. Paper presented at the annual meeting of the Linguistic Society of America, December, New York, New York.

———. (1989). Handshape assimilations in hierarchical phonological representation. In this proceedings.

Goldsmith, J. (1976). Autosegmental phonology. Ph.D. diss., MIT. Reproduced by the Indiana University Linguistics Club, 1976.

Liddell, S. K. (1978). Nonmanual signals and relative clauses in American Sign Language. In *Understanding language through sign language research*, edited by P. Siple, 59–90. New York: Academic Press.

———. (1984). THINK and BELIEVE: Sequentiality in American Sign Language. *Language* 60:372–99.

———, and Johnson, R. (1985). Sign notation workshop. Gallaudet University. Unpublished manuscript.

———, and Johnson, R. (1986). American Sign Language compound formation process, lexicalization, and phonological remnants. *Natural Language and Linguistic Theory* 12:445–513.

Padden, C. A., and Perlmutter, D. (1987). American Sign Language and the architecture of phonological theory. *Natural Language and Linguistic Theory* 5:335–75.

Reinhart, T. (1976). The syntactic domain of anaphora. Ph.D. diss., MIT.

Sandler, W. (1986). The spreading hand autosegment of American Sign Language. *Sign Language Studies* 50:1–28.

Supalla, T. (1986). The classifier system in American Sign Language. In *Noun classification and categorization*, edited by C. G. Craig, 181–214. Philadelphia: John Benjamins Publishing Co.

Wilbur, R. (1986). Why syllables?: An examination of what the notion means for ASL research. In *Theoretical issues in sign language research, I: Linguistics*, edited by S. Fischer and P. Siple. In press.

# Handshape Assimilations in Hierarchical Phonological Representation

## David P. Corina

Phonology is the study of the abstract system underlying the selection and use of minimally contrastive units in natural languages. Traditionally, phonologists have focused on oral languages; however, the recent realization that human languages can evolve outside the oral-aural modality (Klima and Bellugi, 1979) forces a broader understanding of abstract phonological systems. It is assumed here that phonological units will be grounded in the modality in which they are realized. However, the abstract system of constraints and processes affecting these units will be similar across spoken and signed languages, a reflection of the putative human linguistic capacity.

This paper explores the utility of a hierarchical feature system for American Sign Language handshapes and the processes affecting them. I begin with a general discussion of a distinctive feature system for ASL handshapes. This preliminary coding system provides the groundwork for examining the proposed feature hierarchy for ASL handshapes.[1] I then build upon this feature system and present arguments for the arrangement of features. My proposal is motivated by an examination of articulatory and phonological evidence, with a special emphasis on total and partial handshape assimilations.

## DISTINCTIVE FEATURES FOR ASL HANDSHAPES

In describing distinctive feature systems, one attempts to characterize the underlying perceptual and/or gestural components of phonemes in a language. The system of features posited is validated to the extent that it is able to identify uniquely the phonemically contrastive segments of the language and to classify segments in accordance to dimensions extant in phonological processes in that language. In addition, in proposing distinctive feature inventories, one hopes to capture universal phonological distinctions. However, our understanding of phonological processes in signed languages is just beginning, and as these data become available such systems will naturally be subject to revision. In the coding system presented here, a handshape representation consists of features for finger(s) involved in articulating the handshape and features describing the configuration of these fingers. The features proposed here are preliminary and based exclusively on ASL, but they provide a vehicle for understanding how features may be hierarchically arranged in signed languages. With these facts in mind, let us examine the distinctive feature inventory and some consequences of this proposal.

## Configurations

Five binary features are used to describe the configuration of the finger(s) in a handshape. The features [bent], [curved], and [lateral] refer to presence or absence of finger bending. The features [spread] and [crossed] describe relations among fingers. These five features are abbreviated as follows bnt = bent, cur = curved, lat = lateral, spd = spread, crsd = crossed.

The feature [+, − curved] makes reference to the knuckles of the hand that are nonadjacent to the palm. This feature encodes whether these knuckles are unbent [− curved] or bent [+ curved].

The feature [+, − bent] makes reference to the remaining knuckle, that is the knuckle that abuts the palm. The feature [+ bent] indicates a finger configuration in which this knuckle is bent, and conversely [− bent] refers to the nonbent knuckle configuration.

The coding system allows us to capture four principle finger shapes: open, closed, curved (or hooked) and flat-bent (see figure 1 below). This system allows us to distinguish fully closed and open handshapes: [αbent, αcurved] from intermediate forms; [αbent, βcurved]. This distinction has been shown to be important in capturing generalization concerning predictability of handshape change in ASL (Brentari, 1987).

The feature [+ spread] refers to fingers that are nonparallel, or fanned. Conversely, the feature [− spread] codes fingershapes whose lateral surfaces are in contact. The [spread] feature factors significantly in distinguishing a class of handshapes that allow the secondary movement "wiggle" versus that termed "flat bending." We will examine this claim in more detail below.

The feature [lateral] is reserved for thumb specification in ASL because the thumb has more degrees of freedom compared to fingers. [+ lateral] refers to a configuration in which the ulnar side of the thumb is adjacent or parallel to the palm. It is used to distinguish the thumb configurations seen in the handshapes E, M, N, and T.

Last, the feature [crossed] refers to a configuration among fingers. This feature is used to refer to fingers that lie across each other, that is, are crossed. In ASL it is primarily used to describe the index and middle finger, which are crossed in the handshape "R." This feature distinguishes the handshape "R" from "U."

|         | + bnt     | − bnt   |
|---------|-----------|---------|
| + cur   | closed    | curved  |
| − cur   | flat bent | open    |

*Figure 1.* **Principal fingershapes.**

## *Finger Specification*

Monovalent distinctive features are used to encode presence or absence of specified fingers in handshapes. The five features are as follows: Th = thumb, I = index, M = middle, R = ring, P = pinky. Note that we treat the thumb as a finger. The determination of what constitutes a specified finger in an ASL handshape stems from observations of handshape inventories and processes that systematically effect classes within these inventories (see Corina and Sagey, in prep.).

The approach taken here is similar to Sandler's (1987) in that in both analyses specified fingers generally correspond to those fingers that participate in handshape change and secondary movement. The finger features are assumed to be monovalent and to function as class nodes in a hierarchical representation (see ''Organization of Distinctive Features'' below). My approach differs from Sandler's in that the unspecified fingers are not represented in the underlying representation but receive specification through redundancy rules. This treatment is compatible with underspecification theory (Archangeli, 1984), which states that information that is predictable (derivable by rule) is left unspecified and expressed as a rule in the grammar.

A default rule for unspecified fingers can be stated as follows: An unspecified finger receives an open configuration [− bent, − curved], if the specified fingers are closed [+ bent, + curved], otherwise the unspecified fingers receive a closed configuration. The rule is assumed to apply exhaustively to those fingers remaining unspecified in the underlying representation. There is one exception to this rule, the ''open-eight'' handshape, which is articulated with the middle finger bent and all others open. In this handshape, because the specified finger is not fully closed, the redundancy rule assigns a closed configuration to the unspecified fingers. This assignment is, however, incorrect. The unspecified fingers in the open-eight handshape are in fact open. We may attribute this exception to social taboos against articulating a handshape in which the middle finger is bent and all others are closed.[2]

## *Regularities in ASL Handshapes*

The table in figure 2 lists thirty-six contrastive handshapes in ASL (Wilbur, 1987). Absent from the list are handshapes found in the classifier signs that represent the size and shape of objects (SASSES). Handshapes of this class tend to function differently from handshapes listed above. Specifically, for this class of handshapes, the presence or absence of fingers and degree of constriction have a status that is morphemic rather than simply phonemic. (See table 1 for a list of coding conventions.) For an analysis of classifier handshapes, see Supalla (1986).

The system proposed here reveals a number of interesting facts regarding regularities of handshape in ASL. One area that has recently received much attention is the analysis of handshape change in ASL (Sandler 1986b, 1987; Liddell and Johnson, 1985; Corina, 1986; Brentari, 1987). Handshape change refers to the process in which a monomorphemic sign exhibits two distinct handshapes during articulation. The possible pairings of beginning and ending handshapes in monomorphemic signs that permit handshape change are quite restricted (Brentari, 1987; Corina and Sagey, in prep.). It is reasonable to hypothesize that this restricted set constitutes a natural class.

|     | Name | FINGER | BNT | CUR | SPD | LAT | CSD |
|-----|------|--------|-----|-----|-----|-----|-----|
| 1   | C    | TIMRP  | −   | +   | −   | −   | −   |
| 2   | O    | TIMRP  | +   | +   | −   | −   | −   |
| 3   | O>   | TIMRP  | +   | −   | −   | −   | −   |
| 4   | 5    | TIMRP  | −   | −   | +   | −   | −   |
| 5   | 5~   | TIMRP  | −   | +   | +   | −   | −   |
| 6   | 4    | IMRP   | −   | −   | +   | −   | −   |
| 7   | B    | IMRP   | −   | −   | −   | −   | −   |
| 8   | B>   | IMRP   | +   | −   | −   | −   | −   |
| 9   | S    | IMRP   | +   | +   | −   | −   | −   |
| 10  | 1    | I      | −   | −   | −   | −   | −   |
| 11  | 1>   | I      | +   | −   | −   | −   | −   |
| 12  | X/bO | I      | −   | +   | −   | −   | −   |
| 13  | F    | TI     | +   | +   | −   | −   | −   |
| 14  | L    | TI     | −   | −   | −   | −   | −   |
| 15  | L~   | TI     | −   | +   | −   | −   | −   |
| 16  | G    | TI     | +   | −   | −   | −   | −   |
| 17  | U    | IM     | −   | −   | −   | −   | −   |
| 18  | V    | IM     | −   | −   | +   | −   | −   |
| 19  | V~   | IM     | −   | +   | +   | −   | −   |
| 20  | 3    | TIM    | −   | −   | +   | −   | −   |
| 21  | 3~   | TIM    | −   | +   | +   | −   | −   |
| 22  | 8    | TM     | +   | +   | −   | −   | −   |
| 23  | o8   | M      | +   | −   | −   | −   | −   |
| 24  | A    | T      | −   | −   | −   | −   | −   |
| 25  | I    | P      | −   | −   | −   | −   | −   |
| 26  | Y    | IMR    | +   | +   | −   | −   | −   |
| 27  | R    | IM     | −   | −   | −   | −   | +   |
|     |      |        |     |     |     |     |     |
| 28  | D    | TMRP   | +   | +   | −   | −   | −   |
| 29  | E    | TIMRP  | +   | −   | −   | +   | −   |
| 30  | K/P  | TIM    | −/+ | −   | −   | +   | −   |
| 31  | M    | TIMR   | +   | −   | −   | +   | −   |
| 32  | T    | IM     | +   | −   | −   | +   | −   |
| 33  | W    | IMR    | −   | −   | −   | −   | −   |
| 34  | ⊔    | IP     | −   | −   | −   | −   | −   |
| 35  | Ɣ    | TIP    | −   | −   | −   | −   | −   |
| 36  | 7    | TR     | +   | +   | −   | −   | −   |

*Figure 2.* **Preliminary distinctive-feature matrix for ASL handshapes.**

### Handshape Change

Examining the distinctive feature matrix, we note handshapes 1 through 27 participate in handshape change, and that 28 through 33 typically do not. With regard to this distribution, two observations are relevant. First, a handshape that permits handshape change will have identical configuration values for all specified fingers. In contrast, a handshape that does not allow handshape change will often require separate non-identical configuration values for specified fingers. Recall that the thumb is considered a finger under this analysis. As such, handshapes specified for the feature [lateral] will fall into the class of nonidentical finger specifications. Second, handshapes that

***Table 1.*** **Notation Conventions Used in This Chapter**

| Convention | Meaning |
|---|---|
| KNOW | Gloss for an ASL sign |
| PRO-1<br>PRO-2 | First- and second-person pronouns. |
| B> | A flat-bent handshape |
| 5~ | A curved (hooked) handshape. |
| (B → S) | A descriptive representation for a contour segment changing from a B handshape to a fist. Initialized handshapes in the description of contours in this paper do not indicate underlying forms. For a discussion of contour, see Corina and Sagey (in prep). |
| B> = +1 | A descriptive representation of a partially assimilated handshape involving specifications from a flat-bent B handshape and a 1 handshape. |

An example of a specified feature hierarchy in which features for PRM have been omitted for the sake of clarity. It is assumed that these features are also marked [− bnt, − cur].

An example of a contour handshape changing from a closed to an open handshape. As discussed above, features have been omitted for the sake of clarity.

permit handshape change tend to have contiguous fingers specified, whereas those that resist handshape change often have specified fingers that are noncontiguous.

Regarding the first observation, examine the distinctive feature coding for the handshape V, which participates in handshape change (for example, the signs STEAL and FROG), with the K/P handshape, which does not. In the representation for V, we note that both specified fingers, the index and middle finger, receive the feature specification [− bent, − curved] or "open." In contrast, the handshape K/P, which has the thumb, index finger, and middle finger specified, each finger receives a unique specification. Specifically, the index is "open" [− bent, − curved], the middle finger is "flat bent" [+ bent, − curved], and the thumb is "lateral" [− bent, − curved, + lateral].

Regarding the second observation, note that in the handshape V, the specified fingers (index and middle) are contiguous or adjacent. In contrast, a handshape such as ⊔ has nonadjacent finger configuration, that is, the specified fingers jump from the index to pinky, skipping the middle and ring fingers. It appears that handshapes of this type also resist handshape change.

### Secondary Movement

Another process that affects handshape in ASL is secondary movement. In secondary movement a single handshape alternates repeatedly between its specified shape and some restricted degree of closure. This repeated movement of a single handshape is seen as secondary to a sign's path movement. Two examples of secondary movement are flat bending and wiggling. Flat bending takes a handshape such as a B and repeatedly flexes the first knuckle of all fingers simultaneously. This type of movement is noted in the sign HOPE. Wiggling takes a handshape such as a 5 and asynchronously flexes the first knuckle of each finger. The non-path movement form of the sign FINE has a wiggling movement.

The distribution of handshapes that permit secondary movement is restricted to the set described above for handshape change. However, we note additional constraints. The handshapes 1, U, and V can take either flat bending or wiggling (indeed it is ambiguous whether the *1* participates in flat bending or wiggling), whereas the handshapes B and 5 take either flat bending or wiggling, but not both. It appears that those handshapes that are specified for finger combinations of index and middle allow either wiggling or flat bending. In contrast those handshapes specified for additional fingers, ring and pinky, are restricted to only one of these secondary movements. This observation is interesting and may ultimately relate to physiological factors. In the hand, it is well known that there is a separation of motor efferents controlling the radial (index and middle) and ulnar (ring and pinky) fingers. The ulnar/radial division is not directly captured in the distinctive-feature representation; however, the feature [spread] appears to predict the realization of secondary movements in handshapes whose fingers span this ulnar/radial division.[3] Specifically [− spread] handshapes allow only flat bending, whereas those handshapes specified [+ spread] allow wiggling. This suggests that the secondary movements underlying flat bending and wiggling may be different surface instantiations of a single movement (perhaps "repeated flexion of the first knuckle"), its surface form being determined by the presence or absence of the feature [spread] in handshape specified for ulnar and radial fingers. Support for this comes from signs that have allomorphs (or near allomorphs) that differ only in the feature [spread]. For example, we find the sign WAIT₁, when made with a 5 [+ spread] handshape (usually palms up), takes a wiggling secondary movement; whereas in the sign WAIT₂, in which two B [− spread] handshapes face each other, we note flat-bending secondary movement. We find a similar alternation in the signs COOL [− spread] and PLEASANT [+

spread]. Likewise we notice regular alternations of wiggling and flat bending under morphological processes deriving characteristic adjectives. For example DIRTY uses a [+ spread] handshape and wiggles whereas CHARACTERISTICALLY DIRTY uses a [− spread] handshape and flat bends (Klima and Bellugi, 1979).

Distinctive feature systems attempt to represent organizational properties at the level of the phoneme by capturing subphonemic regularities. This subphonemic patterning is thought to reflect articulatory and/or perceptual constraints on language form. We have seen above how the preliminary set of features posited serves to identify contrastive handshapes in ASL and further helps isolate pertinent patterns within the class of ASL handshape. We now examine the organization of these subphonemic features themselves.

## ORGANIZATION OF DISTINCTIVE FEATURES

A desirable outcome of a feature system is its ability to elucidate why certain phonological changes take place only in certain contexts or affect only certain classes of segments. For example, a pervasive process in many of the world's languages is the assimilation of place features in consonants. For example, in English, a nasal will agree in place of articulation features with a following stop consonant. (The asterisk indicates an ungrammatical structure.)

| /iN-/ | indivisible | *imdivisible |
|-------|-------------|--------------|
| /iN-/ | intransitive | *imtransitive |
| /iN-/ | impossible | *inpossible |
| /iN-/ | imbalance | *inbalance |

A similar rule is found in the African language Kpelle, where nasals assimilate in place of articulation to a following stop or fricative, as shown below (from Welmers, 1973).

| /N-polu/ | [mbolu] | 'my back' |
|----------|---------|-----------|
| /N-tia/ | [india] | 'my taboo' |
| /N-koo/ | [ingoo] | 'my foot' |
| /N-fela/ | [mvela] | 'my wages' |
| /N-sua/ | [njua] | 'my nose' |

To the extent that processes like this recur across a wide variety of languages, it would be beneficial to capture this generalization in our distinctive feature representations. Recent proposals along these lines suggest that phonological features are organized formally into classes of features analogous to classes of segments defined by phonological features (Clements, 1985; Sagey, 1986). By positing such classes, we can account for the fact that groups of features that occur together in phonological rules are not random but are limited to certain recurring sets. This treatment of phonological features allows us to distinguish recurring sets of features like [anterior, coronal, high, back] from nonoccurring sets like [voice, coronal, round].

One useful approach for encoding the relationship between classes of features has been to order features hierarchically (see figure 3). Two types of evidence are offered as support for this proposal: physiological and phonological. Physiological support is drawn from the relative degrees of independence between major articulatory structures. For example, the laryngeal structures mediating control of voicing can operate independently of those structures involved in tongue configuration. We would like our feature representations to somehow mirror these facts. One way to capture this independence is to posit structures in which groups of features are geometrically isolable from other groups of features; hierarchical feature arrangements afford this possibility. Physiological facts alone, however, do not constitute the sole evidence for such arrangements; phonological facts must also be considered. Across languages, we find phonological rules that systematically refer to certain classes of features to the exclusion of others. In addition, the scope of processes such as assimilation tends to be rather restricted. That is, in assimilation we find recurring elements that spread in relatively constrained ways. If in our hierarchical feature geometries we are able to encode these facts, we have made progress in capturing important generalizations of natural languages, signed and spoken.

A proposal for a hierarchical representation for ASL handshape features is shown in figure 4. I will motivate this proposal by presenting physiological and phonological evidence from ASL.

### *Handshape Feature Hierarchy: Articulatory Evidence*

Physiological evidence for the feature hierarchy captures relative independence among articulators. First, consider the articulatory independence among the specified fingers.

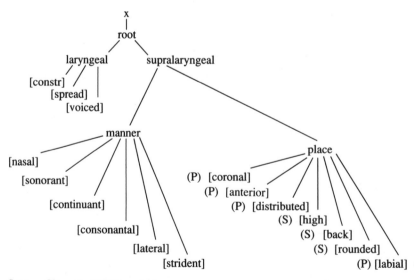

*Source.* Clements (1985), end view.

Key:

(P):   primary
(S):   secondary

***Figure 3.* Spoken-language feature hierarchy.**

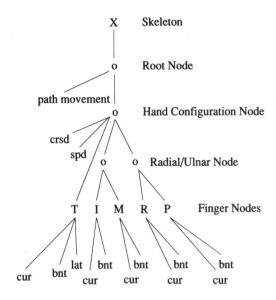

*Figure 4*. **Proposed feature hierarchy for ASL handshapes.**

As we have seen, some ASL handshapes require nonidentical configurations for specified fingers. Figure 5 shows the representation K/P under a hierarchical analysis. Note how the index finger receives a different configuration from the middle finger, which is different from the thumb; that is, each specified finger is to some degree articulatorily independent from the next. A representation in which specified fingers are independently represented allows us to capture the physiological facts.

Physiological factors motivating the nodes dominating radial and ulnar fingers and the effects on secondary movement are discussed above. Articulatory evidence for a hand configuration node derives from the observation that the finger configu-

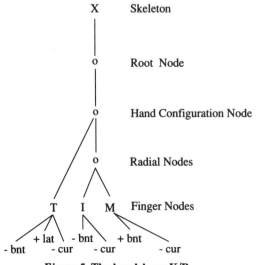

*Figure 5*. **The handshape K/P.**

rations [spread] and [crossed] apply exhaustively to all specified fingers. In ASL, we do not find handshapes where the index and middle fingers and the ring and pinky fingers are specified [− spread] while the middle and ring fingers are specified [+ spread] (the canonical Vulcan greeting). Likewise the feature [crossed], restricted as it is, also applies exhaustively to specified fingers.[4] These features stand in contrast to the features [bent] [curved] and [lateral], which as described above may vary from finger to finger in handshapes such as K/P. Note also that both features [spread] and [crossed] involve the same axis of opposition. The presence of a hand configuration node allows us to encode features that systematically make reference to relations among specified fingers.

It is interesting to note that the handshape R is typically not considered a primary handshape in ASL (see, for example, Sandler, 1987). Sandler considers primary handshapes to be those that involve hand-internal movement (handshape change and secondary movement). However, under the analysis adopted here in which the feature [crossed] attaches to the hand configuration node, R should be able to participate in handshape change. That is, both specified fingers, index and middle, receive identical configurations. This is consistent with the facts. The handshape R does participate in handshape change in the sign TWEEZERS. A representation in which the feature [+ crossed] is allowed to attach a hand-configuration node that dominates the specified fingers allows us to capture this fact.

### *Handshape Feature Hierarchy: Phonological Evidence*

We turn now to phonological evidence for the proposed hierarchy. Two types of evidence are considered: total handshape assimilations and partial handshape assimilations.

Phonological evidence for individual finger nodes is motivated by processes of partial handshape assimilations. Consider a sequence HAVE PRO-2. In this sequence the sign HAVE is articulated with a bent B handshape [+ bent, − curved], fingertips touching the signer's chest. The following pronominal sign is articulated with a straight index finger, a 1 handshape [− bent, − curved]. In this environment, it is not uncommon to see the sign HAVE articulated with a straight, rather than a bent, index finger. We may understand this form as arising from a regressive assimilation of the feature specification from the sign PRO-2. Two possible analyses are illustrated in figure 6.

In the 6a example the feature [− bent] spreads to the index node (I) of the flat B (B>) handshape and "de-links" the original specification. Another possible analysis, shown in 6b, assumes the entire index node (I) of the PRO-2 sign spreads to the hand configuration node of the flat B (B>) de-linking the I node of the B> handshape. The data unfortunately do not allow us to decide between these two hypotheses. A hypothetical case that would allow us to determine whether the feature or the finger node is spreading is illustrated in figure 7. In a sequence like HAVE ONION, spreading of a single feature versus the spreading of an entire finger node results in two different handshapes in the assimilated form. Such sequences, however, do not seem to afford assimilations.[5]

It is important to note that a representation in which finger nodes do not dominate feature configurations will be unable to account for partial handshape assimilation (see figure 8). First consider the case where only the index finger spreads backward

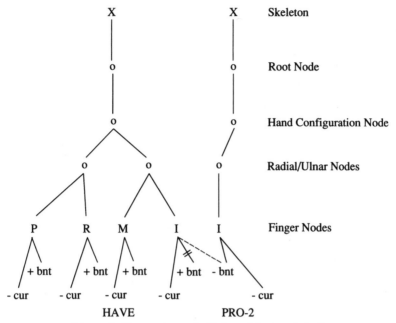

***Figure 6a.* Regressive assimilation of feature [- bnt].**

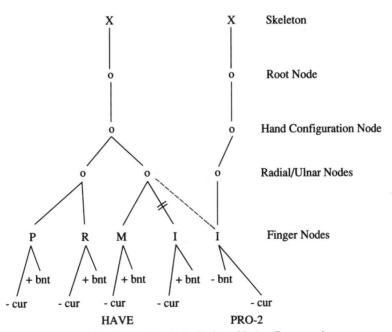

***Figure 6b.* Regressive assimilation of index-finger node.**

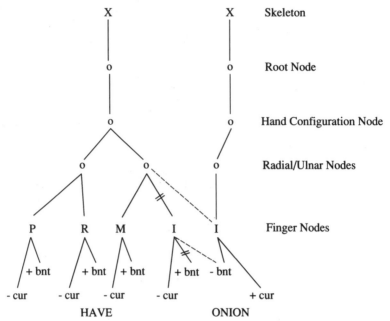

*Figure 7.* **Hypothetical case of feature spread versus finger-node spread.**

from the sign PRO-2 to the sign HAVE (see figure 8b). In this case, the configuration feature [bent] of the sign HAVE dominates the assimilated index finger. Thus no change is evident in the target handshape, that is, HAVE still is specified IMRP [bent]. Second, consider the case where it is the feature configuration that assimilates (see figure 8c). Under this analysis, the configuration feature [open] of the sign PRO-2 spreads backward to the position node of the sign HAVE. In this case, the representation predicts that all specified fingers of the sign HAVE will be [open]. However, as we have seen, partial assimilations in these cases affect only the index finger of the sign HAVE. Both of these accounts are incompatible with the data and thus a hierarchical model in which the finger nodes do not dominate finger configuration features is rejected.

In summary, physiological evidence for independent articulation of individual fingers and phonological evidence from partial assimilations argue for a representation in which individual fingers receive separate feature configurations.

### Redundancy in Representations

I argue above that facts of partial handshape assimilation and articulatory independence of fingers in ASL handshapes require representations where specified fingers dominate configuration features. However, under this proposal, it is clear that fully specified representations of an ASL handshape are wildly redundant. This is particularly true for handshapes that permit handshape change. Here two approaches for removing redundancy are suggested: underspecification and feature spreading.

Underspecification theory assumes that information that is redundant or predictable should be removed from the feature matrix and expressed as a rule in the grammar. Underspecification of configuration features may provide one avenue for

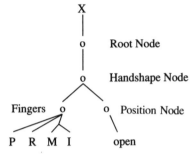

Source. Sandler (1987).

*Figure 8a.* Finger nodes do not dominate feature configurations.

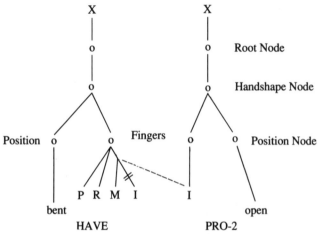

*Figure 8b.* Spreading of index-finger node.

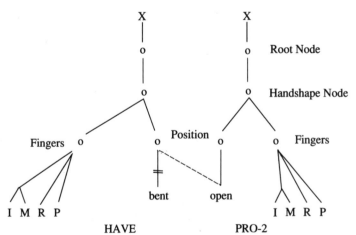

*Figure 8c.* Spreading of feature configuration.

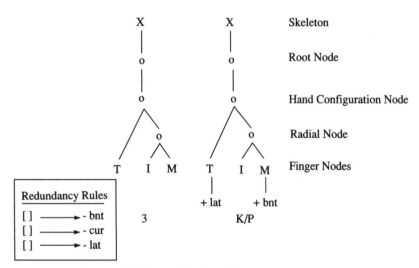

**Figure 9.** **Underspecification of feature configurations.**

removing redundancies in representations of ASL handshapes. Figure 9 compares a possible representation for a 3 and a K/P handshape, and redundancy rules for filling in unspecified features.

A second approach would be to assume that, underlyingly only unique feature configurations are specified, with subsequent associations defined by a spreading rule. Such an approach is illustrated in figure 10, again for the handshape 3 and K/P. This approach is essentially a formalism of Mandel's (1981) observation that in handshapes (and more correctly, handshapes that participate in handshape change), selected fingers will all receive the same feature configurations.

Clearly these two approaches make different predictions for phonological processes affecting handshapes in ASL. The implications of these two approaches or some combination thereof is, however, beyond the scope of the present paper.

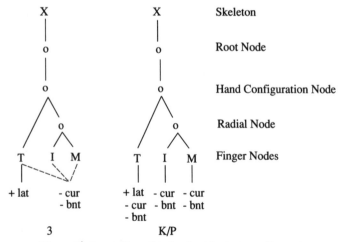

**Figure 10.** **Spreading of redundant feature configurations.**

## Total Handshape Assimilations

Phonological evidence for a hand configuration node derives from two sources: total handshape assimilations and the phonological effects resulting from morphological processes. Newkirk et al. (1976) discuss cases of total handshape assimilation in ASL involving the sequence PRO-1 verb (see table 2, data from Newkirk et al., 1976). For example, in the sequence PRO-1 KNOW, the unassimilated form consists of two independent handshapes, a flat 1 (1>) handshape for the sign PRO-1, which is pointed at the signer's chest, followed by the sign KNOW, a flat B (B>) handshape, fingers touching the forehead. The assimilated form of the sign PRO-1 is signed with a B> handshape, which touches the chest. This total assimilation is illustrated in figure 11. We can account for this regressive assimilation by spreading the hand configuration node from the sign KNOW onto the root node of PRO-1 and delinking its original specification.

Additional evidence for the hand-configuration node is to be found in an examination of sequences where the sign that follows PRO-1 involves handshape change. In this paper, I assume that a handshape that changes during the course of a path movement from one distinct handshape to another constitutes a contour segment. A detailed discussion of the treatment of handshape change as contour is found in Sandler (1987) and Corina and Sagey (in prep.). For the present these contours are represented as branching under the hand-configuration node (see figure 12).

Consider cases where the sign PRO-1 is followed by a handshape change in a sign such as FORGET. In this case only the left-most handshape spreads backward onto the PRO-1 sign. Thus, in the sequence PRO-1 FORGET, where the handshape for FORGET is a contour (descriptively a flat B handshape closing to an S handshape; B>→S), we find only the B> spreading backward onto the PRO-1, and not the entire contour. This derivation is illustrated in figure 13.

A similar phenomenon is seen in a comparison of reduplication versus suffixation in ASL. Reduplication has been used to describe morphological operations that derive

*Table 2.* **Total Handshape Assimilations**

|  | **Assimilating Environment** | | **Assimilated Form** | |
|---|---|---|---|---|
| 1. | 1><br>PRO-1 | B><br>KNOW | B><br>PRO-1 | B><br>KNOW |
| 2. | 1><br>PRO-1 | O><br>TEACH | O><br>PRO-1 | O><br>TEACH |
| 3. | 1><br>PRO-1 | H<br>JOIN | H><br>PRO-1 | H<br>JOIN |
| 4. | 1><br>PRO-1 | C → S<br>GET | C<br>PRO-1 | C → S<br>GET |
| 5. | 1><br>PRO-1 | B> → O><br>LEARN | B><br>PRO-1 | B> → O><br>LEARN |
| 6. | 1><br>PRO-1 | B> → S<br>FORGET | B><br>PRO-1 | B> → S<br>FORGET |

*Source.* Newkirk et al., (1976), Appendix I. Notation for handshapes used here differs slightly from Newkirk, et al.

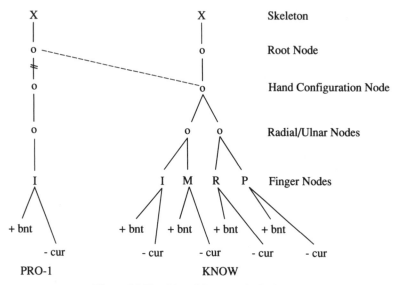

*Figure 11.* **Total handshape assimilation.**

continuative and durative form in ASL (Sandler, 1986a, Corina, 1987). We extend this analysis here to describe the formation of the dual inflection. Following Marantz (1982), an unspecified skeletal slot serves as a target for reduplication. Melodic material from the root is then spread onto this unspecified slot. Under this analysis, spreading of the root node is required, as path movement must spread as well. Note that it follows automatically that whatever handshape(s) is specified in the original segment will show up on the reduplicated segment. This, then, predicts that handshape changes will also be reduplicated. The facts support this analysis. For signs whose root forms contain handshape change, when inflected with morphological inflections that arise from reduplicative processes (continuative, dual, durative), we find the handshape change is rearticulated with each repetition of the inflected form. For example, in the dual inflection, the handshape change occurs twice, once during each unique path movement, as illustrated in figure 14.

Suffixation in ASL behaves differently from reduplication. As evidenced in the multiple inflection, only the second handshape of a contour spreads (Corina, 1986). That is, we observe the handshape change occurring during the first path movement, and then the handshape remains static throughout the rest of the sign. This is particularly evident in signs in which the handshape change is from a closed handshape to an open handshape, as in the sign ASK.

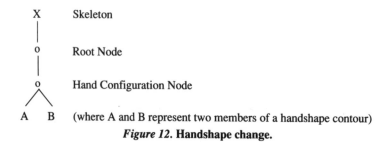

*Figure 12.* **Handshape change.**

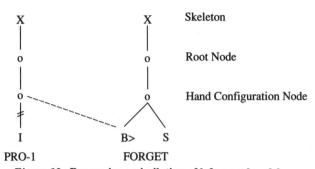

***Figure 13.*** **Regressive assimilation of left-most handshape.**

This follows if path movement is attached to the root node. Suffixes under this analysis are assumed to be prespecified for path movement, and thus a root node is already present. Spreading in these cases is limited to the hand-configuration node and nodes or features existing below this node. As is suggested by the data, the suffix takes only the right-most contour (see figure 15).

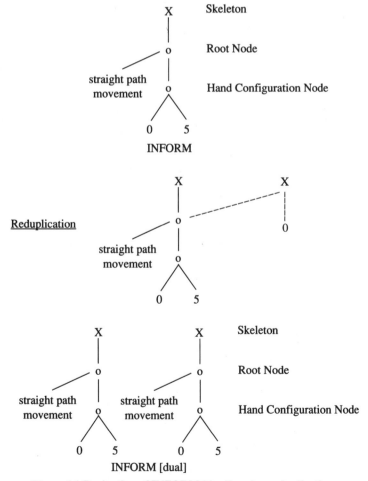

***Figure 14.*** **Derivation of INFORM [dual] under reduplication.**

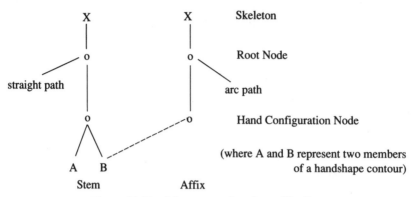

*Figure 15.* **Handshape spread under suffixation.**

Yip (1987) discusses a similar phenomenon with respect to tone contour in Danyang, a Wu dialect of Chinese. In this analysis of Chen's (1986, pp. 10–13) data, we find spreading of the entire contour in a polysyllabic domain. In the case of an underlying HL.LH melody, after the initial edge in association, we find the HL contour spreading rightward to intermediate syllables. This is illustrated below in figure 16.

Contrast the spreading of the entire tone contour shown in figure 16 with the spread of contour melody in figure 17 below. In this case, only the last level toneme spreads. Yip's analysis is similar to that shown for ASL. The presence of a branching under the root node allows one to spread either an entire contour as seen in figure 14 and 16, or alternatively one-half of a contour segment as shown in figures 15 and 17.

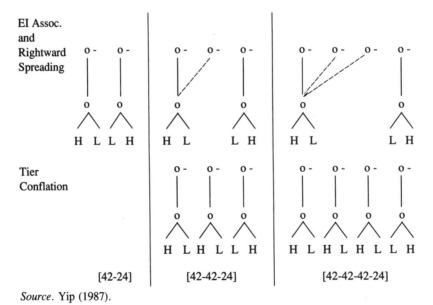

*Source.* Yip (1987).

*Figure 16.* **Tone contours as melodic units: tonal affricates.**

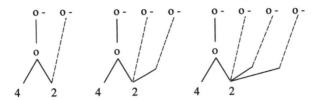

***Figure 17*. Spreading of right-most level toneme in contour tone.**

We have already alluded to the root node in our discussion of morphological processes and their effects on handshapes in ASL. Clements (1985) views the root node as a constituent containing all the features of a segment, which allows him to characterize the "phoneme" as a set of features dominated by a root. Additional support comes from the examination of total assimilation, which creates geminates by spreading root nodes (Clements, 1985). Sagey (1986) argues for a root node based upon association of underspecified segments to skeletal slots in root-and-pattern languages such as Yawelmani. She suggests that unlike the other nodes in a feature hierarchy, root nodes have phonological but not phonetic motivation.

As noted, path movement has been assumed to be directly attached to the root node. We have seen how this produces the correct results for reduplication versus suffixation in ASL. However it is not clear whether the existence of this node is directly important in handshape phenomena. As hierarchical models such as this become more elaborated, additional justification may become apparent (see, for example, Sandler, 1987). We turn now to an examination of an interesting phenomenon related to the blockage of handshape assimilations.

## Blockage of Handshape Assimilations

Recall the environment for partial handshape assimilations discussed above: verb PRO-2. In this environment, the specification for the index finger of the sign PRO-2 may appear in the sign preceding the pronoun, a case of regressive assimilation. Other examples of this type of assimilation elicited for the current study are presented in table 3. Note, however, that in cases 3 through 6, despite the environment where

***Table 3*. Partial-Handshape Assimilations**

| Assimilating Environment | | Assimilated Form | | | |
|---|---|---|---|---|---|
| 1. B> <br> HAVE | 1 <br> PRO-2 | B> +1 <br> HAVE | 1 <br> PRO-2 | | |
| 2. B> <br> KNOW | 1 <br> PRO-2 | B> +1 <br> KNOW | 1 <br> PRO-2 | | |
| 3. S → 5 <br> GAMBLE | 1 <br> PRO-2 | S → 5 <br> GAMBLE | 1 <br> PRO-2 | *S → 5+1 | |
| 4. 5 → O <br> GONE | 1 <br> PRO-2 | 5 → O <br> GONE | 1 <br> PRO-2 | *5 → O+1 | |
| 5. 5 → S <br> MEMORIZE | 1 | 5 → S <br> PRO-2 | 1 <br> MEMORIZE | *5 → S+1 | PRO-2 |

we would expect to find assimilations, no assimilations occur. What is significant about these examples is that all of the signs preceding the PRO-2 involve handshape change. Thus, it appears that regressive assimilation is blocked when the target for the assimilation is a contour segment.

Let us examine whether there is anything inherent in the hierarchical representation of a contour segment that would exclude these patterns. Let us assume that what is spreading in these cases is the entire index-finger node. This situation is shown for the sequence MEMORIZE PRO-1 (see figure 18). Nothing appears to block the assimilation structurally. For example, we do not cross association lines. We could spread the index finger to the right-most branch of the handshape in MEMORIZE and delink the original specification. Why then is the assimilation blocked? One possibility is that it is simply a rule of the grammar of ASL and must be stipulated as such. However, another possibility is that this assimilation is blocked because the representation that would result would no longer be a possible contour in ASL. That is, a contour that starts with a 5 handshape cannot end in a 1 handshape. This view is compatible with one in which a contour change in ASL must affect all specified fingers uniformly. A process of assimilation that would render finger specifications nonidentical in contour segments is blocked. This observation warrants further investigation and may ultimately help constrain representations for handshape change in ASL (see for example Corina and Sagey, in prep.).

### Regressive Assimilation Revisited

The sequence GALLAUDET COLLEGE presents an apparent counterexample to the claim that regressive assimilation is blocked in handshapes where a contour segment serves as a target.[6] The sign GALLAUDET is made with a G, which moves laterally and closes to a closed G handshape at the side of the forehead at about eye level. The sign COLLEGE is a two-handed sign in which the dominant hand, a B handshape palm down, touches the nondominant (also a B handshape) hand palm up and arcs in a sagittal plane. The important point here is that the sign GALLAUDET in this

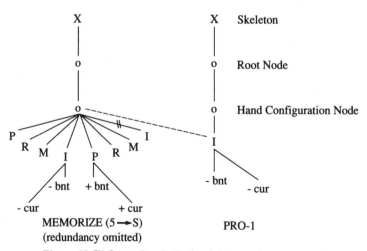

***Figure 18.*** **Ill-formed assimilation into a contour segment.**

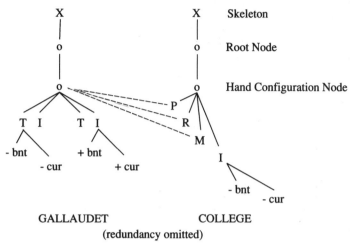

GALLAUDET       COLLEGE
(redundancy omitted)

***Figure 19.* Well-formed assimilation into a contour segment.**

environment is often made with an open F handshape that closes to a closed F handshape, rather than a G-handshape sequence. Apparently the finger specifications from the sign COLLEGE [ − cur, − bent] regressively assimilate to the G handshape. Note, however, an important difference between this example and the examples seen before. In the cases where regressive assimilation is blocked by a contour segment, the target segment underlyingly is specified for the finger that is being assimilated. That is, in the case of MEMORIZE PRO-2 (see figure 17) both signs are underlyingly specified for an index finger node. In the GALLAUDET COLLEGE example, the fingers being affected by the assimilation (M, R, and P) are not underlyingly specified on the target handshape, but are in the following sign (see figure 19). Thus, it appears that the spread of unspecified fingers is not blocked in regressive assimilation.

## CONCLUSION

In this paper I examine a proposal for a hierarchical model of handshape features in ASL. This model is motivated by both articulatory and phonological evidence. I have shown how a model in which individual fingers dominate feature configurations can handle data from partial handshape assimilation in ASL. Further, cases of total handshape assimilation involving signs with handshape change can also be accommodated. Data from these sign sequences are shown to be compatible with a system in which handshape change is represented as a branching contour below the hand configuration node. This phenomenon is similar to the spread of tone contour in a dialect of Chinese. I also examine examples of blockage of assimilation in which contour segments serve as targets. I suggest that contour segments cannot serve as targets in assimilation if they are underlyingly specified for the fingers being spread. However, spread of specified fingers into targets unspecified for those fingers is not blocked.

    The success of hierarchical representation in capturing phonological processes in both signed and spoken languages provides support for the hypothesis that abstract phonological systems, despite surface realization, reflect a basic organizational principle of human language.

## NOTES

This research was supported in part by the National Institutes of Health, grants #NS15175, #NS19096, and #HD13249, as well as National Science Foundation grant #BNS86–09085. I wish to thank Doctors Ursula Bellugi and Howard Poizner at the Salk Institute for Biological Studies. I especially wish to thank Betsy Sagey for extensive discussion of this paper. Lucinda O'Grady, Cheryl Fleck, Freda Norman, Karen Emmorey and Mary Hare provided valuable input.

1. Orientation features are not dealt with in the present paper, and thus are omitted from the diagrams. For a discussion of orientation features in a hierarchical framework see Sandler (1987).
2. The conditioning of handshapes to avoid extant social taboos is attested in some European sign languages, for example, Danish Sign Language. Danish Sign Language uses a version of the one-handed fingerspelling alphabet. However, since the American articulation of "T" (in which the thumb intervenes between the index and middle finger) is considered a vulgar gesture in Denmark, the letter "T" is articulated in Danish Sign Language with the thumb placed at the radial side of the index finger rather than intervening between the index and middle finger. In addition the index finger is not fully closed. I thank Earl Elkins for bringing this point to my attention.
3. Sandler's (1987) hierarchical model of ASL handshape contains a node dominating index and middle fingers (p. 100). Sandler states that this subconstituency represents groups of selected fingers that occur as sets in signs. However, little evidence is presented for this grouping. The facts discussed here provide both phonological and physiological motivation for a subdivision between radial and ulnar fingers.
4. An apparent counterexample may be the novel form of the sign SPACE-SHUTTLE, which appears to be a combination of the sign AIRPLANE ( ⊔ handshape) and ROCKET (R handshape). However, it is possible that this is in fact a polymorphemic classifier sign and thus falls outside the domain of the current analysis.
5. The fact that nearly all of the assimilations discussed in this paper typically involve pronouns and a verb and not just any arbitrary combination of signs is probably not accidental. This fact suggests that these assimilations may be morphosyntactically conditioned, perhaps an example of cliticization.
6. I thank Scott Liddell for bringing this example to my attention.

## REFERENCES

Archangeli D. (1984). Underspecification in Yawelmani phonology and morphology. Ph.D. diss., MIT.

Brentari, D. (1987). Partial predictability in ASL handshape change. Paper presented at the conference, Theoretical Issues in Sign Language Research, II, 18–21 May, at Gallaudet University, Washington, DC.

Chen, M. (1986). An overview of tone Sandhi across Chinese dialects. Paper presented at the Conference on Languages and Dialects of China, Oakland, California.

Clements, G. N. (1985). The geometry of phonological features. *Phonology Yearbook* 2:225–52.

Corina, D. P. (1986). ASL phonology: A CV perspective. Paper presented at the annual meeting of the Linguistic Society of America, December, New York, NY.

———, and Sagey, E. C. (in preparation). Underspecification in ASL handshapes and handshape sequences.

Klima, E., and Bellugi, U. (1979). *The signs of language*. Cambridge: Harvard University Press.

Liddell, S. K., and Johnson, R. E. (1985). American Sign Language: The phonological base. Gallaudet University, Washington, DC. Unpublished manuscript.

Mandel, M. A. (1981). Phonotactics and morphophonology in American Sign Language. Ph.D. diss., University of California, Berkeley.

Marantz, A. (1982). Re Reduplication. *Linguistic Inquiry* 13:435–82.

Newkirk, D., Pedersen, C., Bellugi, U., and Klima, E. S. (1976). Interferences between sequentially produced signs in American Sign Language. La Jolla, CA: The Salk Institute for Biological Studies. Unpublished manuscript.

Sagey, E. C. (1986). The representation of features and relation in nonlinear phonology. Ph.D. diss., MIT.

Sandler, W. (1986a). Aspectual inflections and the hand-tier model of ASL phonology. Paper presented at the conference, Theoretical Issues in Sign Language Research, I, 13–16 June, at Rochester, NY.

———. (1986b). The spreading hand autosegment of American Sign Language. *Sign Language Studies* 50:1–28.

———. (1987). Sequentiality and simultaneity in American Sign Language phonology. Ph.D. diss., University of Texas, Austin.

Supalla, T. (1986). The classifier system in American Sign Language. In *Noun Classes and Categorization*, edited by C. Colette, pp. 181–214, *Typological Studies in Language* 7.

Welmers, W. E. (1973). *African language structure*. Berkeley: University of California Press.

Wilbur, R. B. (1987). *American Sign Language*, 2d ed. Boston, MA: Little, Brown.

Yip, M. (1987). Tone contours as melodic units: Tonal affricates. Brandeis University, Waltham, MA. Unpublished manuscript.

# The Regularity Hypothesis Applied to ASL

## Margaret G. Moser

Gradual language change is a universal fact. Language is organized into two simultaneous, independent levels of structure: the phonology organizes sounds, and the grammar organizes meaningful units. At both levels, separate change processes operate. Regular sound change operates at the phonological level.

In this paper, I claim that regular change in the technical sense of historical linguistics does not occur in sign languages. Such regular change is distinct from the systematic lexical changes that have been observed. To support any claim, I will construct hypothetical examples of regular change in ASL and show that they are fundamentally different from the known changes in historical ASL. Then, I will suggest some facts about ASL are indirect evidence that regular change does not occur.

## REGULAR CHANGE IN SPOKEN LANGUAGE

The description "regular change" is a term for change at the phonetic level. I will use the term "systematic change" to describe other kinds of change that may be exceptionless or formulated by a rule, but that are not regular. For the purposes of this paper, then, a change can be regular or systematic but not both.

The Regularity Hypothesis was first proposed as a working assumption by the neogrammarians in the late 1870s. It accounts for systematic phonetic differences among corresponding words of historically related languages. In regular change, the phonemic system of contrasts in a language can and does change in ways that restructure that system. When a single segment alters its sound, all words containing the segment change their pronunciation without exception and without regard for meaning. Hock explains the Regularity Hypothesis by stating that a "change in pronunciation which is not conditioned by non-phonetic factors is regular and operates without exceptions at a particular time and in a particular speech community, with possible environmental restrictions." (1986, 35). Regular change is often described as "mechanical" because its domain is sound units, not meaning units. So, regular change is uniform change of an element in the phonology. To illustrate, I will give examples of regular change, and then change that is systematic but not regular.

First, a change that has no environmental restrictions is shown in figure 1. This describes the devoicing of stops, a part of Grimm's law. For example, /d/, a voiced stop, changed its pronunciation to that of its voiceless counterpart /t/. So the proto-IndoEuropean word "dekm" changed into Old English "teon." Because the change is at the level of phonology, every word that contained the /d/ sound changed into one with the /t/ sound.

Suppose, counter to fact, that no other changes accompany this one, although historically there were several related changes. Then the distinction between the /d/ and /t/ sounds is useful. This contrast was useful for differentiating words like [den] and [ten], [dip] and [tip], [led] and [let], etc. In modern English, this merger, or loss of contrast, between /d/ and /t/ would create homonyms from all three minimal pairs.

Contrasts can be introduced as well as lost. This process of phonological split occurs when the alternant pronunciations of a segment lose their predictability. For instance, in Old English, the pronunciation of the /f/ phoneme could be an [f] or [v] as shown in figure 2. In word-final position, the /f/ phoneme was an [f] sound. Before a vowel or sonorant, it was a [v] sound. So, in the word "lif," the [f] sound was selected, and in the word "lifyan," the [v] sound was selected. The alternation is conditioned by the environment, that is, the variation was predictable. However, other changes in the language resulted in deletion of the final syllable in words like "livyan." The new form "liv" retained its pronunciation of the /f/ phoneme, the [v] sound. Thus [v] occurred in environments that previously selected the [f] sound, and the alternation was no longer predictable. With both alternants occurring in the same position, they can contrast, as in [layf] versus [layv] or [fin] versus [vin].

Language is dually articulated; the level of phonology is structured independently of the grammatical level. The regular change in phonology contrasts with analogical change, which is systematic at the grammatical level. An example of analogical change is the development of the plural marker "-s" between Old and Middle English. In Old English, the paradigm for a noun like "stone" had six forms as shown in figure 3. Several changes merged the case endings, so the six forms had only two pronunciations. The plural nominative case was reinterpreted to mean just plural. This became a model, the /s/ was used as a plural marker in other paradigms. The incorporation of /s/ into other paradigms is a systematic change that involves the meaning of forms. This kind of change is "mental" or "psychological" compared to mechanical regular change.

In reality, of course, a system as complex as language does not undergo change that is purely mechanical and exceptionless. Although the Regularity Hypothesis

Rule:

$$\begin{bmatrix} + \text{stop} \\ + \text{voice} \end{bmatrix} > [- \text{voice}]$$

Example:

d > t, as in

| PIE | OE | |
|---|---|---|
| *dekm(t) | teon | 'ten' |

*Figure 1.* **Sound merger.**

Rule:

/f/:     [v] / [ + son] ___ {[ + son] or V}
         [f] / [ + son] ___ #

Example:

| OE | NE |
|----|----|
| lif | layf |
| livyan | liv |

*Figure 2.* **Sound split.**

establishes a methodology, exceptions a to regular change must be explained in terms of nonphonetic sources such as analogical change.

## REGULAR CHANGE IN ASL

Now the question is, what would constitute regular change in sign language? And the answer depends on the type of phonology. In sign language, a system of visual contrasts serves the same purpose as the vocal contrasts of speech. To understand regular change in sign language, we need some account of the phonetic factors and environmental restrictions mentioned in the Regularity Hypothesis.

Stokoe (1960) was the first to analyze the subsign organization of ASL. More recent work has greatly refined this analysis. To name just a few such studies: Friedman (1976), Supalla and Newport (1978), Gee and Kegl (1982), Liddell (1984), Liddell (1987), Sandler (1987), and Padden and Perlmutter (1987). It is now generally agreed that ASL phonology requires a sequential nonlinear model. That is, rather than being made up solely of simultaneous phonemes, a sign may have sequential segments. These segments are best described as multiple autonomous segments associated with timing slots. However, the exact content and organization of these autosegments is still being debated.

For the purpose of constructing hypothetical regular changes, I will assume a simplified version of the Hand-Tier model and feature specifications presented in Sandler (1987). The canonical form of a sign in this model, shown in figure 4, consists of a sequence of locations and movements, Ls and Ms. These are timing slots, each with its own feature matrix. In addition, each sign has a single separate hand-configuration autosegment.

Within autosegmental phonology, the identity of the phonemes is not so clear-cut. The question arises as to what unit of analysis is appropriate to describe change. The possibility corresponding most closely to generative phonology is to consider a unit to be all the features associated with a timing slot. Then everything that is simultaneous is part of the same unit, and a unit endures for only one time slot. In the canonical sign there would be three units, each with only a sequential environment, as shown in figure 4a.

| sg. nom. acc | stan | >stone | pl. nom. acc | stanas | >stanes |
|---|---|---|---|---|---|
| dat | stane | >stone | | stanum | >stane |
| gen | stanes | >stones | | stana | >stane |

*Figure 3.* **Analogy.**

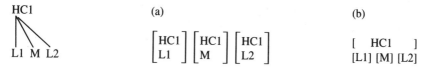

*Figure 4*. **Hand-tier model.**

In keeping with the tradition of ASL phonology, however, handshape, location, and movement are separate units. That is, another possibility is to maintain the autonomy of the autosegments in describing change, as shown in figure 4b. In this case, the unit is an autosegment, as opposed to all the features in a timing slot. Here, the conditioning environment for change may be both simultaneous and sequential. The L1 autosegment, for instance, may be conditioned by HC1 and/or the sequence M,L2. Also, a segment may endure for more than one timing slot. For example, the hand-configuration autosegment, HC1, spreads across three timing slots. It is also possible that the conditioning environment is more limited, confined to autosegments in the same tier. The appropriate description of a conditioning environment within the framework of autosegmental phonology is beyond the scope of this paper.

Now I will construct possible regular changes in ASL that are analogous to the sound changes discussed in the last section. The rule of pinky selection could describe a regular change for handshape, as given in figure 5. Its effect is an unconditioned merger of the handshape A with the handshape Y. The contrast between these two handshapes would be lost. Without exception, every sign previously articulated with an A would now be articulated with a Y. In particular, any signs that previously contrasted only in this handshape would become homophonous. For example, AT-TEMPT, made with an A handshape, and CONTINUE would become homophonous, both looking like the sign for continue.

This rule does in fact describe a recent change. DRUNK, originally made with the 10 handshape, acquired an alternant with the Y handshape. Subsequently, this alternant has been taken to mean VERY DRUNK or BLITZED. Further, the pinky selection has been extended to other signs in order to express extreme degrees. BORING, with a G handshape, can be intensified with pinky selection. However, even if every sign could systematically incorporate this intensifier, this would not be a regular change because it is morphological. The choice of the pinky-selected alternant is meaningful, not environmentally conditioned. The productiveness of this new intensifier is an analogical change, not a regular one.

For a possible phonological split, consider figure 6. Wilbur (1987) discusses predictable variation of the handshapes S and A. The variant with the thumb to the

Rule:

$$\begin{bmatrix} +\text{thumb} \\ -\text{index} \\ +\text{open} \end{bmatrix} > [\,+\text{pinky}\,]$$

Example:

A > Y, as in

| ASL | CHANGE |
|---|---|
| ATTEMPT | ATTEMPT with Y handshape ( = CONTINUE) |

*Figure 5*. **Merger in ASL.**

Rule:

/S/:       [A]/ ___
                 [+ contact]
           [S] otherwise

Example:

ASL        CHANGE
WASH       WASH$_1$ with [A]
           WASH$_2$ with [S]

*Figure 6.* **Split in ASL.**

side is predictable, occurring in environments where the thumb would otherwise block knuckle contact, as in WASH. This is an example of conditioning from the simultaneous environment. The value of the feature [thumb-cross] in the handshape segment is conditioned by the value of the feature [contact] in an L or M segment to which it is associated.

If for some reason the conditioning environment (that is, the type of contact) is lost, the variation would no longer be predictable. For instance, the sign WASH has a [− thumb-cross] feature on its hand segment due to the feature [+ contact] on the associated location segment. Suppose a compound forms from WASH and BASIN. Segment deletion is a common result of compound formation. If the conditioning environment (the base hand) were deleted, A might retain its uncrossed shape. This would leave the handshape A in the noncontacting environment that should condition S. Once the variation has lost is predictability, it would become contrastive.

The discussion so far would suggest that features on the location and movement segments can condition a variation on adjacent segments. However, I have found no clear example of this in the literature, so I will not construct an example of a regular change in ASL with a sequential conditioning environment.

With these examples in mind, consider documented sign change for regularity. Frishberg (1975) identifies five processes or patterns of change between corresponding forms in historical data and modern ASL. First, signs that involved facial expressions, nonmanual movement, touching something in the environment, etc., have lost these extra elements. Such aspects are not part of the phonological system, so lexicalization has deleted them. For example, WONDER transferred head motion to manual motion. Second, signs have altered their locations to more visually convenient positions on the signer's body. Third, signs have been brought in line with the symmetry condition. This has led to change in either handshape or movement. In two-handed signs, the handshape of the base hand has assimilated to that of the articulating hand. For instance, DEPEND has changed from a 1 handshape contacting a B hand to a 1 handshape contacting another 1 handshape. Or, one-handed signs located in the peripheries of the sign space added the other hand with symmetrical handshape and movement.

Siple (1978) suggests that the historical tendency to add or delete a hand is explained by facts about visual acuity. Two-handed signs located near the face became one-handed because this is the area of highest acuity. For example, the two-handed sign for DEVIL became one-handed. Conversely, one-handed signs located in areas of lower acuity became two-handed, as for ANGRY.

Fourth, meaningful segments, both location and handshape, have generalized to other signs. For instance, UNCLE is noted in Woodward (1976) to have moved from neutral location to forehead because this location amounts to a morpheme for "male." Fifth, fluidity has operated on compound signs, smoothing them through assimilation and loss.

All of these processes operate to increase naturalness, redundancy, and systematicity. That is, they result in easier articulation and perception, and they reduce the number of possible phonemic combinations found in the language. Also, these processes operate without regard for iconic elements, so the result of change is to increase the arbitrariness of the sign, favoring systematicity over iconicity.

But are any of these patterns regular, that is, systematic at the phonological level? The answer is no. Instead, they seem to be an incorporation mechanism. As discussed in Klima and Bellugi (1979), new signs may be coined with a reduced p-antomime, fingerspelled loans, and compound formation. When new signs come into the language, they may stretch the constraints of the language. The incorporation mechanism brings them in line with the constraints.

A regular change occurs entirely within the phonological system and may in fact alter that system. That is, regular change involves forms that are stable, conforming to naturalness and redundancy conditions, both before and after the change. Furthermore, the changes in ASL are not exceptionless in the rigorous way required by the Regularity Hypothesis. From the descriptions Frishberg gives, the patterns of change are tendencies. The methodology of requiring an explanation for any exception to the change does not seem to apply here.

On the other hand, two of Frishberg's findings, the generalization of meaningful segments and the reduction of compounds, are related to familiar change processes. The shift of UNCLE to the forehead location implies the segment has been reinterpreted and then extended to other forms. Like the Y handshape intensifier discussed earlier, this parallels the process of analogical change defined in the previous section.

Since Frishberg's work, the process of compound formation has been investigated by Klima and Bellugi (1979) and Liddell and Johnson (1986), among others. By analyzing the sequential segment structure of signs, Liddell and Johnson are able to predict which segments and features will delete in a compound, a morphological process. This is the kind of situation that sets the stage for regular change. That is, if the variation of a segment is conditioned by its sequential environment, then the deletion of segments in a compound could leave the variation in contrast, or at least no longer predictable. In other words, compounds should be an environment in which regular change is initiated.

The lack of documented examples certainly does not prove that regular change does not occur. The Regularity Hypothesis was formulated on the basis of many volumes of comparative grammars of the IndoEuropean languages. Nothing like this exists for sign languages.

However, two properties of ASL provide indirect evidence that regular change does not occur. First, there is a strong tendency in ASL to avoid homonyms. The creation of homonyms is a common effect of regular change. When a merger occurs, homonyms are created wherever the distinction being lost was the only distinctive sound of the pair. Homonym avoidance in ASL suggests that whatever change would have created the homonym is not regular. Second, ASL seems to have very few instances of predictable variation, which is a prerequisite for gaining and losing new contrasts.

## CONCLUSION

In this paper I have discussed the sign language analogue to regular sound change and constructed representative examples. Although there is not enough historical data to be conclusive, the historical change that is documented is not regular. Furthermore, the avoidance of homonyms and rarity of predictable variation in ASL are indirect evidence that regular change does not occur.

## REFERENCES

Friedman, L. (1976). Phonology of a soundless language: Phonological structure of the American Sign Language, PhD. diss. University of California, Berkeley.

———. (1977). Formational properties in American Sign Language. In *On the other hand: New perspectives on American Sign Language*, edited by L. Friedman, 13–57. New York: Academic Press.

Frishberg, N. (1975). Arbitrariness and iconicity: Historical change in ASL. *Language* 51:696–719.

Gee, J., and Kegl, J. (1982). Semantic perspicuity and the locative hypothesis: Implications for acquisition. *Journal of Education* 164:185–209.

Hock, H. (1986). *Principles of historical linguistics*. Berlin, NY: deGruyter.

Klima, E., and Bellugi, U. (1979). *The signs of language*. Cambridge, MA: Harvard University Press.

Liddell, S. (1984). THINK and BELIEVE: Sequentiality in American Sign Language. *Language* 60:372–99.

———. (1987). Structures for representing handshapes and local movement at the phonemic level. Gallaudet University. Unpublished manuscript.

———, and Johnson, R. (1986). American Sign Language compound formation and phonological remnants. *Natural Language and Linguistic Theory* 4:445–513.

Rimor, M., Kegl, J., Lange, H., and Schermer, T. (1984). Natural phonetic processes underlie historical change and register variation in American Sign Language. *Sign Language Studies* 43:97–119.

Sandler, W. (1987). Sequentiality and simultaneity in American Sign Language phonology. PhD. diss. University of Texas, Austin.

Siple, P. (1978). Visual constraints for sign language communication. *Sign Language Studies* 19:95–110.

Stokoe, W. (1972). *Semiotics and human sign languages*. The Hague: Mouton.

Wilbur, R. (1987). *American Sign Language: Linguistic and applied dimensions*, 2d ed. Boston: College Hill Publishers.

Woodward, J. (1976). Signs of change: Historical variation in American Sign Languages. *Sign Language Studies* 10:81–94.

———, and Erting, C. (1975). Synchronic variation and historical change in ASL. *Language Sciences* 37:9–12.

# Licensing in
# ASL Handshape Change

## Diane Brentari

How much handshape change is permitted within an ASL sign and within what domain(s) do such constraints apply? I will be treating constraints on handshape change as static Well-formedness Conditions. I will show that these constraints function at the Word Level (W-level) of a phonological representation (Goldsmith, in press) and may be expressed in two licensing statements. "Licensing" may be defined as the control of a specific node in a phonological representation over a set of features. Both the syllable (as a prosodic unit) and the word will play a critical role in this analysis. Handshape change has been traditionally defined as a single change of handshape within a synchronically monomorphemic sign, such as those shown below.[1]

| | | |
|---|---|---|
| LIKE | THROW | CATCH |
| VANISH | SO-WHAT | ADVISE |
| HATE | WAKE-UP | |

This definition will be altered during the course of this paper.

## THE PROBLEM

Do the two handshapes in each of the signs above belong to one handshape class or two? One analysis of the phenomenon of handshape change, notably that of Liddell and Johnson (1985), says that there are two handshapes in such signs, and that the relationship between the two is unpredictable, and therefore, must be fully specified in the phonological representation. Consider the following signs.[2]

| | |
|---|---|
| CHOOSE | 4 o > 9 o p |
| DESTROY | 4 u > A u |
| MEMORIZE | 4 o > S o |

The first handshape is the same in all cases, but the second handshape varies, indicating that the second handshape cannot be predicted from the first.

Work by Friedman (1977) supports the first part of Liddell and Johnson's analysis, but not the second part. She agrees that there are two handshapes in this class of signs containing handshape change, but says that one must be "neutral." By neutral, she means that the handshapes belong to the group of handshapes discussed thoroughly in Battison (1978) and Boyes-Braem (1981) that may occur as the base hand in two-handed signs like HELP, VOTE, HIT, and AGAINST, and are the most common handshapes used in ASL. These are B, A, S, C, O, 1, and 5. Battison reports that within this class of signs containing handshape change, 87.7 percent include one of these handshapes, and 63.2 percent contain two from this group of seven. The 13 percent that do not conform to this 87 percent are those containing handshapes V, H, and those that have notational variants for 1, like those listed below (1978, 52). Battison uses the notation system developed in Stokoe (1965).

| | |
|---|---|
| NO | V o > V^ o p |
| EJACULATE | V u > V u |
| MOOCH | H o > H^ o   (H > 3 in Stokoe notation) |
| CUT | V o- > H o- |
| WAKE-UP | 1 o p > 1 o   (baby O > L in Stokoe notation) |

From the set of seven neutral handshapes mentioned above, 5, 1, A and S are the handshapes earliest acquired (McIntire, 1977), and 5 is the handshape used most often in nonsign gesturing that accompanies speech.[3] Neutrality and markedness are two notions that will be further explained during the course of this chapter.

The other analysis proposed for such signs states that there are open and closed variants of the same handshape class represented in monomorphemic signs with handshape change (Sandler, 1987; Stokoe, 1965). Sandler calls this "Handshape Internal Movement," and she states that she is following Stokoe's insight that "the beginning and ending shapes in signs with Handshape Internal Movement actually belong to the same underlying class of shapes" (1987, 92).[4] It is true that a "closed 1" and a "closed H" are articulated differently at the phonetic level. But to claim that these two handshapes are in different underlying classes, while "closed H" and "open H" are from the same underlying class, is the important point at which Liddell and Johnson's analysis differs from Sandler's. The following examples show a few signs that demonstrate Sandler's approach as expressed in her notation system.

| | |
|---|---|
| THROW | closed H > open H |
| UNDERSTAND | closed 1 > open 1 |
| LIKE | open 8 > closed 8 |

Sandler postulates a "Handshape Sequence Constraint" (p. 193).
In monomorphemic signs with handshape internal movement:

1. the initial and final handshapes are specified for the same selected fingers, and
2. the first shape may be [ + closed] if the second shape is [ + open]. Otherwise, the first shape is [ + open].

For Sandler, [ + closed] is defined as "bent at bottom two or all three joints, and tips touching thumbtip" and [ + open] as "straight, not bent at any joint" (p. 188).

There are at least two clear sets of counterexamples to this constraint. The first are those like S–O and MELT, which contain [ + closed] feature values in both positions. These are signs that contain flat and closed handshapes.

$$\text{S–O } [+ \text{ closed}] > [+ \text{ closed}] \text{ (S > B\textasciicircum o p)}$$
$$[- \text{ open}] \qquad [- \text{ open}]$$

$$\text{MELT } [+ \text{ closed}] > [+ \text{ closed}] \text{ (B\textasciicircum o p > A)}$$
$$[- \text{ open}] \qquad [- \text{ open}]$$

The feature specifications do not reflect any handshape change in these signs. The second set of counterexamples are signs like ENVISION and WIDE-AWAKE, which begin with a closed handshape and end with a curved one.[5] These begin with a [ + closed] handshape in Sandler's system.

$$\text{ENVISION } [+ \text{ closed}] > [- \text{ closed}] \text{ (S > B\"o)}$$
$$[- \text{ open}] \qquad [- \text{ open}]$$

The Handshape Sequence Constraint wrongly predicts [ + open] in first position. Because the signs above have [ − open] in the second handshape position, they should have [ + open] in first position, yet neither of them do.

Despite these exceptions, there are valuable insights in both of these explanations—the analysis of these signs as having one handshape or two handshapes—and they will be utilized in the analysis I am about to describe. Here, these handshape data will be viewed from an interactive model of perception and production.

## ANALYSIS

### *Choice of Handshape*

One observation about handshape change is that there are actually two notions of markedness that play a role in ASL handshape. The first concerns the choice of individual handshape. The first step in an analysis of handshape change is to identify the group of handshapes that do *not* occur in the class of signs in question. The handshape symbols that are used throughout this analysis are in table 1.[6] Handshapes that do not occur in signs with handshape change are !, D, T, =, N, and M, and these could be considered the relatively marked handshapes as compared with the

### *Table 1.* Handshape Inventory

| Handshape | Description |
|---|---|
| B | all four fingers open [ − spread] |
| B | all four fingers open (commonly known as handshape 4) [ − peripheral] [ − open] |
| A | four fingers closed (unopposed thumb) |
| S | four fingers closed (opposed thumb) |
| 1 | all but index closed |
| 9 | all but index open |
| H | all but index and middle closed |
| H | all but index and middle closed (commonly known as handshape N) [ − peripheral] [ − open] |
| H | all but index and middle closed (commonly known as handshape V) [ + spread] |
| ! | all but middle closed |
| 8 | all but middle open |
| I | all but pinky closed |
| W | all but pinky open ([ + open] fingers selected) |
| W | all but pinky open (commonly known as handshape M) [ − peripheral] [ − open] |
| 6 | all but pinky open ([ − open] finger selected) |
| = | all but pinky and index closed |
| K | ring and pinky closed; index open; middle partly open |
| R | ring and pinky closed; index and middle crossed |
| 7 | all but ring open and spread |
| T | all fingers closed; thumb under index |

seven unmarked handshapes of Battison. According to the analysis I am developing, any time such a marked handshape occurs, it will remain constant throughout the duration of the sign. This is a one-way implication, since the unmarked handshapes occur in signs with no change, while !, D, = , T, and M do not occur in signs with change. This point is illustrated in table 2.

### *Handshape Posture*

The second notion of markedness is ASL handshape concerns handshape posture. Of the possible handshape postures described by Liddell and Johnson (1985), the open ( ) and closed ( − ) handshapes are relatively unmarked as compared with flat (ˆ) and curved (¨) handshapes. Indirect evidence for this distinction comes from work done by Lane et al. (1977). In confusion-matrix analyses done with handshapes was compactness or extension of the hand. [ + compact] was defined as having no extended fingers; [ + broad] was defined as having three or more fingers extended. Although the classes and feature distinctions are not parallel to those used by Liddell and Johnson, the general notion of "broad" could be translated to "open" and "compact" to "closed," respectively.

The types of handshape postures that occur in signs with handshape change are structurally divided using two features: [ ± open] and [ ± peripheral], as shown below. A [ − peripheral] handshape posture is marked, as compared with a [ + peripheral] handshape posture, which is unmarked. Although these are consistent

***Table 2.*** **The Relationship Between Handshape Markedness and the Allowance of Handshape Change**

| Signs with handshape change | | Signs without handshape change | |
|---|---|---|---|
| 1. WIDE-AWAKE | B o | BUS | B o |
| 2. UNDERSTAND | 1 o – | pronouns | 1 o – |
| 3. CHOSE | 9ˆ o p | TRIVIAL | 9ˆ o p |
| 4. ADVISE | 4ˆ o p | HOME | 4 o p |
| 5. TWEEZERS | R o p | CIGAR | R o p |
| 6. WEIRD | W o | WORLD | W o |
| 7. | * | MOCK | = |
| 8. | * | FEMALE- | |
| | | TO-FEMALE SEX | T |
| 9. | * | PANTOMIME | M (initialized) |
| 10. | * | DENTIST | D (initialized) |
| 11. | * | NIECE | N (initialized) |

with phonetic material from the dimensions of production, they are not meant as phonetic descriptions, but rather as structural categories in the spirit of Jakobson, Fant, and Halle in *Preliminaries of Speech Analysis* (1952). Specifically, the notion of distinctive features should optimize language structure and use rather than seek to achieve phonetic description, as in the following examples. (Fant, 1986).

[open]     + : proximal joints of the specified fingers are bent to greater than 90° angle (abducted) with respect to the palm.

– : proximal joints of the specified fingers are bent to less than or equal to a 90° angle (adducted) with respect to the palm.

[peripheral]     + : the fully abducted and fully adducted handshapes with respect to the specified fingers (specifically, open and closed classes in Liddell and Johnson's notation).

– : handshapes that are partially adducted or abducted; 'flat' and 'curved' handshapes in Liddell and Johnson's notation.

The four classes of handshape postures of Liddell and Johnson, expressed using the representation proposed here, are as follows:

|  Liddell and Johnson |  Brentari |
|---|---|
| Open | [+ peripheral], [+ open] |
| Curved | [– peripheral], [+ open] |
| Flat | [– peripheral], [– open] |
| Closed | [+ peripheral], [– open] |

Table 3 represents the possibilities for monomorphemic signs with handshape change with respect to both handshape choice and handshape posture. The initial handshape is plotted on the vertical axis. The second handshape is along the horizontal axis. Within the perimeter cells of table 3, cells (1-1), (1-4), (4-1), and (4-4) contain

**Table 3.** **Possible Handshape Sequences in Signs Containing Handshape Change**

| | | Position 2 | | |
|---|---|---|---|---|
| | **1**<br>**Open (  )** | **2**<br>**Curved ( ¨ )** | **3**<br>**Flat ( ^ )** | **4**<br>**Closed ( − )** |
| **1   Open (  )** | WONDERFUL-4<br>LET'S-SEE-V<br>LICENSE-1<br>SICK-8<br>TRIVIAL-9 | BEAR-4<br>DOUBT-V<br>PERPLEXED<br>*-8<br>*-9 | SHUT-UP-4<br>SAY-NO-TO-V<br>CLOSE-EYES-1<br>LIKE-8<br>CHOSE-9 | TAKE-UP-4<br>STEAL(1)-V<br>DISAPPEAR-1<br>VANISH-8<br>*-9 |
| **2   Curved ( ¨ )** | DON'T-WANT-4<br>EJACULATE-V<br>*-1<br>*-8<br>*-9 | CUP-B<br>STRICT-V<br>WITCH-1<br>*-8<br>*-9 | *-8<br>*-9<br>*-1<br>*-B<br>*-V | MISS-4<br>STEAL(2)-V<br>*-1<br>*-9<br>*-8 |
| **3   Flat ( ^ )**<br><br>Position 1 | INFORM-4<br>WAKE-UP-1<br>*-8<br>EXCELLENCE-9<br>*-V<br>HOSPITAL-H | INFLATE-<br>EGO-B<br>*-8<br>*-9<br>*-1<br>*-V | NONE-B<br>WRITE-1<br>DYE-9<br>*-H/V<br>*-8 | MELT-B<br>*-1<br>*-V<br>VANISH-8<br>*-9 |
| **4   Closed ( − )** | BAWL-OUT-4<br>THROW-H<br>UNDERSTAND-1<br>SCHIZOPHRENIA-B<br>*-8    *-9 | ENVISION-B<br>OOPS-B<br>WIDE-AWAKE-B<br>*-1    *-8<br>*-V    *-9 | S-O-B<br>ASK-1<br>*-V<br>*-8<br>*-9 | SENATE-B<br>*-1<br>*-V<br>*-8<br>*-9 |

signs with two [+ peripheral] handshapes. Cells (1-2), (1-3), (2-1), (2-4), (3-1), (3-4), (4-2), (4-3) contain signs with one [+ peripheral] handshape. More signs are represented in the [+ peripheral] areas than in the cells with only [− peripheral] values: cells (2-2), (2-3), (3-2), and (3-3). Cells having identical values for both positions have no handshape change: cells (1-1), (2-2), (3-3), and (4-4).[7] Consequently, cells (2-3) and (3-2) are the only cells that would contain signs with two [− peripheral] handshapes and would also have the possibility of handshape change.[8] The absence of examples in the cells is an important point of clarification for the phenomenon of handshape change.

### *Formalizing the Constraint*

Let us now discuss the generalizations that can be gleaned from the data in table 3. The various pieces discussed so far can be fit into a single analysis. I propose a

Constraint on Handshape to replace Sandler's Handshape Sequence Constraint, based on these data, and defined as,

A.i. Selected fingers: Both handshapes must contain the same selected fingers,
B.i. Peripherality Constraint: There is a maximum of one [ − peripheral] handshape in a monomorphemic signs, and
 ii. Thumbs will not change counter to other selected fingers.

The type of constraint expressed in the Peripherality Constraint, that is, one that places a maximum of one on the number of times a feature may occur within a given phonological string, has been outlined in Itô and Mester (1986). In their analysis of right-branching Japanese compounds, the feature [+ voice] may only occur once in the right half of the compound. The Peripherality Constraint operates in a similar manner since it places a maximum of one on the number of times [ − peripheral] can occur. The statement referring to thumb position implies three possibilities for thumb positions that may occur in ASL, and all three do occur:

1. Thumbs may remain unchanged if other specified fingers change (for example, RUN, BUG, TAKE-A-PHOTOGRAPH, TWELVE).
2. Thumbs may change redundantly with other specified fingers (for example, WANT, BEAR).
3. Thumbs may change even if other specified fingers remain unchanged (for example, SHOOT-A-GUN).[9]

A discussion of thumb position also involves the notion of contact. In this analysis [+ contact] is defined as contact of the thumb with any part of the hand. [+ open], [+ peripheral] handshapes are redundantly [ − contact]; while [ − open], [+ peripheral] handshapes are redundantly [+ contact]. Flat or curved handshapes may be either [+ contact] or [ − contact]. Restrained contact (Liddell and Johnson, 1985), as seen in signs like TWELVE, THROW, and UNDERSTAND, can be captured by designating that the tumb contacts the back of the finger rather than the tip, pad, or ulnar side of the fingers. In signs in which the thumb is the only selected finger (for example, ELIMINATE), this relationship is reversed: that is, the finger(s) contact the back of the thumb. A "(+)" is used here for restrained contact; a "+" is used to refer to contact of the thumb with either the pads or tips of fingers. Examples of this are

| + | (+) |
|---|-----|
| WAKE-UP (1ˆo + > 1 o) | UNDERSTAND (1 o − (+) > 1 o) |
| INFORM (Bˆo + > B o) | MANY (B o − (+) > B o) |
| TURTLE (A uˆ + > A u) | ELIMINATE (A u (+) > A u) |
| LIKE (8 o > 8ˆ o) | HATE (8 o (+) > 8 o) |

For signs having unopposed thumbs, restrained contact involved contact with the ulnar side of the finger rather than the radial side. I mention contact here only briefly since Sandler utilizes the notion of contact in her definition of [+ closed], and by doing this integrates this feature into the Handshape Sequence Constraint. In this analysis, [+ contact] is an important feature in a sign's phonological representation; however, it plays no role in licensing handshape. Here the handshapes in the signs SO-WHAT and INFORM have identical change

$$\begin{bmatrix} -\text{ peripheral} \\ -\text{ open} \end{bmatrix} > \begin{bmatrix} +\text{ peripheral} \\ +\text{ open} \end{bmatrix}$$

and they differ from each other only in their respective thumb positions.

### Exceptions to the Constraint

There is an apparent exception to the Peripherality Constraint; that is INFLATE-EGO. (The change is from flat > curved, and can be expressed as the following:

$$\begin{bmatrix} -\text{ peripheral} \\ -\text{ open} \end{bmatrix} > \begin{bmatrix} -\text{ peripheral} \\ +\text{ open} \end{bmatrix}^{10}$$

This sign, like those listed below, has a semantic opposite with opposite movement and handshape change:

|              |              |
|--------------|--------------|
| CELL (3-1)   | CELL (1-3)   |
| LIGHTS-ON    | LIGHTS-OFF   |
| GROW         | DISAPPEAR    |
| OPEN-EYES    | CLOSE-EYES   |

It may be the case that the pair INFLATED-EGO / DEFLATED-EGO are members of this class. If this is so, one of the signs in the pair, DEFLATED-EGO, contains the underlying elements (open B) and the other, INFLATED-EGO, contains a surface form (curved B). Another possible explanation is that this sign is a remnant form, a polymorphemic form containing two classifier handshapes. In either case, it is not surprising that such a sign violates the Peripherality Constraint, since it uses the least-marked handshape, namely B/4.

There is one rather large class of exceptions to the Peripherality Constraint, and these come from the realm of fingerspelled borrowings. Although there is one group of fingerspelled borrowings that does conform to the Peripherality Constraint, there is another group of signs that does not—namely those that involve nonselected fingers rather than selected fingers in the initial to final handshape transition. In the following example, list A conforms to the Peripherality Constraint with respect to the initial and final handshapes in these borrowings;[11] list B uses nonselected fingers in the transition process, and does not obey the Peripherality Constraint.

| A | B |
|---|---|
| YES | JOB |
| BREAD | DOG |
| S-O | BACK |
| WHAT | O-K |
| NO | BANK (Long Island dialect) |
| EASY | |
| FAR-OUT | |
| BULLSHIT | |

In addition to those signs in list B that make use of nonselected fingers, those with a K handshape in the second position are especially problematic because K occurs with both [− peripheral] and [+ peripheral] handshapes in initial position. In BACK, it occurs with a [+ peripheral] handshape; in O-K, it occurs with a [− peripheral] handshape. It is likely that fingerspelled borrowings have more flexibility than does the rest of the ASL lexicon, and the discussion below concerning licensing will help clarify this matter.

## LICENSING OF ASL HANDSHAPE

Constraints on handshapes in ASL should have separate statements about handshape choice and handshape posture. In recent work on levels of phonological representation (Goldsmith, in press), discussion has focused on evidence that shows how certain phonological processes may be explained in terms of their occurrence within either the syllable or the word. One example of this is in the vowel-harmony system of Hungarian (Goldsmith, 1985). Without going into details, the feature [front] may spread to vowels of an entire word, while the feature [low] operates within the syllable. It can be said that the word "licenses" the feature [front], and that the syllable "licenses" the feature [low], even though certain suffixes block front/back harmony. Furthermore, while the data concerning a change in value for the feature [front] are particularly useful for explaining the vowel-harmony system of Hungarian, it is not the change that is licensed to appear within a certain phonological unit, but the features themselves. The same relationship is true for ASL: Although changes in certain sets of handshape features are especially useful in analyzing ASL handshape, it is not the change in these features that is licensed by different phonological units, but the feature themselves. It can be shown that features specifying selected fingers and peripherality in the Constraint on Handshape Change are licensed by the syllable and word, respectively, in ASL.

Sandler's Handshape Sequence Constraint and the first formulation of the constraint on handshape change described earlier seem to deal with monomorphemic forms—morpheme structure constraints, if you will. However, work on the ASL syllable by David Perlmutter (1988), has caused me to rethink this matter more carefully with respect to handshape change. The first statement in the Constraint on Handshape Change like the first statement in Sandler's Handshape Sequence Constraint, concerns itself with selected fingers; that is, handshape choice. I would like to argue that this is a set of features that is licensed by the syllable. That is to say, that there is a limit of one handshape class per syllable. For native ASL signs that have no hint of borrowing from English by way of the fingerspelling system there is a one-to-one correspondence of syllable-to-morpheme, and this correspondence is straightforward. This monosyllabic nature of the native ASL lexicon has been argued for in Coulter (1982). But in initialized signs and fingerspelled borrowings, this relationship is *not* straightforward, and Perlmutter has convincingly argued that there are initialized, monomorphemic signs containing two handshape classes. CURRICULUM, BACKGROUND, and PROJECT are members of this class. In order for the language to deal with these borrowings, I suggest that ASL has made the constraint on selected fingers a phonological constraint that operates at the level of the syllable rather than the morpheme. This constraint could explain how totally fingerspelled forms are parsed—as one word with many syllables.

With respect to handshape posture, I suggest that the Peripherality Constraint—that is, handshape posture—is a set of features licensed by the word. This could explain why verbs of motion and location are exempt from both portions of the Constraint on Handshape Change. These forms are morphologically complex native ASL forms, and they can function syntactically as a full verb phrase or even a clause (Padden, 1983). Since compounds function syntactically as words, they are subject to this constraint. In summary, a change in selected fingers is licensed by the syllable. A change in handshape posture is licensed by the word. Thus, I restated the Constraint on Handshape Change in terms of two licensing statements:

A. Selected Fingers: The syllable may license only one set of features that specifies selected fingers.
B. Peripherality Constraint: The world may license a maximum of one [− peripheral] handshape.

## CONCLUSION

Although I have not gone into detail with regard to placing each handshape class and each handshape posture along a hierarchy of markedness, this analysis suggests that both of these dimensions of handshape have marked and unmarked features. Further investigation may produce evidence that such a hierarchy can be found and could prove useful.

In order to determine whether a sign that allows handshape change contains handshapes that are of the same underlying class or of different underlying classes with respect to selected fingers, one must first ask how many syllables the sign contains. If the answer is more than one, the sign may have changes in selected fingers corresponding to the number of syllables in the word. Moreover, regardless of the number of underlying classes of handshapes, if the sign in question is a word, it is subject to Peripherality Constraint and may contain a maximum of one [− peripheral] handshape.

In this analysis, the notion of a syllable in ASL is shown to do important work in differentiating the phonological units where licensing of handshape change occurs.

Furthermore, the analysis has posits that selected finger features and peripherality features may be relevant in defining the syllable and the word in ASL.

## NOTES

1. Liddell (1986) has analyzed local movement as oscillation within a given autosegmental tier, such as hand configuration. In such an analysis, any restrictions on single instances of handshape change also hold for signs with local movement. The analysis presented here is consistent with Liddell's, although a P-Rule would be needed to reduce the excursion of opening or closing in signs with rapid local movement.
2. Handshape designations will follow the format of Liddell and Johnson in the sense that thumb positions are not contained in the main entry of the handshape, but have separate symbols.
3. This information was obtained from data collected in David McNeill's lab at the University of Chicago on hearing adults of several Western and non-Western cultures. In gesturing that accompanies speech during the retelling of stories, the 1 handshape is selectively used as a deictic, but the 4 handshape is the most common. The second most frequently used handshape is reported to be a closed fist; that is, A or S.
4. However, one difference between Sandler's and Stokoe's analyses is that for Stokoe, the second handshape in this class of signs is predictable based on the movement—opening or closing—in the sign, while Sandler's analysis claims that the first handshape is predictable from the second.
5. In a personal communication Sandler has acknowledged only MELT and ENVISION as counterexamples to the Handshape Sequence Constraint. WIDE-AWAKE could possibly be bimorphemic, and therefore, not subject to the Handshape Sequence Constraint. S-O is a fingerspelled borrowing. Although Sandler doesn't consider these subject to the Handshape Sequence Constraint, I feel that any generalizations about the phenomenon of handshape change must include such examples.
6. Although some contrastive handshapes may be expressed in terms of posture features—that is [± spread] and [− open], [− peripheral]—in the text I have used the more common handshape label for convenience. My rationale for doing this in table 1 is to strive to keep selected finger information and posture information in separate symbols in the representation.
7. In this analysis, all [+ peripheral], [− open] handshapes are neutralized to either S or A, and [+ peripheral], [+ open] 9 and 8 are neutralized to B.
8. Within the [+ open] posture, and only the [+ open] posture, there is an additional handshape change that is not represented in table 3. That is, within a monomorphemic sign, the initial handshape can be [+ spread] and the second [− spread] (for example, CUT, CRAB). I propose that [± spread] is dominated by the feature value [+ open], since it occurs only with handshapes that are [+ open]. This is the notion of domination described in Clements (1985). It could be represented three dimensionally related to cell (1-1) in table 3, but since it does not bear on the analysis specific to this paper, I have chosen to omit it.
9. There is one exception to the statement about thumb position in the Peripherality Constraint in some ASL dialects: GAMBLE, which changes from an opposed thumb position to an unopposed one. For this reason, the statement about thumb position is limited to posture features. I am grateful to Robert Johnson and Scott Liddell for pointing this counterexample out to me.
10. This sign is a counterexample only in some ASL dialects. For many signers, INFLATE-EGO is made with a handshape change from flat > open like those listed on page 64.
11. It is not yet clear just how many of the handshapes of the fingerspelled alphabet are contained in these forms.

# REFERENCES

Battison, R. (1978). *Lexical borrowing in American Sign Language*. Silver Spring, MD: Linstok Press.

Boyes-Braem, P. (1981). Distinctive features of the handshape of American Sign Language. Ph.D. diss., University of California, Berkeley.

Coulter, G. (1982). On the nature of ASL as a monosyllabic language. Paper presented at the Annual Meeting of the Linguistic Society of America, San Diego.

Fant, G. (1986). Features: Fiction and facts. In *Invariance and variability in speech processes*, edited by J. Perkell and D. Klatt, 480–88. Cambridge, MA: MIT.

Friedman, L. (1977). Formational properties of American Sign Language. In *On the other hand: New perspectives in American Sign Language*, edited by L. Friedman, 13–56. New York: Academic Press.

Goldsmith, J. (in press) *Autosegmental and metrical phonology*. New Yrok: Basil Blackwell.

————. (1985). Vowel harmony in Khalkha Mongolian, Yaka, Finnish and Hungarian. *Phonology Yearbook* 2:253–75.

Itô, J., and Mester, R. A. (1986). The phonology of voicing in Japanese: Theoretical consequences for morphological accessibility. *Linguistic Inquiry* 17:49–73.

Jakobson, R., Fant, G., and Halle, M. (1972; reprint from 1951). *Preliminaries to speech analysis*. Cambridge, MA: MIT Press.

Lane, H., Boyes-Braem, P., and Bellugi, U. (1976). Preliminaries to a distinctive feature analysis of handshapes in American Sign Language. *Cognitive Psychology* 8:263–89.

Liddell, S. (in press) Structures for representing handshape and local movement at the phonemic level. In *Theoretical Issues in Sign Language Research* edited by S. Fischer and P. Siple. Chicago: University of Chicago Press.

————, and Johnson, R. E. American Sign Language: The Phonological Base. Gallaudet University. Unpublished manuscript.

McIntire, M. (1977). The acquisition of American Sign Language hand configurations. *Sign Language Studies* 16:247–66.

Padden, C. (1983). Interaction of morphology and syntax in American Sign Language. Ph.D. diss., University of California, San Diego.

Perlmutter, D. (1989). A moraic theory of American Sign Language syllable structure. Unpublished manuscript.

Sandler, W. (1987). Sequentiality and simultaneity in American Sign Language phonology. Ph.D. diss., University of Texas at Austin.

Stokoe, W., Casterline, D. and Croneberg, C. (1965). *A dictionary of American Sign Language on linguistic principles*. Silver Spring, MD: Linstok Press.

# PART

# II

# MORPHOLOGY

# The Morphology of Classifier Handshapes in Italian Sign Language (LIS)

Serena Corazza

This chapter analyzes the classifier system of Italian Sign Language (LIS), a topic that has not previously been addressed. However, such studies have been made for other sign languages, for eample, ASL (Boyes-Braem, 1981; Padden, 1983; Supalla, 1986; for a review Wilbur, 1987) Danish Sign Language (Engberg-Pedersen, and Pedersen, 1983), and Swedish Sign Language (Wallin, 1988). These studies propose various classifications and different terminologies. In the present analysis, I adopt the theoretical framework outlined by Liddell and Johnson (1987) in their analysis of spatial locative predicates of ASL. I became familiar with Liddell and Johnson's theory during the academic year I spent in Washington, D.C., at Gallaudet University, in the Department of Linguistics and Interpreting.

## LIDDELL AND JOHNSON'S ANALYSIS OF CLASSIFIER PREDICATES IN ASL

In their analysis, Liddell and Johnson isolate, according to the meaning of the individual movements, three categories of predicates: process roots, stative-descriptive roots, and contact roots.

In the first category, the process roots, the movement of the hand corresponds to movements of entities. For example, in

(1) 3-CL (move right to left)

the movement of the hand corresponds to the movement of a vehicle. In another example,

(2) 1-CL (move right to left),

the movement of the hand corresponds to the movement of a person.

In the second category, the stative-descriptive roots, the sign describes a state rather than an action or a process. In these signs, the movement of the hand corresponds to physical attributes of the object being described. For example, in

(3) B B (lumpy surface),

one hand remains stationary while the other traces out the shape of a surface. In this example, the movement of the hand does not correspond to any change in the entity, but shows the form of the object being described.

In the third category, the contact roots, the movement consists of a single, short, typically downward movement followed by a hold that establishes the location and orientation of the entity being represented by the handshape. For example, in

(4) 3-CL (contact root),

the sign locates a vehicle but does not correspond to any movement of the vehicle. If a movement should be represented, it would become a process root.

To summarize, the three categories share the following three characteristics: hand configuration is meaningful; location of the hand is meaningful; orientation of the hand is meaningful. Furthermore, Liddell and Johnson propose a classification of the hand configurations that are used in these productive predicates into six categories: whole entity, surface, instrument, size, width-depth, and perimeter shape.

## ANALYSIS OF CLASSIFIER PREDICATES
## IN LIS

I identify Liddell and Johnson's three categories of predicates in LIS. In the following examples I use the notational system adopted for LIS in Corazza et al. (1985) and Volterra (1986).

An example of a process root is

(5) B-CL (move to right)

in which the handshape can represent a surface or a vehicle or an animal turning to the right.

An example of a stative-descriptive root is

(6) B B (lumpy surface).

In this case, as in the ASL sign, only the shape of a surface is represented.

An example of contact root is

(7) B-CL (short downward movement).

In this case, the handshape can represent the location of a surface or a vehicle or an animal.

I identify the following categories of meaningful hand configurations: grab, surface, descriptive, perimeter, and quantity.

## Grab

The first category is very similar to the category called "instrument" by Liddell and Johnson. It contains handshapes where the grasping hand acts as an instrument or represents the instrument itself. The characteristics of this class of handshape morphemes are as follows:

- They can be used only with a process root, for example,

    (8)  T (FISHING-LINE), C (GLASS), L (CLOTHES-PEG).

- They can operate on body locations and they allow other handshapes to be located on them, for example,

    (9)  B B (PRESS-SANDWICH), 5 H (BEND-KNIFE).

- They show control over some other entity, for example,

    (10)  C (pick up a glass and release it).

A first list of handshapes in this category are found in table 1 and figure 1. The corresponding meaning is reported with each handshape.

## Surface

The handshapes in this category represent surfaces. They have the following characteristics:

- They are used with a contact root and a process root, for example,

    (11)  B-CL (CAR).

- They can operate on body locations and they can represent a surface upon which other entities can be located, e.g.

    (12)  V-CL (PERSON).

This category contains various types of vehicles represented by different handshapes, for example,

(13)  Y-CL (AIRPLANE).

Different handshapes represent also the number of people

(14)  4-CL (FOUR PERSONS).

Table 2 and figure 2 contain a list of handshapes included in this category.

*Table 1.* **Representative Grab Morphemes**

| Handshape | Meaning |
|-----------|---------|
| G | finger |
| H | knife |
| $\overset{...}{3}$ | crane |
| $\hat{L}$ | small object |
| $\overset{...}{L}$ | round, small cup |
| $\overset{\#}{L}$ | clip |
| $\overset{...}{5}$ | ball |
| $\overset{\#}{5}$ | postcard |
| $\hat{B}$ | sandwich |
| C | glass |
| G | hook, scratch |
| As | suitcase |
| $\overset{\circ}{F}$ | coin |
| V | hooks |
| I | string |
| $\overset{\#}{F}$ | sheet of paper |
| $\overset{\#}{T}$ | fishing line |

## Descriptive

The handshapes in this category contain information about shape and size of entities and sometimes other information as well. This category is similar to what Liddell and Johnson call "depth and width morphemes." These handshapes share the following characteristics:

• They are used only with a descriptive root, for example,

(15) B B (DESERT).

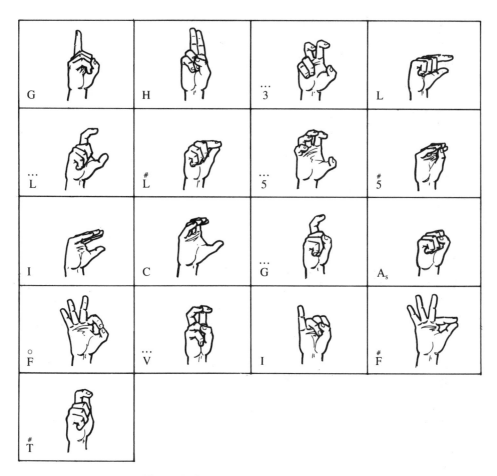

*Figure 1.* **Representative grab morphemes.**

• They can operate on body locations, but they will not allow any other handshape to be located on them, for example

    (16) G (LINES),

    (17) C C (COLUMNS).

The handshapes of this category are reported in table 3 and figure 3.

### Perimeter

The handshapes in this category provide information about the perimeter of single entities. They have two characteristics, the first distinguishes them from descriptive handshapes; the second distinguishes them from surface handshapes:

*Table 2.* **Representative Surface Morphemes**

| Handshape | Meaning |
|-----------|---------|
| G | person, pole, knife, leg |
| H | plank, person, knife |
| Y | airplane |
| V | two persons, standing |
| 3 | three persons |
| $\overset{...}{3}$ | crane, pimple |
| L | gun |
| $\hat{L}$ | small objects |
| $\overset{...}{L}$ | glass, little cup |
| 5 | five persons |
| $\overset{...}{5}$ | ball, cupola |
| $\overset{\#}{5}$ | tulip |
| 4 | four persons |
| B | frame, book, car, motorcycle |
| $\hat{B}$ | book, sandwich |
| C | glass |
| $\overset{...}{G}$ | hook |
| As | handle |
| $\overset{\circ}{F}$ | coin |
| $\overset{...}{V}$ | on one's knees |

- They are used with a process root and a contact root, for example

    (18) L L (PLATE).

- They can operate on body locations but they will not allow other handshapes to be located on them, e.g.

    (19) L L (PLATE-ON-HEAD).

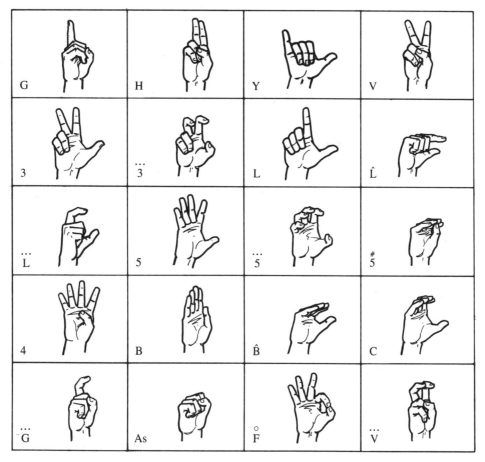

*Figure 2*. **Representative surface morphemes.**

When other handshapes are located on it, the same hand is classified as surface morpheme. A list of handshapes from this category is reported in table 4 and figure 4.

### Quantity

This category is very similar to what Liddell and Johnson called "Extent morphemes." The handshapes in this category contain information about change in length, height, or volume. The change described can represent a decrease or an increase. I have chosen the term "quantity," but I am not yet sure that this term describes the meaning of the category in the right way.

The handshapes of this category have the following characteristics:

• They are restricted to use with a process root, for example,

*Table 3*. **Representative Descriptive Morphemes**

| Handshape | Meaning |
|---|---|
| G | dot, line, liquid, path |
| H | wide line |
| V | two lines |
| 3 | three lines |
| L → L̷ | rectangle |
| L̂ | tape |
| L̈ | vase |
| L̷ | thin line |
| 5 | five lines |
| 5̈ | freckles |
| 4 | four lines |
| B | wall |
| B̈ | cupola |
| B̂ | thickness |
| C | column |
| G̈ | hook |
| O | tube |
| F̊ | tube |
| V̈ | scratches |
| I | line |
| F̷ | thin |

(20)  L ] L (cigarette-becomes-shorter),

(21)  L ] L (liquid-in-a-glass-diminishing),

(22)  Bo ] B (pile-of-papers-reducing),

(23)  C ] B (pile-of-papers-reducing).

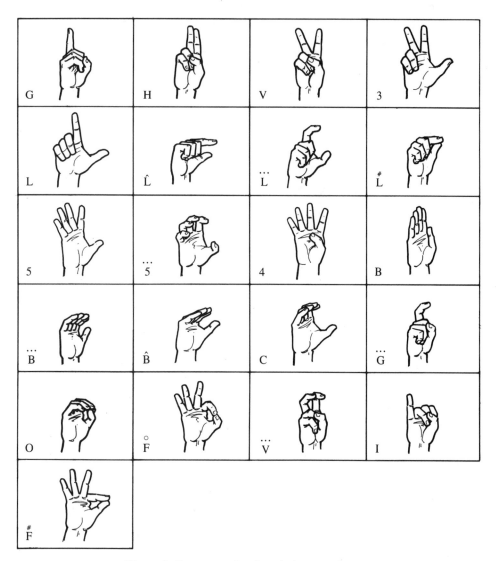

*Figure 3*. **Representative descriptive morphemes.**

Examples (20), (21), and (22) refer to length, depth of a liquid and volume respectively. The choice between examples (22) and (23) depends on the sign previous used in the sentence, but the meaning remains the same.

- They can operate on body location but they will not allow other handshapes to be located on them (see example [20]).

Table 5 and figure 5 report the complete list of handshapes in this category.

*Table 4.* Representative Perimeter Morphemes

| Handshape | Meaning |
|-----------|---------|
| L | frame |
| L̈ | plate |

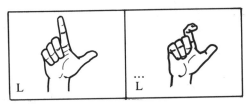

*Figure 4.* Representative perimeter morphemes.

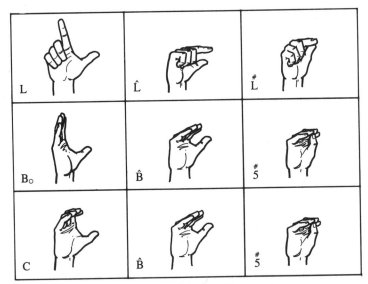

*Figure 5.* Representative quantity morphemes.

*Table 5.* Representative Quantity Morphemes

| Handshape | Meaning |
|-----------|---------|
| L → Ĺ | liquid, person, cigarette |
| Bo → 5̆ | thickness |
| C → 5̆ | idem |

## CONCLUSION

In this analysis I divide predicate roots into three categories, and I proposed five categories of handshape morphemes. I have found interesting rules on the combinability of predicate types and handshape morphemes. Some of the categories and some of the restrictions are similar to those found for ASL, but sometimes they look different.

I have not identified in LIS the category called "whole entity" by Liddell and Johnson. Examples in ASL are

(24) 3-CL (vehicle),

(25) V''-CL (animal).

In LIS, I have found handshapes that can represent groups of entities but not the whole category. These include:

(26) B-CL (car or animal),

(27) G-CL (long-thin-animal),

(28) 5̈-CL (big-animal or group-of-animal).

These handshapes do not have the same characteristics of those predicates in Liddell and Johnson's whole-entity category. In ASL, it is ungrammatical to place any other handshape morpheme on one of the surfaces of a whole entity classifer. In LIS, all the handshapes listed in examples (26), (27), and (28) allow other handshapes to be located on them.

More data on signers' intuitions and on spontaneous production are needed in order to make a complete analysis of the classifier system in LIS. Furthermore, a better understanding of the classifier system of a sign language can help us to understand the formational rules of the signs in that language.

## NOTE

I am deeply grateful to Emanuela Cameracanna, Scott K. Liddell, Ceil Lucas, Paolo Rossini, Clayton Valli, and Virginia Volterra for this work. The earlier version of this paper was outlined at Gallaudet University where I spent the academic year 1987–88 sponsored by the Mason Perkins Fund.

## REFERENCES

Boyes-Braem, P. (1981). Distinctive features of the handshape in American Sign Language. Ph.D. diss., University of California, Berkeley.

Corazza, S., Radutsky, E., Santarelli, B., Verdirosi, M. L., Volterra, V. and Zingarini, A. (1985). Italian Sign Language: General summary of research. *SLR 1983 sign language research*, edited by W. Stokoe and V. Volterra, 289–98, Silver Spring, MD: Linstok Press, and Rome, Italy: Istituto di Psicologia, CNR.

Engberg-Pedersen, E., and Pedersen, A. (1985). Proforms in Danish Sign Language. *SLR 1983 sign language research*, edited by W. Stokoe and V. Volterra, 202–9. Silver Spring, MD: Linstock Press, and Rome, Italy: Istituto di Psicologia, CNR.

Liddell, S., and Johnson, R. (1987). An analysis of spatial-locative predicates in American Sign Language. Paper presented at the Fourth International Symposium on Sign Language Research, 15–19 July, Lappeenranta, Finland.

Padden, C. (1983). Interaction of morphology and syntax in American Sign Language. Ph.D. Diss., University of California, San Diego.

Pizzuto, E., Anselmo, G. and Volterra, V. (in press). Langue Italienne des signes: structures lexicales et morphologigues. In *Recherches en langues des signes Europeenes*, Brussells: Edirsa.

Supalla, T. (1986). The classifier system in American Sign Language. In *Noun classes and categorization*, edited by C. Craig, pp. 181–214. Philadelphia: John Benjamins.

Volterra, V., ed. (1987). *La Lingua Italiana dei segni*. Bologna, Italy: Il Mulino.

Wallin, L. (1988). Polymorphemic verbs. Paper presented at the conference Theoretical Issues in Sign Language Research, II, at Gallaudet University, 18–21 May, Washington, DC.

Wilbur, R. (1987). *American Sign Language: Linguistic and applied dimensions*, 2nd ed., Boston, MA: College Hill Press.

# Manual and Nonmanual Morphology in Italian Sign Language: Grammatical Constraints and Discourse Processes

Elena Pizzuto, Enza Giuranna, and Giuseppe Gambino

This paper focuses on some of the morphological and morphosyntactic regularities of Italian Sign Language (LIS). In particular, we shall explore and describe the behavior of manual nouns, verbs, and pronouns, and the relationship between these manual signs and a specific class of nonmanual pronominal markers. Our main objective is to clarify features of LIS morphology that are related to discourse structure, specifically, the mechanisms governing the marking of person and grammatical roles, the specification of deictic and anaphoric reference in both isolated sentences and connected text, and the indication of the coreferential ties that may link different referential expressions across sentences.

The information provided by previous studies on the topic is limited to verb signs and to the relation between verbs and nonmanual pronouns (Corazza, Franchi, and Voltera, 1984; Pizzuto, 1986, 1987). Part of this information will be discussed in this paper. It must be noted, however, that previous studies have left three main questions unexplored, namely:

1. What is the morphological behavior of LIS nouns? In particular:
2. What is the relation, if any, between noun and verb morphology in the context of both isolated sentences and connected discourse?
3. What is the relation, if any, between the morphology of manual nouns and verbs, on one hand, and manual as well as nonmanual pronouns in sentences and connected discourse?

The exploration of these questions is directly relevant to a clearer understanding of LIS morphology and discourse patterns. The evidence to be reported below provides some preliminary answers to these questions.

## DATA AND METHODOLOGY

The data used for this study consist of a corpus of approximately 400 LIS noun and verb signs produced by native signers. These are listed in tables 1 and 2. Most of the signs were taken from the context of free conversation or narrative monologue texts that were videorecorded for later analysis. The remaining signs or sign utterances were collected while interacting with the informants during the analysis: after noting features of interest in some of the signs under analysis, the signers often produced other signs, or sign utterances, as additional illustrations of the relevant features. We kept written records of these latter productions using both the revised version of the Stokoe's notation used for LIS (see Voltera, 1987; Corazza, this volume), and a particular notation of the sign glosses that will be described below.

A large number of the verb signs we studied were collected and analyzed in Palermo, Sicily. Thus, although our observations of these signs were discussed with signers of other Italian regions (Rome and Trieste) and appear to be generalizable, it must be remembered that at least part of our database represents the variety of LIS used in Palermo, Sicily.

In order to distinguish the classes of nouns, pronouns, and verbs both among themselves and from other classes of signs, we employed semantic, morphological,

***Table 1.*** **List of the LIS Nouns Investigated, Distinguished in Two Morphological Classes***

| Class 1: Uninflective type. Citation form noted as noun | | | |
|---|---|---|---|
| ALMOND | DEVIL | MAN | SEED |
| ANGER | DOCTOR | MEAT | SKIRT |
| APPLE | DOG | MEMORY(1) | SMELL |
| BINOCULARS | DONKEY | MEMORY(2) | SNAIL |
| BIRD | DOOR-MAN | MOON | SOLDIER |
| BISHOP | EGG | MORNING | SON |
| BLOOD-PRESSURE | EVENING | MOTHER | SOUP |
| BONES(1) | FATHER | NECKLACE | SPY |
| BUTTON | FOG | NIGHT | SORROW |
| BRACELET | FROG | NUN | SUN |
| CAMERA | GLASS | OFFENSE | SURPRISE |
| CANDLE | GLASSES | OLD-MAN | SWEAT |
| CAP | GOAL-KEEPER | PAIN | SWEATER |
| CAT(1) | GOVERNMENT | PANTS | TELEPHONE |
| CHIEF | GRANDMOTHER | PERFUME | TELESCOPE |
| CLOWN | HAT | PEASANT | TIE |
| COFFEE | HEARING-PERSON | PENITENCE | TOURISM |
| COLLAR | HOOD | PIG | TRUST |
| COMB | HUNGER | PIPE | UNCLE/AUNT |
| COMMUNION | IDEA | PRIEST | UNIVERSITY |
| COMPUTER | INDIAN | QUEEN | VACATION |
| CONFIRMATION | JEWISH-PERSON | REMORSE | VERB |
| COWBOY | KING | REST | VIPER |
| DAWN | LADY | SACRIFICE | WOLF |
| DEAF-PERSON | LAWYER | SATISFACTION | WOMAN |
| DENTIST | LIFE | SCARF | WINE |

*Table 1 continues on the next page.*

Table 1 continued from previous page.

| Class 2: Inflective type. Citation form noted as $_0$noun | | | |
|---|---|---|---|
| AIRPLANE | DOOR | MARRIAGE | SNAKE |
| BALL | DOOR-BELL | METER | SNOW |
| BICYCLE | EMPLOYEE | MIRROR | SOCKS |
| BILL | ENGINE | MONEY | SQUARE |
| BONES(2) | ERASER | MONTH | STREETCAR |
| BOOK | FIRE | MOUNTAIN | STRIKE |
| BOY | FISH | NAME/NOUN | SWORD |
| BOX | FORM | OIL | SWORD-FISH |
| BREAD | FRIEND | PAINTING | TABLE |
| BRIDGE | FUN | PLAINS | TAP |
| BROTHER/SISTER | GASOLINE | PLATE | TAX |
| BROTHER-IN-LAW | GNOCCHI | PROVINCE | TEA |
| BUS | GUN | PUPPET | TELEGRAM |
| BUTTER | HOLE | RAIN | THREAD |
| CAR | HOTEL | REGION | TICKET |
| CAT(2) | HOUSE | RELATIVES | TOMATOES |
| CHAIR | ITALIAN | RENT | TRAIN |
| CHEESE | KEY | SALAMI | TREE |
| CHILD | KITCHEN-STOVE | SALT | TYPEWRITER |
| CHURCH | KNIFE | SCALES | WALL |
| CINEMA | LAMP | SCHOOL | WAR |
| CITY | LAW | SCISSORS | WIND |
| COLLEAGUE | LOUNGE | SEA | WINDOW |
| DIPLOMA | LOVER | SENTENCE | WORK |
| DOG(2) | MAIL | SHOES | WORLD |

*Each LIS noun is represented by a distinct English gloss in caps (for example, MAN). Nouns requiring more than one word to translate are in hyphenated gloss (for example, BLOOD-PRESSURE). Single glosses followed by (1) and (2) indicate two distinct LIS nouns that correspond to a single English gloss. Noun classes and additional notational conventions are described in the text.

and morphosyntactic criteria. These are discussed in part in Pizzuto (1987), and cannot be considered in detail within the limits of this paper. In order to uncover the morphological and morphosyntactic regularities of the signs being analyzed, we noted and compared formal features of the signs in the following different contexts: (1) in the original context of production, taking into account the nonmanual markers co-occurring with the signs, if any; (2) out of context, as we elicited the citation forms of the signs from the informants; (3) in the context of elicited sentences of different types. Albeit certainly artificial, we found that this third type of context was particularly useful for exploring what morphological alterations a sign can or cannot take depending upon both its formal features and/or its context of production.

Some of the terms we employ in describing LIS morphology need to be defined. We use the term ''inflection'' for any regular morphological alteration of the citation form of a sign that conveys specific discourse or grammatical information. Accordingly, signs that can exhibit such alterations will be defined as ''inflective,'' and signs that cannot do so will be defined as ''uninflective.'' Two points should be

*Table 2*. **List of the LIS Verbs Investigated, Categorized by Verb Classes***

**Class 1: Uninflective, citation form noted as verb**

| | | | |
|---|---|---|---|
| ADVISE | DRINK | LEARN | SMELL |
| BE-AFRAID | EAT | LIKE | SWALLOW |
| BE-BORED | EAT-SANDWICH | LISTEN | TAKE-IN |
| BE-CAPABLE | EAT-SOUP | LOOK-FOR | TAKE-OFF-CAP |
| BE-INATTENTIVE | EAT-WITH-FORK | LOOK-ALIKE | TAKE-OFF-HAT |
| BE-FORCED | EAT-WITH-SPOON | MISS | TAKE-OFF PANTS |
| BE-SAD | FALL-ASLEEP | PERFUME | TAKE-OFF-SHIRT |
| BE-SORRY | FORGET(1) | PUT-ON-BOOTS | TASTE |
| BE-SURPRISED | FORGET(2) | PUT-ON-CAP | TELEPHONE(1) |
| BE-STUCK | GET-DRESSED | PUT-ON-COAT | THINK |
| BE-TIRED | GET-UNDRESSED | PUT-ON-GLASSES | TOUR |
| BE-WORRIED | HAVE | PUT-ON-HAT | TRY-HARD |
| BRUSH-ONESELF | HEAR | PUT-ON-PANTS | UNCOVER |
| BRUSH-TEETH | HOPE | REMEMBER | UNDERSTAND |
| COMB-ONESELF | IMAGINE | RUN(1) | WAIT |
| COVER-ONESELF | INVENT | SAY | WAKE-UP(1) |
| CRY | KISS | SCREAM | WAKE-UP(2) |
| DISLIKE | KNOW(1) | SEEM | WANT |
| DOUBT | KNOW(2) | SING | WONDER |
| DREAM | LAUGH | SLEEP | YELL |

**Class 2A: Inflective for two arguments where initial point of articulation marks subject, final point of articulation marks object. Citation form noted as $_1$verb$_2$**

| | | | |
|---|---|---|---|
| ANSWER | FIGHT | INFORM(1) | SCOLD |
| ASK | FOLLOW | INFORM(2) | SEE |
| BITE | FORCE | KILL | SHOOT |
| BLOCK | GIVE | LOOK-AT | SHOW |
| BOTHER | GIFT | MEET | SIGN |
| CATCH | GIVE-THIN-OBJECT | ORDER | TEACH |
| CHAT | GO(1) | PAY | TELEPHONE(2) |
| COME(1) | GO-OUT | PUSH | TELL |
| CRITICIZE | GO-AWAY | QUARREL | TELL-STORY |
| DESPISE | HATE | REPROACH | THROW-AT |
| EXPLAIN | HELP | RUN | VISIT |

**Class 2B: Inflective for two arguments where initial point of articulation marks object, final point of articulation marks subject. Citation form noted as $_2$verb$_1$**

| | | |
|---|---|---|
| CHOOSE | GATHER | SUCK |
| COME(2) | INVITE | TAKE |
| COPY | STEAL | TAKE-ADVANTAGE |

*Table 2 continues on next page.*

*Table 2 continued from previous page.*

---

**Class 3A: Inflective for one argument where the verb only point of articulation marks the semantic patient as its subject. Citation form noted as $_0$verb**

| | | | |
|---|---|---|---|
| ACCEPT | DISAPPEAR | MUST | TRY |
| BEGIN | DRIVE | PLAY | WAIT(2) |
| BE-WRONG | ENJOY | SIT | WORK |
| CAN | GO(2) | STAND-UP | |
| DIE | GROW | STUDY | |

---

**Class 3B: Inflective for one argument where the verb only point of articulation marks the semantic patient corresponding to, respectively, the subject of intransitive verbs, and the object of transitive verbs. Citation form noted as $_0$verb**

| | | | |
|---|---|---|---|
| BREAK | CLOSE-WINDOW | FUNCTION | READ |
| BRUSH | CLOSE-WITH-KEY | HIDE | SEW |
| BUILD | COLLAPSE | KNOCK | STIR |
| BURN | COMB | MAKE | STOP |
| BUST | COOK | MELT | SWITCH-OFF |
| CARESS | CUT-WITH-KNIFE | OPEN | SWITCH-ON |
| CHANGE | CUT-WITH-SCISSORS | OPEN-CURTAIN | TAKE-AWAY |
| CLEAN | DISCOVER | OPEN-TAP | TEAR |
| CLIMB | DRESS | OPEN-WINDOW | WASH |
| CLOSE | FINISH | OPEN-WITH-KEY | WET |
| CLOSE-TAP | FIX | PUSH-BUTTON | WRITE |

---

*Each LIS verb is represented by a distinct English gloss in caps (for example, ADVISE). Verbs requiring more than one word to translate are in hyphenated glosses (for example, BE-BORED). Single glosses followed by (1) or (2) indicate two different LIS verbs that correspond to a single English gloss. Verb classes and additional notational details are specified in the text and illustrated in figures 1 through 6.

stressed. First, according to our working definition, the citation form of a sign is considered its basic, unmarked form. Second, our distinction between inflective and uninflective signs should not be interpreted in absolute terms, but only relative to those aspects of LIS structure considered here, namely the marking of person and grammatical roles. This implies that signs that we define as uninflective in the context of this paper may well be inflective under other aspects not considered here. There are, in fact, many verb signs that cannot be inflected for person and grammatical roles. We will classify such signs as uninflective in the present context, but they can nonetheless be inflected to convey aspectual modulations of their meanings (see Pizzuto, 1987 for details).

Finally, a few remarks are necessary on the terms "subject" and "object." "Subject" will refer to one of the following: (1) the semantic agent or experiencer of a typically transitive verb such as, for example, the sign for "woman" in the sentences meaning "The woman eats the cookie" or "The woman sees the man"; (2) the semantic experiencer or patient of a verb typically intransitive, or intransitively used, as, for example, the sign for "child" in a sentence meaning "The child grows," or the sign for "chair" in a sentence meaning "The chair is broken." "Object" will refer to the semantic patient, beneficiary or recipient of any verb used transitively, as, for example, the signs for "child" or "chair" in sentences such as "The woman saw the child" or "He broke the chair."

## RESULTS AND DISCUSSION

We shall first outline the more general information concerning LIS noun and verb morphology. We will then consider the relation between noun and verb morphology at the manual level of expression, and the relation between manual morphology of nouns and verbs and certain nonmanual markers used in sentences and discourse.

### *Typological Features of LIS Noun and Verb Morphology*

In general, we found that the morphology of both nouns and verbs in LIS can be described by accounting for two major elements, namely the points of articulation of the signs in their citation forms, and the morphological alterations of those points of articulation that nouns or verbs can or cannot exhibit in different contexts, depending upon specific circumstances. We also found that the relation between noun and verb morphology can be described with respect to conventional "person reference points," which in LIS, as in other sign languages, permit the "position" in the signing space of the referents that are introduced in discourse. Since different locations of the signs in space appear to be the crucial element in describing the morphological regularities observed, we devised a notation to indicate the points of articulation of the signs that are relevant from a morphological standpoint and their morphological alterations in the signing space. To this end, we use a modified version of the notation employed by several authors in describing ASL, in particular Padden (1981, 1983, 1986). Some illustrative examples are provided in figures 1 to 4 below.

Note that all the signs are illustrated in their citation forms. These figures represent LIS signs in capitalized English glosses marked with subscripts. Each subscript shows the point or points of articulation of the sign and/or its most relevant morphological features according to the following conventions:

* indicates a point near to or on the signer's body, as, for example, in the nouns $_*$WOMAN or $_*$SON or in the verbs $_*$TELEPHONE and $_*$THINK, illustrated in figure 1.

0 stands for a point in any unmarked or neutral position in front of, or at the sides of the signer, as, for example, in the nouns $_0$CHILD and $_0$TOWN, or in the verbs $_0$GROW and $_0$BREAK, illustrated in figure 2.

1 and 2 indicate, respectively, a point near the signer in a position that marks first-person reference, and a point away from the signer, in the direction of his addressee, in a position that marks second-person reference, as, for example, in the LIS pronouns for first- and second-person reference singular, illustrated in figure 3.

3 stands for any point away from both the signer and his addressee in a position marked for third-person reference. Since spatially distinct points can be used to mark likewise distinct third-person referents in space, we used

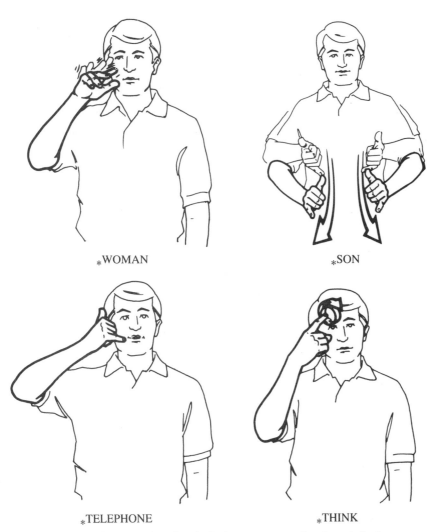

*Figure 1.* **Point of articulation on or near the signer's body.**

markers such as 3a, 3b, 3c, to identify these spatially distinct points. This is illustrated in figure 3 by two forms of the LIS third-person singular pronoun, marked at points 3a and 3b, which can be used to indicate two distinct third-person referents.

Finally, note that when only one subscript is used, either at the beginning or at the end of a sign gloss, the sign illustrated has only one point of articulation, as illustrated by all the signs in figures 1 through 3. But when two subscripts are used, the sign has two points of articulation, a beginning one and an ending one, with a movement in between. In this case, the first subscript on the gloss shows the sign's

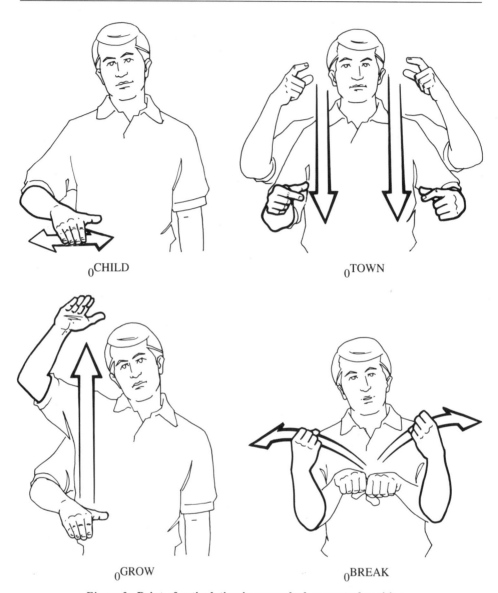

$_0$CHILD                                    $_0$TOWN

$_0$GROW                                    $_0$BREAK

*Figure 2*. **Point of articulation in unmarked or neutral position.**

beginning point, and the second subscript shows its ending point. This is illustrated in figure 4 by the verbs $_1$TEACH$_2$ and $_2$TAKE-ADVANTAGE$_1$. In $_1$TEACH$_2$, subscript 1 indicates that this verb form begins in a first-person position, and subscript 2 indicates that it ends in a second-person position. But in $_2$TAKE-ADVANTAGE$_1$ the order of the subscripts indicates that the verb begins in a second-person position and ends in a first-person position.

From a morphological perspective, all the LIS nouns we have analyzed thus far, listed in table 1, appear to be characterized by only one point of articulation. Two major morphological classes can be distinguished:

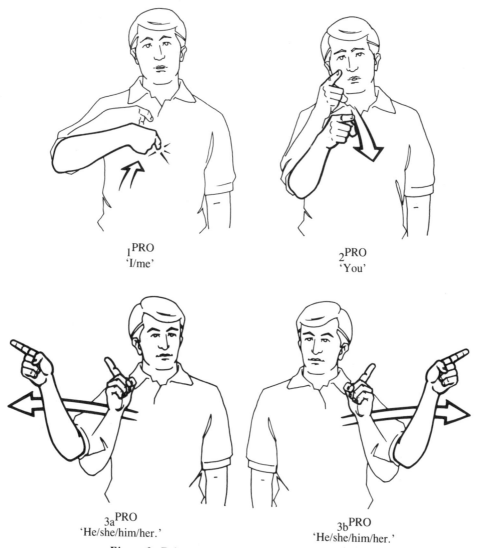

*Figure 3.* **Point of articulation marking reference.**

Class 1 comprises uninflective nouns like \*SON, which in citation form are typically articulated near or on the signer's body, and which maintain their citation form regardless of the context in which they occur.

Class 2 comprises inflective nouns like $_0$CHILD, which in citation form are articulated in neutral space, and which can change their point of articulation in context to assume marked positions in the third-person reference space. The different behavior of these two classes of nouns is illustrated in figure 5. Note how, in the context of the same type of sentence with the verb $_0$GROW, the noun $_0$CHILD changes its point of articulation to assume the marked position 3a, while the noun \*SON retains its citation form.

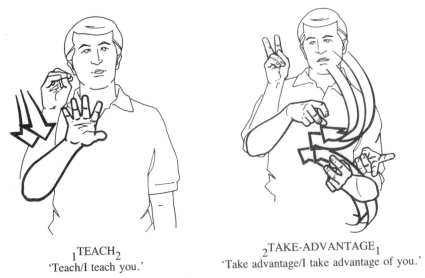

$_1$TEACH$_2$<br>'Teach/I teach you.'

$_2$TAKE-ADVANTAGE$_1$<br>'Take advantage/I take advantage of you.'

***Figure 4.* Signs with two points of articulation.**

In some ways, verb morphology resembles noun morphology. Three major classes and four subclasses of verbs can be distinguished, depending upon whether or how verbs can be inflected in space to agree with their arguments. We shall discuss only the major classes here. Additional details are provided in table 2, along with a list of the verbs we have examined, and in Pizzuto (1986, 1987).

A first, rather large class of verbs comprises uninflective signs that in citation form are typically articulated near or on the signer's body. These verbs retain their form regardless of the person and grammatical role of their arguments, as illustrated in figure 6 by the verb $_*$KNOW.

Class 2 comprises inflective verbs that typically have two points of articulation, a beginning one and an ending one, with a movement between the two. With few exceptions that will not be considered here (see Pizzuto, 1987), these verbs can alter one or both of their points of articulation according to the person and grammatical role of their arguments. This is illustrated in figure 6 by the verb $_1$GIVE$_2$. Compare the verb's citation form with the inflected form meaning "He/she gives to him/her." It should be noted that the citation form of these verbs coincides, in most cases, with the form marked for a first-person subject and a second-person object (direct or indirect).

Finally, Class 3 comprises inflective verbs that, however, in their citation form possess only one point of articulation in neutral space. Accordingly, these verbs can change their only point of articulation to agree with only one of their potential arguments. Most commonly, these verbs agree with their semantic patient or experiencer. This can surface as the verb subject when the verb is intransitive (for example, $_0$GROW), or is used as intransitive (for example, $_0$BREAK in a sentence meaning "That is broken"), but it can also surface as the verb object when the verb is used

Citation
forms:

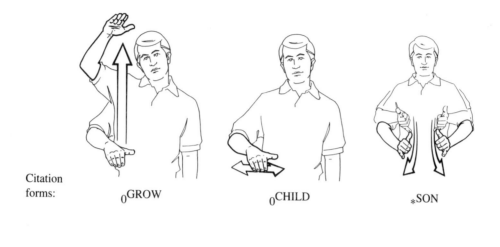

₀GROW          ₀CHILD          *SON

Forms
in context:

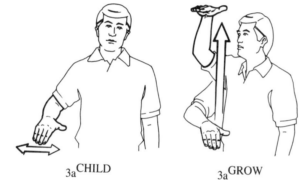

3ₐCHILD          3ₐGROW          'The child
                                grows/has grown.'

*SON          ₀GROW          'The son
                            grows/has grown.'

*Figure 5.* **Uninflective versus inflective nouns.**

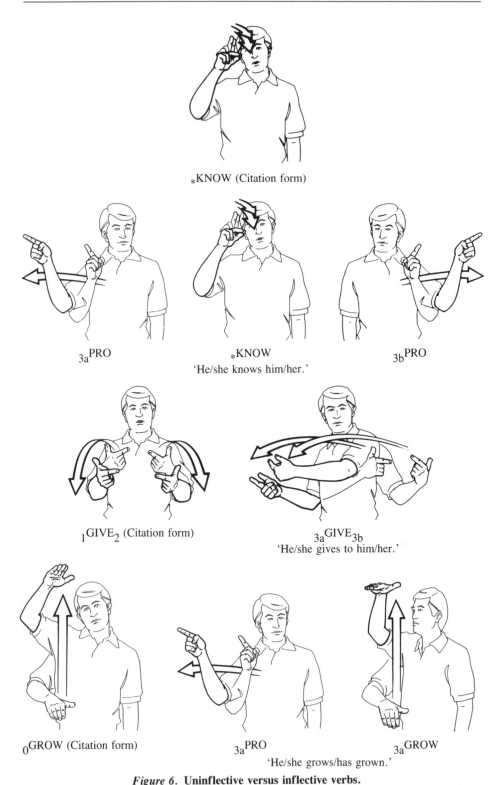

*Figure 6.* **Uninflective versus inflective verbs.**

transitively (for example, the same verb $_0$BREAK in a sentence meaning "He broke that," where the verb agrees with the object "that"). One illustrative example of Class 3 inflectional pattern is provided in figure 6 by the verb $_0$GROW.

These data demonstrate that the morphology of LIS nouns and verbs is complex and heterogeneous, including uninflective, and inflective patterns of different types.

### The Relation Between Noun and Verb Morphology

In order to assess the effect of Class 1 or Class 2 nouns on verbs of different classes, we compare sentences where a verb of the same class occurs in two different contexts: (1) with nouns of either Class 1 or Class 2; and (2) with two distinct third-person pronouns. The results of our observations provide evidence that the different morphology of Class 1 and Class 2 nouns indeed has a significant effect on verb morphology, especially on the behavior of fully inflective verbs. This can be best illustrated by referring to the examples in table 3, where the inflective verb $_1$CALL$_2$ (citation form) occurs with either third-person pronouns, or with Class 1 nouns (for example, $_*$MAN, $_*$WOMAN, $_*$MOTHER), or with Class 2 nouns (for example, $_0$BOY, $_0$CHILD).

Looking at the elicited sentences 1 and 2 as compared with 1a and 2a, we observe that when both nouns and verbs are inflective, all of them can be morphologically modified to mark in space the discourse and grammatical relations among the elements of the sentences. In this case, verb behavior is the same in sentences with third-person pronouns or inflective nouns. We note interesting differences however, in sentences 3 through 6 as compared with 3a through 6a. In 3 and 4, where

*Table 3.* **Examples of the Behavior of LIS Inflective Verbs in Sentences with Class 1 and Class 2 Nouns (1–6) and in Sentences with Pronouns (1a–6a)**

| LIS sentences | English translations |
| --- | --- |
| 1. $_{3a}$BOY $_{3a}$CALL$_{3b}$ $_{3b}$CHILD | 'The boy calls the child.' |
| 1a. $_{3a}$PRO $_{3a}$CALL$_{3b}$ $_{3b}$PRO | 'He calls him.' |
| 2. $_{3a}$CHILD $_{3a}$CALL$_{3b}$ $_{3b}$BOY | 'The child calls the boy.' |
| 2a. $_{3a}$PRO $_{3a}$CALL$_{3b}$ $_{3a}$PRO | 'He calls him.' |
| 3. $_*$MAN $_1$CALL$_0$ $_*$WOMAN | 'The man calls the woman.' |
| 3a. $_{3a}$PRO $_{3a}$CALL$_{3b}$ $_{3b}$PRO | 'He calls her.' |
| 4. $_*$WOMAN $_1$CALL$_0$ $_*$MAN | 'The woman calls the man.' |
| 4a. $_{3a}$PRO $_{3a}$CALL$_{3b}$ $_{3b}$PRO | 'She calls him.' |
| 5. $_{3a}$CHILD $_1$CALL$_0$ $_*$MOTHER | 'The child calls the mother.' |
| 5a. $_{3a}$PRO $_{3a}$CALL$_{3b}$ $_{3b}$PRO | 'He calls her.' |
| 6. $_*$MOTHER $_1$CALL$_0$ $_{3a}$CHILD | 'The mother calls the child.' |
| 6a. $_{3a}$PRO $_{3a}$CALL$_{3b}$ $_{3b}$PRO | 'She calls him.' |

*Descriptive categories and notational conventions as described in the text, in tables 1 and 2 and in figures 1 through 6.

the verb occurs with two Class 1 uninflective nouns, we find that the verb is not inflected at specific third-person positions. In fact, the verb beginning point remains the same as in its citation form (that is, "1"), while its ending point is in an unmarked "0" position. The verb exhibits the same morphological behavior in sentence 5 where the subject noun, $_0$CHILD, in inflective but the object noun, $_*$MOTHER, is not inflective. Quite differently, in sentence 6, the verb appears partially inflected: its beginning point is still the same as in citation form, but its ending point agrees with the point of the object noun $_{3a}$CHILD.

These data provide a clearer understanding of morphosyntactic patterns in LIS. Pizzuto has found (1986) that the inflective verbs of LIS, quite differently from the inflective verbs noted in many verb-inflecting spoken languages such as, for example, Italian, are not always and obligatorily inflected. Rather, the use of morphological inflections in LIS appeared to be "flexible," depending in part upon linguistic and in part upon "pragmatic" factors. All of these factors remain to be ascertained and described. The present evidence helps us to specify some of the linguistic factors that can influence the production of verb inflections, namely the presence of Class 1 or Class 2 nouns.

In addition, although this issue cannot be extensively addressed here, it seems to us that our results are relevant to a clearer understanding of the relation between verb behavior and the order of signs within sentences, at least in regard to the manual level of linguistic expression. Observational as well as experimental studies conducted on LIS indicate that the use of verb inflections permits more variability in the order of signs within the sentence (Laudanna, 1987; Volterra, Laudanna, Corazza, Radutzky, and Natale, 1984). However, most of the work generating these results has been conducted without taking into account noun morphology or the relation between noun and verb morphology, or, in more general terms, the presence of a certainly large number of uninflective elements in the language. The present results indicate that all of these variables are relevant for an appropriate description of verb behavior, and certainly they cannot be disregarded in future explorations of verb morphology and, more generally, of morphosyntactic patterns.

### LIS Verb and Nouns in Relation to Nonmanual Markers

Thus far we have considered only the morphology of manual signs. We shall now focus our attention on LIS nonmanual markers, and on the relation between these markers and the morphology of manual nouns and verbs. We limit our observations here to only one of the several types of nonmanual markers that have been identified in LIS, namely to "body markers" (see also Franchi, 1987; Corazza et al, 1984; Pizzuto, 1986). Note that what we call here "body markers" have also been described, in research on LIS as well as on other sign languages, as "role-taking" or "role-playing" devices. These devices have been likened in function to "direct-quotation" markers that may be used in spoken languages. In the following, drawing from evidence on LIS, we propose a somewhat different analysis of the functions of these nonmanual markers.

From a morphological standpoint, body markers can be characterized as particular combinations of body shifts and facial expressions that uniquely identify some of the referents introduced in discourse. These nonmanual behaviors are marked with respect to neutral or unmarked postures and facial expressions that are observed in ordinary signing. A specific semantic constraint regulates the use of body markers in LIS: body markers can be used for animate referents, most typically for people or animals, but not for inanimate referents. This constraint does not apply to other nonmanual markers such as simpler gaze shifts, which can be employed for either animate or inanimate referents. From a syntactic standpoint, note that body markers fulfill somewhat different functions depending upon the context in which they are produced: in isolated sentences they appear to mark the subject of the sentences; in connected discourse they mark the main topic of a series of related sentences. In either case, they are significantly related to the morphology of manual nouns and verbs, as will be illustrated in the following discussion.

Table 4 shows some examples of the working body markers in isolated sentences. Note that all the sentences were spontaneously produced by native signers to illustrate two different manners in which a given sentence meaning could be coded in LIS. The sentences 1 through 5 include body markers, and sentences 1a through 5a are without body markers.

The notation used for the manual signs in the sentences is the same specified previously. In sentences 1 through 5 we show with our notation some of the formational features of body markers: in each sentence, single boldface square brackets indicate the production of a body marker. The scope of the brackets shows the temporal duration of the marker: it encompasses the entire sentence. Finally, the first manual sign of each sentence is also shown in boldface characters: this indicates that in time, as well as due to its formational features, the body marker specifies this sign, and not the other signs in the sentence. Thus, for example, when producing sentence 1,

*Table 4.* **Illustrative Examples of the Morphology of LIS Nouns and Verbs in Sentences with and without Body Markers***

| Sentences with body markers | Sentences without body markers |
|---|---|
| 1. $\left[ _0\textbf{SNAKE}\ _*\text{EGG}\ _*\text{EAT} \right]$ | 1a. $_0\text{SNAKE}\ _*\text{EAT}\ _*\text{EGG}$ |
| 2. $\left[ _*\textbf{VIPER}\ _*\text{EGG}\ _*\text{EAT} \right]$ | 2a. $_*\text{VIPER}\ _*\text{EAT}\ _*\text{EGG}$ |
| 3. $\left[ _0\textbf{CHILD}\ _*\text{GRANDMA}\ \text{EMBRACE}_{3a} \right]$ | 3a. $_0\text{CHILD}\ \text{EMBRACE}_0\ _*\text{GRANDMA}$ |
| 4. $\left[ _{3a}\textbf{BOY}\ _{3b}\text{CHILD}\ _{3a}\text{GIVE}_{3b} \right]$ | 4a. $_{3a}\text{BOY}\ _{3a}\text{GIVE}_{3b}\ _{3b}\text{CHILD}$ |
| 5. $\left[ _*\textbf{MAFIOSO}\ _*\text{WOMAN}\ _1\text{KILL}_0 \right]$ | 5a. $_*\text{MAFIOSO}\ _1\text{KILL}_0\ _*\text{WOMAN}$ |

*Descriptive categories and notational conventions as described in the text, in tables 1 and 2, and in figures 1 through 6. The English translation of the LIS sentences illustrated is as follows:
1 and 1a: 'The snake eats the egg.'
2 and 2a: 'The viper eats the egg.'
3 and 3a: 'The child embraces grandmother.'
4 and 4a: 'The boy gives to the child.'
5 and 5a: 'The mafia-man kills the woman.'

meaning "The snake eats the egg," the signer shifts her body into a marked position, and assumes a facial expression appropriate to represent a snake at precisely the same time as she produces the noun $_0$SNAKE. Similarly, in sentence 3, meaning "The child embraces grandmother," the signer shifts her body, and assumes a facial expression appropriate to represent a child at the very same time as she produces the sign $_0$CHILD.

Referring to the examples in table 4, note first that body markers cannot be easily compared to direct quotation markers such as those found in speech. The function of direct quotation in speech is that of specifying "who says something to whom," with the speaker playing the role of first or second person while uttering the reported speech. However, in none of the sentences illustrated in table 4 do body markers indicate discourse participants (that is, the signer and/or his/her addressee), or other referents in the role of third persons who say something to each other. Rather, body markers seem to provide a particularly effective demonstration or deictic specification of the subject of each sentence.

Second, note that all the sentences with body markers are consistently characterized by a subject-object-verb pattern. On the contrary, the sentences without body markers show a subject-verb-object pattern. Aside from other considerations that could be made under a closer scrutiny, this fact in itself shows that the use of body markers has a significant effect on sign-order patterns within sentences.

Finally, it is of particular interest to relate the use of body markers to the morphologically different types of nouns and verbs discussed earlier. These are all represented in the sentences in table 4. Observe that body markers can be temporally superimposed in the same manner on all types of nouns and verbs: they occur, in fact, with inflective nouns like $_0$SNAKE, $_0$CHILD and $_0$BOY, as well as with uninflective nouns like $_*$VIPER, $_*$MAN, $_*$WOMAN, $_*$MAFIOSO; they can occur with different types of inflective verbs like $_0$EMBRACE or $_1$GIVE$_2$, $_1$KILL$_2$, or with uninflective verbs like $_*$EAT. In all these cases, body markers can convey rather homogeneously grammatical information that the manual signs in some cases do not express, as, for example, in sentences 1 and 2, where nouns and verbs belong to the uninflective type or are at any rate uninflected in space (for example, $_0$SNAKE); or express it in a different manner, depending both upon the type of verb being used (whether Class 2 or Class 3 inflective), and upon the context in which the verb occurs (whether with inflective or uninflective nouns, and in which order, for example, sentences 3 to 5). In other words, body markers in some sense "neutralize" the morphological diversity proper of LIS manual signs. This aspect of the working of body markers is even more readily apparent in connected discourse. Table 5 shows a sequence of utterances taken from a larger narrative, monologue text: the rendition by a Sicilian deaf native signer of "The Snowman" story (Briggs, 1980).

The notation for the manual signs and for the body markers illustrated in table 5 is the same as previously specified. The other notation marks in the table (that is, round brackets, exclamation points, small circles), stand for other kinds of nonmanual behaviors identified in the text, including particular gaze shifts, facial expressions, and postures. These, however, will be disregarded for the purposes of the present discussion. We shall instead focus our attention on the body markers, shown in single and double embedded square brackets. Note that the letters "S" and "C" next to the square brackets indicate that the signer produced two distinct body markers, each identifying a separate referent: body marker "S" identifies the referent "snowman,"

*Table 5.* **Illustrative Examples of the Relationship Between the Morphology of Manual Signs and Nonmanual Markers in Connected Text Utterances***

1. $$S\left[\; _0SNOWMAN\; _*MOVE\; _*LIFT\text{-}CAP\;\right]$$

2. $$\overset{-!-}{C\left[\; _0CHILD\;\right]}$$

3. $$S\left[\; _*STEP\text{-}FORWARD\; GREET_{3a}\;\right]$$

4. $$C\left[\; SHAKE\text{-}HAND_{3b}\;\right]$$

5. $$S\left[\;\;\right]\quad C\left[\; _2COME_1\; _2COME_1\;\right]$$

6. $$\overset{-\,mm\,-}{S\left[\;\;\right]}\quad C\left[\;\;\right]$$

7. $$S\left[\;\;\right]\quad C\left[\; _2COME_1\; _2COME_1\;\right]$$

8. $$S\left[\; _*TAKE\text{-}OFF\text{-}CAP\; _0WALK\text{-}IN_{3c}\;\right]$$

9. $$\overset{-\,oo\,-!-}{S\left[\;\overset{(3d\;)}{_*SEE_{3d}}\;\right]}$$

10. $$_{3c}HOUSE\; _0LOUNGE\; _0LARGE$$

11. $$_0CAT\; _*ANIMATE\text{-}BEING\text{-}CROUCHED$$

12. $$\overset{-----!---}{S\left[\;\overset{(3d}{_*NICE\; CARESS_{3d}}\; _{3d}GO\text{-}AWAY_0\;^{)}\right]}$$

*Descriptive categories and notational conventions as described in the text, in tables 1 and 2, and figures 1 through 6. The English translation of the LIS text illustrated is as follows: The snowman moves, lifts his cap. The child goes, "Oohh!" The snowman steps forward and greets the child, who shakes his hand. Then "Come in, come in," says the child to the snowman. The snowman nods. "Come in, come in," the child says again to the snowman. And the snowman takes off his cap and walks into the house. The lounge is large. "Hhmmm, beautiful." Then the snowman sees something, a cat lying asleep. "That's nice," he thinks, and he caresses it, but (to his surprise!) it runs away.

and body marker "C" identifies the referent "child." These are the two main characters of the story narrated by the signer.

Referring to the text in table 5, we can make several observations. First, note that body markers can be used in two distinct, related manners: as deictic specifiers of the nouns with which they initially co-occur; and as anaphoric pronominal markers. The first function can be observed in utterances 1 and 2, where body markers "S" and "C" are produced simultaneously with, respectively, the nouns $_0$SNOWMAN and $_0$CHILD. This use of body markers is similar to that noted in the isolated sentences described in table 4. The anaphoric function is apparent in all the subsequent eight utterances of the text, where body markers occur without their associated nouns: they anaphorically reintroduce in discourse the "snowman" and the "child" referents previously named.

Regarding the discourse functions fulfilled by body markers, note the following: Seven of the ten body markers in the text (noted in table 5 with simple square brackets) are comparable in function to either deictic specifiers or to anaphoric third-person pronouns that can occur in indirect discourse. The remaining three body markers (noted in utterances 5 to 7 with double embedded brackets) are different; these body markers are in fact comparable to direct quotation marks observable in speech. In fact, they are equivalent in meaning to such spoken expressions as "and he says to him." Note that although signers clearly distinguish this direct-quotation type of body markers from the one described above, it is very difficult to capture with a written description the differences between the two types. Further investigations need to be done to specify both the morphological features of each of the two types (for example, gaze and posture orientations and shifts), and the morphosyntactic, semantic, and pragmatic constraints that regulate the use of each type. A promising line of research we are currently pursuing is extending to LIS the analysis of role shifting proposed by Padden (1986) for ASL.

Another interesting feature of body markers is their relationship with the manual signs occuring in the text. Looking at table 5, observe that in the majority of cases, the manual signs of the text do not convey sufficient lexical or morphological information to specify the subjects or even the main topics of the text utterances, or the referential and discourse relations linking these topics across utterances. This information is in fact provided almost exclusively at the nonmanual level, by the body markers of the text. To see how this is the case it will suffice to note the following:

- Although all the nouns in the text are inflective, only one of them, namely $_0$HOUSE, is actually inflected in space, in the form $_{3c}$HOUSE, to mark a locative relation with the partially inflected verb $_0$WALK-IN$_{3c}$. The remaining nouns, instead, are produced in neutral, unmarked space, much as in their citation forms (see $_0$SNOWMAN, $_0$CHILD, $_0$LOUNGE, $_0$CAT).
- Ten different verbs have as their subjects either the snowman or the child referent. However, only two of these are fully inflective verb forms ($_2$COME$_1$ and $_2$WALK-IN$_{3c}$), and only one of these morphologically marks its subject, namely $_2$COME$_1$. Furthermore, note that simply on the basis of the specific body marker co-occuring with this verb, we can establish referential identity of this verb's second-person subject as the snowman, and not as, for example, the signer's addressee, or as the child-referent.

- The remaining verbs of the text comprised four uninflective, Class 1 verbs ($_*$MOVE, $_*$LIFT-CAP, $_*$STEP-FORWARD, $_*$TAKE-OFF-CAP), three inflective verbs of Class 3, which, however, specify only their object (GREET$_{3a}$, SHAKE-HAND$_{3b}$, CARESS$_{3d}$), and finally one irregular Class 2 verb that also specifies its object, but not its subject ($_*$SEE$_{3d}$).
- As a consequence of what is explained above, almost no morphological information is given in the utterances to identify the subjects of the verbs.
- In addition, in all cases except utterance 1, in which the verbs $_*$MOVE and $_*$LIFT-CAP are explicitly connected with the noun $_0$SNOWMAN, information on the subjects of the verbs is also missing at the lexical level: no other manual nouns or pronouns accompany the remaining verbs of the text. (See, for example, the verbs $_*$STEP-FORWARD, GREET$_{3a}$, SHAKE-HAND$_{3b}$.)
- However, all the discourse and grammatical information that is "missing" at the manual level is reliably and clearly provided at the nonmanual level of expression, precisely by the two body markers in the text. Regardless of the types of signs upon which the body markers were temporally superimposed, they actually permit the identification of the subject or the main topic of each utterance, the referential identity of the referents symbolized in the text (that is, whether reference is made to the snowman or to the child), and the specific discourse relations among the referents, as well as the coreferential bounds linking the different utterances. Thus, for example, it is the occurrence of body marker S for the snowman that informs the text-addressee that this referent, and not the referent child or any conceivable other, "steps forward" and "greets" someone. The co-referentiality of the verbs in utterances 1 and 3 with all the others having the snowman as their subject ($_*$TAKE-OFF-CAP, $_0$WALK-IN$_{3c}$, $_*$SEE$_{3d}$, CARESS$_{3d}$), is likewise ensured, across utterances, by the presence of one and the same body marker "S." In contrast, in utterance 4, the occurrence of the distinct body marker "C" informs the text-addressee that the referent child, and not the snowman, is the subject of the verb SHAKE-HAND$_{3b}$.

## CONCLUSION

Our results confirm and extend those of previous, but more limited, studies. In particular, we provide further evidence on the existence, in LIS manual morphology, of a variety of morphologically distinct patterns, and we show that these influence each other in significant ways, especially along the inflective/uninflective dimension. We note that due to morphological variety and the relative optionality of certain inflectional processes, it is often very difficult to disambiguate grammatical and discourse relations on the basis of the lexical, and/or morphological information carried by manual signs alone, most notably by the noun and verb types discussed above.

In this context, nonmanual markers, and particularly the body markers described in this paper in some detail, appear to play a fundamental role: they can specify and disambiguate relevant grammatical and/or discourse information that is in part, or at times even entirely, missing at the manual level of expression. In so doing, these markers in part neutralize the morphological diversity of manual signs. Body markers also appear to exert a significant influence on syntactic patterning and to do so at the level of both isolated sentences and connected discourse. Further investigations are certainly necessary to reach a clearer understanding of the complex interplay between manual and nonmanual morphology as well as to assess its relevance in the framework of comparative, cross-linguistic research on signed- and spoken-language structure.

## NOTE

Part of the data described in this paper have also been discussed in Pizzuto (1986, 1987), and Pizzuto, Giuranna, and Gambino (1987). The authors are deeply grateful to Serena Corazza, Maria Luisa Franchi, Anna Maria Peruzzi, and Virginia Volterra for many helpful comments and constructive criticism during the preparation of this paper.

## REFERENCES

Briggs, R. (1980). *The Snowman*. London: Puffin Books.

Corazza, S. (1989). The morphology of classifier handshapes in Italian Sign Language. In this proceedings.

———, Franchi, M. L., and Volterra, V. (1984). *Syntactic mechanisms in Italian Sign Language (LIS)*. Paper presented at the Bristol International Sign Language Workshop, Bristol, England.

Franchi, M. L. (1987). Componenti non manuali. In *La Lingua Italiana dei Segni*, edited by V. Volterra, 159–77. Bologna, Italy: Il Mulino.

Laudanna, A. (1987). Ordine dei segni nella frase. In *La Lingua Italiana dei Segni*, edited by V. Volterra, 211–30. Bologna, Italy: Il Mulino.

Padden, C. A. (1981). Some arguments for syntactic patterning in American Sign Language. *Sign Language Studies* 32:239–59.

———. (1983). *Interaction of morphology and syntax in American Sign Language*. Ph.D. diss., University of California, San Diego.

———. (1986). Verbs and role shifting in American Sign Language. In *Proceedings of the Fourth National Symposium on Sign Language Research and Teaching*, edited by C. A. Padden, Silver Spring, MD: National Association of the Deaf.

Pizzuto, E. (1986). The verb system of Italian Sign Language (LIS). In *Signs of life. Proceedings of the Second European Congress on Sign Language Research*, edited by B. T. Tervoort, 17–30. Amsterdam: University of Amsterdam.

———. (1987). Aspetti morfo-sintattici. In *La Lingua Italiana dei Segni*, edited by V. Volterra, 179–209. Bologna, Italy: Il Mulino.

———, Giuranna, E., and Gambino, G. (1987). Morphology of manual signs and nonmanual components in Italian Sign Language (LIS). Paper presented at the Fourth International Symposium on Sign Language Research, 15–19 July, 1987, Lappeenranta, Finland.

Volterra, V., ed. (1987). *La Lingua Italiana dei Segni*. Bologna, Italy: Il Mulino.

———, Laudanna, A., Corazza, S., Radutzky, E., and Natale, F. (1984). Italian Sign Language: The order of elements in the declarative sentence. In *Recent Research on European Sign Languages*, edited by F. Loncke, P. Boyes-Braem, and Y. Lebrun, 19–48. Lisse, Holland: Swets and Zeitlinger B. V.

# Spatial-Locative Predicates in Thai Sign Language

## Marianne Collins-Ahlgren

Many of the young deaf people in Chiang Mai, Thailand, acquired literacy in Thai language simultaneously with acquisition of Thai Sign Language (THAISL). This chapter investigates the intriguing question of whether these bilingual individuals borrowed Thai classifiers ad hoc into their use of THAISL, or whether Thai classifiers influenced THAISL classifiers diachronically.

## TYPES OF CLASSIFIER LANGUAGES

Both Allan (1977) and Dixon (1968) describe two types of classifier languages. The first type is characterized by a noun-classification system including numeral classifiers. This classification system is typified by Thai, spoken language, (henceforth, Thai). In this system, noun classes are represented by gender and concordial systems. Gender systems are usually correlated with isolating languages where large sets of classifiers are free morphemes in discourse-sensitive reference. Concordial systems are compatible with languages characterized by an inflectional morphology where smaller finite sets of noun classes are obligatory.

A second type of noun-classification system, usually correlated with polysynthetic languages, is a noun-incorporation or predicate-classifying system. The primary function of this system is to qualify the verb rather than to classify the noun.

Cross-linguistic studies show that typologically and geographically diverse systems of classifying exhibit similarities so remarkable as to suggest that such similarities are due not to chance or accident, but rather to common semantic organizational principles. Craig suggests that classifiers define categories; therefore, they are linguistic devices for overt categorization. The world is categorized "in terms of the various types of interactions that human beings carry out with the objects of their environments. These interactions being social, physical and functional" (1986, 5). Craig's critical focus is on how people interact with their environment rather than how things are in the environment. Cross-linguistic studies also suggest that, as Craig writes, "an implicational scale can be established among semantic features of classification which states that linguistic classifications mark humanness and animacy first, then shape, then use and consistency'' (1986, 5). This scale may account for similarities noted in repertoires of languages throughout the world.


## SPATIAL-LOCATIVE PREDICATES IN
## THAISL

The informants for this study were young adult members of the Northern Thai Association of the Deaf in Chiang Mai, Thailand. They attended elementary school at the Sethsatian School, a school for the deaf in Bangkok, Thailand, which from 1953 to recently was the only school for the deaf in the country. The recent history of THAISL is associated with the Sethsatian School because most deaf people who did not have deaf parents learned to sign from the model of their peers while attending this school. Khun Kasemsri and Khunying Kamala Krairisksh, graduates of Gallaudet College in Washington, D.C., were the first teachers in this school. Apparently these teachers, among others, invented signs using the American one-handed manual alphabet to represent the initial sound of a Thai word such as *nam* ''water.'' Some ASL signs were incorporated into use at the school also. Despite these instances of ASL influence, the deaf community in Chiang Mai claim that ASL is not the substrate language of THAISL. This issue is raised because the polymorphemic predicates of THAISL are very similar to those of ASL. Considering the similarities noted between classification systems in various spoken languages, perhaps it is not surprising that two, signed, predicate-classifier languages are similar. But the similarities suggest that widespread principles may operate across signed languages, at least across ASL and THAISL, if this research is borne out.

To my knowledge, the geneology of THAISL has never been established. The deaf community insists that THAISL is an old sign language and that it is different from the signed languages of Burma, Laos, Kampuchea, and Malaysia, Thailand's neighboring countries. This claim is particularly interesting because Li (1977), who describes the three branches of the Thai language family, claims that southwestern Thai branch includes Thai, Lao, Shan (spoken in Burma), White Thai, and others. Consultants report that THAISL also differs greatly from Chinese Sign Language but note that it shares some lexical and structural similarities with the signed languages of Hong Kong, Singapore and Taiwan, which have Chinese populations. Analysis of spatial-locative predicates in THAISL has not been presented, but examples have been published in the *Thai Sign Language Dictionary* (National Association of Deaf, 1986).

ASL spatial locative verbs have been described by Liddell (1980), Liddell and Johnson (1987), and Padden (1981, 1983). Ted Supalla (1986) has proposed three types of movement roots: an existence root, a location root, and a motion root, along with several classes of handshapes in synthetic predicates of ASL. Boyes-Braem (1981) describes classifiers for handling entities. McDonald (1982) presents an analysis of handling verbs in which the handshape, not the movement, is the root for productively formed signs.

The analysis of ASL spatial locative verbs presented by Liddell and Johnson (1987) is very similar to what I find in THAISL. I use their terminology in order to facilitate future cross-linguistic study.

# POLYMORPHEMIC PREDICATES IN THAISL

Spatial locative predicates are used in THAISL to establish an entity in space or to establish the relationship between entities in space. The signer articulates a contact root for a stative function. The contact root does not describe an action, event, or process, but rather it produces a stative predicate that establishes the location and orientation of an entity represented by the handshape morpheme. A short single movement, usually downward, followed by a holding segment expresses the stative predicate.

Spatial locative predicates are used to describe the physical appearance or dimensions of an entity or unit of mass, or the arrangement of multiple entities under discussion. The signer articulates the stative-descriptive root to describe the shape and/or inherent characteristics of an entity that has been introduced into the discourse. Unlike in the contact root, in the spatial locative predicate the movement itself is meaningful; it corresponds to the perceived physical attributes of the object being described through spatial contour. This predicate consists of a meaningful movement path; meaningful location of articulation; meaningful hand configuration, which describes dimensions; and meaningful hand orientation. Its hold segments, however, are not meaningful. The signer often articulates a spatial locative predicate with two hands; one hand remains stationary to maintain a point of reference while the other moves meaningfully.

A spatial locative predicate may describe an action, event or process between points in space or in relation to another entity. For this function, the signer articulates the process root. The process root describes the action or process of a human or animal or their action on an inanimate object. In the process root, the handshape morpheme represents the entity integral to the action. The hand configuration is also meaningful, as are movement path and hold segments.

Because handshape morphemes qualify the verb, all three root types share the characteristics of meaningful hand configuration. The handshape morpheme's orientation and the location of articulation in signing space are also meaningful. Function of and type of movement and significance of hold segments distinguishes the three types.

The predication intended by the signer is obviously the heart of the spatial locative predicate. He chooses a root that is appropriate for the type of predication he intends. In some instances, the subject and object of this type of predication have been introduced into the discourse before the signer represents them as entities qualifying the verb. The handshape morpheme ususally represents a basic-level category of entities. For example, if the noun phrase, ''an old hooded lady,'' is the subject in a process of walking somewhere, the signer will qualify the process of walking either with a basic-level upright-person morpheme or a person-on-legs morpheme depending on his emphasis regarding the walking. The handshape morpheme retains the basic-level category person in the process.

Preliminary investigations indicate the following types of basic-level categories or classifier handshape morphemes used with predicate roots in THAISL.

## *Whole-Entity Handshape Morphemes*

Whole-entity handshape morphemes represent a class of whole entities with the same essence. This category makes basic distinctions between human, animate, inanimate, and shape. The criteria for judging a handshape morpheme to belong to this whole entity type are semantic. The handshape morpheme is used with all three types of predicate roots.

For example, figure 1 shows a signer locating an upright person and locating an animal (buffalo) in space. The process of the buffalo's movement toward the person and the person's movement from the buffalo is shown in process roots. The cessation of action of one or both is shown intermittently through hold segments.

Whole-entity classifiers are used in stative-descriptive roots where the hand movement does not correspond to the physical activity of the entity represented but to the spatial contour of the entity or arrangement of multiple entities. Figure 2 shows the handshape morpheme for general inanimate object used in a stative-descriptive root to predicate an arrangement. The following handshapes are whole-entity morphemes:[1]

| | | |
|---|---|---|
| Person upright | $Y_{T<}$ | or $G_{<\wedge}$ |
| Person sitting | $\dot{I}_{T<}$ | (contracted Y) or $\ddot{V}_{b\vee}$ |
| Person lying | $Y_{a\perp}$ | |
| Person on legs | $V_{b\vee}$ | |
| Two to four Persons | $2_{<\wedge}$ | $3_{<\wedge}$     $4_{<\wedge}$ |
| Many people | $5_{<\wedge}$ | |
| Animal | $Y_{b\vee}$ | |
| Many Animals | $5_{b\perp}$ | |
| General inanimate | $B_{\perp\wedge}$ | |
| One-dimensional entity | $B$ | |
| Two-wheeled vehicle | $B_{b\perp}$ | (figure 3) |
| Three-or-more-wheeled vehicle | $B_{<\perp}$ | (figure 4) |
| Boat/ship | $B_{a\perp}$ | |
| Airplane | $\sqcup_{b\perp}$ | |

**Figure 1.** Whole-entity handshape morphemes (right, animal; left, upright person) located in contact roots.

**Figure 2.** Whole-entity handshape morphemes (general, inanimate) described in orderly arrangement in stative-descriptive roots. Function appears to be deictic.

*Figure 3*. Whole-entity handshape morpheme (two-wheeled vehicle) moving in a process root.

*Figure 4*. Whole-entity handshape morphemes (four-wheeled vehicles) moving in process roots. Vehicle arrangement is indicated.

Two features noted in the articulation of general inanimates and in multiples need additional research. The palm orientation of the general inanimate morpheme appears to face toward the entity when there is a deictic function, but to face toward the signer when the function is anaphoric (see figure 5). The feature of disorderly arrangement of multiple animate, inanimate entities is indicated by repeated finger wiggling (see figure 6).

*Figure 5*. Whole-entity handshape morphemes (general, inanimate) described in orderly arrangement in stative-descriptive roots. Function appears to be anaphoric.

*Figure 6*. Whole-entity handshape morphemes (playing cards) described in disorderly arrangement in stative-descriptive root.

### Surface Handshape Morpheme

Surface morphemes represent a surface upon which other entities may be located. They are used with process or contact roots. The forearm functions as a long surface morpheme, as shown in figure 7, in which a person is seated on a *naga*, "snake-dragon."

The flat hand (B) represents a wide surface and the orientation of the handshape is significant. For instance, in figure 8, which shows a person seated on an elephant's head, the palm is turned downward, since the back of the hand represents the flat surface. In figure 9, on the other hand, which shows a person walking on a red carpet, the palm is upward because the flat surface and starting point for the walk was the forearm.

It seems that the surface root may be used with a process root. For example, a rider may be standing on a surface morpheme to windsurf or skateboard over space. Figure 10 shows the broad surface of the sea in undulating action. During upward swings. this is a surface for a boat.

The following are surface handshape morphemes:

| | |
|---|---|
| Long surface | Forearm |
| Wide, flat surface | B |
| Narrow surface | H |
| Thin surface | 1 |
| Multiple, thin surfaces | 2, 3, 4 |

*Figure 7*. Whole-entity handshape morpheme (seated person, right) located in contact root on surface handshape morpheme (back of dragon, left) located in contact root.

*Figure 8*. Whole-entity handshape morpheme (seated person, right) located in contact root on surface handshape morpheme (head of elephant, left) located in contact root.

*Figure 9*. Whole-entity handshape morpheme (upright person, right) moving in process root on surface handshape morpheme (red carpet, left) located in contact root.

*Figure 10*. Whole-entity handshape morpheme (boat, right) in movement-process root comes into contact with surface handshape morpheme (undulating sea, left) in process root.

### Depth, Width, and Shape Handshape Morphemes

Handshapes that represent the depth, width, or shape of an entity are used with a stative-descriptive root. When used in this root, depth, width, or shape morphemes are not used as surface morphemes.

The signer's perception about the physical attributes of an entity dictates his choice of handshape. For example, if he views a rainbow as a broad but shallow entity spanning an arc or as a combination on many narrow bands of light, he will trace the arc with either an index and parallel thumb handshape or with a spread-finger handshape, as shown in figure 11. As shown in figure 11, the nondominant hand often holds a point of reference at the initial point of movement.

Smooth texture is indicated by a flat hand, and rough texture by fingers bent at two joints. These handshapes are used to contrast a thatched roof with a tiled roof, and smooth cloth with a rough-weave textile.

The following handshapes serve as depth, width, and shape morphemes:

| | |
|---|---|
| Curved or rounded surfaces | C 9 $\overline{\overline{\text{B}}}$ $\overline{\overline{\text{G}}}$ $\overline{\overline{\text{H}}}$ |
| Medium width, and small depth | H |
| Twisted | R |
| Narrow or outlined | 1 |
| Strips | 2, 3, 4 |

The handshape may change during the articulation of the predicate to reflect the shape of an entity. For instance, an entity may narrow in width as height increases.

### Perimeter Handshape Morpheme

The perimeter handshape morphemes describe either the shape of a single entity's perimeter or the bounded but unspecified shape of an entity. The perimeter morpheme is used only with the contact root. Figure 12 shows the perimeter of a house established in a contact root. Figure 13 shows the establishing of upper and lower limits perimeter. Figure 14 illustrates the unspecified perimeter as it is used to establish the locations of two villages. Both hands are often used to establish the perimeter of a single entity in a contact root.

### Extent Handshape Morphemes

Extent handshape morphemes describe volume or the amount of an entity. They are used with process predicates, typically without movement path. A change in amount of a contained mass noun such as liquid in a bottle is reflected from containing full volume (B), as shown in figure 15, to lack of volume ($\hat{O}$). Levels midway between these extremes are described by the relationship between the fingertips and the thumb. A change in the amount of a mass noun in a mound such as a pile of rice on a plate is described through an extent morpheme, $5_{b\perp}$ [$\hat{O}$]. An increase or decrease in the number of count nouns is indicated by the morpheme, $5_{a\perp}$ [$\hat{O}$]. For example, the nondominant hand may describe the movement and stops of a bus, and the dominant hand the increased number of passengers.

### Instrument Handshape Morphemes

Instrument handshape morphemes represent instruments, including the hand when it acts as an instrument. The predicate may articulate both types with one type in each hand, as, for example, in figure 16 where the signer drinks from a mug. Present

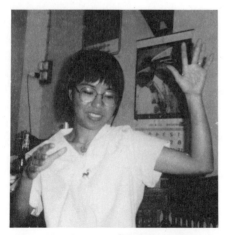

*Figure 11*. **Width handshape morphemes (rainbow bands) described in arc movement of stative-descriptive root with right hand; left hand "holds" base of rainbow.**

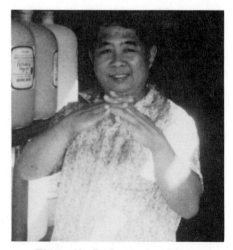

*Figure 12*. **Perimeter handshape morphemes (house roof) established in contact root.**

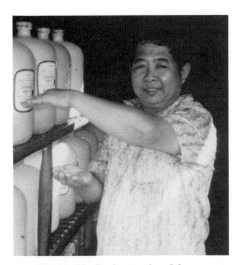

**Figure 13.** Perimeter handshape
morphemes establish upper and lower
limits (jar) in contact root.

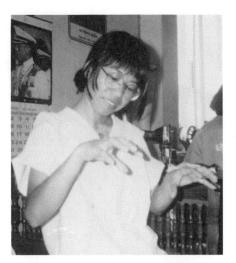

**Figure 14.** Perimeter handshape
morphemes (two villages) established in
contact roots.

research suggests that instrument handshape morphemes are used only with process roots. These morphemes contact the signer's body in predicating a process, for example, in drinking from a mug.

Both hands may represent the same entity in a process such carrying an entity by holding the top and bottom of it or each hand may represent a different entity such as a container and a lid, as shown in figure 17.

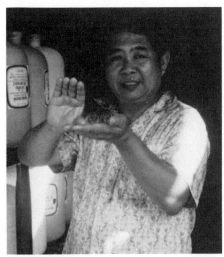

**Figure 15.** Extent handshape morpheme
(volume of contained liquid) changes
shape in process root to show change in
volume.

**Figure 16.** Instrument handshape
morphemes (hand as instrument, right;
hand representing mug, left) in lifting-to-
mouth process roots.

***Figure 17.*** **Instrument handshape morphemes (lid, right; container, left) in moving-process roots.**

This investigation suggests clearly that THAISL informants choose a predicate root to focus deliberately on some process, action, event, or change of state; to describe the characteristics of a referent; or to establish and locate an entity in space. They choose predicate either to convey expected meaning or to gain special effect. The predication is the heart of the spatial-locative predicate and certain entities appropriate for each type of predication are represented by handshapes used in the predicate. The following types of compatibilities are apparent. Whole-entity morphemes occur with all three types of roots. Surface morphemes occur with contact and process roots. Shape, depth, and width morphemes occur with stative-descriptive roots. Extent and instrument morphemes occur with process roots.

## THAI CLASSIFIERS

Thai classifiers serve a classifying and quantifying function. In so far as the classifiers refer to a group or class of things or set of individuals, they function to support the correct choice of verb (Denny, 1986). For instance, a volitional verb is appropriate if a class of humans is indicated but not for classes of animals or inanimates. Thai noun classifiers refer to the individuals being enumerated within their class. The quantification of these individuals is the principal function of Thai classifiers. The classifiers are hypernyms in so far as the variables within these classes extend over the whole class of things and define membership within the class. The types of classes may be termed units, parts, multiples, kinds, and measures.

A noun phrase usually introduces an entity into the discourse. The classifier that names the class to which the individual belongs may be used in subsequent discourse without the noun. To identify the noun as an individual of a given class, a numeral follows the noun and precedes the classifier so it will be clear in subsequent discourse how many individuals of the class are relevant. In repeated reference to the same individual entity, the noun is usually deleted and only the classifier is used. However, if the numeral in a sentence does not actually enumerate individuals of a class, the classifier is dropped and the noun is retained. Conklin (1981) observes that classifiers are used with a demonstrative when their use strengthens its anaphoric reference. Classifiers precede demonstratives.

Thai, which is essentially a noun-classifying language, demonstrates an ambiguous area between prototypical noun-classification systems and noun-class systems, because class names are used in some Thai compound nouns. Delancey describes a continuum between nouns that serve no classifying function, through nouns that serve a classifying function as class terms and/or classifiers, to pure classifiers, which are free morphemes serving only to classify. He suggests the following diachronic evolution of classification morphemes:

> The more probable sequence of starting as a noun with simultaneous class term use, later acting as a classifier in one or two semi-lexicalized constructions, gradually expanding its repertoire of classifier uses, perhaps abandoning some of its nominal uses as these are replaced by a compound of which it is the head, and finally being caught in some attested language having some marginal use as a noun, a semi-productive use as a class term, and a productive classifier use in which, however, it classifies a different set of nouns that it does as a class term (1986, p. 444).

In many instances, there is an obvious semantic connection between individuals within a classification. But some classifiers have a less translucent semantic link, as is noted in table 1.

The speaker's choice of classifier depends on the individual entity being sorted and enumerated, but the speaker may choose to focus deliberately on some characteristic of the entity. Because the characteristics of the referent are compatible with more than one classification, the speaker has options. However, innovation is usually restricted by convention. Though the speaker's interaction with the world of things he classifies and his notions about the situation predicated influence his choices, some choices become grammaticized or fossilized, and the noun dictates the choice of classifier. Choice of classifier is also influenced by the register or style of discourse or writing. For instance, fruit is classified by *phŏn* in formal style, but by *lûuk* (round object, offspring, seeds) in colloquial speech; unmarked person is classified by *khon* in normal register, but in colloquial style one counting heads may use the classifier for heads of tubulars, *hŭa*.

## COMPARISONS BETWEEN THAI CLASSIFIERS AND THAISL CLASSIFICATION

Group type classifiers of Thai express a group of indefinite number of some entity. A specific number of groups may be enumerated. THAISL uses an indefinite plural-number handshape for animals and humans. To specify a definite number of groups, the sign group ($B_{>\perp}$ $B_{\leq\perp}^{>\times}$) may be articulated in different spaces a given number of times or the signer may follow the group sign with a numeral.

*Table 1*. **Sample of Types of Thai Classifiers**

| Unit | Parts | Multiples/Groups | Kind | Measure |
|---|---|---|---|---|
| Khon (person) | | glûm (crowd) | chán | |
| oŋ (revered person) | | | | |
| tua (animal) | | fǔuŋ (flock) | | |
| chyâk (elephant) | | | | |
| an (inanimate) | chín (piece) | | jàaŋ | caan (filled bowl) |
| sên (one-dimensional) | klìip (clove, petal) | | chaníd | khùat (filled bottle) |
| phèen (two-dimensional) | | | | thuây (cup) |
| phy̌yn (flexible, one-dimensional) | khǎaŋ (one side of a pair) | | | |
| baj (flexible, two-dimensional) | | | | kêew (glass) |
| | | mát (bunch tied) | | thǎŋ (bucket) |
| méd (small, round) | | phuaŋ (bunch of) | | mɔ̂ɔ (pot) |
| lûuk (large, round) | | kɔɔŋ (disorderly pile) | | tàd (flat pan) |
| thɔ̂ɔ (hollow cylinder) | | | | |
| tôn (plant) | | | | sɔɔŋ (soft pack) |
| baan (mirror, door, window) | | tâŋ (stack) | | tung (bag) |
| klɔ̂ɔŋ (camera, binoculars, opium pipe) | | thɛ̌ɛw (rows of) | | metric measures |
| muan (cigar, cigarette) | | khûu (pair) | | |
| sǎay (river, street, line) | | chúd (matching group) | | |
| dâam (pen) | | | | |
| lêm (book, comb, candle) | | | | |
| dɔ̀ɔk (flower, key, firecracker, joss stick) | | | | |

In multiple arrangements a specific number is indicated by slowly and deliberately repeating the contact root a given number of times in a row or stack arrangement. Similarly, a specific number of articulations of entities, usually up to four, located deliberately indicates that specific number of things in an arrangement.

Kind type classifiers of Thai such as *jaàŋ* and *chaníd* do not appear to have counterparts in THAISL. The signs associated with deictic reference in THAISL seem to serve this function; however, additional research is needed in this area.

Part type classifiers such as *chín* in Thai do not appear as such in THAISL. In THAISL, parts are usually indicated by an action on a whole followed by a stative-descriptive root description of the resulting parts or a contact root location of perimeters of resulting parts.

Measure type classifiers share the common principle of containing a mass in some unit or container that is the designated unit of measure. Because speakers of Thai and signers of THAISL are containing the same mass in real-world experience, the measures chosen are similar but not always identical. For instance, Thai classifies a plate of rice, *caán*, and THAISL measures rice by the spoonful. Several THAISL measures are designated by a stative-descriptive root using appropriate dimensional handshapes or by process roots using instrument classifiers.

Unit type classification in both languages demonstrates the implicational scale that Craig (1986) finds to be typical of all classifier languages. After animacy and inanimacy are distinguished, human and animal are distinguished, then shape and dimension are distinguished, and finally consistency. Unlike spoken Thai, shape is relevant to all types of classification and units in THAISL. While many of the unit type classifiers employ the same or similar semantic units, the expressions are not always identical.

One aspect of classifier use that is the same in both languages is the fact that those who use classifiers with skill in rich and extensive selections are admired by other speakers. Adults learning the languages have difficulty incorporating classifier use with the facility of native speakers, and children learn to incorporate classifiers relatively late in their acquisition of language, even in the presence of a good adult model speaker.

In both THAISL and spoken Thai, the level of discourse, or of text in Thai, influences the variety and frequency of classifier use. In spoken Thai, generally, the more formal the register, the more extensive and richly dotted is classifier use. Usually a smaller set of classifiers is used in informal speech. In THAISL, however, a high degree of formality is correlated with less classification, and informality correlates with more classification.

The great importance of social status in Thai society is reflected in spoken Thai. This is seen, for example, in the distinctions between the unclassified person *khon* and the high-status person *oŋ*. The elephant, which historically was owned by royalty and is thus high status, is classified *chyâk*, while all other animals are classified *tua*. Social status is not similarly marked in THAISL, however.

I suggest above that Thai classifiers began their diachronic evolution as nouns or noun classes. In THAISL, however, nouns appear to be historically related to spatial-locative predicates that have become frozen or fossilized over time. Several established lexicalized nouns may have evolved diachronically from predicates.

In both Thai and THAISL, the noun or noun phrase usually places the entity into the discourse. In subsequent discourse, the noun is often omitted and represented by a Thai classifier or by a THAISL handshape morpheme.

The primary function of the THAISL handshape morpheme is to qualify the verb by implying the basic class of entity involved in the predicate. The handshape morpheme thus not only restricts the scope of the predicate but reminds the addressee of the limiting entity during the discourse. The handshape morpheme functions like a classifier in so far as it implies features characteristic of the entity involved in the predication.

The primary function of the Thai noun classifier is to classify certain features of a specific noun and to enumerate a number of individuals of that class. Classifiers are the principal means used to quantify in spoken Thai, whereas THAISL has alternative means of quantifying and indicating plural number.

THAISL, a predicate-classifier language, uses handshape morphemes that share some fundamental characteristics with the classifiers of Thai, most notably a numeral classifier system with free-morpheme classifiers. But these similar repertoires of classifiers for unit, measure, and multiple status seem to be due to the nature of categorization of the world noted in cross-linguistic studies, and not due to the influence of Thai language on THAISL. Thus, my research supports the intuition of native informants that THAISL is a separate language from Thai and that those who are competent in both languages are bilingual.

## NOTE

1. The alphabet handshape symbols are from Stokoe (1976) and from Brennan et al. (1980). The subscript symbols from palm (first) and finger (second) orientation are from Brennan et al. (1980).

## REFERENCES

Allan, K. (1977). Classifiers. *Language* 53:285–311.

Boyes-Braem, P. (1981). A study of the acquisition of the DEZ in American Sign Language. Ph.D. diss., University of California, Berkeley.

Brennan, M., Colville, M., and Lawson, L. K. (1980). *Words in hand*. Edinburgh: Moray House College of Education.

Conklin, N. F. (1981). The semantics and syntax of numeral classification in Thai and Austronesian. Ph.D. diss., University of Michigan.

Craig, C., ed. (1986). *Noun classes and categorization*, pp. 1–10. Philadelphia: John Benjamins Publishing Co.

Delancey, S. (1986). Toward a history of Thai classification. In *Noun classes and categorization*, edited by C. Craig, 437–51. Philadelphia: John Benjamins Publishing Co.

Denny, J. P. (1986). The semantic role of noun classification. In *Noun classes and categorization*, edited by C. Craig, 297–308. Philadelphia: John Benjamins Publishing Co.

Dixon, R. M. W. (1968). Noun classes. *Lingua* 21:104–25.

Li, F. K. (1977). *A handbook of comparative Thai*. Honolulu: University of Hawaii.

Liddell, S. (1980). *American Sign Language syntax*. The Hague: Mouton.

———, and Johnson, R. (1987). An analysis of spatial-locative predicates in American Sign Language. Symposium conducted at the Fourth International Symposium on Sign Language Research, 15–19 July, Lappeenranta, Finland.

McDonald, B. (1982). Aspects of the American Sign Language predicate system. Ph.D. diss., University of Buffalo, New York.

National Association of Deaf in Thailand. (1986). *The Thai Sign Language dictionary*, book one. Thailand: Thai Watana Panich Press.

Noss, R. B. (1964). *Thai reference grammar*. Washington, DC, Foreign Service Institute.

Padden, C. (1981). Some arguments for syntactic patterning in American Sign Language. *Sign Language Studies* 32:239–59.

———. (1983). Interaction of morphology and syntax in American Sign Language. Ph.D. diss., University of California, San Diego.

Stokoe, W. C., Casterline, D. C., Croneberg, C. G. (1976). A dictionary of American Sign Language on linguistic principles, rev. ed. Silver Spring, MD: Linstok Press.

Supalla, T. (1986). The classifier system in American Sign Language. In *Noun classes and categorization*, edited by C. Craig, 181–214. Philadelphia: John Benjamins Publishing Co.

# The Relation Between Space and Grammar in ASL Verb Morphology

Carol A. Padden

One of the more traditional approaches to analysis of signed languages has been to examine the ways in which modality interacts with language structure (Klima, Bellugi, et al., 1979; Wilbur, 1979; Bellugi and Studdert-Kennedy, 1980). Perhaps the most compelling feature of signed languages, certainly one that has attracted much discussion, is their ability to exploit the visuo-spatial dimension. Unlike oral languages where space is referred to, in sign languages, space is physically available for representation. The space around and on the signer's body is exploited at all levels: formationally similar signs may contrast only in location; verb agreement is marked using spatial position; and discourse topics are distinguished from one another by where the signs are articulated.

The availability of this dimension begs the question of whether it affords signed languages grammatical possibilities that are not otherwise available in oral languages. Given a set or subset of grammatical markers, perhaps sign languages exceed the number within any set found in oral languages. It has been suggested elsewhere that ASL has unusually rich pronominal and agreement distinctions that may not be matched in oral languages (Lacy, 1974; Lillo-Martin and Klima, to appear). Since these distinctions are largely made spatially, perhaps this difference is due to the fact that space is implicit in oral languages, but explicit in signed languages. Alternatively, it is possible that the spatial dimension in signed languages exists only as an epiphenomenon of grammatical structure. Spatial contrasts and distinctions can be accounted for by grammatical features that already exist in the class of natural languages.

Drawing on an analysis of verb morphology in ASL, I address the question of whether spatial possibilities of ASL verbs can be predicted from grammatical features. ASL has at least three major verb classes, which differ with respect to which morphemes can be added to them. I show that certain spatial possibilities in these verb classes can be predicted from constraints on verb agreement systems in natural languages. As such, these data show that at least with respect to one domain of verb morphology—agreement—spatial contrasts are predictable from grammatical contrasts needed in grammars of natural languages.

## ASL VERB MORPHOLOGY

In an earlier description of ASL verbs (Padden, 1988), I identified three classes of verbs on the basis of which affixes may be added to them. The first category of verbs, called "plain verbs," do not inflect for person or number, nor do they take locative affixes. Some have inflections for aspect.[1] Examples include LOVE, CELEBRATE, LIKE, TASTE, THINK, WONDER. A second category, "inflecting verbs," inflect for person, number, and aspect, but do not take locative affixes. Examples are GIVE, SHOW, TELL, ASK, SEND, BAWL-OUT, INFORM, ADVISE, FORCE, PERSUADE. A third class, "spatial verbs," do not inflect for person, number or aspect, but instead have locative affixes. Different subclasses of spatial verbs also add other affixes, including manner and noun-class morphemes. The three classes capture generalizations across verbs that display a particular pattern of morphology exclusively. Inflecting verbs are those that display person and number morphology; spatial verbs are those that display locative morphology.

In a recent paper, Johnson (1987) suggests that the label "inflecting verbs" is misleading because plain verbs also inflect, not for person and number, but for aspect. He suggests that the class be renamed "agreement" verbs to signify their most outstanding feature. His correction keys in on a central point underlying the distinction between classes: verb-agreement morphology appears only in one class of ASL verbs. I concur with this correction and shall henceforth refer to "inflecting verbs" as "agreement" verbs.

### Spatial Verbs

All spatial verbs have locative affixes, but they fall into one of several subclasses depending on which combination of affixes they display. Supalla (1986, in press) has provided a detailed description of one large subset of spatial verbs, those he calls "verbs of motion and location," or "classifier verbs." In my analysis, which focuses on the presence of commonly shared morphology, the class of spatial verbs is larger than the class of classifier verbs. Spatial verbs include verbs that lack the highly detailed noun-classifier morphemes, but like classifier verbs, have locative morphemes. Except for subclass 1, the subclasses of spatial verbs below are analyzed extensively in Supalla (1986, in press).

> Subclass 1: Predicates that take locative affixes: MOVE, PUT.
> Subclass 2: Predicates that take locative, instrument-classifier, and manner affixes: CARRY-BY-HAND, HOLD-ERASER-BY-HAND.
> Subclass 3: Predicates that take locative, manner, and noun-classifier affixes: VEHICLE-MOVE-IN-STRAIGHT-PATH, PERSON-MOVE, FOUR-LEGGED-ANIMATE-MOVE.
> Subclass 4: Predicates whose locative affixes are on the body: GUN-DIRECTED-TO-TORSO, GUN-DIRECTED-TO-HEAD, HIT-IN-THE-EYE. (Supalla [1986] refers to these as "body-classifier verbs.")
> Subclass 5: Predicates with locative affixes and body-part noun classifiers: OUTSTRETCHED-WINGS, PAWS, CLENCHED-FIST. (Supalla [1986] refers to these as "bodypart classifiers.")

### Agreement Verbs

Agreement verbs are those that contain agreement affixes for person and number of the subject and/or final object (Padden, 1988), but not all verbs mark both. The verbs GIVE, SHOW, SEND, ASK, FORCE, PERSUADE, INFORM inflect for person and number of both the subject and final object. NAB, OPPRESS, CON/CONVINCE inflect for person and number of the final object only.

**Person Agreement.**    Traditionally, person agreement in ASL is described as having three forms: first, second, and third. First-person agreement forms are located near the signer's body, second-person in the direction of the addressee, and third, any other location (Padden, 1988). Meier (in press) observes that unlike first-person agreement, which is always located near the signer's body, second- and third-person agreement forms do not have fixed locations. Second-person forms involve eye contact with the addressee while pointing in the direction of the addressee. Third-person pronouns index any other location not involving eye contact with the addressee. Meier argues that since second- and third-person referents are disambiguated largely by eye contact, the conditions are pragmatic, not grammatical. Because the lexicon cannot enter "position of the addressee" as part of the phonological form of the second- and third-person pronoun, there can be no entries in the lexicon for second- and third-person pronouns. Consequently, Meier proposes that person in ASL falls into two categories: first- and non-first-person pronouns. Meier notes that although the lexicon may not have all three person categories, they are semantically distinct in ASL.

Lillo-Martin and Klima (in press) note the same difficulty as Meier and ask what form of the second- or third-person pronoun is to be entered in the lexicon. Further, they note that first-person pronouns have different locations during "role shifting" (discussed below); the body to which the first-person pronoun references shifts from side to side to indicate a change in subject identity. Consequently, a third-person locus under one body shift can become a first-person in another body shift. To handle the complex constraints needed to handle coreference across discourse units, Lillo-Martin and Klima propose no distinction between first- and non-first-person pronouns; instead they enter a single pronoun root in the lexicon, specified for handshape and movement but unspecified for location. The discourse representation component in the grammar interprets the index for coreference.

The proposals of Meier and Lillo-Martin and Klima differ in terms of whether first-person (and by extension, non-first-person) categories are grammatically marked. Meier argues that they are; Lillo-Martin and Klima argue that they are not.[2] The strength of Meier's argument rests on his observation that in ASL there is a set of fixed first-person pronoun forms: I (first-person singular), MY (first-person possessive), WE (first-person plural), OUR (first-person plural possessive).

The form of person agreement markers in ASL is similar to person pronouns: first-person agreement forms are located near the signer's own body and second- and third-person forms are elsewhere. In the absence of a persuasive argument against Meier's observation that first person is marked independently in ASL, I shall assume a contrast between first and other categories of person.

**Number Agreement.**    Number agreement in ASL falls into two categories: singular and plural. Plural agreement has a number of subforms, including dual, ("two"), exhaustive ("each"), and multiple ("them") (Klima and Bellugi, 1979).

The form of singular or unmarked number agreement is a single point in neutral space; plural agreement involves displacement, that is, movement away from a single point. Some forms of plural agreement are marked only on the final absolutive: the multiple and one form of the dual plural.[3]

A summary of the morphological differences between the three classes of verbs in ASL appears in table 1.

### Plain Verbs and Agreement Morphology

There are forms of plain verbs that potentially challenge the categorization in table 1; they contain indexic points, as do agreement markers. An example appears in sentence 1 below; the plain verb WANT is articulated twice, once at some specific locus (a, b). Like agreement verbs, the verb does not involve contact with the body, but is articulated in neutral space, using some specific locus. These forms resemble agreement verbs with deleted subject agreement, for example, OWE, CRITICIZE, which lack path movement and are executed at some point in the area around the signer's body (called "neutral space"). Note that sentence 1 is ambiguous, referring to either subject or object. Sentence 2 involves three iterations of WANT, and again is ambiguous as to whether subject or object is marked.

(1) WOMAN $_a$WANT; MAN $_b$WANT.[4]
'The woman$_i$ is wanting and the man$_j$ is wanting, too.'
'The woman wants it$_i$ and the man wants it$_j$.'

(2) WOMAN $_a$WANT $_b$WANT $_c$WANT.
'The women$_{i,j,k}$ are each wanting.'
'The woman wants this$_i$, that$_j$ and that one$_k$, too.'

Instead of expanding the class of agreement verbs to include some plain verbs, I demonstrate below that these forms in question do not contain agreement morphology, despite their surface similarity to agreement verbs; instead, the correct analysis is that they contain pronoun clitics.

## THE ARGUMENT FOR PRONOUN CLITICS

All verbs containing pronoun clitics can also appear with overt pronouns. In sentences 3 and 4 the citation form of WANT is executed by the strong hand (S), and the

*Table 1.* **Morphology of Verb Classes in ASL**

|  | Plain | Agreement | Spatial |
|---|---|---|---|
| Morphology |  |  |  |
| person | no | yes | no |
| number | no | yes | no |
| locative | no | no | yes |
| noun classifier | no | no | yes |
| instrument classifier | no | no | yes |

pronouns by the weak hand (W). Sentences 3 and 4, too, are ambiguous as to whether subject or object is marked. For each indexic point, there is a separate iteration of the sign WANT.

(3) S: WOMAN WANT; MAN WANT.
    W:        $_a$PRO          $_b$PRO
    'The woman$_i$ is wanting and the man$_j$ is wanting, too.'
    'The woman wants it$_i$ and the man wants it$_j$.'

(4) S: WOMAN WANT WANT WANT.
    W:        $_a$PRO  $_b$PRO  $_c$PRO
    'The women$_{i,j,k}$ are each wanting.'
    'The woman wants this$_i$, that$_j$ and that one$_k$, too.'

The key, crucial fact about these structures is that they are not restricted to plain verbs but can also be found in nouns and adjectives, as in sentences 5 through 8. Like plain verbs, they appear in plain, citation form.

(5) S: I SEE DOG DOG DOG.
    W:        $_a$PRO $_b$PRO $_c$PRO
    'I saw a dog here, there and there, too.'

(6) I SEE $_a$DOG $_b$DOG $_c$DOG.
    'I saw a dog here, there and there, too.'

(7) S: HAVE CAR LINE-OF BLUE  BLUE  BLUE.
    W:                      $_a$PRO  $_b$PRO  $_c$PRO
    'There's a line of blue cars.'

(8) HAVE CAR LINE-OF $_a$BLUE $_b$BLUE $_c$BLUE.
    'There's a line of blue cars.'

The distribution of these pronoun clitics mirrors that proposed for simple clitics in Zwicky and Pullum's (1983) analysis of the English "n't" affix. Relevant for the present discussion is their observation that clitics "exhibit a low degree of selection with respect to their hosts while affixes exhibit a high degree of selection with respect to their stems." Inflectional affixes are restricted to a single grammatical category, for example, the English plural "-s" is confined to nouns, the past tense "-ed" to verbs. Clitics, in contrast, can appear across categories, for example, the English "'ve" contraction can be attached to verbs, prepositions, or nouns. Sentences 1, 2, 6, and 8 demonstrate that the mutable forms are not selective as to grammatical category and can appear without semantic restriction.

There is, however, one restriction on forms with pronoun clitics, a strictly phonological one. Pronoun clitics cannot attach to "body-anchored" signs, or signs that involve contact with the body (sentences 9 and 10). Examples of such signs are: HAVE, HUNGRY, CAT, MOUSE, CHINESE, SUSPICIOUS, LIVE, etc. With body-anchored signs, only sentence 9 is a possible structure.

(9) S: WOMAN HAVE; MAN HAVE.
    W:        $_a$PRO          $_b$PRO
    'The woman has it and the man does, too.'

(10) *WOMAN $_a$HAVE; MAN $_b$HAVE.
    'The woman has it and the man does, too.'

The restriction on signs like HAVE, again, is not selective; it can apply across grammatical categories to any form having a certain phonological shape. The noun CAT is likewise a body-anchored sign, and it disallows dislocation to neutral space, but it can be accompanied by simultaneous pronouns. This restriction is similar to the one found in the English ''-d'' contraction for ''would/had''; the contraction appears only with forms ending in a vowel.

There are structures where agreement verbs are accompanied by simultaneous pronouns. However, the verbs cannot appear in an uninflected or citation form; agreement is obligatory as shown in sentence 12. Furthermore, unlike clitics in sentences 1 through 4, there is no unambiguous interpretation of the agreement marker.

(11) *S: WOMAN GIVE   GIVE   GIVE.
     W:         $_a$PRO  $_b$PRO  $_c$PRO
     'The woman gave it to her, him and her, too.'

(12) S: WOMAN GIVE$_a$   GIVE$_b$   GIVE$_c$.
     W:         $_a$PRO  $_b$PRO  $_c$PRO
     'The woman gave it to her$_i$, him$_j$ and her,$_k$ too.'

In conclusion, the apparent similarities between pronoun clitics and agreement affixes are misleading. The special mutability allowed in forms such as sentences 1, 2, 6, and 8 are best represented in terms of pronoun clitics, not as agreement, thus preserving the generalization that person and number affixes are highly restricted, appearing only with verbs, and that plain verbs in ASL lack agreement morphology.

## AGREEMENT VERBS AND SPATIAL VERBS

Having determined that there is only one class of verbs in ASL that displays agreement morphology, the question now is how the spatial possibilities of these verbs differ from spatial verbs, which contain not agreement, but locative morphemes. There are two relevant facts about agreement verbs: first, agreement morphology cannot co-occur (following Supalla [1986] and Liddell [1984], cannot be arranged simultaneously, or vertically) with locative, manner, instrument, or nominal morphemes. Unlike spatial verbs, where rich combinations of simultaneously occurring locative, nominal, instrument and manner affixes are possible, agreement affixes are exclusive of these affixes.[5]

Second, agreement verbs and spatial verbs use the space in front of the signer's body in very different ways. Agreement verbs have certain spatial restrictions that do not apply to spatial verbs; the spatial possibilities of agreement verbs are far more constrained. This second fact, I later argue, follows from properties of verb agreement morphology in natural languages.

## THE SPECIAL CONSTRAINTS OF PERSON AGREEMENT

There are a number of pairs of verbs that are phonologically similar, even identical, and contrast only in morphology. The similarity between pairs like these led earlier investigators of ASL verb structure such as Friedman (1975) to propose a single category "directional verbs" for all verbs that involve a path movement from one location to another. But the similarity based on path movement is misleading. For example, compare GIVE, an agreement verb, and CARRY-BY-HAND, a spatial verb. Although their forms are identical, their morphologies are distinct.

(13) $_1$GIVE$_a$
'I give you.'

(14) $_a$CARRY-BY-HAND$_b$
'I carried it from here to there.'

In sentence 13, the first segment of the verb involves a location near the signer's body, likewise in sentence 14. However, in 13 at the first position ($_1$) is a person-agreement morpheme; in 14, it is a locative morpheme ($_a$). First-person agreement forms can phonetically vary from any location near the signer's chin, down to the upper torso, and to the middle torso. However, each of these same locations are distinctive for the class of locative morphemes in ASL. In sentence 15 below, the first segment is a locative morpheme whose location is near the signer's chin. Sentences 16 and 17 reveal contrastive meanings.

(15) $_c$CARRY-BY-HAND$_d$
'I took the paper I had near my chin and carried it there.'

(16) $_e$CARRY-BY-HAND$_d$
'I took the paper I had near my chest and carried it there.'

(17) $_f$CARRY-BY-HAND$_d$
'I took the paper I had near the lower part of my body and carried it there.'

Likewise, compare the agreement verb CATCH and the spatial verb CATCH-BY-HANDS. The form of the agreement verb does not vary according to scale or identity, as sentences 18 and 19 show.

(18) POLICE CATCH$_a$ MAN, BIG-SHOULDERED.
'The police arrested a large man.'

(19) POLICE CATCH$_a$ WOMAN, THIN.
'The police arrested a slender woman.'

But the spatial verb, CATCH-BY-HANDS, with the instrument classifier: -BY-HANDS varies in scale and location depending on features of the object.

(20) POLICE CATCH-BY-HANDS MAN BIG-SHOULDERED.
'The police grabbed hold of a big-shouldered man.'

(21) POLICE CATCH-BY-HANDS WOMAN, THIN.
'The police grabbed hold of a slender woman.'

(22) POLICE CATCH-BY-HANDS-NEAR-WAIST.
'The police grabbed him at the waist.'

(23) POLICE CATCH-BY-HANDS-NEAR-HEAD.
'The police grabbed him at the throat.'

The spatial contrast between person agreement and locative morphology can be characterized in this way: the phonetic representation of location in person agreement involves reference to vectors, not specific points. First-person agreement involves a vector located toward the upper center of the signer's body. Non-first-person agreement likewise involves general direction of movement away from the signer's body. Locative morphemes, in contrast, access specific locations.

Up to this point, the terms "person agreement," "index," and "spatial location" have been used to reference a spatial location on or around the signer's body. A careful distinction among the three will make clearer the special nature of person agreement. A "spatial location" is any physical point on or around the signer's body. It is neutral with respect to agreement or pronoun morphology. An "index" is referential; it exists in contradistinction to some other index. Person morphemes simply distinguish between first- and non-first-person. First person occupies a vector near the signer's body; non-first, vectors apart from the signer's body.

## THE SPECIAL CONSTRAINTS OF NUMBER AGREEMENT

Another instructive way to compare the spatial possibilities of agreement morphology and locative morphology is with number inflections. Compare below GIVE, an agreement verb and PUT, a spatial verb. GIVE is inflected for the plural, exhaustive number agreement, and there is a phonologically similar form with PUT. In sentences 24 and 25 below, the movement of the verb forms is nearly identical. Both GIVE and PUT involve three iterations, each evenly spaced with respect to the other.

(24) I $_1$GIVE$_d$, exhaus.
  'I gave one to each of them.'

(25) I $_c$PUT$_d$; $_c$PUT$_e$, $_c$PUT$_f$.
  'I put one in each of those places.'

Contrast sentence 25 with sentence 26, where the distance between the end points is variable. The distance between the first two points is shorter than between the second and the third. The meaning is entirely different:

(26) $_c$PUT$_d$; $_c$PUT$_g$, $_c$PUT$_h$.
  'I put one here; I put one at close distance to the first, and I put a third item at some distance from the other two.'

There is no comparable contrast with GIVE. A form of GIVE that is phonetically similar to sentence 26 would have no change in meaning. It would be within the range of permissable phonetic variation for exhaustive agreement. Its phonetic form can vary from three locations evenly spaced apart or three locations of variable distance from each other. The spatial verb PUT does not inflect for plural agreement; instead, the nearly identical form is actually made up of three distinct verb phrases ('I put one here; I put one there; and I put one over there'), each one with a different locative morpheme. Sentence 24 contains a single verb phrase; sentences 25 and 26 contain three VPs each.

Compare also GIVE in sentence 27, where the final object is marked for reciprocal agreement (a type of dual agreement of the subject and final object), and the forms of PUT in sentences 28 and 29. Reciprocal agreement has one of two possible forms: in one, the two hands cross and terminate at the other's beginning point; in the other, the end point of the two hands' path movements is adjacent. There is no contrast in meaning. However, this same phonetic variation is contrastive with PUT.

> (27)  $_{a-b}$GIVE$_{b-a}$.
>     'They gave each other something.'
>
> (28)  $_a$PUT$_b$; $_b$PUT$_a$.
>     'I put one in each other's places.'
>
> (29)  $_a$PUT$_b$; $_c$PUT$_d$.
>     'I put the two of them next to each other.'

These examples demonstrate that while the phonological forms of plural agreement may be similar to a series of spatial verbs, each with locative morphemes, their morphologies are not at all identical. Number-agreement morphemes in ASL are complex and numerous but all involve fixed trajectories of movement. The reciprocal number-agreement form, for example, can vary in possible end positions, where the hands are near each other, or in each other's places. Locative morphemes, in contrast, are drawn from a rich class of forms, each varying finely one from the other in range of possible locations. Consequently, what is phonetic variation for number agreement is distinctive for locative morphology.

It appears that number agreement can be accompanied by pronoun clitics. In sentence 30 below, there are two iterations of GIVE, each inflected for exhaustive plural. The two inflected forms of GIVE are articulated in different locations, one in location marked (a), and the other marked (b). The first plural refers to one group, and the second to a second, distinct group.

> (30)  C-O $_0$GIVE$_{a, exhaus}$ ; FINISH $_0$GIVE$_{b, exhaus}$.
>     'The company gave one to everyone in that group$_i$ and one to everyone in the other group$_j$.'

Instead of entering each possible form of a particular number inflection in the lexicon, a reasonable solution would be to isolate the indexic element, which is then interpreted elsewhere in the grammar. The result is a set of number-agreement morphemes that are constrained in movement and spatial range, capturing, as with person morphemes, the generalization that verb-agreement morphemes are constrained in an unusual way. A fuller discussion of how agreement morphemes and clitics are combined is left for a future paper.

In summary, agreement morphology is distinguished by spatial constraints of a particular kind. Like locative morphology, agreement morphology exploits the space around the signer's body, but the spatial possibilities are much more limited. In particular, agreement morphology accesses broader chunks of space. Non-first person contrasts with first person, but the individual person morpheme has the form of a vector. Although person and locative morphemes in ASL are remarkably similar, a closer analysis shows that these similarities are superficial, masking deeper morphological differences.

## AGREEMENT SYSTEMS IN NATURAL LANGUAGES

The preceding sections show that a distinction can be drawn about the different ways that agreement and locative morphology exploit the space around the signer's body: agreement morphology uses vectors, but locative morphology draws from a much richer inventory of loci. The crucial point here is that this distinction is not accidental but follows from properties of natural-language agreement systems. Specifically, the special restrictions on ASL verb morphology can be accounted for by more general restrictions on verb agreement in natural languages.

Verb agreement constitutes a subset of agreement structures. Other types of agreement include agreement of quantifiers, modifiers, determiners, and anaphoric pronouns with nouns in gender, number, person, case, and definiteness (Moravcsik, 1978). Moravcsik defines agreement broadly as "a grammatical constituent A is said to agree with a grammatical constituent B in properties C in language L if C is a set of meaning-related properties of A and there is a co-variance relationship between C and some phonological properties of a constituent $B_1$ across some subset of the sentences of language L, where constituent $B_1$ is adjacent to constituent B and the only meaning-related noncategorial properties of constituent $B_1$ are the properties C," (1978, 333). Moravcsik further specifies that among the class of structures that are excluded from "agreement" are the set of semantic/selectional restrictions that apply to specific lexical items, for example, *pour* in English. Although *pour* requires that there be an appropriate receptacle, the two do not "agree." There must be a "grammatical or semantic syntagmatic relation" between two sets of lexical items, a fact absent from this particular example—the verb *pour* does not contain a marker from a category of agreement forms, nor does it appear in a class of lexical items which vary in the same way.

In natural languages, verb agreement has three traditional categories: person, number, and gender. As the previous section demonstrates, ASL marks person and number agreement, but does not mark gender. There are, however, other sign languages that do, for example, Taiwanese Sign Language (Smith, in press).

What is crucial for the facts about agreement morphology in ASL is a central claim about verb agreement morphology in natural languages: the possible categories are made up of a very small number of elements, specifically no more than three, sometimes only two. Number agreement is typically characterized in terms of two categories: singular and plural. There have been proposals for a third category: paucal (more than one but less than many). Person agreement is first, second, and third. Gender is masculine, feminine, and neuter.

There have been reports of languages that counter this claim, as in a proposal for fifteen gender classes in Serbo-Croatian argued against by Corbett (in press). Corbett argues that the "maximalist" proposal, or one that posits more than the traditional three genders, can be reanalyzed positing only three genders. In the case of Serbo-Croatian, the gender system can be analyzed as made up of three "controller" genders: masculine, feminine, and neuter, with two subgenders in the masculine—animate and inanimate. Subgenders are predictable morphological variations for the same gender class, usually for noun class such as animacy. Corbett concludes that in cases where upward of four, eight, or fifteen genders are proposed for a single language, a reanalysis can usually be carried out reducing the number to no more than three genders.

It appears that number and person are likewise constrained to a small number of contrastive categories. Moravcsik (1978), in her review of number agreement across languages and across language families, has argued that there are basically two number-agreement forms: singular and plural, with several subdistinctions within the plural category: dual, trial, plural of paucity, and plural of abundance. And Greenberg (1966) has proposed a universal stating that all languages distinguish, at least semantically, between three person categories.

## VERB AGREEMENT IN NATURAL
## LANGUAGES AND ASL VERBS

Corbett's careful reanalysis of various gender systems points to the common confounding in oral languages between gender and noun class (for example, animacy). Based on claims by Friedman (1975) and others, what seems to be common in analyses of signed languages has been uncertain distinctions between person agreement and locative morphology because their phonological forms are so similar. But as Corbett, Moravcsik, and Greenberg argue, what distinguishes verb agreement morphology from other types of morphology is the small number of possible markers within each agreement category.

The outstanding property of agreement systems appears to be their contrastive properties. Each category has at most a three-way contrast, sometimes only two. If we take this to be a basic definition of agreement, then the spatial restrictions of agreement morphology in ASL can be accounted for in an interesting way. If we translate the fact about the three-way contrast of agreement systems into spatial terms, it follows then that person-agreement morphology as in $_1GIVE_a$ use a vector space, in contrast to locative morphology in verbs like $_aCARRY-BY-HAND_b$, which use a three-dimensional space. Number agreement, likewise, involves trajectories in a certain direction, but locative morphology can appear at any point along each of the three dimensions.

Agreement verbs in ASL as a whole restrict spatial possibilities compared to spatial verbs. What this special example from ASL demonstrates is that the sharp distinction in spatial possibilities between the two classes of verbs is not merely a fact about two different verb classes in ASL, but can be seen in terms of contrastive possibilities in verb-agreement morphology.

## "ROLE-SHIFTING" AND LOCATIVE
## MORPHOLOGY IN ASL

The preceding sections demonstrate that the apparently limitless spatial possibilities of ASL verbs are actually quite constrained and the constraints can be characterized in terms of universal restrictions on verb-agreement morphology in natural languages.

There is another set of structures in ASL that seems to have limitless spatial possibilities; these structures fall into the category of what has been generally referred to as ''role-shifting,'' structures in which the body shifts out of an unmarked position into some other location, either to the side or slightly forward. But, as will be shown, even these structures can be accounted for by a more general characterization of morphology in natural languages.

The term ''role-shifting'' is an unfortunate one because it suggests that the structures are accounted for in terms of play-acting or role-changing principles. It also suggests a global description for what are most certainly several different structures (Padden, 1986). One common role-shifting structure is the type that resembles ''direct quotation'' or ''reported speech'' in English (Partee, 1973). Shown below in sentences 31 and 32, direct quotation in ASL involves a shift to one side followed by another sequence where the body is shifted to an opposite position. These positions can be from side to side as in sentence 31 or from front to back, as in sentence 32. All involve certain facial features marking signing intonation, similar to speaker intonation, which Partee identified as distinctive about direct quotation. Signing intonation is accompanied by various signing cues, which not only mark question formation but also mimick actual signing behavior such as eye contact, head nodding, and squeezed eyebrows requesting confirmation.

(31) WOMAN SAY [I GIVE-YOU NEXT-WEEK]; (body shift) I [NO, GIVE-ME
   TOMORROW.]
   'The woman said, ''I'll give it to you next week.''
   'I replied, ''No, give it to me tomorrow.'' '

    --------raised brows--          ------shake head----
(32) [YOU WORK NOW?]; (body shift) [NO, NOT WORK.]
   'Are you working?'
   'No, I'm not working.'

The conditions that govern body shifting in the above structures are stated in terms of discourse topics, speaker perspective, etc. No constraints need be stated in terms of verb class. But there is another set of role-shifting structures that are constrained in a different way. These also involve body shifting but are not direct quotation. In each of the verb pairs in sentences 33 through 35 below, the verbs are spatial verbs: the first a body classifier (the body holding the gun, the body with the syringe, the body yielding a closed fist), followed by an another classifier verb involving contact with the body: GUN-HELD-BY-HAND-TO-HEAD, SYRINGE-INJECTED-IN-REAR, FIST-GRAZES-CHEEK. The body shift appears between the two verbs.

(33) MAN [GUN-IN-HAND]; (body shift) [GUN-HELD-BY-HAND-TO-HEAD.]
   'The man held a gun to another's head.'

(34) NURSE [INJECTS-SYRINGE-IN-HAND]; (body shift) [SYRINGE-
   INJECTED-IN-REAR.]
   'The nurse gave him a shot in the buttocks.'

(35) MAN [SWINGS-FIST]; (body shift) [FIST-GRAZES-CHEEK.]
   'The man swung at his cheek.'

The role-shifting structures in sentences 33 through 35 involve "shifting locative grids." A locative grid, first defined by Supalla (1982), is a set of interconnected locative points. Locative grids are located on or around the signer's body. When the body is a locative grid, each point on the body is a location, connected in scale to some other point on the body. To specify locations other than those on one locative grid, a body shift is needed.

Two restrictions apply to body locative grids (Supalla, 1986): (1) The body is to scale. Any body classifier involving contact or proximity with the body follows its actual scale. (2) There is exactly one body per body classifier. What follows from the above restrictions is that the body cannot be used for more than one locative grid. Sentence 36 has only one possible meaning: there is a single head, attached to the same hand that is holding a gun, and there is another gun held by another person and held to the same head.

(36) MAN [GUN-IN-HAND]; [GUN-HELD-BY-HAND-AT-RIGHT-TEMPLE].
 *'The man$_i$ held a gun and a gun was held to his$_j$ head.'
 'The man$_i$ held a gun and a gun was held to his$_i$ head.'

However, if there is a body shift between the two verbs, the unacceptable meaning in sentence 37 becomes possible:

(37) MAN [GUN-IN-HAND]; (body shift) [GUN-HELD-BY-HAND-AT-RIGHT-TEMPLE].
 'The man$_i$ held a gun and a gun was held to his$_j$ head.'
 *'The man$_i$ held a gun and a gun was held to his$_i$ head.'

Using locative morphemes, signers can access not only a single three-dimensional space, but also additional related spaces that are connected by rules of anaphora. In structures such as sentences 33, 34, 35, and 37, there are complex spatial verbs with locative morphemes of different locative grids. Agreement morphology, in contrast, disallows these kinds of shifts. A structure comparable to sentence 37 but with agreement verbs results in "odd" structures that consultants say are "pointless" like sentence 38 because agreement morphology does not have the same kind of combinatory or grid "chaining" possibilities as does locative morphology.

(38) MAN [$_1$GIFT$_a$]; (body shift) [$_a$GIFT$_1$].
 'The man gave it to her; someone gave it to her.'

If space indeed were to offer limitless possibilities in ASL, then structures like sentence 38 should be permissible; as it turns out, only locative morphology allows these special kinds of body-shifting structures.

## CONCLUSION

The spatial possibilities in sign languages lend themselves in interesting ways to the question of how modality interacts with language structure. The case of agreement morphology in ASL offers one piece of evidence showing that at least with respect to verb morphology in ASL, the spatial possibilities are shaped by restrictions on verb-agreement morphology in natural languages. Spatial verbs exhibit morphology that has locations along any number of three-dimensional spaces; agreement morphology, in contrast, is highly constrained. Agreement morphemes use a space composed of vectors and fixed trajectories of movement. Locative morphology exploits a richer set of locations, and new sets are available through body shifting. This spatial restriction is consistent with properties proposed for verb agreement in general: they are made up of a very small number of elements, either two or three, and are categorical and contrastive rather than detailed.

These data reveal another observation about the dimension of "space" in ASL. It has been observed elsewhere (Klima and Bellugi, 1979) that the space around the signer's body has different dimensions at each level of analysis, from phonological space (phonemically contrastive locations), morphological space (agreement morphology) to syntactic and discourse space (indexing and anaphora). What these data illustrate is that even within a single grammatical class—verbs in ASL—space takes contrastive forms, from the rich detailed space found in spatial verbs to the sparse and categorical space found in agreement verbs. Further, it demonstrates that rich body-shifting possibilities are in fact limited to a certain set of structures. Agreement verbs fail to access these structures.

Finally, there remains one set of elements that exploit the spatial dimension and appear to do so in a way unmatched in oral languages: the indexic segments. The challenge to those constructing a grammar of ASL will be to account for these segments in a principled way.

## NOTES

This paper took fuller shape following its first presentation at the Second International Conference on Theoretical Aspects of Sign Language Research. I owe thanks to Freda Norman and Cindy O'Grady, who helped me to refine the distinctions between verb classes, and to Diane Lillo-Martin, David Perlmutter, and Karen van Hoek for additional discussions. They may still disagree with certain points in this paper.

1. There are semantic restrictions: HAVE cannot take aspect, but CRY can inflect for habitual, continuative, and other temporal markers.
2. A potential problem for Lillo-Martin and Klima, one that they recognize, is that Lyons (1977) has argued that all natural languages grammatically mark the distinction between first and non-first persons.
3. Dual agreement has one of two forms: a one-handed form with a displaced path movement and two end points; or a two-handed form, each hand's path movement executed either simultaneously or in sequence. The first form is possible only on the final absolutive. The second form is possible for both subjects and final direct objects. I am not sure if the second form is indeed an inflection; if so, it would be an exception to the final absolutive rule.
4. Notation of first person in sign glosses is by the subscript "1" all other person categories will be marked by the letters "a, b, c. . . ." Same person is marked by identical subscripts. Identity is marked by the subscripts "i, j, k. . . ." In structures where the two hands are used to execute signs simultaneously, glosses appearing on a line preceded by "S" indicate that the signs are articulated with the strong hand, the right hand for a right-handed person, and the left for a left-handed person. The following line, preceded by "W" represents signs articulated on the weak hand, or the nondominant hand, that is, the left hand for a right-hander, etc.
5. Agreement morphology interacts with aspectual morphology but this interaction is not relevant for the purposes of this paper.

# REFERENCES

Bellugi, U., and Studdert-Kennedy, M., eds. (1980). *Signed and spoken language: Biological constraints on linguistic form.* Weinheim: Verlag Chemie.

Corbett, G. (in press). An approach to the description of gender systems. In *Studies in syntax and universals of language,* edited by M. Atkinson et al. Oxford: Oxford University Press.

Greenberg, J. (1966). Language universals. In *Current trends in linguistics,* vol. 3, edited by T. Sebeok, 61–112. The Hague: Mouton.

Friedman, L. (1975). Space, time and person reference in ASL. *Language* 51:940–61.

Johnson, R. E., and Liddell, S. K. (1987). A morphological analysis of subject-object agreement in American Sign Language. Paper presented at the Fourth International Conference on Sign Language Linguistics, 15–19 July, Lapeenranta, Finland.

Klima, E., and Bellugi, U. (1979). *The signs of language.* Cambridge, MA: Harvard University Press.

Lacy, R. (1974). Putting some of the syntax back into semantics. Paper presented at the Linguistic Society of America Annual Meeting, 28–30 December, New York.

Lillo-Martin, D., and Klima, E. (in press). Pointing out differences: ASL pronouns in syntactic theory. In *Theoretical issues in sign language research I: Linguistics,* edited by S. Fischer and P. Siple. Chicago: University of Chicago Press.

Liddell, S. (1984). THINK and BELIEVE: Sequentiality in ASL. *Language* 60:372–99.

Meier, R. (in press). Person deixis in ASL. In *Theoretical issues in sign language research, I: Linguistics,* edited by S. Fischer and P. Siple. Chicago: University of Chicago Press.

Moravcsik, E. (1978). Agreement. In *Universals of human language,* vol. 4, edited by J. Greenberg, 331–74. Stanford: Stanford University Press.

Padden, C. (1986). Verbs and role-shifting in ASL. In *Proceedings of the fourth national symposium on sign language research and teaching,* edited by C. Padden, 44–57. Silver Spring, MD: National Association of the Deaf.

———. (1988). *Interaction of morphology and syntax in ASL.* Garland Outstanding Dissertations in Linguistics, Series 4. New York: Garland Press.

Partee, B. (1973). The syntax and semantics of quotation. In *A festschrift for Morris Halle,* edited by S. Anderson and P. Kiparsky, 410–18. New York: Holt, Rinehart and Winston.

Siple, P., ed. (1978). *Understanding language through sign language research.* New York: Academic Press.

Smith, W. (in press). Evidence for auxiliaries in Taiwan Sign Language. In *Theoretical issues in sign language research I: Linguistics,* edited by S. Fischer and P. Siple. Chicago: University of Chicago Press.

Supalla, T. (1986). The classifier system in ASL. In *Noun classes and categorization: Typological studies in language,* edited by C. Craig, 181–214. Philadelphia: John Benjamins Publishing Co.

———. (in press). *Structure and acquisition of verbs of motion in ASL.* Cambridge, MA: MIT Press/Bradford Press.

Wilbur, R. (1979). *American Sign Language and sign systems.* Baltimore: University Park Press.

Zwicky, A., and Pullum, G. (1983). Cliticization vs. inflection: English *n't. Language* 59:502–13.

# Polymorphemic Predicates in
# Swedish Sign Language[1]

## Lars Wallin

I would like to begin by expressing my gratitude for being invited to this conference. It is a great honor for me to be invited to Gallaudet University. I would also like to take this opportunity to congratulate Gallaudet on its first deaf president and its deaf chairman of the Board of Trustees. It is an important achievement not only for deaf people in the United States, but for deaf people all over the world. Such victories inspire us to continue the fight to achieve equality.

## THE IMPORTANCE OF SIGN LANGUAGE
## RESEARCH

At Gallaudet University a great deal of knowledge about sign language teaching, sign language research, deaf culture, etc. has been accumulated. "Gallaudet" is truly a well-known concept within deaf communities all over the world. Gallaudet was the place where sign language research started with William C. Stokoe in 1955. In 1960 Stokoe published the first linguistic analysis of American Sign Language and it was followed by *A Dictionary of American Sign Language on Linguistic Principles* in 1965, the first dictionary of its kind.[2] The research paved the way for acceptance of sign language as a language.

The same chain of events occurred in Sweden. Sign language research started in 1972 with Brita Bergman. Largely as a consequence of this research, Swedish Sign Language was acknowledged by the Swedish Parliament in 1981. Deaf people's right to be bilingual was legally established, stating that Swedish Sign Language should be our primary language and Swedish the second language. There is now a new curriculum for schools for the deaf, stating that sign language should be the language of instruction and a scheduled subject of its own. It became possible for deaf people to study sign language at the university level in 1981, and for hearing people in 1987. There is a Department of Sign Language within the Institute of Linguistics at Stockholm University. Both research and instruction is financed by the government. Research is an important tool in our struggle for the acceptance of Sign Language as one of the languages in society.

So far only one dissertation has been published on Swedish Sign Language. Now one more is on its way: mine. I am enrolled in a Ph.D. program in Swedish Sign Language and I have full financial support to write a dissertation and get my degree. The preliminary title of my dissertation is "Polymorphemic Predicates in Swedish Sign Language."

## VERBS IN SWEDISH SIGN LANGUAGE

Before looking at polymorphemic predicates, let us look at verbs in Swedish Sign Language in general. They can be divided into three groups according to number of morphemes (Bergman, 1987): monomorphemic verbs, bimorphemic verbs, and polymorphemic verbs. Monomorphemic verbs consist of only one meaningful unit, that is, one morpheme. An example of a sign from this group is the sign EXIST ('exist,' 'have,' 'be') (figure 1). Bimorphemic verbs are verbs created by compounding. These verbs consist of two morphemes. An example of a compounded sign is the sign PROMISE/GIVE ('permit') (figure 2). Polymorphemic verbs consist of several morphemes. This group can be subdivided into three semantic subgroups. One group consists of verbs denoting the manipulation of an object. An example of a sign from

*Figure 1.* **EXIST ('exist,' 'have,' 'be').**

*Figure 2*. **The first and second sign of the compound PROMISE/GIVE ('permit').**

this group is the sign TAKE-DOWN (figure 3). Another semantic group consists of verbs denoting size and/or shape of an object. An example of a sign denoting size is BIG (figure 4), and an example of a sign denoting shape is OVAL (figure 5). The third group consists of verbs of motion and location. An example of a sign expressing a motion is TWO-DIMENSIONAL (2D)-OBJECT-MOTION (figure 6). An example of a sign denoting a location is 2D-OBJECT-TO-BE-LOCATED (figure 7).

My work focuses on the third subgroup of polymorphemic verbs: verbs of motion and location. I started my analysis quite recently and so far have looked at stative predicates expressing location and existence. My work is restricted to the analysis of possible morphemes of the hand. There has not yet been a great deal of investigation of this type of predicates in Swedish Sign Language. We are of course familiar with the work of Supalla (1978, 1982, 1986), McDonald (1982), Liddell and Johnson (1987), and others regarding ASL. Their work has influenced my thoughts and the discussion in Sweden. But since my analysis is far from complete, I am not ready to make a comparison of these predicates in Swedish Sign Language and in ASL.

## ANALYSIS

When I started my work I set up a number of questions: Can handshapes be said to function as morphemes? Can parts of the hand be said to function as morphemes?

*Figure 3*. Initial and final positions of the moving hand in TAKE-DOWN, as in, for
example, 'take down a book.'

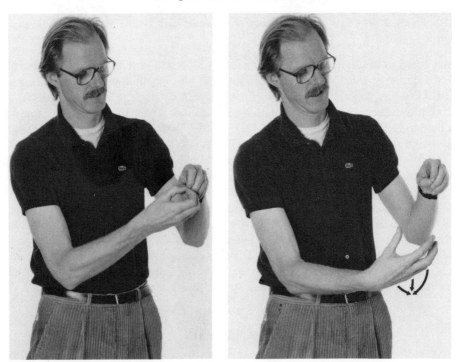

*Figure 4*. Initial and final positions of the moving hand in BIG when describing, for
example, 'a giant strawberry.'

*Figure 5*. Initial and final positions of the moving hands in OVAL when describing, for example, 'an oval frame.'

*Figure 6*. Initial and final positions of the moving hand in 2D-OBJECT-MOTION, as in, for example, 'a paper blows away.'

**Figure 7.** **Position of the hand in 2D-OBJECT-BE-LOCATED, as in, for example, 'a painting on a wall.'**

Can orientation (of fingertips and palm) be said to function as morphemes? Does the set of morphemes include combinations of handshape and orientation? What do the morphemes denote? My paper will address the following three issues: handshape as a possible morpheme, orientation as a possible set of morphemes, and the possible morphemic status of various parts of the hand. I will restrict myself to the discussion of one handshape: the flat hand.

### Handshape as a Morpheme

Let us first look at the handshape as a possible morpheme. The flat hand is used when referring to objects like a painting (figure 7), a car or a table (figure 8), a piece of paper or a book (figure 9), a plate or a piece of paper (figure 10), a rifle or a postcard (figure 11), or a bicycle (figure 12). It will be helpful to look at some other handshapes in comparison (figures 13 and 14).

There seem to be similarities between how handshapes are chosen in Swedish Sign Language and the morphological markers called "classifiers" in descriptions of ASL (Supalla 1978, 1986). However, a more thorough analysis is needed before I am ready to adopt that concept for polymorphemic predicates in Swedish Sign Language.

In Swedish Sign Language the flat hand is used to refer to objects that are saliently two-dimensional. Objects such as a painting and a paper have two dimensions that are more salient than the third. But why, then, is the flat hand used to refer to

*Figure 8.* The handshape in the predicate 2D-OBJECT-BE-LOCATED, as in, for example, 'car' or 'table.'

*Figure 9.* The handshape in the predicate 2D-OBJECT-BE-LOCATED, as in, for example, 'a piece of paper' or 'a book.'

*Figure 10.* The handshape in the predicate 2D-OBJECT-BE-LOCATED, as in, for example, 'a piece of paper' or 'a plate.'

*Figure 11.* The handshape in the predicate 2D-OBJECT-BE-LOCATED, as in, for example, 'a rifle' or 'a postcard.'

*Figure 12*. The handshape in the
predicate 2D-OBJECT-BE-LOCATED, as
in, for example, 'a bicycle' or 'a suit-case.'

*Figure 13*. The handshape in the
predicate 3D-OBJECT-BE-LOCATED, as
in, for example, 'a stone' or 'a bun.'

*Figure 14*. The handshape in the
predicate 1D-OBJECT-BE-LOCATED, as
in, for example, 'a pencil.'

objects such as a plate and a rifle, which have distinctly different shapes, the plate being round and the gun having a barrel. Swedish Sign Language seems to classify these objects as saliently two-dimensional.

So, apparently, in "the flat hand" is a morpheme denoting objects that are saliently two-dimensional, "the clawed 5" seems to denote saliently three-dimensional objects, and "the index finger" saliently one-dimensional objects.

### Orientation

Now let us consider whether orientation can be said to have morphemic status. We will first take a look at fingertip orientation and then palm orientation.

**Fingertip Orientation.** If we look at figures 15a and 15b we see that in 15a the fingertip orientation is perpendicular to the frontal plane of the signer's body. In figure 15b the fingertip orientation is parallel to the frontal plane of the signer's body. Can these different orientations be said to constitute different morphemes?

The orientation of the fingertips denotes the orientation of the object in the room, seen from the signer's perspective. That is, the largest dimension of the hand

*Figure 15a*. **Fingertip orientation in the predicate 2D-OBJECT-BE-LOCATED, as in, for example, 'a car' or 'a table.'**

*Figure 15b*. **Fingertip orientation in the predicate 2D-OBJECT-BE-LOCATED, as in, for example, 'a car' or 'a table.'**

(base to fingertips) represents the largest dimension of the object. So the sign in figure 15a means that the largest dimension of the object is perpendicular to the signer's body, and in figure 15b that it is parallel to the frontal plane of the signer's body. The signs therefore express different orientations of the objects.

**Palm Orientation.** Let us now look at palm orientation to see whether that can be said to constitute a set of morphemes (figures 16a and 16b). In figure 16a the palm is oriented toward the signer and in figure 16b away from the signer.

In these two signs, the orientation of the hand does not denote orientation in the room but rather whether the object referred to is easily movable, like a painting on a wall (figure 16a) or not easily movable, like a tile on a wall (figure 16b).

From the above discussion, we can infer that orientation constitutes a set of morphemes. Fingertip orientation expresses orientation in the room, and palm orientation denotes whether the object is easily movable. Furthermore, the sign in figure 16a, in which the palm is directed toward the signer, seems to include some kind of visibility factor. That is, the orientation of the palm in this sign also seems to imply that the text or the face of the painting is visible to the signer. But I have not found the same clear contrast of visible versus not visible as there seems to be with movable versus not movable.

*Figure 16a*. Palm orientation in the predicate 2D-OBJECT-BE-LOCATED, as in, for example, 'a painting.'

*Figure 16b*. Palm orientation in the predicate 2D-OBJECT-BE-LOCATED, as in, for example, 'a tile.'

### Parts of the Hand

Now let us look at the different parts of the hand. It seems as if the fingertips and the base of the hand also can be said to constitute morphemes. They apparently denote the short sides of a saliently two-dimensional object, for example, a table, and their orientation in the room as seen from the signer's perspective. In figure 15a, then, one of the short sides is farthest away from the signer and the other short side, the base of the hand, is closest to the signer. In figure 15b, the short sides are to the left and the right of the signer.

In reference to an object with an intrinsic front and back, for example, a car, there does not seem to be a clear connection between its front end and the fingertips, and the back and the base of the hand. The hand arrangement in figure 17 with the addition of an outward movement of the right hand is usually used when referring to many cars. But such a hand arrangement does not necessarily imply that the cars are all parked in the same direction, only that they are parked side by side. The same hand arrangement can be used to refer to two cars, but now without the movement of the right hand. In this case, too, nothing more than the fact that they are parked side by side is implied.

The previous examples have all been examples in which the fingertips were oriented away from the signer's body. Now let us look at the sign in figure 18, where the fingertips are oriented toward the signer's body, the sign still referring to a car. With this shift in orientation, more prominence is given to the front of the car. The bent flat hand in figure 18 may look like a different handshape, but it is interpreted as an extended flat hand. The bent flat hand is articulatorily conditioned and perceived as an allomorph of the flat hand. That is, the flat-hand morpheme has two allomorphs, extended flat hand and bent flat hand.

*Figure 17.* **The hands in the predicate TWO-2D-OBJECT-BE-LOCATED, as in, for example, 'two cars side by side.'**

*Figure 18.* **The hand in the predicate TWO-2D-OBJECT-BE-LOCATED, as in, for example, 'a car.'**

Let us now return to the different parts of the hand and look at another example where the front is given prominence (figures 19a and 19b). The examples refer to two cars parked front to front, seen from two different perspectives. However, the fingers do not always denote the front end when the bent flat hand is used. By moving both hands in figures 19a and 19b, either away from the body or to the right, a signer can refer to cars parked in a double row, seen from two perspectives. This does not, however, mean that all the cars are necessarily parked front to front, merely that the cars are parked opposite each other in a double row, and not side by side as in the earlier example.

When the fingers of both hands are oriented toward each other it denotes the fact that something is opposite something else rather than side by side with it.

**Other Aspects of the Possible Morphemic Status of Parts of the Hands.** There are other aspects of the possible morphemic status of parts of the hands. In figures 20a, b, and c, we have three different hand arrangements: the right hand next to the fingertips of the left hand in figure 20a, next to the inner knuckles in figure 20b, and next to the base of the hand in figure 20c. These hand arrangements express the spatial relation of a person (the right hand) to a saliently two-dimensional object, for example, a car (the left hand). When the right hand is positioned next to the fingertips of the left hand, the front of the car is given prominence; when the right hand is positioned by the inner knuckles, the middle of the car is given prominence; and

*Figure 19a–b.* **The hands in the predicates TWO-2D-OBJECT-BE-LOCATED seen from different perspectives.**

*Figure 20a–c.* **Different hand arrangements in predicates expressing PERSON-BE-LOCATED-BY-2D-OBJECT.**

when the right hand is positioned by the wrist of the left hand, the rear of the car is given prominence. The spatial relations of the hands give possible morphemic status to parts of the flat hand.

Contact is another possible parameter that may give parts of the hand morphemic status. Let us look at figures 21a through f. When the right hand touches the fingertips of the left hand as in figure 21a, something like 'one car (the right hand) hitting the front end of another car (the left hand) from the side' is expressed. In figure 21b, the right hand touches the right side of the metacarpal part of the left hand and 'one car driving into the midsection of the side of another car' is expressed. In figure 21c, the right hand touches the base of the left hand, and 'one car driving into the rear end of another car from the side' is expressed. If the fingertips of both hands touch each other, as in figure 21d, 'a head-on collision' is expressed. In figure 21e, the right hand touches the carpus of the left hand and here 'one car driving into another car from behind' is expressed. Finally, when the bases of the hands touch each other, as in figure 21f, 'two cars backing into each other' is expressed.

To sum up, if both hands are used, and in contact, and if the object denoted has an intrinsic front and back, the fingertips denote the front and the base of the hand denotes the back.

*Figure 21a–f.* **Different hand arrangements in predicates expressing**
**2D-OBJECT-CONTACT-2D-OBJECT.**

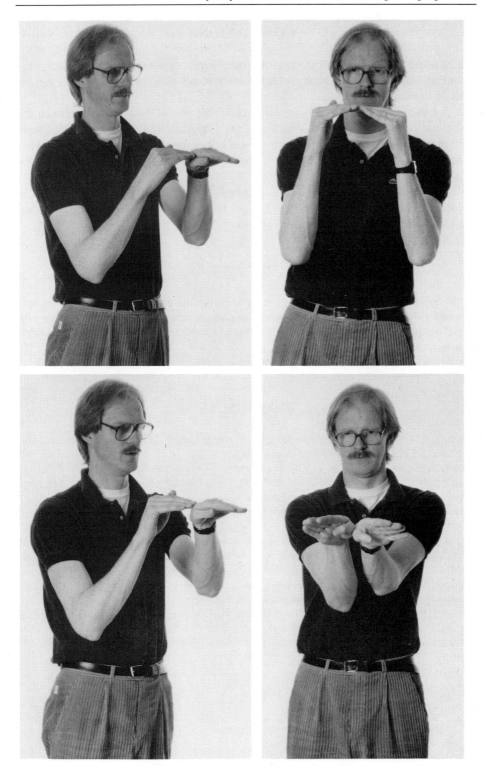

*Figure 21a–f.* (Continued from page 146.)

# CONCLUSION

We have now discussed some possible morphemes of the hand in Swedish Sign Language, including handshape, fingertip orientation, palm orientation, and various parts of the hand.

To this I have added parameters such as the spatial relationship between the hands and contact. I have also mentioned the importance of perspective. But there are a great many more parameters that must also be considered, such as various types of movements, direction of movement, positions of the hands, and at what level the sign is performed.

All in all, the evidence of a highly complex morphemic structure indicates that a much more thorough analysis is needed before we can truly say that we understand this rich and complex morphological structure.

# NOTES

1. This paper was translated from Swedish Sign Language into English by Anna-Lena Nilsson. I would also like to thank Brita Bergman for comments on earlier versions of this paper, and the photographer who provided the illustrations, Sven Calissendorff, of the University of Stockholm.
2. Being a Swede, maybe I can take some pride in the fact that Sweden contributed one of the coauthors, Swedish-born C. G. Croneberg.

# REFERENCES

Bergman, B. (1987). Föreläsningsanteckningar om verbmorfologi. Stockholms Universitet, Institutionen för lingvistik. Unpublished manuscript.

Liddell, S. K., and Johnson, R. E. (1987). A analysis of spatial-locative predicates in American Sign Language. Paper presented at the Fourth International Symposium on Sign Language Research, 15–19 July, Lappeenranta, Finland.

McDonald, B. (1982) Aspects of the American Sign Language predicate system. Ph.D. diss., University of Buffalo, Buffalo, NY.

Supalla, T. (1978). Morphology of verbs of motion and location in American Sign Language. In *Proceedings of the Second National Symposium on Sign Language Research and Teaching*, edited by F. Caccamise and D. Hicks, 27–45. Silver Spring, MD: NAD.

———. (1982). *Structure and acquisition of verbs of motion and location in American Sign Language*. Ph.D. diss., University of California, San Diego.

———. (1986). The classifier system in American Sign Language. In *Noun classes and categorization: Typological studies in language*, 7, edited by C. Craig, 181–214. Philadelphia: John Benjamins Publishing Co.

# Predicate Argument Structure
# and Verb-Class Organization in
# the ASL Lexicon

Judy Kegl

This paper proposes an argument-structure typology for ASL that identifies and distinguishes verbs based upon the number and types of arguments (usually NPs) they take: transitives ($x<y>$), double-object constructions ($x<y$ $z<$), three-place predicates ($x<y$ $Pz>$), unaccusatives ($<y>$), unergatives ($x< >$), psych(ological) verbs ($<y$ $z>$), and predicate-complement constructions ($<y_i>w_i$); where $x$ = external argument, $y$ = direct argument, $z$ = indirect argument, and $w$ = VP adjunct. Terms and notations are introduced as they become relevant. Using evidence from agreement and the argument-taking properties of verbs, I identify semantic classes that exhibit systematic transitivity patterns and participate in transitivity alternations.

The earliest work on verb-class organization in ASL appears in Edge and Herrmann (1977) and Fischer and Gough (1978). Their papers consider not only morphosyntactic, but also semantic bases for classification. In fact, Fischer and Gough were first to point to the existence of different types of intransitives in ASL. This work follows Fischer and Gough's original agenda of classifying and providing syntactic tests for verb classification, but I will not adopt their classification.

Since the Fischer and Gough study, research on ASL has focused on morphological and syntactic characteristics of verb-class organization to the exclusion of more semantic bases for classification. Recent studies employ the organization of verb classes proposed by Padden in her 1983 dissertation (published in 1988). Padden proposes three classes of verbs on the basis of their agreement patterns: inflecting, plain, and spatial. Inflecting verbs inflect for person and number (GIVE, SEND, ASK, TELL, FORCE, TEASE, TEACH, SELL, DEFEAT, BLAME, BORROW, COPY, INVITE, etc.) Plain verbs do not inflect for person and number (THINK, LOVE, CELEBRATE, LIKE, EXERCISE, REQUEST, etc.). Spatial verbs agree with location, allowing agreement with a wider range of spatial points around the signer's body (GO-TO, DRIVE-TO, MOVE, MOVE-AWAY, PUT, BRING/CARRY, CL:V-WALK, etc.). Meier (1982) demonstrates the validity of Padden's verb-class typology with acquisition data.

Although Padden's classification system gives us important information about ASL, it doesn't give us quite the information we need in order to determine the place of ASL agreement in a larger cross-linguistic typology of agreement phenomena. Furthermore, the classification is not designed to capture systematic argument-taking regularities within semantically coherent verb classes. Subsequent studies such as Shepard-Kegl (1985), Kegl (1987), and Lillo-Martin (1985, 1986) examine how the agreement properties of ASL verbs condition the presence of null arguments, but no studies to date have examined the interaction between agreement properties of ASL verbs and their argument-taking possibilities. For example, some plain verbs take two syntactic arguments (LIKE, LOVE, SEE), while other take only one (LAUGH, CAREFUL, LIPREAD). Some spatial verbs take a single argument (FALL, SIT, STAND). Others take more (INSERT, CARRY-BY-HAND, SCRUB, PUT). Some verbs take NP complements (HIT, BUY, MEMORIZE), and others take sentential complements as well (DECIDE, PERSUADE, CONVINCE).

## A SEMANTIC/SYNTACTIC APPROACH TO VERB-CLASS ORGANIZATION

Following analyses of English by Levin (1985) and Rappaport, Levin, and Laughren (1988), and of Italian by Belletti and Rizzi (1986, in press), this account of verb-class organization is sensitive to both the lexical semantic and the syntactic properties of verbs. Examining interdependencies between agreement, syntactic position of arguments, and semantic verb class information can yield insights into the structure of the ASL verb lexicon that the study of these properties in isolation has thus far failed to highlight.

A verb class is a set of verbs that share some aspect of their meaning (for example, change of state, creation, perception, consumption, emotion, etc.) and, as a result, behave similarly in terms of the kinds of sentences they appear in. Certain verb classes exhibit systematic syntactic alternations, having both a transitive and an intransitive construction associated with the same sense (meaning) of the verb. These syntactic alternations can be used as evidence for class membership.

### *Transitivity*

Before proceeding, it is necessary to look more closely at transitivity. In traditional grammar terms, a "transitive" verb has both a subject and a direct object, an "intransitive" has only a subject, and a "ditransitive" has a subject, direct object and indirect object. The transitive verb *hit* has a subject and object (the hitter and the hittee). The intransitive verbs *arrive* and *sleep* have only subjects (the arriver and sleeper, respectively). The ditransitive verb *give* has a subject, direct object, and indirect object (the giver, the thing given, and the receiver).

Identifying the number of arguments (NPs required by the verb) and the grammatical relations (subject, object, indirect object) they hold at S-structure (the syntactic level at which all overt movement transformation have applied) is insufficient for characterizing verb types. We also need to consider the thematic/semantic role borne by a verb's arguments and the syntactic positions it occupies at both S-structure and D-structure (the level of the initial phrase marker associated with the verb). For the verb and its obligatory arguments, the initial phrase marker (syntactic tree) is a direct projection of the VP tree from the lexicon.

The lexical entry of every verb lists its obligatory arguments and the syntactic position they occupy at D-structure. Distinguishing arguments in terms of their initial syntactic position yields three argument types: external ($x$), direct ($y$), and indirect ($z$) arguments. In addition, any obligatory adjuncts ($w$) are also listed. These are required XPs (phrases of any category) that do not behave as arguments. They never occur in subject, object, or indirect-object position at S-structure. These adjuncts appear Chomsky adjoined (see the structural configuration in figure 1), and as a result, are neither internal to nor fully external to VP (see Kegl and Fellbaum, 1988). Figure 1 illustrates the syntactic D-structure positions occupied by the three types of arguments as well as by the VP adjunct.

### Different Types of Intransitives

Although members of verb classes systematically associate thematic/semantic roles such as agent, causer, experiencer, source, goal, theme, etc. to their arguments, once the D-structure position of these arguments is determined, these roles play no part in the syntax. Syntactic rules do not distinguish types of external, direct or indirect arguments by the thematic/semantic roles they are linked to lexically. The syntax cannot be sensitive to whether an external argument is an agent versus an experiencer versus a causer. Syntactic alternants (transitive and intransitive constructions associated with a single verb sense) exhibit consistent D-structure associations between arguments and semantic roles across both members of the pair. The following sentence pairs illustrate a syntactic alternation between members of the class of change-of-state verbs in English.

Change of state: *break, smash, melt, freeze, bake, wilt,* etc.
(1) Marisa broke the stick./The stick broke.
(2) Antonio baked the chicken in the oven./The chicken baked in the oven.
(3) The heat melted the ice./The ice melted.
(4) The cold wind froze the lake solid./The lake froze solid.

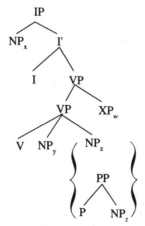

*Figure 1.* **D-structure positions of arguments and obligatory adjuncts.**
**Key: $NP_x$ = external, $NP_y$ = direct, $NP_z$ = indirect; $XP_w$ = Obligatory adjunct**

Change-of-state verbs participate in the causative/inchoative alternation. Both forms involve an entity that undergoes a change of state (the thing that breaks, bakes, melts or freezes). In the inchoative alternant, the entity undergoing the change is the only argument and no agent is presumed. The causative alternant, however, is transitive, involving an additional argument that is a causer (Marisa, Antonio, the heat, or the cold).

Change-of-state verbs contrast with creation verbs, which participate in a different transitivity alternation: the indefinite-object alternation. The following sentence pairs exemplify the alternation between creation and activity characteristic of the creation class.

Creation: *paint, sew, sculpt, knit, write, compose, bake,* etc.
(5) The artist was painting a portrait./The artist was painting.
(6) The seamstress was sewing a new dress./The seamstress was sewing.
(7) The author was writing a book./The author was writing.
(8) The pastry chef was baking cakes./The pastry chef was baking.

The argument left behind in an intransitive construction involving a creation verb differs from the argument left behind in an intransitive construction involving a change-of-state verb. The surface object of the transitive change-of-state verb shows up as the surface subject of its intransitive counterpart, but the surface subject of the creation verb remains the surface subject of its intransitive alternant. Also, the semantics of the alternation exhibited by creation verbs is creation/activity rather than causative/inchoative.

The verb *bake* participates in both verb classes and yields a different interpretation in each context. In the transitive change-of-state construction, the chicken exists at the beginning of the event and undergoes a change of state, going from unbaked to baked. In the transitive creation verb, the baker begins with raw ingredients and creates a new entity, a cake. The intransitive of the change-of-state verb does not presume an agent, but the intransitive of the creation verb does presume some created flour-based entity. Figure 2 presents two contrasting senses of the verb *bake*.

Verb classes, not the individual verbs themselves, are the unit of organization in the lexicon. Frequently a single word (such as *bake*) can have multiple senses, and can therefore participate in more than one verb class. Looking for generalizations that cover words that map onto multiple classes can obscure a more general picture of the semantic architecture of the verb lexicon. Table 1 presents several verb classes and some of their representative members. Atkins, Kegl and Levin (1986, 1988) discuss several verb classes and their transitivity patterns.

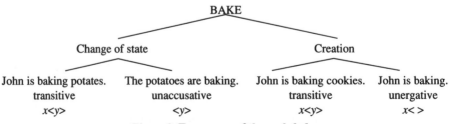

*Figure 2.* Two senses of the verb *bake*.

### Transitivity Patterns

Verb classes like creation and change of state differ in terms of their semantics and in terms of the transitivity patterns with which they associate. These transitivity patterns are represented in terms of sets of argument-structure schemas where variables represent the argument types: Creation: $x<y>$, $x< >$; Change of State: $x<y>$, $<y>$. The schemas are called "Predicate-argument structures" (PASs). The two verb classes yield semantically and structurally distinct transitivity alternations. The change-of-state class expresses a causative/inchoative distinction by alternating a transitive with an unaccusative construction. "Unaccusative verbs" take only a single direct argument at D-structure. The creation class, on the other hand, expresses a creation/activity distinction by alternating a transitive with an unergative construction. "Unergative verbs" take only a single external argument at D-structure (see table 2). The transitive PASs for both classes are identical, but their specific semantic interpretations differ.

A PAS is used to indicate the number and type of arguments a verb requires to be present in the sentence in order for it to be well formed. Arguments are noun phrases or clauses obligatorily selected for by a verb, which, if NPs, must receive "case" (appear in or be linked to argument positions at S-structure). Verbs take from zero to three arguments and at most one obligatory VP adjunct (but only in verbs where there is a co-occurring direct argument in the PAS (see Simpson, 1983). A detailed discussion of predicate argument structure is beyond the scope of this paper, but a comprehensive examination with respect to the English lexicon appears in Kegl and Levin (in press) and with respect to the ASL lexicon in Kegl (to appear). Table 3 presents the range of possible PASs and an example English sentence that illustrates each construction.

*Table 1.* **Representative Verb Classes**

| Verb class | Representative members |
|---|---|
| Change of State | *break, smash, melt, freeze, bake, wilt, tear, bend, stretch* |
| Creation | *sew, knit, paint, bake, write, invent, draw, whip-up, compose* |
| Consumption | *eat, drink, imbibe, breathe, smoke, snort* |
| Appearance | *appear, arrive, pop-up, disappear, emerge, vanish, show-up* |
| Contact | *hit, slap, punch, scrape, touch, finger, poke, jab, prod, tap, rub* |
| Cognition | *think, know, wonder, ponder, consider, remember, imagine* |

*Table 2.* **Transitivity Alternations: Change-of-state vs. Creation Class**

| Verb class | Example | PAS | Pattern | Semantics |
|---|---|---|---|---|
| Change of State | Mary is sewing a dress.<br>x          y | $x<y>$ | transitive | creation |
| | Mary is sewing.<br>x | $x< >$ | unergative | activity |
| Creation | John broke the bottle.<br>x          y | $x<y>$ | transitive | causative |
| | The bottle broke.<br>   y | $<y>$ | unaccusative | inchoative |

*Table 3*. **Typology of Predicate Argument Structures (English)**

| PAS | Pattern | Sample Sentence |
|---|---|---|
| x<y> | transitive | The $dog_x$ bit the $boy_y$. |
| x< > | unergative | The $woman_x$ slept. |
| <y> | unaccusative | The $ship_y$ appeared. |
| | passive | The $baseball_y$ was hit. |
| x<y, Pz> | three-place predicate | The $man_x$ gave the $book_y$ to the $woman_z$. |
| x<y, z> | double object | The $man_x$ gave the $woman_z$ the $book_y$. |
| <y, z> | psych-verb | The $play_y$ amused the $children_z$. |
| < > | weather verb | It rained. |
| <y>w | measure verb | The $chicken_y$ weighed 3 $pounds_w$. |
| | copular | $Mary_y$ is a $doctor_w$. |

## THE ASL LEXICON

Cross-linguistically, the same range of PASs and the same types of semantic classes found in English appear in other languages as well. However, the pairing of specific PASs or transitivity pairs with semantic classes of verbs such as change of state, creation, appearance, etc. admits much variability. In the remainder of this paper, I will consider aspects of how the typology of PASs and verb-class organization apply to the ASL lexicon. I will focus upon three ways ASL appears to differ from English: (1) the realization of the causative/inchoative alternation; (2) the range of intransitive types and the apparent lack of passive; and (3) the argument-taking properties of three types of psych-verb constructions.

This material is drawn from a larger body of ongoing research on the ASL lexicon that proposes a preliminary typology of PASs for ASL verbs taking NP complements as shown in table 4.

The typology presents each PAS followed by a typical label associated with the kind of construction exemplifying that pattern. One or more ASL sentences exemplify each construction and each example sentence is followed by its English translation. Numerous examples appear because a single PAS is often associated with several different types of constructions. For example, the unaccusative PAS (<y>) is associated with both the inchoative and passive constructions, which differ from each other in terms of their clitic-taking properties and their sublexical structure.

### A Digression on Notational Conventions

ASL morphology, which includes sublexical morphological regularities, agreement, incorporation, and various aspectual modulations, is extremely complex. Noting this information in a comprehensive manner requires understanding MOVE-LOC notation (see Shepard-Kegl, 1985) or any notation equal in morphological detail. But most researchers are unfamiliar with this notation.

English glosses not only obscure the morphological and syntactic structures of ASL, they can be misleading. The choice of English gloss for ASL sign has been determined over the years by random consensus; the most frequently used gloss associated with a given sign wins out. This association is generally tied to frequency of use in translation, but the ASL sign and its English gloss may not pattern alike syntactically at all. For example, the sign glossed by GIVE, unlike the English verb from which its gloss comes, does not allow an alternation between a construction with a prepositionally licensed indirect argument (V NP to NP) and a double-object

*Table 4.* **Typology of Predicate Argument Structures (ASL)**

| PAS | Pattern | ASL Sentence | English Translation |
|---|---|---|---|
| x<y> | transitive | MARY$_4$, JOHN$_5$ (SBP$_5$)#cl$_4$#$_{(5)}$HIT$_4$ | John$_x$ hit Mary$_y$. |
| | | JOHN$_5$ (SBP$_5$) SCARE$_4$ MARY$_4$ | John$_x$ scared Mary$_y$. |
| | | STICK$_{10}$, JANE$_0$ SBP$_0$#$_{10}$ | John$_x$ broke the stick$_y$. |
| | | CL:HAND + BREAK | |
| | psych-verb (temere) | MARY$_{10}$ SBP$_{10}$#CL:8 + HATE$_{20}$ SUE$_{20}$ | Mary$_x$ hates Sue$_y$. |
| x< > | unergative | JANE$_{10}$ SBP$_{10}$# CL:G + RUN | Jane$_x$ ran. |
| | | JOHN$_{10}$ SBP$_{10}$#CL:B + DIE | John$_x$ died. |
| | | RUTH$_{10}$ SBP$_{10}$#cl[f]# | Ruth$_x$ is sewing. |
| | | CL:HAND[F] + SEW[redup.] | |
| <y> | unaccusative | ICE$_{10}$ CL:G[plural] + MELT | The ice$_y$ melted. |
| | | BOX$_{10}$ CL:S/S + EXPLODE | The box$_y$ exploded. |
| | | STICK$_{10}$ CL:G + BREAK[inchoative] | The stick$_y$ broke. |
| | | GHOST$_{10}$ $_{10}$DISAPPEAR | The ghost$_y$ disappeared. |
| <y> | passive | POLICEMAN$_{10}$ SBP$_{10}$# AT-HIT$_{10}$[passive] | The policeman$_y$ got hit. |
| | | SUE$_{10}$ SBP$_{10}$# AT-KISSED$_{10}$[passive] | Sue$_y$ got kissed. |
| | | JOHN$_9$ SBP$_9$#$_0$CL:[8] + AT-TOUCHED$_{9[head,stom]}$ | John$_z$ became sick$_y$. |
| | | [*TOUCH in this sense usually glossed as SICK*] | (John$_y$ was touched by sickness) |
| x<y Pz> | three-place pred. | SUE$_5$ SBP$_5$# KNIT SOCKS SBP$_0$#$_0$FOR$_4$ ED$_4$ | Sue$_x$ knitted socks$_y$ for Ed$_z$. |
| | | ED$_5$SBP$_5$#BUY$_0$SHOES$_0$ $_0$FOR$_4$ SUE$_4$ | Ed$_x$ bought shoes$_y$ for Sue$_z$. |
| x<y z> | double obj. | MARY$_9$(SBP$_9$)#$_{(8)}$BOOK + GIVE-TO$_7$ BILL$_7$ | Mary$_x$ gave Bill$_z$ a book$_y$. |
| <y Pz> | psych-verb | ED$_9$ SBP$_0$#$_0$ CL:HAND[B] + PLEASE$_{9[chest]}$MUSIC$_8$ | Music$_y$ pleases Ed$_z$. |
| | (piacere) | [*PLEASE in this sense usually glossed as ENJOY*] | (On Ed$_z$ pleases music$_y$) |
| | | ED$_9$ SBP$_9$#$_{[heart]9}$CL:HAND[8] + LIKE MUSIC$_8$ | Ed$_z$ likes music$_y$. |
| | | | (From Ed$_z$ pulls music$_y$) |
| <y z> | psych-verb (preoccupare) | *do not occur (see psych-verb discussion)* | |
| <y>w | predicates | BALL$_{10}$ Ø RED | The ball$_y$ is red$_w$. |
| | | MARY$_{10}$ Ø DOCTOR | Mary$_y$ is a doctor$_w$. |
| | psych-pred. | SUE$_{10}$ Ø AT$_0$-SBP$_i$# CL:HAND[claw] + ANNOY$_{i[chest]}$ | Sue$_x$ was depressed$_w$. |
| | light verbs | BOOK$_{10}$ COST 5 DOLLAR | The book$_y$ costs 5 dollars$_w$. |
| <y> | weather verbs | CL:G[plural] + MOVE-DOWNWARD[redup.] | It is raining. |
| | | CL:G[plural,individuated] + MOVE-DOWNWARD[redup] | It is snowing. |

construction (V NP NP). The sign glossed as UPSET does not function as a two-argument psych-verb (*NEWS UPSET$_{i[stomach]}$ JOHN$_i$ 'The news upset John.'), but instead appears only as an adjectival passive (JOHN$_i$ AT$_i$-SBP$_0$#UPSET$_{0[chest]}$ 'John was upset.'). The sign glossed as MELT does not participate in a causative/inchoative alternation like the English verb *melt* (The butter melted./The cook melted the butter.) Instead, in ASL, MELT only appears as an inchoative (BUTTER$_0$ MELT 'The butter melted'/*COOK$_i$ SBP$_i$#MELT BUTTER 'The cook melted the butter.'). Even a gloss like CRY posed problems since the sign is more precisely 'at John tears fell from the eyes': JOHN$_i$ SBP$_i$#$_{[eyes]i}$CL:G + MOVE-DOWNWARD [iterative]. In even the most figurative reading, it would be difficult to translate 'John cried a river' with a single ASL clause. It is important to refrain from transferring to a sign the syntactic and semantic characteristics of its English gloss.

For purposes of expediency tempered by an awareness of the inadequacy of simple glossing, ASL verbs have been transcribed using supplemented glosses that include indexes for verb agreement, matrix clitics (SBP, the role-prominence clitic; and cl, the classifier/ground clitic), theme classifiers (CL:$X$, where $X$ is a variable that can be filled in by any number of classifiers, for example, G = long thin object [lto]; s = round solid object [rso] HAND = handling classifier indicating causation/manipulation, etc.), and morphological markers such as [reciprocal] or various aspect markers (reduplicated: iterative, reduplicated: continual).

Particular attention should be paid to the SBP, or role-prominence clitic (RP clitic). If the SBP appears in parentheses, its presence is optional and it may appear on other arguments of the verb as well. If the SBP is not in parentheses, its presence is obligatory and is necessarily associated with the argument with which it is co-indexed. Obligatory presence of the SBP picks out the traditional class of body-anchored verbs. The absence of an SBP indicate those verbs that do not allow role prominence clitics, except under special circumstances: to mark optional adversative or ethical dative arguments as in sentence 9, or to indicate denied responsibility or awareness as in sentence 10. (Actual numbers rather than variables are used in the examples. These indicate association with distinct points in space, or if set to zero, indicate neutral agreement).

(9) $\overline{\text{FRED}_{20}\text{ ICE-CREAM}_0}^{\text{topic}}$ SBP$_{20}$#MELT
Fred$_{20}$ ice cream$_0$ RP$_{[Fred]}$ x$_0$-melt
'The ice cream melted on Fred' (not physically on him, but adverse to his wishes)

(10) STICK$_{10}$ $\overline{\text{SBP}_0\text{#CL:G/G-BREAK}}^{\text{avert}}$ [inchoative]
stick$_{10}$ RP$_{[negated]}$ - lto - break
'The stick broke by itself/on its own.'

The line over the verb in example 10 labeled ''avert'' indicates a posture/facial gesture that involves averting the eyes and head. This negates the SBP and indicates non-agentivity or nonresponsibility.

Transcriptions in full MOVE-LOC notation require much space and explanation, but full MOVE-LOC transcriptions and videotaped presentations of the examples used here are available on request. Examples 11 and 12 are presented both in supplemented glosses and MOVE-LOC notation as an indication of the content of the more elaborate transcription system.

### Agreement Patterns and Argument-Taking Properties

The remaining sections use verb agreement and the number and surface positions of arguments selected by certain classes of ASL verbs to begin to determine the organization and typological characteristics of the ASL lexicon. Transitivity patterns for change-of-state verbs, the range of existing intransitives, and the types of argument patterns available for the expression of psych-verbs and psych-predicates highlight significant differences between the English and ASL lexicons and reveal interesting argument taking and agreement properties of ASL verbs.

**Causatives and Inchoatives in ASL.**   The causative/inchoative alternation exists in ASL, but the transitive verb is explicitly marked with causative morphology, which involves the presence of a handling classifier in the position of the verb generally associated with the theme (the element that undergoes the change of state). This classifier is articulated coextensive with the movement of the verb. It indicates involvement of both a causer and an affected element, thereby signaling the addition of a causer argument. Kegl (1985) discusses causative marking in ASL. Example 11 involves $SBP_i\#_iCL:HAND[S/S] +$ BREAK [causative].

(11)  $\overline{STICK_{10}},$ $\overline{M\text{-}A\text{-}R\text{-}I\text{-}S\text{-}A_0\ SBP_0\#_{10}CL:HAND[S/S] + BREAK}$
stick-topic Marisa RP-(rso)causative-break
'Marisa broke the stick.'

*(with "topic" over $STICK_{10}$ and "head nod" over the rest)*

The MOVE-LOC notation for sentence 11 appears in figure 3.

The articulation of sentence 11 involves four complex gestures: (1) The sign for "stick at location$_{10}$" involves locating the hands at location$_{10}$ while two F handshapes, initially contacting each other at the index-finger edge with palms facing downward, horizontally move apart (SASS for long thin object). (2) The fingerspelled letters "M," "A," "R," "I," "S," "A" are used to spell the name Marisa in a neutral, nonindexed, position—indicating that Marisa is not being set up for future use in the discourse. (3) The RP clitic, which marks the person from whose perspective the action of the verb is viewed, involves movement of the signer's body to agree with some position. In this case it remains in neutral position, leading us to construe coreference with M-A-R-I-S-A$_0$. (4) The sign BREAK is located at position$_{10}$ (agree-

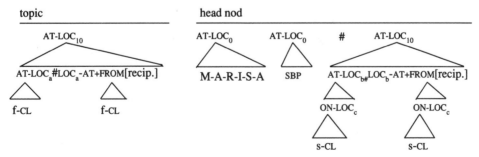

*Figure 3.* MOVE-LOC **representation for sentence 9, 'Marisa broke the stick.'**

ing with STICK$_{10}$) and involves two fists (CL:HAND[S/S], oriented palm downward, that separate and turn upward and inward in a quick, twisting gesture. These fists indicate handling and serve to mark causation.

The inchoative counterpart of SBP$_i$#$_j$CL:HAND[S/S] + BREAK [causative] appears in sentence 12 and its MOVE-LOC representation appears in figure 4. Sentence 12 is identical to 10 except for the absence of a negated RP marker. The difference in interpretation is that the stick broke, but responsibility for the action is left unspecified and unpresumed.

$$\overset{\text{topic}\qquad\text{avert}}{(12)\ \overline{\text{STICK}_{10},\ \text{SBP}_{0\#10}\text{CL:G/G} + \text{BREAK}_{[\text{inchoative}]}}}$$
stick-topic RP-negated-lto-break
'The stick broke.'

Sentence 12 is similar to 11 except that there is no argument corresponding to the agent/causer. The RP clitic is accompanied by a head twist and aversion of the eyes that indicate noninvolvement of an agent. The handshape in SBP$_i$#$_j$CL:G/G + BREAK[inchoative] involves two index fingers (CL:G/G) that are classifiers associated with long thin objects. Thus the thing broken, rather than the agent of the breaking, fills the theme position of the verb.

The two examples above are fully transcribed, indicating the sublexical morphology associated with the causative (agent argument, SBP handling-CL/causative marker) and inchoative (only a theme argument, averted SBP, regular classifier) forms of verbs. For purposes of expediency, rather than fully transcribe future examples, I will mark the verb as [causative] versus [inchoative] and will indicate the presence of a role-prominence marker with the gloss ''RP clitic.'' Other verbs in ASL with same alternation include *SPILL, OPEN, SLIDE, MOVE,* and *CLOSE.*

**A Variety of Intransitive Types in ASL.**    Transitive verbs have both an external and a direct argument. These NP arguments are overt at S-structure. They appear in, or are linked to, the argument positions for subject and direct object. The most general way of characterizing intransitives states that these constructions fail, for one of several reasons, to satisfy the criteria for being transitive. Intransitives can lack an external argument, a direct argument, or both.

The analysis of intransitives in ASL is not immediately obvious and because the framework employing PASs is probably unfamiliar to most readers, I will first consider the range of intransitive constructions in English and then compare and contrast them with what is to be found in ASL. Some striking differences and surprising similarities are revealed.

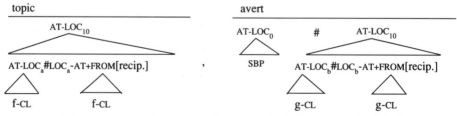

***Figure 4.*** MOVE-LOC **representation for sentence 10, 'The stick broke.'**

*Preliminary Background on Intransitives in English.* Because of the extended projection principle (EPP) (Chomsky, 1981), a constraint on S-structure representations that requires all sentences to have an overt subject, all intransitive sentences in English have one argument[1] and that argument shows up in subject position. The type of argument that shows up in the subject position of intransitives varies, as examples 13 through 18 illustrate. Recall that $x$ = external argument and $y$ = direct argument. An additional subscripted 0 indicates a dummy (a pleonastic pronoun, *it*, that fills an empty subject position at S-structure when the EPP is not satisfied by some movement rule).

(13) The bottle$_y$ broke.          (inchoative)
(14) The ship$_y$ sank.             (appearance verb)
(15) The child$_x$ ate.             (pseudo intransitive with implied object)
(16) The boy$_x$ ran.               (activity verb)
(17) The man$_x$ slept.             (experiencer verb)
(18) It$_0$ rained.                 (weather verb)

All of the constructions in 13 through 18 are intransitives and have subjects at S-structure that have received nominative Case.

Case (nominate, accusative,etc.) is a property assigned by a verb or preposition to an NP holding a particular structural relation to it. Receiving Case allows an NP to occupy a particular syntactic position (subject position, object position, or object of a preposition). All verbs assign nominative Case to subject position (SPEC of IP [specifier or inflection phrase]), therefore, all verbs allow subjects.

Only verbs that already have an external subject can also assign accusative Case to an NP in object position. This is called Burzio's Generalization (Burzio, 1986). Verbs that assign both nominative and accusative Case are transitive. Some verbs, like those in sentences 15 through 17 have an external argument, but do not subcategorize for a second NP that needs to be assigned accusative Case. These constructions are referred to as unergatives ($x< >$). The term "unergative" comes from ergative case, which in some languages is assigned to only the subject of a transitive verb.[2] Being an ergative construction means having an external argument and a direct argument. "Unergative" labels those constructions that have an external argument, but lack a direct argument. Interestingly, unergatives generally allow an alternant with a direct argument. Examples 19 through 22 present such transitive alternants and suggests that Burzio's Generalization not only predicts that accusative Case cannot be assigned if there is no external argument, but also that the presence of an external argument suggest the potential for an alternant with a direct argument.

(19) The girl ate the cardboard. (definite object)
(20) The girl ate food. (indefinite object)
(21) The woman ran a marathon. (semantically restricted object)
(22) The man slept a restful sleep. (cognate object)

Examples 19 through 22 represent a variety of transitive alternants of unergative verbs ranging from relatively semantically free to highly lexically determined. Sentence 19 shows a true transitive form of *eat* and is not the construction that alternates with sentence 15. Sentence 20 is the alternant of 15.

Resultatives like 23 through 25 are especially interesting because they require a pseudo-reflexive.

(23) The man ran himself ragged. $x<y=$self$>w$/*John ran ragged. $x< >w$
(24) The woman laughed herself silly. $x<y=$self$>w$/*The woman laughed silly. $x< >w$
(25) John's mother worried herself sick. $x<y=$self$>w$/*John's mother worried sick. $x< >w$

The difference between the unergative-based resultatives in sentences 23 through 25 and the resultatives in sentences 26 through 31 follows from the presence versus absence of a direct argument in their PASs.

(26) The sun became orange. $<y>w$
(27) The lake froze solid. $<y>w$
(28) Mary fell flat on her face $<y>w$
(29) Mary painted the walls red. $x<y>w$
(30) John loaded the wagon full. $x<y>w$
(31) The student wiped the chalkboard clean. $x<y>w$

The resultative construction gives us a test for distinguishing two types of intransitives: those with D-structure objects (direct arguments) and those with D-structure subjects (external arguments). For a discussion of resultative constructions and their need for direct arguments see Simpson (1983). Unfortunately for us, ASL doesn't seem to tolerate resultative constructions, a property it seems to share with many romance languages (Spanish, French, etc.).

Examples like 13 and 14 and 26 through 28 are called "unaccusatives" because their subjects come from D-structure object position (the syntactic position that receives accusative Case). Accusative Case can be assigned by a verb only if it has both an external and a direct argument (that is, if it is transitive). Since unaccusative verbs lack an external argument, they cannot assign accusative Case. Therefore, they do not allow an NP to remain in object position (that is, to remain accusative), and therefore they have been termed "unaccusatives" (Perlmutter, 1978).

The passive construction is unaccusative as well. It differs from inchoatives and middles by virtue of the fact that the verb is marked with a special passive morphology. Semantically, the passive also presumes an agent even though one need not be present in the sentence. Sentences 32 through 34 present some passives with their corresponding D-structure representations. ([$t_y$] is the trace left by movement of the direct argument to subject position.)

(32) Albert$_y$ was hit [$t_y$] (by Mary).          DS: [e] was hit Albert (by Mary).
(33) The window$_y$ was broken [$t_y$] (by the boy).    DS: [e] was broken the window (by the boy).
(34) Bill$_y$ was arrested [$t_y$] (by the police).     DS: [e] was arrested Bill (by the police).

The optionality of the oblique-agent phrases is indicated not only as evidence that agent NPs are no longer required at S-structure, showing that a passive has one less argument than its transitive counterpart, but also to highlight the ambiguity between a passive sentence like 33, which implies agency, and its corresponding adjectival passive, which does not. Distinguishing between passives and their adjectival counterparts proves important to our discussion of ASL.

The best test for transitivity in English is alternation of a sentence with a passive alternant. The best tests for distinguishing between a true agentless passive and an adjectival passive are (1) co-occurrence with a *by*-phrase, and (2) ability of the adjectival passive to occur prenominally. The first test is not infallible as examples with *sewn by hand* and *made by dwarves* show. The second test reveals passives only without an adjectival counterpart, but many verbs co-occur with both regular passives and adjectival passives. Adjectival passives, by the way, would have the $<y>w$ PAS characteristic of predicate adjectives and predicate nominals.

Finally, we have "weather constructions," which get their name from the fact that the typical verbs associated with this type of PAS refer to weather phenomena: *rain, snow, sleet, pour*. Weather constructions do not select for any arguments. Therefore, except for the fact that the EPP would be violated because subject position would be left empty, such verbs should be able to stand alone as a sentence. Because of the EPP English requires the dummy pronoun *it* (a semantically empty place filler for an absent subject) to appear in subject position as in sentence 18. Sentences 32 through 34 illustrate a variety of constructions that require the presence of a pleonastic/dummy pronoun.

(32) It snowed. $(<\ >)$
(33) It seemed that John didn't want to be at the party. $(<y=S>)$
(34) It bothered Mary that she had forgotten her best friend's name. $<y=S, z>$

Sentence 33 has no argument present that could fill subject position. Sentence 34 has a sentence as its direct argument and, since sentences need not receive Case, it is not forced to move to subject position. Sentence 35 is a sentential psych-verb construction, which is problematic to explain. Although this construction also has a sentential direct argument, it nevertheless also has an indirect argument (Mary) that becomes the direct argument. However, since by Burzio's Generalization the verb should not be able to assign accusative Case to *Mary* because *bother* lacks an external argument, it is not at all clear why *Mary* can remain in direct-object position. Belletti and Rizzi (1988) stipulate inherent Case assignment for psych-verbs that such behavior might force us to adopt.

*ASL Intransitive Types.* This section reverses the order of presentation used in the discussion of English intransitives, beginning with weather constructions, moving to several types of unaccusatives, and finally to a range of psych-verb constructions.

Weather verbs in ASL exhibit no agreement, are not anchored to the body, and take no arguments. Sentences 35 through 37 show that ASL requires no pleonastic pronoun in subject position, indicating its immunity to the EPP.

(35) CL:G[plural] + MOVE-DOWNWARD [reduplicated]
   lto -plural + fall - repeatedly (Is raining)
   'It is raining.'

(36) CL:G[plural,individuated] + MOVE-DOWNWARD
   lto - plural,individuated + fall (Is snowing)
   'It is snowing.'

(37) CL:5 + MOVE-SIDEWAYS [reduplicated]
    permeable substance - blow - repeatedly (Is blowing)
    'The wind is blowing.'

ASL is not unique in being immune to the EPP. It shares this property with many of the world's languages: Italian, Spanish, Turkish, Slovene, Chinese, Russian, etc. Furthermore, immunity from the EPP is independent of ASL's status as a pro-drop language. The presence of non-overt subject and object pronouns is conditioned by the presence of agreement on the verb and accounts for the systematic absence of certain obligatory arguments as S-structure. The insertion of pleonastic pronouns to satisfy the EPP only comes into play in a language when no argument, overt or non-overt, fills subject position at S-structure. The insertion of pleonastic pronouns to satisfy the EPP has no relation to the presence or absence of agreement on the verb. Weather verbs are simply lexically specified for taking no arguments, and because ASL does not have the EPP, the surface realization of sentences involving weather verbs will not require any NPs.

Unaccusatives, on the other hand, select for a single argument, and unless verb agreement or a zero topic allows a non-overt pronoun, such sentences will have a single NP at S-structure. The inchoative examined earlier in sentences 10 and 12 provides the clearest, but not the only, example of an unaccusative construction ($<y>$) in ASL. We see from the preverbal surface position of the single NP argument that the D-structure direct argument moves to subject position to receive case. Thus, ASL must be subject to both Burzio's Generalization and the "case filter" (a requirement that all overt NPs receive case). The subject of an unaccusative is associated with the theta-role "theme" (the object that moves, is located, or changes). The subject of the inchoative is not body anchored and the action of the verb is either at the index point of the subject NP or is in neutral position.

Motion/location verbs are translatory (from $x$, to $x$, from $x$ to $y$) or nontranslatory (in $x$, on $x$, at $x$) forms of the verb MOVE. They vary in terms of either their theme classifier or incorporated NP, and they pattern exactly like the class of change-of-state-verbs (BREAK, OPEN, CLOSE, etc.) The inchoatives involve a classifier or fully incorporated NP in theme position, but the causatives contain a handling classifier instead. Nice sets of causative versus inchoative motion-verb pairs can be found by comparing the data in dissertations by Bernstein (1980) and Supalla (1982). Both these theses focus on the acquisition of motion/location verbs from an experimental perspective. Bernstein's experiments involved the presentation of stimuli (the moving and locating of objects in space) by a live experimenter, while Supalla's experiments made use of animated videotape presentations. Bernstein's experimenters had to handle objects to move them around, but Supalla could present objects moving on their own. As might be expected, Bernstein elicited a greater number of causatives, and Supalla elicited a greater number of inchoatives. There still remains some variability with respect to which transitivity alternant subjects chose to use. Sentences 38 and 39 present a causative/inchoative motion-verb pair parallel to the examples in 11 and 12.

(38) (BOTTLE$_0$), SUE$_{30}$SBP$_{30}$#CL:HAND[B/S] + $_{10}$ MOVE$_{20}$ [causative]
    bottle-indef. Sue bottle __ handling + source $_{10}$-move-goal$_{20}$
    'Sue moved a bottle from location 10 to location 20.'

(39) BOTTLE$_0$ CL:[C] + $_{10}$MOVE$_{20}$ [inchoative]
   bottle-indef. object __ taller __ than __ wide + source$_{10}$-move-goal$_{20}$
   'A bottle moved from location 10 to location 20.'

Causative/inchoative motion verb pairs often have one strange member. Since bottles tend to be moved rather than to move on their own, sentence 39 seems a bit odd. Sentences 40 and 41 present a more common causative/inchoative pair, which also serves to demonstrate that handling moves beyond simple carrying and truly marks causation.

(40) SUE$_{10}$SBP$_{10}$#CL:HAND [S/S] + MOVE$_{10}$ STORE$_{10}$
   Sue$_{10}$RP$_{10}$ car __ handling + move-goal$_{10}$ store$_{10}$
   'Sue drove (the car) to the store.'

(41) (CAR$_0$) CL:[3] + MOVE$_{10}$ STORE$_{10}$
   car vehicle + move-goal$_{10}$ store$_{10}$
   'The car drove/went to the store.'

Notice that in sentence 40 the independent NP argument corresponding to CAR is absent from the sentence. The handling classifier "car-handling" already incorporates this NP. In sentence 41 CAR is also optional because the unmarked interpretation of the vehicle classifier is "car". Another type of vehicle like TRUCK or BUS would be obligatory unless specified previously in the discourse.

ASL has very few prepositions. For the most part, locative relations are expressed as verbs or as part of a verb. The benefactive FOR is the only consistently freestanding preposition in ASL. It still differs from the English preposition *for* in that FOR agrees with its object. Notice that in sentences 38 through 41 the locative relations that would be expressed by independent pronouns in English are expressed as part of the verb—not just as part of the meaning, but registered by virtue of their locative agreement as part of the verb. These locative advancement structures (in relational grammar terms [Perlmutter and Postal, 1974; Dryer, 1983]) or applicative constructions (Baker, 1985, 1988) obscure parallels between argument-structure types in ASL and English. Where English takes an independent PP, ASL often incorporates a locative relation into the verb appearing to take a locative object as its direct object. Baker (1988) terms these "APPLIED OBJECTS."

Verbs of appearance in ASL (cl[5]$_i$#POP-UP/APPEAR + P$_i$, cl[C]$_i$#$_i$DISAPPEAR + P, (cl[B]$_i$#$_i$THUP + P[3], cl[5]$_i$#$_i$DROWN + P. etc.) are applicative verbs. The applied objects in the intransitives in sentences 42 and 43 are all NPs referring to surfaces. Furthermore, each verb has a classifier clitic indicating object agreement with a surface/visual barrier of some sort: cl[B] "unspecified surface" and cl[5] "permeable __ flat __ surface."

topic
(42) $\overline{\text{WATERSURFACE}_{20}}$, BOY cl[5]$_{20}$#CL:[G] + $_{20}$DROWN
   boy permeable__flat__object long__thin__object + go__down__beneath
   'A boy went beneath the surface of the water.'

topic
(43) $\overline{\text{HORIZON}_{20}}$, cl[B]$_{20}$#CL:F + $_{20}$RISE
   horizon flat__surface round__flat__object + go__up__from__behind
   'The sun rose above the horizon.'

These applicative-verb constructions pattern like typical ASL transitives, which select for classifier clitics. Kegl (1986, 1987) distinguishes two types of object-agreeing verbs in ASL: both agree spatially with their direct objects by associating the verb's final point of articulation with the position at which the object NP was indexed previous in the sentence or discourse, but one set (cl[G]$_i$#CL:S + HIT$_i$, cl[flatO]$_i$#CL:flatO + KISS$_i$, cl[B]$_i$#CL[8] + TOUCH$_i$, etc.), in addition to agreeing spatially with the position associated with the direct object, is preceded by a classifier clitic (cl[x]#) that functions as the direct object. This classifier clitic receives the accusative Case assigned by the verb and as a result prevents any full NP from receiving Case. Such clitics are said to be "Case absorbers." Since no full NP can receive accusative Case, no NP can occur in direct-object position (after the verb). If a corresponding NP occurs at all, it will be in topic position agreeing spatially with the classifier clitic.

The verbs in sentences 42 and 43 are similar in behavior to transitives classifier clitics. They pattern alike in having a classifier clitic that blocks the appearance of a NP in object position, but they differ in having a subject that is a non-agentive theme. Verbs of appearance always have a regular classifier in their theme slot and never a handling classifier or part of the body. The subject of a transitive can usually be coindexed with an RP clitic, but the subject of an appearance verb never can (except in rare, highly marked, instances that border on personification and occur most frequently in an art form called visual vernacular). The object of a transitive is generally a patient/affected element, but the applied object of an appearance verb is a location. Transitives have a passive (or at least adjectival passive) alternant, appearance verbs do not.

Are the appearance constructions in sentences 42 and 43 transitive (x<y>) like cl[G]$_i$#CL:S + HIT$_i$, or intransitive (<y>) like MELT? Despite surface similarities, I would vote for the latter. These applicative verbs seem to be intransitives that allow an additional applied object. ASL seems sensitive to ergative subjects, namely, subjects that are agentive and act upon or affect some patient. Such subjects are distinguished by causative marking and co-occur with a verb that has both subject and object person agreement as well as a passive alternant. Such transitives also require two arguments, unless the clitic is semantically strong enough to imply one. Appearance verbs lack these characteristics. Despite spatial agreement with some relevant surface location, the semantics associated with their objects fits more with oblique arguments than with the traditional external (agent), direct (affected/moving or located element), or indirect (recipient/experiencer/benefactor) arguments.

However, these "nontransitives" seem to alternate with a clearly intransitive alternant. In fact, this alternant is the more frequently occurring form of the verb. Compare sentences 44 and 45 with 42 and 43.

(44) BOY AT$_0$-cl[5]$_i$#CL:[G;] + $_i$DROWN
     boy permeable__flat__object long__thin__object + go__down__beneath
     'A boy drowned.'

(45) AT$_0$-cl[B]$_i$#CL:[F] + $_i$RISE
     flat__surface round__flat__object + go__up__from__behind
     'The sun rose.'

These verbs exhibit internal agreement between the source or goal of the verb and its classifier clitic, yet this internal agreement is irrelevant, in fact it is opaque to any agreement between the verb and an independent NP in the sentence. The verbs in sentences 44 and 45 are produced differently from their counterparts in 42 and 43. Their movements are constrained and are signed at a single location. They do not move to or get located at a specific end point. The phenomenon seen in these sentences is discussed in Kegl and Schley (1986). Basically, the Kegl and Schley paper argues that certain verbs can be embedded within other verbs and that when this happens the agreement points of the embedded verb become opaque with respect to syntactic agreement. They can no longer be co-indexed with syntactic arguments, although co-indexing between a verb and its lexically selected for classifier clitic remains. The embedded verb and its clitic are not opaque with respect to each other because they occur at the same level of embedding. The simplest way of turning a two-argument verb into a one-argument verb is to embed it in a one-argument verb.

The applicatives in sentences 44 and 45 are embedded in a single argument-taking $AT_i$ verb. This verb can have neutral agreement, which would result in a verb with no agreement that we would construe as coreferential with a non-indexed, or null-topic subject. Or, the $AT_i$ matrix verb can agree with the spatial location assigned as the index of the subject. In sentence 42 we get a reading like 'at a/the boy a moving down below a surface occurred.' In sentence 43, where the sun would not easily be indexed in the sentence or discourse, we get only a reading like 'a round object rising occurred.' I have represented the embedding of verbs inside $AT_i$ by prefixing $AT_i$ - to the entire verb complex and leaving the internal co-indexing marked with variables instead of real numbers, indicating their consistent relation to each other but irrelevance to syntactic agreement. The variable on the matrix $AT_i$ verb itself will either be co-indexed with the subject or left null.

Embedding in an $AT_i$ verb seems to be just another type of applicative construction; this time one that reduces the number of arguments rather than adding one. We can look at the applicatives in sentences 41 and 42 similarly. Sentence 41 is embedded in a cl $[5]_i\#_i$FROM verb. It already had its theme argument and it adds a source argument. Theme arguments never have spatial agreement anyway. Sentence 42 is embedded in a cl$[B]_i\#$FROM verb. When we strip the applicative form from its basic appearance unaccusative, we see the parallels to the inchoative motion and change unaccusatives. None of these basic unaccusatives agrees with an independent NP. It is the applicative verb that shows location agreement and imparts this agreement to the basic verb. The choice of applicative affix/embedder is a matter of lexical selection. Notice that the appearance verbs as a class select for a surface source or goal. Even $_i$THUP, which is not a two-handed sign, has a beginning motion that indicates contact with a surface.

Unaccusatives easily lend themselves to being embedded within other verbs. Consider CL:G/G + BREAK and applicative cl[5]$_{10}$#CL[G] + $_{10}$ APPEAR + P. Each can involve no agreement with the subject (*x* broke, or *x* appeared) or the signing of the entire verb at the subject's location with no other agreement (a breaking occurred at *x*'s location, or an appearing occurred at *x*'s location). The potential for an entire unaccusative verb to fill the theme slot of a locative verb obscures the basic property of unaccusatives, which select for a single direct-theme argument ($<y>$). In ASL themes never have spatial agreement with an independent NP. Therefore, once we can identify applicative constructions, we find that unaccusatives invariably take a single direct argument and no agreement. This contrasts with the weather verbs, which take no arguments and no agreement.

Does ASL have a passive construction? If so, is it unaccusative as in English? Examining only verb agreement, we find little evidence of a passive PAS in ASL, but examining subtle aspects of agreement in conjunction with the argument taking properties that a verb has reveals a morphologically distinct passive form in ASL. What has been called the "passive" equivalent is signaled by a shift in the agreement of the RP clitic with one NP versus the other as in sentence 46 and 47. Notice that role prominence is on *the thief* in sentence 46 and on *the policeman* in sentence 47 even though their roles with respect to the verb do not change.

(46) $POLICEMAN_{20}$, $THIEF_{10}$ $SBP_{10}\#cl[G]\#CL{:}S +_{10}HIT_{20}$.
policeman thief $_{RP}$ RP - lto - rso - source$_{10}$ hit goal$_{20}$
'The thief (with role prominence) hit the policeman.'

(47) $POLICEMAN_{20}$, $THIEF_{10}$ $SBP_{20}\#cl[G]\#CL{:}S +_{10}HIT_{20}$.
policeman$_{RP}$ thief RP - lto - rso - source$_{10}$ hit goal$_{20}$
'The thief hit the policeman (with role prominence).'

Sentence 47 cannot be considered the passive alternant of 46 for several reasons. First, there is no passive morphology on the verb. The only change is in the agreement of the RP clitic. Second, there is no change in the number of arguments the verb selects for. Both sentences 46 and 47 are transitive. Generally, the passive eliminates the agent argument or relegates it to the status of an oblique argument (in English, the object of a *by* phrase). All we have here is a shift in role prominence.

However, consider sentences 48 and 49, where we clearly do have an intransitive sentence that has been reduced by one argument and that clearly resists the presence of a second NP.

(48) $POLICEMAN_{20}$, $AT_{20}$ - $SBP_i\#cl[G]_i\#CL{:}S +_jHIT_i$ [passive]
policeman $_{RP}$ their PASS - RP - lto - rso - source$_j$ - hit - goal$_i$
'The policeman got hit.'

(49) *$POLICEMAN_{20}$, $THIEF_{10}$ $AT_{20}$ - $SBP_i\#cl[G]_i\#CL{:}S +_jHIT_i$ passive
policeman$_{RP}$ thief PASS - RP - lto - rso - source$_j$ - hit - goal$_i$
'The policeman got hit the thief.'

The articulation of the passive verb in sentence 48 differs from the articulation of the transitive verb in sentence 47. The transitive agrees with two distinct points in space, but the passive is articulated with reference to only one syntactically relevant index point. The entire verb in sentence 47 is embedded within a locative verb $AT_i$ in sentence 48.

In sentences 48 and 49, I have labeled as passive morphology the process of embedding a transitive verb with role prominence on its direct argument inside of an intransitive locative verb $AT_i$-. This detransitivizing passive morphology reduces by one the arguments a verb requires/permits at S-structure.

Passives characteristically involve handling classifiers, the ASL causative marker that signals a truly ergative transitive construction (one where an agent acts upon some patient). Thus we can see that passive is the detransitivization of a truly ergative construction. The orientation of the hands in a passive is the opposite of its transitive alternant with role prominence on the external argument. Passives are articulated close to the signer's body with a constrained, minimal movement that does not agree with any position other than the SBP (signer's body). Nevertheless, the constrained movement that does exist is a translatory movement from some neutral position to a final position on, at, or oriented toward the signer's body.

The passive sometimes shows up in an optional, stylistic, verb-doubling construction that is used when a discourse shift in role prominence is desired or there is a need to assign role prominence to both syntactic arguments. Only one role-prominence marker can exist per verb complex and these sentences double the verb to allow double role prominence or to shift it.

(50) POLICEMAN$_{20}$,  THIEF$_{10}$  SBP$_{10}$#cl[G]#CL:S + $_{10}$HIT-AT$_{20}$  AT$_{20}$-
SBP$_i$ + cl[S] + CL:S + $_j$HIT$_i$.
policeman thief RP$_{thief}$-lto-rso-source$_{10}$ hit-at goal$_{20}$RP$_{policeman}$-lso-rso-PASS-source$_{10}$
hit goal$_{20}$
'The thief (with role prominence) hit - the policeman (with role prominence) got hit.'

The first verb cl[G]#CL:S + $_j$HIT-AT in sentence 50 differs from cl[G]#CL:S + $_{10}$HIT$_{20}$ in sentence 46 in one respect: It doesn't make complete contact with the classifier clitic, yielding a reading more like *hit at* (orient toward *x* with a movement of the fist).

In some languages the association of a particular NP with subject position (or with prominence) is conditioned by a control hierarchy that ranks nouns with respect to their ability to serve as the agent or controller of the action in a sentence. In Navajo, such phenomena have been analyzed by Hale (1973), Creamer (1974) and Witherspoon (1977). They tied the obligatory inversion of subject and object in certain Navajo sentences to violations of a hierarchy of control that was roughly as follows: speakers > callers (sound makers) > corporeal > incorporeal. If the subject in Navajo ranks lower in this hierarchy than the object, the two are inverted and the inversion is registered by a *bi-* prefix rather than the usual *yi-* prefix on the verb. Compare sentences 51 through 53.

(51) Hastiin łįį' yiztał
man horse it-it-kicked
'The man kicked the horse.'

(52) *Łįį' hastiin yiztał.
horse man it-it-kicked (violation of the control hierarchy)
'The horse kicked the man.'

(53) Hastiin łįį biztał (inversion of subject and object)
man horse it-it-kicked
'The man let the horse kick him.'/'The man was kicked by the horse.'

ASL has such a hierarchy and requires that the NP associated with role prominence (the one co-indexed with the SBP) be superior on the hierarchy to any other argument in the sentence. The hierarchy is arranged as shown in table 5. Sometimes when a violation of the control hierarchy will occur, the verb-doubling option becomes the only option available for expressing a given utterance. Examples 54 through 56 parallel 51 through 53 and illustrate the effects of the control hierarchy in ASL.

*Table 5*. **ASL Control Hierarchy (highest to lowest)**

First person
Second person/third person
Animate
Inanimate
Moving
Nonmoving
Three-dimensional
Two-dimensional

(54) $JOHN_{10}$, $(PRONOUN_{1st\ per.})$ $SBP_{1st\ per.}\#cl[G]_{10}\#CL:S +_{1st\ per.}HIT_{10}$
John I $_{RP}$ RP lto - rso - source$_{1st\ per.}$ - hit - goal$_{10}$
'I (with role prominence) hit John.'

(55) $(PRONOUN_{1st\ per.})$, $JOHN_{10}$ $SBP_{10}\#cl[G]_{1st\ per.}\#CL:S +_{10}HIT_{1st\ per.}$
me John$_{RP}$ RP lto - rso source$_{1st\ per.}$ - hit - goal$_{10}$
'John (with role prominence) hit me.'

(56) $JOHN_{10}SBP_{10}\#cl[G]_0\#CL:S +_{10}HIT\text{-}TOWARD_0$ $AT_{1st\ per.}$ - $SBP_i\#cl[G]_i\#$
$CL:S +_jHIT_i$
John $_{RP_{John}}$lto-rso + source$_{10}$-hit-at-goal$_0$ (someone) PASS-source$_j$-hit-
goal$_{1st\ per.}$
'John hit at (someone), I got hit.'

Sentence 54 is a simple transitive with the role-prominent subject highest on the hierarchy. Sentence 55 violates the control hierarchy by having a third person role prominent when the remaining argument (first person) is higher on the hierarchy. Finally, the verb-doubling construction in sentence 56 resolves the violation of the hierarchy by reducing sentence 51 to a single-argument-taking passive construction and establishing the third person's role prominence in the preceding half of the verb-doubling construction, which leaves the object unspecified.

This section demonstrates that the unaccusative PAS ($<y>$) is shared by a number of verb types: inchoative change of state and motion/location verbs, appearance verbs, and passives. Furthermore, passives are distinguished from other unaccusatives, and from transitive constructions involving a shift in role prominence, on the basis of their morphology. Passive morphology is the embedding of a transitive with role prominence on the direct argument under an intransitive $AT_i$ verb. The observable differences exhibited by passives are the selection of a single argument; the reduction of the movement of the verb, which signals its articulation at a single index point; and the nonagreement of the source of the embedded intransitive, which indicates its detransitivization and resulting opacity with respect to syntactic agreement. The same articulation is also found in constructions involving psych-verbs and adjectival passives.

**Psych-Verbs.** I will conclude the paper by discussing three types of ASL psych-verb constructions because their analysis makes use of the observations concerning predicate-argument structure and verb-class organization we have made thus far while also introducing two new PASs we have not yet considered: the unaccusative double-object construction with a prepositionally licensed indirect argument ($<y$ $Pz>$), and its nonprepositionally licensed counterpart ($<y$ $z>$). The two new constructions are the intransitive equivalents of the more familiar ditransitive constructions found in the English dative alternations like "Mary$_x$ gave a book$_y$ to $_p$ Sue$_z$." ($x<y$ $Pz>$) versus "Mary$_x$ gave Sue$_z$ a book$_y$. ($x$ $<y$ $z>$)." Psych-verbs are particularly troublesome because, despite differing semantic interpretations and syntactic behavior, they all select for two arguments and they all look transitive at S-structure. This is true of English, Italian, and ASL alike; except that ASL and Italian have enough verb morphology to aid us in making distinctions between the various forms.

*Psych-Verbs in Italian.* Belletti and Rizzi (1988, in press) observed three types of psych-verbs in Italian. The three types are given in sentences 57 through 60 and are followed by the PASs I would associate with them. Sentences 59 and 60 are variant realizations of the same PAS.

(57) Gianni$_x$ teme questo$_y$. (B&R's ex. 1, 1988; 291)  $x<y>$
'Gianni fears this.'
(58) Questo$_y$ preoccupa Gianni$_z$. (B&R's ex. 2, 1988; 291)  $<y$ $z>$
'This worries Gianni.'
(59) A$_P$ Gianni$_z$ piace questo$_y$. (B&R's ex. 3a., 1988; 291)  $<y$ $Pz>$
'To Gianni pleases this.'
(60) Questo piace a Gianni. (B&R's ex. 3b., 1988; 292)  $<y$ $Pz>$
'This pleases to Gianni.'

Example 57 is a transitive verb whose surface subject is an experiencer and whose surface object is a theme. Example 58 is an unaccusative double-object intransitive verb whose surface subject is a theme and whose surface object is an experiencer. Under Belletti and Rizzi's analysis, the construction in sentence 58 lacks an external argument and therefore cannot assign Case to its direct argument, forcing the direct argument to externalize to subject position to receive Case. They argue that the stranded indirect argument receives inherent Case by virtue of a lexically stipulated property of the verb. Sentences 59 and 60 have the same structure as 58 except for the fact that the indirect argument (the experiencer) is structurally licensed by a preposition. It is the independent licensing of this argument by a preposition that accounts for its freedom in terms of the surface position in which it may occur. The interesting feature of psych-verbs is the fact that the experiencer is the subject of the transitive and the object of the intransitive double-object psych-verb. Since there isn't sufficient space here to fully explicate their analysis, the reader is referred to Belletti and Rizzi's articles for a detailed discussion of the intricacies of the semantics, agreement properties, and syntactic behavior of psych-verbs in Italian and in English.

*Psych-Verbs in ASL.* ASL has three types of psych-verb constructions. They parallel the Italian constructions, although not exactly. Table 6 presents a list of properties exhibited by each type of psych-verb.

Only true transitives ($x<y>$) have passive alternants. This allows us to pick out only type 3a as a transitive construction in ASL. Notice that in all but Type 3a the subject of an ASL psych-verb construction is an experiencer with role prominence. Type 3a is problematic for ASL in the same way that a verb like *amuse* is problematic for English. When a subject is nonhuman it is clearly a theme, but when it is human some verbs allow both a theme and an agent reading for the surface subject. Compare

**Table 6.  ASL Psych-Verb Constructions**

Type 1: Subject$_i$ = experiencer Role Prominence$_i$ VERB$_j$ Object$_j$ = theme {HATE, FEAR, etc.} $x<y>$

Type 2: Subject$_i$ = experiencer Role Prominence$_i$ VERB + Prep$_i$ Object$_0$ = theme {ENJOY, LIKE, etc.} $<y\ Pz>$

Type 3a: Subject$_i$ = theme Role Prominence$_i$ VERB$_j$ Object$_j$ = experiencer {BOTHER, SCARE, etc.} $x<y>/<y\ z>$

Type 3b: Subject$_i$ = experiencer Role Prominence$_i$ AT$_0$-VERB(adj. passive) {DEPRESSED, UPSET, etc.} $<y>w$

'The toy amused the children' with 'The clown amused the children.' Type 3a would compare to the agent reading of 'The clown amused the children.' In English, little structural evidence supports a different PAS for the agent reading. In ASL, however, themes are never co-indexed with an SBP and agents are always external arguments. Agents never even appear as oblique arguments (that is, in a *by* phrase). This would suggest that the verb in sentence 61 is transitive.

(61)  JOHN$_{10}$ SBP$_{10}$ + CL:5 + SCARE$_{20}$ MARY$_{20}$
      John$_{RP}$-subj. RP—clitic with—hands scare Mary-d. obj.
      'John scared Mary.' (as in jumped out from behind a tree in order to cause fear)

The focus in sentence 61 is on John's action, not Mary's response. In this respect, SBP$_i$ + CL:5 + SCARE$_i$, although transitive, may not really qualify as a psych-verb.

It is type 1 verbs in ASL that correspond to the *temere*-type (fear-type) transitive psych-verbs in Italian. Compare the Italian example in sentence 57 with the ASL example in sentence 62. The difference between types 1 and 3a are that type 1 has an experiencer in subject position and type 3c has an agent that is not an experiencer. Furthermore, type 3a allows a passive alternant and type 1 does not. Nonetheless, SBP$_i$#CL:8 + HATE$_i$ patterns like a transitive in terms of agreement. Its role-prominence marker agrees with the subject and the verb agrees with the object.

(62)  JOHN$_{10}$ SBP$_{10}$#CL:8 + HATE$_{20}$MARY$_{20}$
      John$_{RP}$-subj RP emotion + hate(repel) Mary-d. obj.
      'John hates Mary.'

The verb SBP$_i$#CL:8 + HATE$_i$ allows a shift in role prominence to its object, but it does not seem to allow a single-argument-taking passive form.[4] The analysis as it stands predicts that sentence 62 should have a passive alternant and I have no explanation for why it does not, unless only ergative transitives can have passive alternants—ones that truly affect their objects. Generally, experiencers seem obligatorily body anchored. If this were the case, then passive alternants of psych-transitives would be thrown out for independent reasons. However, reciprocals with HATE and the shift in role prominence in the transitive forms argue against this.

ASL has two intransitive psych-verb constructions. The first is an unaccusative plus "prepositionally licensed" indirect argument ($<y\ Pz>$). The second is a copular construction taking as its predicate an adjectival passive ($<y>w$ = adjectival passive). The copular construction is also unaccusative. Examples 63 through 65 illustrate the unaccusative-plus-indirect-argument PAS.

(63) $JOHN_{10}$ $SBP_{10}$#CL:B/B + ENJOY + $ON_{[chest]10}$ $MUSIC_0$ $<y\ Pz>$
John$_{RP}$ RP flat—surface + enjoy/please/rubs + on music
"John enjoys music." ("On John pleases music.")

(64) $JOHN_{10}$ $SBP_{10}$#$_{10[chest]}$CL:HAND[middle-thumb] + FROM + LIKE
$MUSIC_0$ $<y\ Pz>$
from-John$_{RP}$ RP from + like/draws—feeling music
"John likes music." ("From John's chest pulls feeling music.")

(65) $JOHN_{10}$ $SBP_{10}$#LOVE + $TO_{[heart]10}MARY_0$ $<y\ Pz>$
to-John$_{RP}$ RP love/endear Mary
"John loves Mary." ("To John endears Mary.")

The unaccusative-plus-indirect-argument psych-verb construction might at first glance appear to have the $<y\ z>$-*type* PAS because of the absence of an explicit prepositional licenser, but remember the applicative constructions found in appearance verbs where the verb incorporates a preposition and appears to agree spatially with an oblique object as its direct object. In fact, this spatial agreement is obligatory in ditransitive constructions. The direct argument (theme) is incorporated into the verb, or is relegated to a nonargument position at the end of the sentence (placed *en chomage* in relational grammar terms), and the indirect argument shows up with spatially realized person agreement on the verb as in example 66.

(66) $MARY_9$ $SBP_9$#($_9$FROM + )BOOK + CL:HAND[flat0 ] + GIVE-$TO_7$ $BILL_7$
Mary$_{RP}$-subj. (source$_9$-)book-incorp + causative + give-to-goal$_7$ Bill-applied object
"Mary gave Bill a book." `

It could be that all prepositions (except maybe $FOR_i$) are incorporated in this manner. Notice that verbs never agree spatially with direct (theme) arguments. Verbs also never agree spatially with their subject arguments; they agree with a role-prominence clitic, and they agree with a source or goal. The spatial agreement we see on verbs may be an indication that they are applicative constructions. An example like 66 would have an incorporated-goal postposition and an optional incorporated-source preposition. (The optionality is pointed out in Padden [1988], although she would reject the claim that these verbs involve spatial agreement.) Transitives with classifier clitics could be reanalyzed as having applicative sources and goals as well. This would account for both the scarcity of independent propositions in ASL and for lack of agreement on all theme and some agent arguments.

If examples 63 through 65 are applicative and have a $<y\ Pz>$-type PAS, a question arises as to why the most common type of psych-verb pattern does not seem to occur in ASL. This is the unaccusative double-object PAS ($<y\ z>$) exhibited by the *preoccupare*-type psych-verbs in Italian (see example 58). This PAS seems to be the one most frequently used by new psych-verbs entering a language (Maurice Gross, personal communication, November 1986). A quick thought back to the control hierarchy in ASL tells us exactly why these constructions cannot occur. The themes in these psych-verb constructions are nonhuman and the experiencers are human. A sentence of the *preoccupare*-type would violate ASL's language-specific control hierarchy. The few verbs that might slip through (for example, verbs like

SBP$_i$#BOTHER$_j$, SBP$_i$#SCARE, etc., where the subject is typically a person) either do occur or have been reanalyzed as transitives as in type 3a in table 6.

How could such a reanalysis occur? Kegl and Fellbaum (1988) point out that unaccusative psych-verbs with a stranded indirect argument are perfect candidates for such a reanalysis. That paper argues for a movement of the unlicensed indirect argument to a position adjacent to and governed by the verb where it will be able to receive structural Case. In this position it is structurally indistinguishable from a direct argument. The previous direct argument is stranded by this operation, but it is saved by externalizing to subject position where it can receive Case from INFL. Here it is structurally indistinguishable from an external argument. Thus, the two movements triggered by the stranding of arguments in a psych-verb construction like this serve to create a derived transitive structure. If such a derived transitive structure allows a passive alternant, we can imagine it quickly being reanalyzed as a basic transitive.

Consider a little evidence that the derived structure could without reanalysis constitute a transitive of sorts. Belletti and Rizzi (1988, 333) point out that one problem for them is the fact that *preoccupare*-type verbs take the aspectual auxiliary *avere* (to have) rather than *essere* (to be). The ability to take *avere* is considered to be a reliable diagnostic for a verb that is able to assign accusative Case. Unaccusative verbs cannot assign accusative Case and characteristically take *essere*, except in the case of the unaccusative psych-verb with a stranded indirect argument. These psych-verbs take *avere* while passing a myriad of other tests that indicate that their surface subject was a D-structure direct argument. By assuming derived transitives to be assigners of accusative case, we find support for the Kegl and Fellbaum proposal of the movement of internal arguments adjacent to the verb in order to receive structural case over Belletti and Rizzi's proposal of a special inherent case-marking rule for these constructions, and we find an explanation for the occurrence of passives corresponding to these apparently unaccusative constructions and thereby an explanation for the occurrence of adjectival passives both preverbally (*the amused children*) and postverbally (*the children were thoroughly amused*). The presence of an adjectival passive indicates the presence, at least at some stage in the language, of a corresponding passive.

ASL doesn't have auxiliaries like *essere* and *avere* that can serve as diagnostics for transitivity (basic or derived) versus unaccusativity, but it does have adjectival passives. They show up in sentences like 68, which would relate to the passive counterpart sentence 67 of the causative change of state verb SBP$_i$#CL:HAND[S] + BREAK[causative] that appears in sentence 11.

(67) POSSESSIVE$_{1st per.}$ KNEE$_0$ AT$_{[knee]1st per.}$-SBP$_i$#$_i$ CL:HAND[C/C] + BREAK [passive]

        my            knee   passive-broken

    'My knee was broken (by someone intentionally).'

(68) LEG$_0$ POSSESSIVE$_{2nd per.}$AT$_0$-SBP$_i$#$_i$CL:HAND[C/C] + BREAK [adjective passive]

    leg   your           broken

    'Your leg is broken.'

The adjectival passive is distinguished from the passive in having no agreement on the AT-prefix. Further evidence of its adjective rather than verb status comes from its ability to occur in preverbal position as in sentence 69. Its PAS is $<y>w$. This structure contains a zero verb.[6]

(69) $AT_0$-SBP$_i$#CL:HAND[C/C] + BREAK$_i$ [adjectival passive] LEG AWFUL
broken                                                   leg awful
'A broken leg is awful.'

Thus we have an explanation for why in the absence of a $<y\ z>$-type psych-verb construction we do have the expected set of verbs appearing as adjectival passives as in sentences 70 through 73.

(70) MARY$_{10}$ AT$_0$-SBP$_i$#CL:HAND[5] + SCARE$_{i[chest]}$        Mary$_y$ was frightened$_w$.
(71) MARY$_{10}$ AT$_0$-SBP$_i$#CL:HAND[8] + DEPRESS$_{i[chest]}$   Mary$_y$ was depressed$_w$.
(72) MARY$_{10}$ AT$_0$-SBP$_i$#CL:HAND[claw] + UPSET$_{i[chest]}$   Mary$_y$ was upset$_w$.
(73) MARY$_{10}$ AT$_0$-SBP$_i$#CL:HAND[claw] + ANNOY$_{i[chest]}$  Mary$_y$ was annoyed$_w$.

All of these psych-verbs have transitive counterparts outside of the domain of emotion verbs where subjects are not required to be experiencers.

## CONCLUSION

I have been speculative in this paper at the expense of detailed argumentation in the hopes of conveying the benefits to be gained, or at least the new questions to be raised, from examining the organization of the ASL lexicon from the point of view of verb-class membership, predicate argument structure, and transitivity alternations. A number of interesting hypotheses are suggested by this research including the possibility that the marking of grammatical relations in ASL is done configurationally rather than morphologically; that verbs, even apparent transitives like GIVE and HIT, might include only theme and manner, whereas relations like source, goal, location, and even their person-marking counterparts are the result of applicative operations in the syntax. Furthermore, the range of PASs found cross-linguistically, including passive, have their realization in ASL, but a close look at these PASs and the constraints on their S-structure realizations will move us away from the confusion imposed by inappropriate and nonisomorphic English glosses and toward a comprehensive typological characterization of the ASL lexicon.

## NOTES

1. There are some intransitive constructions with two arguments, for example, psych-verb constructions ('The toy amused the children') and copular construction ('Mary is a genius.'). These are intransitive in the sense that they lack an external argument. In such constructions, the surface subject is actually a D-structure direct argument (a deep object). We will not concern ourselves with these constructions until the section on psych-verbs.
2. The term "ergative" is problematic because it is used at least two ways in the government and binding literature. In speaking of ergative/absolutive versus nominative/accusative language types, ergative is a type of case marking that appears on the subject of a transitive verb. This notion of ergative, which is the sense I intend in this discussion is explained in detail in Levin

(1983) and subsequent publications. Burzio (1986) introduces the term "ergative" as a synonym for Perlmutter's term "unaccusative," probably for symmetry between unergative $<y>$ vs. ergative $x < >$. This use is misleading and clashes with the notion of ergativity that appears in traditional grammars. The reader should bear in mind that this use of the term is being avoided since the term "unaccusative" suffices without confusing matters.

3. I have no idea what the English gloss for $(cl[B]_i)\#_i THUP$ might be. This is the verb that refers to a pile of objects suddenly disappearing, presumably as the result of rapid consumption or sucking up in some manner. I have taken the gloss from the concurrent mouth gesture that rapidly sucks in the tongue making a sound akin to $\theta ap$. This sign usually occurs without a base hand, but can occur with an unspecified flat-surface classifier. Even in the absence of a classifier clitic referring to a surface, the movement of this verb suggests contact with a surface and a postverbal NP corresponding to the applied object is prohibited.

4. An example with ASL $SBP_i \# CL:B/B + FEAR_i$ that is directly comparable to Italian *temere* (fear) also exists but it is less common and I am not sure what English gloss is associated with it. Since this verb tends to take only generic objects, has neutral agreement, and doesn't tolerate a shift in role prominence, it doesn't serve as a clear example and may not even by analyzed appropriately.

> (i) $CHILD_{10}$ $SBP_{10}\#CL:B/B + FEAR_0$ $BEAR_0$[redup.]
> $child_{RP}$ RP__clitic flat__surfaces + fear/ward-off bear-plural/generic
> 'The child fears bears.'

5. The same is true of the English predicate complement construction. It has a zero verb as well. The verb *to be* that occurs is an auxiliary as its ability to undergo subject/Aux inversion (i) and negative contraction (ii) demonstrate. Compare the behavior of the auxiliary is with the true verb *break*.

> (i) Is John depressed?/*Broke John the bottle?
> (ii) John isn't depressed./*Breakn't John the bottle.

## REFERENCES

Atkins, B., Kegl, J., and Levin, B. (1986). Explicit and implicit information in dictionaries. Lexicon Project Working Papers 12. Cambridge, MA: Center for Cognitive Science, MIT. Also CSL Report 5. Princeton, NJ: Cognitive Science Laboratory, Princeton University.

———, Kegl, J., and Levin, B. (1988). Anatomy of a verb entry: From linguistic theory to lexicographic practice. *International Journal of Lexicography*, 84–126.

Baker, M. (1985). *Incorporation: A theory of grammatical function changing*. Chicago: University of Chicago Press.

———. (1988). The syntax of applicatives in Chichewa. *Natural Language and Linguistic Theory* 6:353–389.

Belletti, A. and Rizzi, L. (1988). Psych-verbs and θ-theory. *Natural Language and Linguistic Theory* 6:291–352.

———, and Rizzi, L. (in press). Notes on psych-verbs, θ-theory, and binding. In *Proceedings of the Princeton workshop on comparative grammar*, edited by R. Freidin, Cambridge, MA: MIT Press.

Bernstein, M. Acquisition of locative expressions by deaf children learning American Sign Language. Ph.D. diss., Boston University, Boston, MA.

Burzio, L. (1986). *Italian syntax: A GB approach*. Dordrecht: D. Reidel.

Chomsky, N. (1981). *Lectures on government and binding*. Dordrecht: Foris Publications.

Creamer, M. H. (1974). Ranking in Navajo nouns. *Diné Bizaad Nánílííh (Navajo Language Review)* 1:29–38.

Dryer, M. (1983). Indirect objects in Kinyarwanda revisited. In *Studies in relational grammar*, vol. 1, edited by D. Perlmutter, Chicago, University of Chicago Press.

Edge, V., and Herrmann, L. (1977). Verbs and the determination of subject. In *On the other hand*, edited by L. Friedman, 137–79. New York: Academic Press.

Hale, K. (1973). A note on subject-object inversion in Navajo. In *Issues in linguistics: Papers in honor of Henry and Renee Kahane*, edited by B. Kachru et al., 300–09. Urbana: University of Illinois Press.

Fischer, S., and Gough, B. (1978). Verbs in American Sign Language. *Sign Language Studies* 18:17–48.

Kegl, J. (1985). Causative marking and the construal of agency in American Sign Language. In *CLS21*, part 2: *Papers from the parasession on causatives and agentivity*, edited by W. H. Eilfort, P. D. Kroeber, and K. L. Peterson, 120–37. Chicago: University of Chicago.

———. (1986). Clitics in American Sign Language. In *The syntax of pronominal clitics*, edited by H. Borer, 285–309. *Syntax and Semantics*, vol. 19: New York: Academic Press.

———. (1987). Coreference relations in American Sign Language. In *Studies in the acquisition of anaphora*, vol. 2: *Applying the constraints*, edited by B. Lust, 135–170. Dordrecht: D. Reidel.

———. A typology of ASL argument structure. Swarthmore College, Swarthmore, PA. Unpublished manuscript.

———, and Fellbaum, C. (1988). Noncanonical argument identification. *Proceedings of WCCFL VII*. Irvine, CA: University of California at Irvine.

———, and Fellbaum, C. (in press). An analysis of obligatory adjuncts: Evidence from the class of measure verbs. In *Proceedings of ESCOL '88*. Columbus: Ohio State University.

———, and Levin, B. (in press). Entries for a government-binding lexicon. In *Towards a polytheoretical lexical database*, edited by D. Walker, A. Zampolli, and N. Calzolari. Pisa, Italy: Istituto di Linguistica Computazionale, CNR.

———, and Schley, S. (1986). When is a classifier no longer a classifier? In *Proceedings of the Twelfth Annual Meeting of the Berkeley Linguistics Society*, edited by V. Nikiforidou, M. VanClay, M. Niepokuj, and D. Feder, 425–41. Berkeley, CA: Berkeley Linguistics Society.

Levin, B. (1983). On the nature of ergativity. Ph.D. diss., MIT, Cambridge, MA.

———, ed. (1985). *Lexical semantics in review*. Lexicon Project Working Papers, No. 1. Cambridge, MA: MIT, Center for Cognitive Science.

Lillo-Martin, D. (1985). Null pronouns and verb agreement in American Sign Language. In *Proceedings of NELS 15*, edited by S. Berman, J.-W. Choe, and J. McDonough, 302–18.

———. (1986). Two kinds of null arguments in American Sign Language. *Natural Language and Linguistic Theory* 4:415-44.

Meier, R. (1982). Icons, analogues, and morphemes: The acquisition of verb agreement in ASL. Ph.D. diss. University of California, San Diego.

Padden, C. (1988). Interaction of morphology and syntax in American Sign Language. Outstanding Dissertations in Linguistics, Series 4. New York: Garland Publishing.

Perlmutter, D., and Postal, P. (1974). *Lectures on relational grammar*. Amherst, MA: Summer Institute of the Linguistic Society of America, University of Massachusetts.

Rappaport, M., Levin, B., and Laughren, M. (1988). Niveaux de representation lexicale. *Lexique* 7. [An English version appears as Rappaport, M., Levin, B., and Laughren, M. (1987)]. Levels of Lexical Representation. Lexicion Project Working Papers, No. 20. Cambridge, MA: MIT, Center for Cognitive Science.

Shepard-Kegl, J. (1985). Locative relations in American Sign Language word formation, syntax, and discourse. Ph.D. diss., MIT, Cambridge, MA.

Simpson, J. (1983). Resultatives. In *Papers in Lexical-Functional Grammar*, edited by L. Levin, M. Rappaport, and A. Zaenen, 143–57. Bloomington, IN: IULC.

Supalla, T. Structure and acquisition of verbs of motion and location in American Sign Language. Ph.D. diss., University of California, San Diego.

Witherspoon, Gary. (1977). *Language and art in the Navajo universe*. Ann Arbor: University of Michigan Press.

# Four Functions of a Locus: Reexamining the Structure of Space in ASL

## Scott K. Liddell

This paper reinvestigates the structure and use of space in ASL. Most of the discussion will focus on the behavior of agreement verbs, but it will become evident that the behavior of agreement verbs is not independent of other uses of space including, for example, the use of classifier predicates.

Verbs like ASK, in which the form of the verb itself makes spatial reference to the subject, object, or both subject and object, have been referred to as "directional verbs" (Fischer and Gough, 1978), "multidirectional verbs" (Friedman, 1976), "inflecting verbs" (Padden, 1983), and "agreement verbs" (Johnson and Liddell, 1987). I will refer to verbs in this class as "agreement verbs." Consider the two forms of the sign ASK in figure 1. When ASK begins close to the signer and then moves toward the addressee (figure 1a), the meaning is 'I ask you.' When the movement is reversed, so is the meaning.

The signs in figure 1 are directed toward referents who are physically present (the signer and addressee). When a referent is not present, a signer can "set up" a location for that referent by "establishing an index." One way that this can be done is illustrated in figure 2. In figure 2a the signer mentions the referent which is to be "established" in space. In figure 2b, the signer designates the locus at which the referent is "established."

The concept of a locus is central to virtually all the discussion that follows. I will use the term "locus" to refer to a point on the body or in the signing space that serves an articulatory function. The sign DOG, for example, is produced at a spatial locus a foot or so ahead of the trunk. It happens that the spatial locus for the sign DOG and the location of the hand in the signing space coincide. This is a rather complicated way to say that a locus a foot or so ahead of the body is the significant point in the signing space for this sign, and that the hand is located at that point. This might seem too obvious to mention, but in other signs, this does not always happen. The sign MY, for example, begins by moving toward the chest and ends after it contacts the chest. During the course of its movement the hand traverses several inches of space on its way to the chest. The path taken by the hand could be

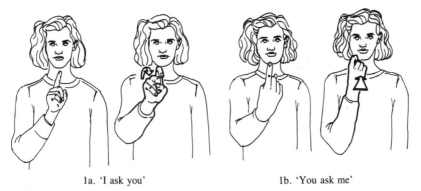

1a. 'I ask you'          1b. 'You ask me'

*Figure 1*. **Two forms of the verb ASK.**

described mathematically as being composed of an unbounded number of separate points. But it seems necessary to specify only a single locus as being linguistically significant in the production of this sign. That locus is the point on the chest that the hand contacts. Viewed in this way the production of the sign MY can be described as beginning its movement ahead of that body locus and ending its movement in contact with that body locus.

I will also talk about the point in space at which an index is established as a locus. What is generally said about a locus at which an index has been established is that subsequent reference to this locus makes reference to the referent "established" at that locus. For example, since the sign ASK in figure 3 is directed to the right, where the index in figure 2 was established, it means, 'I asked the girl.'

In the literature on verb agreement in ASL this concept of "establishing an index" has received considerable attention and gained widespread acceptance. Virtually all researchers agree that establishing an index sets up a relationship between the locus and a referent. The literature has treated this relationship as one of referential equality between the locus and the referent. Consider the following from Friedman: "An act of pronominal reference consists in indexing a point in the signer's body-space which has been pre-established as *designating* a particular person, object, or location" (emphasis added) (1975, 947). Clearly Friedman intends that the relation-

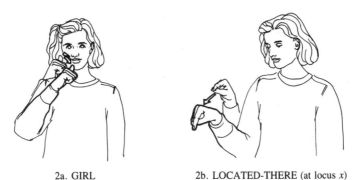

2a. GIRL          2b. LOCATED-THERE (at locus *x*)

*Figure 2*. **Establishing an index.**

*Figure 3.* **'I asked (the person established in space on my right).'**

ship is a type of equality between the locus and the referent. In a sense, the locus substitutes for the nonpresent referent. Loew makes a similar characterization: "A single locus normally *stands for* a single referent (or a group of spatially related referents, such as a house and its occupants)" (emphasis added) (1984, 11). Wilbur says essentially the same thing: "It is predominantly single individuals or objects that are *represented* by these location points" (emphasis added) (1987, 116). The above descriptions of the relationship between a locus and a referent are all basically the same in that a locus is said to represent a referent.

Klima and Bellugi (1979) and Poizner, Klima, and Bellugi (1987) treat this system of spatial reference as an abstract association between a locus and a referent that is distinct and separate from what they describe as "topographical" uses of space in ASL. DeMatteo (1977) describes some of those topographical uses of space in detail. In his analysis the space in front of the signer serves as a space in which the placement of classifier handshapes corresponds analogically to real-world placement of the entities represented by those classifiers. One might imagine the space in front of the signer as a stage upon which "actors" will occupy certain positions. For example, imagine a scene in which there is a table on the left at which someone is seated. A second person enters from the right and approaches the first person, the two exchange words, then the second person goes back to where he came from. This interaction could be described in ASL by placing a classifier representing the table placed in the left side of the signing space followed by a classifier representing the person seated at the table. A classifier representing the second person would enter the scene from the right side of the signing space, and move to the left side of the signing space. After describing their interaction, the classifier representing the second person would then move away to the right. This topographical use of space is primarily associated with classifier predicates (Supalla, 1978, 1986; Liddell and Johnson, 1987).

Syntactic and topographical uses of space are conceived of as being quite distinct. In the former a locus is treated as representing a referent and in the latter a referent is at a location. These two relationships between a locus and a referent are contrasted in figure 4. Referential equality can be easily explained with a legal analogy. In a contract, one of the participants (Mr. Jones) might be identified as "the borrower." All subsequent occurrences of "the borrower" make reference to Mr. Jones. This is the relationship described in figure 4a. A referential equality is established between a referent and a locus. This is equivalent to the descriptions cited

a. REFERENTIAL EQUALITY   $referent_a = locus_a$
b. LOCATION FIXING         $referent_a$ is at $locus_a$

*Figure 4*. **Two possible relationships between a locus and referent.**

from Friedman (1975), Loew (1984), and Wilbur (1987). Compare this with an actor told to stand at a certain mark on a stage. When the actor stands on that mark then he is located on that mark. There is a relationship between the actor and the mark, but it is not a relationship of referential equality, but a physical locative relationship. The actor is physically located on that mark. This is the relationship described by figure 4b.

Classifier predicates are assumed to locate entities in the signing space (location fixing). Agreement verbs are treated by Klima and Bellugi (1979) and Poizner, Klima, and Bellugi (1987) as operating within a separate abstract space that is not topographical, but that does involve setting up a referential equality between referents and loci. But suppose a signer uses a classifier predicate to place a person in the right side of the signing space (location fixing). There is a sense in which one could say that an "index" has been established since it is possible to use an agreement verb to refer to the person represented by the classifier. To do so, the argument verb would be directed toward the right. How is this possible if topographical space and the space of spatial syntax are distinct? Further, Padden (1983) observes that if a classifier predicate is used to "move" that person to the other side of the signing space, subsequent reference to that person through a pronoun of agreement verb will be to the new location, not the old one.[1]

The above example of locus shifting provides evidence that topographical uses of space and syntactic uses of space interact. This presents a problem to the view that syntactic space is separate from topographical space.

The main aim of this paper is to describe the relationships between a locus and a referent that come into being when an index is established. This description will call into question the notion that establishing an index in space establishes a referential equality between a locus and referent and will also call into question the idea that there is a syntactic space used for verb agreement and a separate topographical space used with classifiers.

## AGREEMENT VERBS VERSUS
## SPATIAL VERBS

Verbs that use space to refer to locations rather that subjects or objects are called spatial verbs (Padden, 1981, 1983). The general category of spatial verbs includes within it the very large class of signs referred to as classifier predicates (Supalla, 1978). An agreement verb and a spatial verb are illustrated in figure 5. The sign GIVE is an agreement verb, and MOVE-FLAT-OBJECT is a spatial verb (Padden, 1983). In figure 5a GIVE moves from one side of the signing space to the other side. Its initial location indicates its subject and its final location indicates its object. In figure 5b MOVE-FLAT-OBJECT also moves from one side of the signing space to the other side, but the significance of the beginning and end points of the movement differs from that described for GIVE. The beginning and end points of the movement indicate the initial and final location of the thing being moved. If the initial and final locations for these two signs were reversed, their meanings would also be affected. The sign in figure 5a would mean, 'person$_y$ give to person$_x$.' The sign in figure 5b would mean 'move object from y to x.'

The two signs in figure 5 are highly similar in form. They are both made with the same hand configuration and both move with respect to two spatial points of articulation. In spite of their similarity in form, however, the two signs illustrated above make use of space in quite different ways. In figure 5a the sign GIVE makes reference to the subject and object of the verb. In figure 5b, the sign MOVE-FLAT-OBJECT makes reference to two locations (initial and final location of thing being moved). Distinguishing between agreement verbs and spatial verbs can pose problems since both types of verbs can be produced at numerous places in the signing space. Padden (1983) distinguishes agreement verbs from spatial verbs by their ability to inflect for person and number. In her analysis, agreement verbs have the ability to inflect for person and number, but spatial verbs do not. For example, when ASK moves from one side of the signing space to the other, the initial placement and orientation of the hand identifies the subject of the verb and the final placement and orientation identifies the object of the verb. This is what Padden describes as ''person agreement.''[2]

The form of GIVE in figure 5a means, 'referent$_x$ gives (something) to referent$_y$.' The significance of the loci for a spatial verb is different. When the spatial verb MOVE-FLAT-OBJECT (figure 5b) moves from one locus in the signing space to another, the first locus signifies the initial location of the entity being moved, and the final locus signifies the final location of that entity. Similarly, for the spatial verb 3-CL:MOVE (from x to y), shown in figure 6a, locus x signifies the initial location of the vehicle and locus y signifies the final location of the vehicle.

Liddell and Johnson (in preparation) observe an additional difference between agreement verbs and spatial verbs. Although spatial verbs and agreement verbs are located and move with respect to loci, they differ with respect to whether or not the hand must actually be at a specified locus.[3] For example, to say that a vehicle was

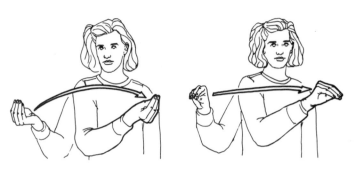

5a.  x-GIVE-y                    5b.  MOVE-FLAT-OBJECT-FROM-x-TO-y
     'person$_x$ give to person$_y$'      'move object from x to y'

*Figure 5*. **An agreement verb and a spatial verb.**

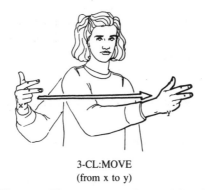

3-CL:MOVE
(from x to y)

*Figure 6.* **The movement of a spatial verb.**

driven from a starting point, represented by $x$ in the right side of the signing space, to an ending point represented by $y$ on the left side of the signing space, the hand begins its movement at $x$ and ends its movement at $y$ (figure 6). If the sign in figure 6 were to be modified by ending the movement only halfway to $y$, that would represent a different event than that described in figure 6, where a vehicle moves all the way to $y$.

An agreement verb, on the other hand, typically does not begin at one agreement locus and end its movement at a second agreement locus. Using the same two points, we can locate a person at $x$ and another person at $y$ (figure 7). The sign moves with respect to the same two points, but does not begin at $x$ nor does it end at $y$. Instead, it begins by being nearer to $x$ then moves to a location closer to $y$. One difference, then, between ASK (agreement verb) and 3-CL:MOVE (spatial verb) is whether or not the hand must move from one locus to another (3-CL:MOVE) or whether it must move (less restrictively) between the two loci (ASK).[4]

The criteria described so far that help to distinguish between agreement verbs and spatial verbs are (1) whether the hand must move to be at a specific locus in space, and (2) whether that locus identifies the subject or object of the verb or signifies the initial and/or final location of an entity. Agreement verbs, in general, do not

x-ASK-y

*Figure 7.* **Movement properties of the verb ASK.**

move all the way to or from specific loci, but nevertheless, they identify the subject or object of the verb. How this is done will be described later. This contrasts with spatial verbs where placing the hand *near*, *far from*, or *at* a locus all contrast.

## AGREEMENT-VERB BEHAVIOR

### Agreement Verbs and Present Referents

When another person is physically present with the signer, an agreement verb can be used to refer to that person. The most obvious person that fits this description is the addressee. Signers do not typically establish an index, as was done in figure 2, in order to refer to the addressee.[5] Three forms of 1-ASK-addressee are illustrated in figure 8. In figure 8a the signer and addressee are the same height and the sign moves horizontally at roughly chin level between the speaker and addressee. However,

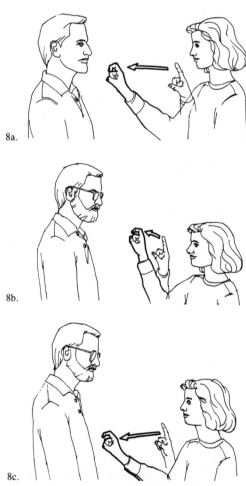

8a.

8b.

8c.

*Figure 8.* **Three forms of 1-ASK-addressee.**

if the addressee were significantly taller than the signer, figure 8b shows that the sign moves upward toward the addressee's chin.[6] If the signer directs the sign ASK horizontally between his chin and the addressee's chest (figure 8c), the result is ungrammatical, in spite of the fact that the signer is doing exactly the same movement as figure 8a (which is grammatical in the other situation). The toe-to-head height of the addressee is not the issue here. What is important is the relative height of the addressee's face from the point of the view of the signer. If a tall addressee were seated, 1-ASK-addressee would be directed downward toward the addressee's head, even though the addressee was tall. Thus, when agreement verbs are used with present referents, the height of the other person with respect to the signer becomes important.

Every agreement verb has a specific body height at which it moves. The sign ESP-WITH (figure 9a) is directed toward the forehead level; SAY-NO-TO (figure 9b) is lower, moving at roughly the level of the nose; GIVE (figure 9c) is lower still, moving at the chest level. Klima and Bellugi state, "The actual positions of the signer and addressee determine the locations of their indexic loci in the indexic plane" (1979, 277). Lillo-Martin and Klima (in press) make essentially the same claim, stating that the presence of the addressee "determines an R-locus" (a referential locus). In their terminology an R-locus is a spatial locus that is associated with a referent. Both these claims associate a locus with the addressee. Klima and Bellugi go on to claim that "to inflect for indexic reference, as in 'I ask you', the sign moves toward the second-person target locus" (1977, 277).

The evidence presented above contradicts the claim that there is a locus on the indexic plane that is associated with the addressee. There is no single point in space

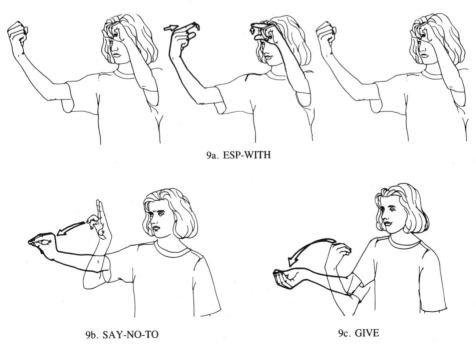

9a. ESP-WITH

9b. SAY-NO-TO                    9c. GIVE

*Figure 9*. **Differing heights of agreement verbs.**

toward which agreement verbs and pronouns are directed. For example, if one were to suppose that such a locus were at chin height, then although ASK would be directed toward that locus, GIVE, which is directed at chest level, would not. Pronominal reference to the addressee would also not be directed at that locus. It too is directed at chest height. ESP-WITH would be directed at the forehead level, well above the locus at chin height. No matter which level one were to select as the level for such a locus, many agreement verbs would not be directed at that locus. Thus, there does not seem to be any real evidence in support of a spatial locus anaphorically associated with the addressee.

### Agreement Verbs and Referents Imagined as Present

When referents are imagined to be present, agreement verbs act as if an invisible referent were physically present. To direct the verb ASK toward an imagined referent, the signer must conceive of the location of the imaginary referent's head. For example, if the signer and addressee were to imagine that Wilt Chamberlain was standing beside them ready to give them advice on playing basketball, the sign ASK would be directed upward toward the imagined height of Wilt Chamberlain's head (figure 10a). It would be incorrect to sign the verb at the height of the signer's chin (figure 10b). This is exactly the way agreement works when a referent is present. Naturally, if the referent is imagined as lying down, standing on a chair, etc., the height and direction of the agreement verb reflects this. Since the signer must conceptualize the location of body parts of the referent imagined to be present, there is a sense in which an invisible body is present. The signer must conceptualize such a body in order to properly direct agreement verbs.

The phenomenon of "body shifting" is frequently mentioned in the ASL literature. (Friedman, 1975; Baker and Cokely, 1980; Liddell, 1980; Padden, 1983; Wilbur 1987). It has been described as a process by which a signer shifts (rotates) the body, thereby adopting the role of another signer (Friedman, 1975).[7] Suppose, for example, that two loci have been established: a boy on the right and a girl on the left. If the signer rotates his body to the left (facing the girl's locus) then he "adopts the role" of the boy. This is a form of direct discourse. While in the role, first person reference refers to the boy rather than the signer. In figure 11, the boy

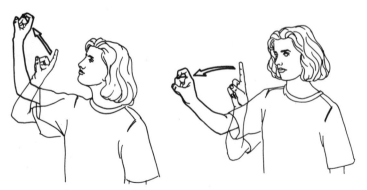

10a. addressee-ASK-imagined tall referent   10b. * addressee-ASK-imagined tall referent

*Figure 10.* **Agreement verbs and referents imagined as present.**

*Figure 11.* **1-ASK-addressee (in role of boy asking girl).**

tells the girl, "I asked you." In this example the boy is equated with the signer and the girl is treated as the addressee. This is typical of cases of "adopting a role." The signer is operating as if a nonpresent addressee were present.[8] In figure 11 the verb moves horizontally. This is appropriate if the boy and girl are the same height. If the boy were talking to a child, the signer would treat the imagined addressee as shorter and direct the sign downward. With real or imagined persons in the environment of the signer, agreement verbs move toward designated heights on those persons.

### Agreement Verbs and Spatial Loci

The behavior of agreement verbs with respect to established loci has received considerable attention in the ASL literature. Klima and Bellugi (1979) describe a horizontal indexic plane at about the level of the lower chest upon which indexes are established. As they describe it, agreement verbs then move toward or away from these indexes. However, Johnson and Liddell (1984) show that agreement verbs do not necessarily move toward or away from an index. They observe that often agreement verbs move at a height that may be obviously different than the height at which the index was established.

In figure 3 the agreement verb ASK moves "in the direction" of the locus but at a higher level. The fact that the sign ASK is made at chin height is a lexical property of the verb rather than a reflection of the height of the locus at which an index was established. Table 1 presents a representative list of verbs and the heights at which they would be made with respect to a locus established at trunk height. These heights are the heights at which these signs would be produced if the referent were physically present. When no referent is present or conceived of as present the

*Table 1.* **Lexically Specified Heights for Some Agreement Verbs**

| Verb | Height |
|------|--------|
| ESP-WITH | forehead |
| SAY-NO-TO | nose |
| ASK | chin |
| REMIND | shoulder |
| GIVE | chest |

signer produces these verbs at heights corresponding to heights on the signer's own body. This type of data demonstrate clearly that agreement verbs (as a class) are not directed toward a locus at which an index has been established. Individual verbs may be directed toward such a locus if the lexically specified height of the verb coincides with the height of that locus. But this is a result of the lexically specified height matching the height of the locus, rather than features of the locus determining the height of the verb.

The evidence above strongly suggests that the relationship between the spatial loci discussed above and their referents is not referential equality but location fixing. Establishing an index serves as a way of saying where the referent is, not what point is referentially equivalent to the referent. Evidence for this conclusion comes from the fact that agreement verbs were not directed toward the locus at which the index was established, but directed to points in space whose height was a function of the lexical properties of the verb rather than a function of the height of the locus.

An agreement verb can refer to a nonpresent referent, even without having established an index at a locus in space. This occurs in figure 12, where the referent is mentioned for the first time after the agreement verb. Since the verb ASK is directed toward the right, without anyone having been located in that direction, the signer identifies the object by producing a nominal object of the verb with the sign MOTHER.[9] Signers know that the verb ASK is directed toward the person being asked and they also know that the person asked was "mother." It is not difficult then, to make a connection between space on the right side of the signing space and the referent "mother." This appears to locate "mother" on that side of the signing space.

### Agreement Verbs and Loci on the Body

It is possible to locate entities on the body. This can be done easily with classifier predicates. For example, figure 13 shows how a signer could talk about an ant on someone's forearm using a classifier predicate. Locus $z$ represents a location on someone's forearm. We can assume that the ant is being described as on the signer's own forearm. If the ant associated with locus $z$ was a very intelligent ant capable of understanding questions, figure 14 shows how the signer could talk about asking the ant a question.

ASK (right)                    MOTHER

*Figure 12.* **An agreement verb used without a previously established index.**

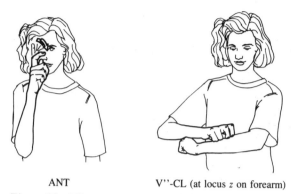

ANT        V''-CL (at locus *z* on forearm)

*Figure 13.* **'There was an ant on (someone's) forearm.'**

In this example it looks like the sign is directed toward the locus where the ant is located, thereby making reference to the ant. But this is an illusion. In order to demonstrate this it is necessary to deal with animals larger than an ant. Suppose that a signer was talking about a falcon on his arm at the same locus *z*. Figure 15a shows how one would talk about asking the falcon a question. The sign is directed at the location of the imagined falcon's head. This is exactly the way that agreement verbs behave with a present entity (real or imagined) as opposed to a spatial locus. If the sign ASK is directed at the locus *z*, the result is ungrammatical for the intended meaning.

But what about the ant on the forearm? The ant is so small that the location of its head is indistinguishable from the locus *z*. Directing the sign ASK toward the location of the ant's head is not physically distinguishable from directing the sign toward the locus *z*.

Establishing an index at *z* on the forearm with a classifier can have quite different consequences from establishing an index at a spatial locus *x* with a classifier. Establishing an index at a spatial locus does not necessitate the conceptualization of an invisible body. Based on evidence such as that presented above, however, establishing an index on the body does involve the conceptualization of an invisible body. Earlier we saw that persons or entities imagined as present involved conceptualizing a body

*Figure 14.* **1-ASK-(ant on arm).**
**'I asked the ant on my forearm.'**

**Figure 15**. **1-ASK-(falcon).**
**'I asked the falcon on my forearm.'**

for that person or entity. Locating a bird on one's arm certainly seems to place it in the signer's presence. It makes sense, then, that the bird would acquire a conceptualized body.

The evidence described above demonstrates that, as before, the relationship between a referent and a locus on the body is one of location fixing. It is perhaps even easier to see with a body locus, since in the examples presented the referent associated with the locus acquired a body. It is not the locus on which the body was placed that represents the referent, but the invisible body that is imagined to be located at that locus. One correctly makes reference to the referent by directing an agreement verb toward the appropriate part of the invisible body, not by directing the agreement verb toward the locus on the signer's body on which the referent is imagined to be located.

### Classifier Handshapes Located at Spatial Loci

The previous example, where a spatial locus was established, did not necessitate the conceptualization of an invisible body for the referent associated with that locus. The next example (figure 16) also makes use of a spatial locus, but this time the weak hand is at that locus while the active hand produces the agreement verb.

This type of example might arise if the signer had been using the 1-classifier to describe the someone's movements. The 1-classifier could be left at its locus and the verb ASK could then be directed toward it. In this example the 1-classifier is located at $y$, representing a standing person. Notice that the agreement verb is directed toward the classifier handshape.

In the previous example of an agreement verb and a spatial locus (without a classifier handshape involved) each verb had a lexically specified height toward which it was directed. This does not occur when a classifier handshape is present. Instead, agreement verbs are directed at the classifier handshape. The agreement verb does not appear to be directed at the top or the bottom of the 1-classifier, but at the middle of the extended index finger. Agreement verbs seem to be directed at the finger as a whole rather than different parts of the finger. Thus, although the three agreement verbs INFORM, TELL, and GIFT$_v$, are each made at a different height in the presence of a referent or spatially established index, there are no height differences when directed toward a 1-classifier.

*Figure 16.* **ASK-(1-CL)-at-y**
**'(Someone) asked (the person established on my left).'**

Since agreement verbs are directed toward the classifier handshape, this provides evidence that the handshape is functioning as the body of the referent. In contrast to real or imagined bodies, however, the classifier body does not appear to have body parts toward which agreement verbs can be directed. An agreement verb is simply directed at what appears to be the center of the extended finger.

This phenomenon of directing an agreement verb at the center of an object also occurs when an agreement verb is directed toward a physically present entity which has no discernible body parts (Fischer and Gough, 1978, 27). For example, if a signer were describing asking a boulder (which has no anthropomorphic character- istics) the sign ASK would be directed (more or less) toward the center of the boulder. Placing a classifier handshape at a spatial locus seems to provide a body toward which agreement verbs can be directed. The classifier body, however, does not provide us with evidence that it is treated as having discernible body parts toward which different agreement verbs are directed.

Once again, the relationship seen here between a locus and a referent is one of location fixing. The assumption being made here is that the base of the classifier handshape is located at the locus in question. This seems like a reasonable assumption since this is what can be seen when the classifier is located on a visible surface such as the forearm. Reference is made by directing an agreement verb toward the classifier handshape rather than to the place at which the classifier is located.

### Ordinal Loci on the Thumbtip and Fingertips

The tip of the thumb and four fingers of the hand (when placed as in figure 17) allow associations to be made between them and individual referents. It is possible to make associations with up to five entities depending on how many fingers are extended in addition to the thumb. When entities are associated with these loci, they have an inherent order. The tip of the thumb is first, the tip of the index finger is second, and so on until the tip of the little finger, which is last.

One typical use of this type of ordinal enumeration is to list siblings in the order of their birth. The utterance illustrated in figure 17 illustrates the beginning of such an enumeration of siblings. This would normally be followed by stating who was second born, third, fourth, and last. The two signs in figure 17 establish a relationship between the brother in question and the tip of the thumb. That relationship is estab-

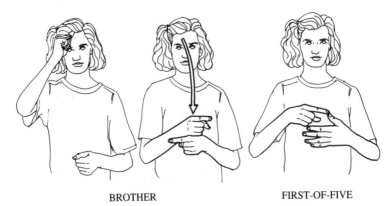

BROTHER                    FIRST-OF-FIVE

*Figure 17.* **'(My) brother is the first of five (oldest).'**

lished by naming the referent and then touching the tip of the thumb. Reference is subsequently made by directing the agreement verb toward the tip of the thumb. Figure 18 demonstrates this with the verb 1-GIFT-(thumb locus). This might look like earlier examples in which an agreement verb is directed at a classifier (figure 17), but the behavior of the agreement verb is not the same. When an ordinal tip locus is used a pronoun or agreement verb is directed toward the tip of the thumb or finger, not at the whole thumb or finger.

Of all the examples examined in this paper so far, this is the only one in which agreement verbs are directed toward the locus at which an index has been established. There is also another important difference between the thumbtip and fingertip loci and all other loci described above. The thumb locus and fingertip loci do not correspond to locations in abstract space. This requires some explanation.

A locus can also *represent* a spatial location. That is, the locus that we have been referring to with the letter *x* is roughly a foot or so ahead of the signer's shoulder. But signers are quite comfortable uttering a statement such as that in figure 19, CAR 3-CL:BE-LOCATED-AT-x. This simple clause does not mean 'a vehicle is suspended in air roughly a foot ahead of my shoulder.' The signer is making a statement that a vehicle is located in a certain position someplace other than just ahead of the shoulder. In the physical situation that prompts the utterance, the vehicle might be

*Figure 18.* **1-GIFT-(thumb locus).**
**'I give (it) to [referent associated with thumb locus].'**

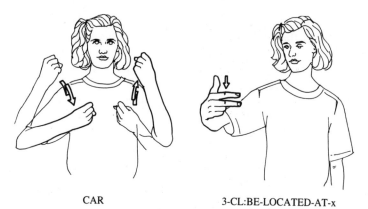

CAR                    3-CL:BE-LOCATED-AT-x

*Figure 19.* **'A car is there on my right.'**

several yards away, but the actual distance is simply not mentioned in figure 19. Signers understand that the vehicle was further away than twelve or fourteen inches. This makes it clear that a locus represents a much more abstract location than just "the space in front of the signer." In fact, the signing space can be conceived of as representing an abstract three-dimensional space. A locus $x$ that is physically lower in the signing space than a locus $x'$ represents a location that is lower than that represented by locus $x'$. The spatial relationships between the locations represented by spatial loci work in all three dimensions (up-down, left-right, and in-out).

In figure 19, the verb 3-CL:BE-LOCATED-AT-x locates a car (since CAR is the subject of that verb) in a three-dimensional abstract space. The articulatory space in front of the signer can represent an abstract space unrelated to the singer of an abstract space in which the singer is present.[10] In 3-CL:BE-LOCATED-AT-x, the signer is making use of the latter space, stating that the vehicle was located to her right.

Ordinal tip loci provide evidence that they do not correspond to locations in an abstract three-dimensional space. After establishing an index for "brother" at the tip of the thumb, it would be ungrammatical to attempt to say that a man was standing next to my brother (figure 20). This example is ungrammatical and nonsensical. The

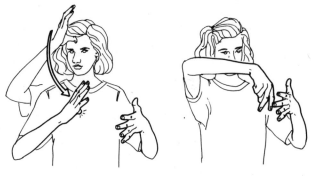

*Figure 20.* *   MAN            **V-CL:BE-LOCATED-AT-y**
                                **FIVE-ENTITIES ⎯⎯⎯→**

ill-formedness of this example demonstrates that although it is possible to establish an index at the tip of the thumb, that locus is not capable of being related to points in abstract space.

The tip of the thumb (or finger) is also not capable of serving as the location for a classifier predicate. It is grammatical to locate a 1-classifier at a locus ahead of the signer (figure 21a), but it is not possible to locate the same classifier at an ordinal tip locus as in figure 21b. Based on the ungrammaticality of 21b, there must be a requirement that a classifier predicate is required to make use of a three-dimensional space. Such a space is not available when the tip of the thumb is functioning as an ordinal index.

In contrast to the examples in all the previous sections, the relationship between ordinal tip loci and their referents seems to be one of referential equality. For anaphoric purposes a locus is designated as being equivalent to a referent. To make reference to that referent an agreement verb or pronoun is directed toward that locus.

## THE RELATIONSHIP BETWEEN A LOCUS
## AND A REFERENT

The term ''index'' has been used in this paper to refer to a locus that is associated with a referent. I have attempted to distinguish two distinct senses that could describe the relationship between the locus and referent: referential equality and location fixing. The majority of the cases examined above were best described as location fixing rather than referential equality.

The traditional evidence for referential equality rested on the claim that pronouns and agreement verbs point toward an index, thereby referring to the referent associated with that index. But with the exception of ordinal tip loci, all of the other examples contradict this description of an index.

A summary of the behavior of agreement verbs with respect to the various types of loci and referents is presented in table 2. In cases a and b, where a referent is present or imagined to be present, there is no evidence at all for a relationship between a locus and a referent. There is no need for such a relationship. Since the referent is present or conceived of as present, the signer merely directs the verb or pronoun at the referent or its visualized substitute.

21a.  1-CL-at-x                           21b.  *1-CL-at-thumbtip
(contact root)                                  (contact root)

***Figure 21*. Two versions of the contact root.**

**Table 2. Summary of Agreement-Verb Behavior**

|  |  | Index established | Type of index | Goal of verb's movement |
|---|---|---|---|---|
| a. | Present referent | no | — | Referent [height on referent lexically determined] |
| b. | Imagined referent | no | — | Visualized substitute referent [height on substitute lexically determined] |
| c. | Spatial locus | yes | Location Fixing | Nonvisualized substitute referent [since substitute has no body, height of verb determined by height of signer] |
| d. | Body locus | yes | Location Fixing | Visualized substitute referent [height on substitute lexically determined] |
| e. | CL at spatial locus | yes | Location Fixing | Visible substitute referent [referent represented by classifier] |
| f. | Ordinal tip locus | yes | Referential Equality | Visible substitute referent [locus = referent] |

In cases c through e a substitute referent is conceived of as located at a locus. In two of those cases (d and e) there is a visualized referent or classifier toward which the agreement verb can be directed. Case c is the most abstract case since there is no conceptualized body nor is there a classifier or other physical object toward which the verb can be directed. The claim made in table 2 is that the verb is directed toward a substitute referent with no body (real or conceptualized). If a real body were present, the sign ASK would be directed at the chin level of the referent. Since there is no body (real or conceptualized) toward which to direct the verb, the verb is produced at the signer's own chin height in the direction of the nonvisualized substitute referent.

The most general statement that can be made with respect to agreement verbs is that they are directed toward their actual or substitute referents. In only one of the cases in table 2 does that mean directing the verb toward the locus at which an index has been established. When this occurs (case f), there is reason to say that the locus and the referent are associated through referential equality.

## FOUR FUNCTIONS OF A LOCUS

### *Articulatory Function*

I have been using the term "locus" to refer to a point on the body or in the signing space that serves an articulatory function. The hand can be at that point (as in DOG) or not at that point (as in the beginning of the sign MY). Such a locus need not have any semantic import whatsoever. When it serves as a phonologically significant point in articulatory space, it is being used with an articulatory function.

### 3-D Function

A locus can also represent a spatial location. This was referred to earlier in the paper when mention was made of the concept of a stage upon which referents were placed. For example, suppose a signer makes a statement such as CAR 3-CL:BE-LOCATED-AT-x, where the locus $x$ is roughly a foot or so ahead of the signer's shoulder. The signer is making a statement that a vehicle is located in a certain position someplace other than just ahead of the shoulder. Physically the classifier handshape is located at $x$, but semantically it means that the car is located at some other place. So $x$ seems to be performing a semantic function, in addition to its articulatory function. The locus $x$ represents a location other than itself. In fact, the signing space can be conceived of as representing an abstract three-dimensional space.

The verb 3-CL:BE-LOCATED-AT-x locates a car (since CAR is the subject of that verb) in a three-dimensional abstract space. Loci in the signing space ahead of the fingertips represent positions ahead of the vehicle. The space beside the palm represents space to the side of the vehicle. The space beside the back of the hand represents space to the other side of the vehicle. Finally, the space above and below the vehicle handshape represents space above and below the car.

Using loci in the space ahead of the signer to represent other locations is common in ASL, occurring in all the examples of classifier usage in this paper. Translations of classifier predicates typically contain the word "there" (for example, A car was over there). The hand moves to a specific locus in the signing space to produce such a sign, but that locus is not the "real" location of the car. This use of loci in the three-dimensional signing space to correspond to locations in a three-dimensional abstract conceptual space is the "3-D" function of a locus.

### Location-Fixing Function

This function came into play in all the examples of "establishing an index" described above except for the thumbtip and fingertips. A substitute referent is "placed" at a location through the use of a classifier predicate (including the contact root), or through other locative signs, such as the index finger pointing and moving downward toward a locus, as in GIRL THERE$_x$. This utterance actually involves three functions simultaneously. The locus $x$ serves an articulatory function since that is the point in articulatory space toward which the index finger is directed. It also serves the location fixing function since the girl is now "located" at that locus. The locus $x$ also serves the 3-D function since it corresponds to a location in an abstract three-dimensional space.

### Referential Equality Function

This is the function that has generally been assumed to be in play whenever an index is established. When this function of a locus is operating there is a referential equality set up between a locus and a referent. This occurs in the discussion above where an index is established at an ordinal tip locus (at the tip of the fingers or thumb). Subsequently directing an agreement verb toward that locus makes reference to that referent.

Only two functions of a locus are at play with an ordinal tip locus: the articulatory function and the referential equality function. The tip of the thumb and fingers do not correspond to any points in an abstract space nor do they serve (in this usage) as places upon which entities are located.

## SYNTACTIC VERSUS TOPOGRAPHICAL SPACE

Poizner, Klima, and Bellugi (1987) analyze space in ASL as composed of two nonoverlapping and distinct spaces. "Clearly, the internal representation for mapping relies heavily on the inherent spatial relationships among objects described in the real world, whereas the internal representation for syntax is based on abstract linguistic syntactic properties, despite their realization in a spatial medium" (1987, 211). In the first, loci are related to one another in a three-dimensional sense. In the second, agreement verbs move toward, from, and between loci indicating their subjects and objects. In this conception these loci have no locational (that is, topographical) import. They are simply points associated with referents.

The evidence presented in this paper contradicts this view. First, I argue that with the exception of the ordinal tip loci, establishing an index locates an entity. Second, classifier predicates can be used to locate entities and agreement verbs can make reference to those same entities at those locations. Conversely, a locus established without a classifier (by pointing for example) can serve as a location toward which or from which other classifier predicates can move. This could take the form of a new referent entering the scene or the movement of the established referent. This should not be possible if there were not already a topographical (locative) component present in the first place.

Interestingly, I find five points (not a space) that behave nontopographically: the tip of the thumb and four fingertips. For these loci a referential equality can be established between each locus and a referent. These loci have no topographical import and are not related to one another in a spatially significant way. Since these loci do not have a topographical component, it is not possible to locate a classifier predicate on them or near them.

## CONCLUSION

The model of the structure of space in ASL, particularly as it relates to agreement verbs, has revolved around the notion of establishing an index. It has been assumed that establishing an index means making an association between a locus and a referent. The purpose of this association has been to facilitate subsequent reference to that referent, which could be accomplished through directing a sign toward the particular locus. The problem with this model is that, in general, agreement verbs and pronouns are not directed toward such loci.

In the model that this paper begins to outline, a locus can perform one or more of four functions: articulatory, 3-D, location fixing, and referential equality. The most important of these for agreement verbs are the location-fixing and the referential-equality functions. Of these two, referential equality is the easiest to describe. A locus is associated anaphorically with a referent. Subsequently directing an agreement verb toward that locus makes reference to the referent associated with that locus.

Location fixing is more difficult to describe because agreement verbs operate differently depending on the particular locus. Establishing an index at a spatial locus fixes the location of a substitute referent at that locus. This means that there is an entity "there" at that locus. But this does not set up a referential equality between the entity and the locus. Instead of being directed toward the locus (on an indexic plane), agreement verbs are directed toward the substitute referent that is "at" that locus. This may take the form of an imagined body at that locus, a classifier at that locus, or even no body at all at that locus. In the last case, the verb is directed at body heights equal to body heights on the signer's own body. The heights at which the agreement verbs are produced are a lexical property of those verbs.

When referents are present, or conceived of as present, agreement verbs are directed at them. Exactly where the agreement verb is directed is a property of the agreement verb itself. Each verb has its own height on the body toward which it is directed. In several of the cases described above, a spatial image of the referent is necessary in order to be able to produce the agreement verb. One of the inescapable conclusions of this paper is that spatial imagery plays a much more central role in the grammar of ASL than has been previously thought.

Finally, the evidence supports the idea that space is not divided into a syntactic space and a topographical space. Instead, what seems to be a syntactic space may really be topographical, and agreement verbs make significant use of that topographical space by being directed toward their referents (or substitutes). Under very restricted circumstances, when a referent is equated with an ordinal tip locus, the agreement verb is directed toward the locus, which stands for the referent.

## NOTES

This is a revised version of a paper originally entitled "Three Functions of a Locus," which was presented at the second Theoretical Issues in Sign Language Research Conference, Gallaudet University, May 1988. I am grateful to Robert E. Johnson, Ceil Lucas, and Elisabeth Engberg-Pedersen for reading and commenting on earlier drafts of this paper. Their comments led to substantive improvements in the final version. The illustrations in this paper are by Paul M. Setzer. The production of the illustrations was supported by the Gallaudet Research Institute.

1. Padden (1983) refers to this process as "locus shifting."
2. ASL agreement verbs agree with their referents, but the basis for that agreement does not seem to be person. The description of the type of agreement involved, however, goes beyond the scope of this paper. In the text I will refer to this simply as "agreement."
3. Not all spatial verbs and not all agreement verbs move with respect to two loci. I have selected an agreement verb and a spatial verb that each have important beginning and end points. As Supalla (1978) points out, some classifier predicates move from a locus, some move to a locus, and some move past a locus.
4. Loci determine the path that agreement verbs like ASK take, but the agreement verbs do not necessarily move between or toward the loci that were originally established. For the moment I will talk about them as if they did.

5. This is possible, but setting up an index for the addressee (or any other present referent) simply adds another ''third person'' referent to the conversation. That referent happens to be identified with the addressee, but reference to that index works like reference to other nonpresent entities.
6. Fisher and Gough (1978) mention that signs move upward if the addressee is taller than the signer or down if the addressee is shorter. They do not mention that individual verbs have specific heights at which they are produced.
7. Padden (1986) calls this ''role shifting.''
8. Not enough types of data have been examined to determine whether this always happens when a role is adopted.
9. It is clear that MOTHER is the object of the verb ASK because of its syntactic position. Had the signer produced the utterance MOTHER ASK (right), it would mean 'mother asked someone.'
10. The distinction between classifier predicates that make spatial representations unrelated to the signer versus those that include the signer as perceiver or participant (predicates of perceived motion) is made in Lucas and Valli (in press).

# REFERENCES

Baker, C. and Cokely, D. (1980). American Sign Language: A teacher's resource text on grammar and culture. Silver Spring, MD: T.J. Publishers.

DeMatteo, A. (1977). Visual imagery and visual analogues in American Sign Language. In *On the other hand*, edited by L. Friedman, 109–36. New York: Academic Press.

Fischer, S. and Gough, B. (1978). Verbs in American Sign Language. *Sign Language Studies* 18:17–48.

Friedman, L. (1975). Space, time, and person reference in American Sign Language. *Language* 51:940–61.

————. (1976). Phonology of a soundless language: Phonological structure of American Sign Language. Ph.D. diss., University of California, Berkeley.

Johnson, R. E., and Liddell, S. K. (1984). Structural diversity in the American Sign Language lexicon. In *Papers from the parasession on lexical semantics*, edited by D. Testen, V. Mishra, and J. Drogo, 173–86. Chicago, IL: Chicago Linguistic Society.

————, and Liddell, S. (1987). A morphological analysis of subject-object agreement in American Sign Language. Paper presented at the Fourth International Conference on Sign Language Research, 15–19 July, Lapeenranta, Finland.

Klima, E., and Bellugi, U. (1979). The signs of language. Cambridge, MA: Harvard University Press.

Liddell, S. (1980). American Sign Language syntax. The Hague: Mouton.

————, and Johnson R. (1987). An analysis of spatial-locative predicates in American Sign Language. Paper presented at the Fourth International Conference on Sign Language Research, 15–19 July, Lapeenranta, Finland.

————, and Johnson, R. (in preparation). Aspects of American Sign Language phonology and morphology. Gallaudet University. Unpublished manuscript.

Lillo-Martin, D. and Klima, E. (in press). Pointing out the differences: ASL pronouns in syntactic theory. In *Theoretical issues in sign language research, I: Linguistics* edited by S. Fisher and P. Siple. Chicago: University of Chicago Press.

Loew, R. (1984). Roles and reference in American Sign Language: A developmental perspective. Ph.D. diss., University of Minnesota.

Lucas, C. and Valli, C. (in press). Predicates of perceived motion. In *Theoretical issues in sign language research I: Linguistics*, edited by S. Fischer and P. Siple. Chicago: University of Chicago Press.

Padden, C. (1981). Some arguments for syntactic patterning in American Sign Language. *Sign Language Studies* 32:239–59.

————. (1983). Interaction of morphology and syntax in American Sign Language. University of California, San Diego.

Poizner, H., Klima, E., and Bellugi, U. (1987). *What the hands reveal about the brain*. Cambridge, MA: MIT Press.

Supalla, T. (1978). Morphology of verbs of motion and location in American Sign Language. *Proceedings of the Second National Symposium on Sign Language Research and Teaching*, edited by F. Caccamise, 27–45. Silver Spring, MD: National Association of the Deaf.

————. (1986). The classifier system in American Sign Language. In *Noun classes and categorization*, edited by C. Craig, 181–214. Philadelphia: John Benjamins Publishing Co.

Wilbur, R. (1987). *American Sign Language, linguistic and applied dimensions*, 2d ed. Boston, MA: College Hill Press.

# PART

# III

# SYNTAX

# A Class of Determiners in ASL

## June Zimmer and Cynthia Patschke

This paper examines a particular class of pointing signs in ASL. It will be shown that this class of signs is distinct from other pointing signs in several ways. The analysis provided here gives support to the idea that these signs act as determiners.

Sign language researchers who discuss pointing signs in ASL have arrived at diverse conclusions as to their syntactic, semantic, and pragmatic functions. Lacy (1973) finds that signers establish referents in particular locations in signing space and use pointing signs that act as pronouns to reference these locations. O'Malley (1975) distinguishes two types of pronouns: deictic, which refer to objects that are physically present; and anaphoric, which refer to objects that are not actually present.

Mandel (1977) and Wilbur (1979) propose that the pronoun is the point in space rather than the pointing gesture, and that the pointing gesture merely indicates which referent is meant. However, most researchers (Coulter, 1977; Liddell, 1980; Pettito, 1983; Padden, 1983) agree that these signs do function as pronouns. Liddell (1980) has shown that they appear in the syntactic positions reserved for subjects and objects, thus acting in the same way as personal pronouns in spoken languages like English.

Freidman (1975) speaks of these signs in terms of "proforms," which are used to achieve all pronominal, most locative, and some temporal references. Edge and Herrman (1977) and Hoffmeister (1977) also use the term "proforms." Edge and Herrman state that proforms can reference people, objects, time, and locations. Like Mandel (1977) and Wilbur (1979), they claim that the pointing sign merely functions as an indicator rather than a lexical item. In their view, the proforms consist of locations in space or of "markers," which can take the form of the signer's body or hand "which are understood or explicitly labeled to take on the identity of referents" (1977, 142). Hoffmeister (1978), on the other hand, calls the pointing sign itself the proform and says that it functions as a personal pronoun, a demonstrative pronoun, or a prolocative.

Several researchers (Liddell, 1980; Padden, 1983; Aramburo, 1986) have studied pointing signs used as locatives. Ingram (1978) notes that the pointing of the finger is one of the many possible markers for ASL topics. Hoffmeister (1977, 1978) and Wilbur (1979) briefly mention that pointing signs also function as determiners.

From this discussion it is obvious that descriptions of the forms and uses of pointing gestures are diverse and ambiguous. One might assume from the literature that one sign performs many different functions, and that this sign is made by pointing to a particular location in neutral space. However, a close examination indicates that pointing signs constitute several different lexical items.

This paper focuses on a class of pointing signs that are phonologically and syntactically distinguished from other pointing signs. The analysis and discussion support the notion that this class of signs act as determiners.

## METHODOLOGY

The data for this project come from two main sources. The first set comes from videotape recordings of ten deaf native signers of ASL. The tapes were transcribed using a system of written English glosses, and drawings were made to document the various forms pointing signs could take.

The second set of data comes from work with several deaf informants. The time spent with the informants was mainly used to elicit particular types of data, to ask specific questions, and to check hypotheses. These data were collected in the form of notes in which ASL signs were recorded using English glosses.

In the analysis of these written transcripts and notes, each occurrence of a pointing sign was described according to its phonological form, placement in a clause or phrase, signs preceding or following it, and apparent meaning and function.

## PHONOLOGICAL ANALYSIS

Although the pointing signs mentioned in the literature are composed of a variety of movements, locations, and orientations, the category of signs examined in this paper is quite restricted in form. The vast majority of these signs point slightly upward (see figure 1). These signs, made with the nondominant hand, are often simultaneous with a sign on the dominant hand. In this case, they are sometimes lowered (see figure 2). Eye gaze is variable, sometimes remaining on the addressee, sometimes following the direction of the point.

These signs are phonologically distinct from other pointing signs with arcing or jabbing movements. Aramburo (1986) describes varying forms of locative pointing signs, all of which involve an arcing movement. Other pointing signs in our data have a jabbing movement, which is often repeated. Neither of these classes of pointing signs will be discussed here. This paper focuses on signs that move slightly or not at all, never arc or jab, and most often point slightly upward.

## SYNTACTIC ANALYSIS

A large corpus of signs with this particular phonological form were analyzed according to their syntactic function. It soon became apparent that these signs could be divided into two syntactic categories: pronouns and determiners.[1]

The use of pointing signs as pronouns has been well documented, but will be briefly reviewed here. Pronominalization in ASL has been said to involve the indexing of a particular area in signing space. A pointing sign acting as a pronoun is distin-

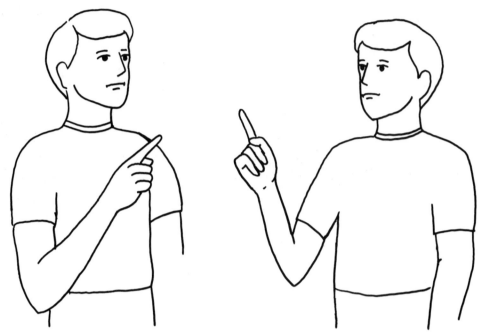

*Figure 1.* **Pointing signs on dominant hand.**

guished by its function and by its placement within a clause. In ASL, the first-person-singular pronoun is signed with the tip of the index finger moving to make contact with the chest (transcribed as PRO.1). Describing the syntactic function of this pronoun helps to identify other pronouns in ASL, and to help discriminate them from other uses of pointing signs. Examples 1 and 2 are examples of first-person-singular pronouns.

(1) PRO.1 CL:PICK-UP-PIECES
'I picked up the pieces.'
(2) NEVER SEE BOY BREAK-INTO-TEARS FOR PRO.1
'I'd never seen a boy burst out crying over me.'

The pronouns all stand alone. In accordance with the definition of pronouns, they are "noun phrases of the simplest possible structure, which, as a rule, allow neither premodification nor postmodification" (Aarts and Aarts, 1982, 49). ASL pronouns function in a similar way to English pronouns, except that there is no gender marking or case marking.

Pointing signs acting as pronouns are shown in sentences 3 and 4. (Henceforth [p.s.] will be used to indicate a pointing sign).

(3) [p.s.] COOK THAT GREEN CL:SMALL-CYLINDER
'He cooked celery.'
(4) PRO.1 LIKE [p.s.]
'I liked him.'

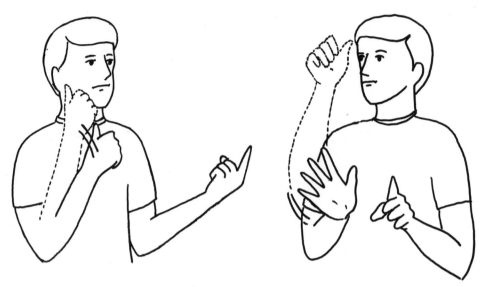

*Figure 2*. **Pointing signs on nondominant hand simultaneously produced with sign on dominant hand.**

In accordance with the definition of third-person pronouns, these signs can be replaced by the noun phrase for the person, place, or thing to which they refer. The pointing sign constitutes the whole noun phrase. This is illustrated in the phrase structure trees of sentences 3 and 4 (see figure 3).

Many of the pointing signs in this corpus do not act as pronouns. A pronoun, as mentioned above, must stand alone in a noun phrase. However, pointing signs sometimes occur with nouns rather than replacing them, as in sentences 5 and 6.

(5) [p.s.] GIRL ALL-DAY WORK
'The girl worked all day long.'
(6) OTHER MAN [p.s.] STEAL
'The other man had stolen it.'

The data collected for this study are consistent with the notion put forward by Hoffmeister (1977) and Wilbur (1979) that pointing signs may act as determiners. The tree diagrams of sentences 5 and 6 indicate that the pointing sign, together with the noun, constitutes the noun phrase (see figure 4).

## POINTING SIGNS AS DETERMINERS

Since the pointing signs discussed above occur with nouns in noun phrases, they serve to modify nouns. They don't contain a great deal of semantic content nor do they describe nouns. Thus they do not function as adjectives. When asked why these signs were being used, the informants stated that they "specify" the noun. These observations indicate that these signs function as some type of determiner.

In English, determiners are usually considered to include the articles "a" and "the," the demonstrative pronouns ("this," "that," "these," and "those"), pos-

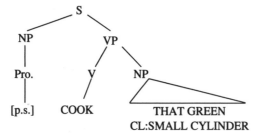

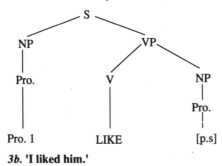

*3a.* **'He cooked celery.'**

*3b.* **'I liked him.'**

***Figure 3.*** **Phrase structure trees for 'He cooked celery' and 'I like him.'**

sessive pronouns, and quantifiers like "any," "other," "some," "none," etc. (Stockwell, Schachter, and Partee, 1973; Huddleston, 1984; Givon, 1984). They help "determine" which object is being referred to. Determiners can be either definite or indefinite. The factors that dictate whether a definite or an indefinite determiner will be used have not been fully described. However, it is generally agreed that a definite determiner is used when the interlocutor can be expected to be able to locate a referent (for example, "the girl," "that book," "my mother") because such a determiner is anaphoric (makes reference to prior discourse) or deictic (makes reference to an entity that is present). An indefinite determiner will be used when the particular referent cannot be identified (for example, "a girl," "some books," "anyone's mother"). A noun phrase in English can contain up to three determiners as in "all her many friends" (Huddleston, 1984).

The data examined for this study support Wilbur's (1979) claim that pointing determiners may occur before, after, or simultaneously with a noun, as in sentences 7 through 10: (Pointing determiners will be labeled "DET" throughout the rest of the paper.)

(7) Before the noun
SEE DET GIRL
'He saw a girl.'
(8) After the noun
OTHER SISTER DET COME
'The other sister came over.'
(9) Simultaneously with the noun
SAME MAN/DET CL:ONE PERSON-MOVES-TOWARD-ANOTHER
'The same man was walking towards her.'

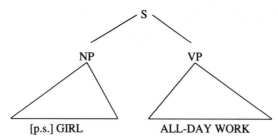

*4a.* **'The girl worked all day long.'**

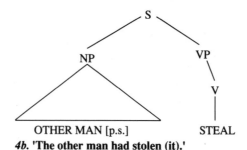

OTHER MAN [p.s.]                    STEAL
*4b.* **'The other man had stolen (it).'**

***Figure 4.* Tree diagrams indicating pointing signs.**

As in English, ASL permits more than one determiner to occur in a noun phrase. Many examples of a pointing determiner occurring with other signs that act as determiners, such as OTHER and THAT, were found in these data, as in sentence 10:[2]

(10) OTHER MAN DET THAT^DET ENTER
'The other man, that one, came in.'

Wilbur (1979) hypothesizes that the definite/indefinite distinction in ASL may be made by the contrast between the existence of a surface determiner (in which case a noun phrase is definite) or the lack of a surface determiner (in which case it is indefinite). The data in this study, however, are not consistent with this hypothesis. One clear case in which one would expect to see an indefinite determiner is that in which a character in a story who is unknown to the interlocutor is being mentioned for the first time. But, we found many instances in which a noun being mentioned for the first time does occur with a determiner. In sentence 11, one of the signers is telling a story about an experience he and a friend had at the beach. A clumsy man walks by and spills a can of soda on his friend. In this utterance, the man is being mentioned for the first time.

(11) DET FAT-KLUTZ MAN CL:WALK-CLUMSILY
'A fat klutzy guy was walking clumsily toward us.'

We found several instances in which a newly mentioned noun occurs without a determiner, but by far the most usual case was that in which a determiner is present.

## Determiners with Specific and Concrete Nouns

We found no instances of pointing signs being used with generic nouns. The informants in this study indicated that pointing determiners are used to describe only specific entities. Sentences 12 and 13 provide examples of a permissible utterance and an ungrammatical utterance:

(12) MY CAR DET BETTER THAN POSS.3 CAR DET
'My car is better than his car.'
(13) *TOYOTA DET BETTER THAN HONDA DET
'The Toyotas are better than the Hondas.'

In addition, we found no instances of pointing determiners being used with abstract nouns. The informants also judged as ungrammatical the use of pointing signs simultaneously with signs such as CONCEPT and THEORY.

These data seem to indicate, therefore, that pointing determiners in ASL are used only with concrete nouns that refer to specific entities. It is also possible that pointing determiners are used only with count nouns, although this needs to be investigated further. As yet, we have identified no process marking the definite/indefinite distinction. Our original hypothesis was that this distinction is marked by whether the determiner occurs before or after the noun, but a thorough investigation proved this hypothesis to be unfounded.

## Arbitrary Direction of the Point

One particularly interesting discovery is that the direction of the point is most often insignificant. It has been generally accepted that signers set up entities at different locations in space. In a story with several different characters, the claim has been that each character is identified with one particular location in the signing space. In this view, the location remains constant until the signer indicates that the character has moved to a new location (Padden, 1983). This view also claims that a pointing gesture in the direction of a location associated with a character is used when referring back to this character.

The characters in the stories we examined, however, are typically not set up in this way. In most cases, the determiners used with many different characters point to the same location. In fact, the data indicate that signers tend to have a preferred location that they use consistently for their determiners. When we asked one of the informants to tell the story of "Cinderella," the determiners used with nouns to indicate each of the characters were most often identical in form—that is, handshape, orientation, and (most notably) location were the same. These observations show that the locations to which these signs point do not distinguish characters from one another. Furthermore, even determiners occurring with nouns indicating places (for example, HOME and B-A-L-L) show no distinction in location. Also the determiners used with one character are not consistently directed toward one location. Occasionally the determiners used with GIRL (indicating Cinderella), were directed toward a different location, with no apparent semantic or pragmatic reason for doing so. It appears, then, that the direction in which a determiner points is arbitrary. One particularly clear example of this occurs in sentence 14. This utterance occurred in a story in which one of the characters was a woman sitting in the back seat of a car. The story teller, referring to the woman in the back seat signed the utterance (LOC here refers to a pointing sign functioning as a locative).

> (14) DET (to the left) WOMAN LOC (to the back)
> 'The woman in the back . . . '

The determiner in this case points toward the left, whereas the locative points toward the back.

### Determiners with Plural Nouns

We also found determiners of the same form used with plural nouns, as in sentence 15.

> (15) FLIRT MANY GIRL DET SERVE KING
> 'He was flirting with the king's serving girls.'

In sentence 15 the determiner follows the noun GIRL, which is pluralized by the addition of the sign MANY. However, the form of the determiner is the same as that used with a singular noun. Plural pronouns, on the other hand, use an arcing movement as in sentence 16.

> (16) PRO.1 ASK PRO.3 (arcing movement).
> 'I asked them.'

### Determiners with Personal Names and Possessives

We found that pointing signs can occur with personal names, indicating another difference between English determiners and ASL determiners. We observed occurrences of ASL determiners being used with proper nouns in both the videotaped narratives and in the work with informants. Sentence 17 is one example of a determiner used with a personal name:

> (17) BILL DET TAKE-ADVANTAGE ANN
> 'Bill took advantage of Ann.'

ASL determiners also appear with possessives, as in sentence 18:

> (18) MY CAR DET BETTER THAN POSS.3 CAR DET
> 'My car is better than his car.'

## SUMMARY

In this study, pointing signs that act as determiners have been phonologically and syntactically distinguished from other pointing signs. Evidence has been provided that indicates that such pointing signs occur with nouns in a noun phrase and are used to mark specific entities in a discourse. This analysis shows how ASL determiners are similar to and different from English determiners. Unlike English determiners,

ASL determiners can occur with proper nouns and possessives, and apparently cannot occur with generic or abstract nouns. It is particularly interesting that the direction in which a determiner points is generally insignificant.

This is a preliminary study of how pointing determiners behave in one visual/ gestural language, ASL. Areas for future research include the exploration of the definite/indefinite distinction, the interaction of pointing determiners with other determiners like THAT and OTHER, and the possibility that some pointing signs (possibly those with a jabbing movement) act as demonstratives. Finally, it would be of interest to examine whether pointing signs are ever used to "set up" entities in space for later reference, and if so, whether these signs act as determiners or have some other syntactic function.

## NOTES

The authors wish to thank Scott Liddell for his guidance and encouragement.

1. The fact that pronouns and determiners have the same phonological form is not unique to ASL. As noted by Sera de Vriendt (personal communication), this phenomenon is also found in other languages. In French, for example, the masculine "le" and feminine "la" are used as both pronouns and determiners.

2. The form THAT$^\wedge$DET, although not addressed in this paper, is worthy of special note. It may be that it is one lexical item since it appears that the two parts cannot be interrupted by additional details or by a pause. Its function warrants further investigation. One possibility is that it acts as some type of discourse marker.

## REFERENCES

Aarts, F., and J. Aarts. (1982). *English syntactic structures: Functions and categories in sentence analysis*. Oxford: Pergamon Press, Ltd.

Aramburo, A. (1986). *Locative features of deictics in American Sign Language*. Gallaudet University. Unpublished manuscript.

Coulter, G. (1977). Continuous representation in American Sign Language. In *Proceedings of the national symposium on sign language research and teaching*, edited by W. Stokoe, 247–57. Silver Spring, MD: National Association of the Deaf.

Edge, V. and Herrman, L. (1977). Verbs and the determination of subject. In *On the other hand: New perspectives in American sign language research*, edited by L. Friedman, 137–79. New York: Academic Press.

Friedman, L. (1975). Space, time, and person reference in American Sign Language. *Language* 51:940–61.

Givon, T. (1984). *Syntax: A functional-typological introduction*, vol. 1. Philadelphia: John Benjamins Publishing Co.

Hoffmeister, R. (1977). The influential point. In *Proceedings of the national symposium on sign language research and teaching*, edited by W. Stokoe, 177–91. Silver Spring, MD: National Association of the Deaf.

———. (1978). *The development of demonstrative pronouns, locatives, and personal pronouns in the acquisition of ASL by deaf children of deaf parents*. Ph.D. diss., University of Minnesota.

Huddleston, R. (1984). *Introduction to the grammar of English*. Cambridge: Cambridge University Press.

Ingram, R. (1978). Theme, rheme, topic and comment in the syntax of American Sign Language. *Sign Language Studies* 20:193–218.

Lacy, R. (1973). Directional verb marking in the American Sign Language. Paper presented at the Summer Linguistic Institute, Linguistic Society of America, 3–5 August, University of Michigan, Ann Arbor.

―――. (1974). Putting some of syntax back into semantics. Paper presented at the Linguistic Society of America Annual Meeting, December, New York.

Liddell, S. (1980). *American Sign Language syntax*. The Hague: Mouton.

Mandel, M. (1977). Iconic devices in American Sign Language. In *On the other hand: new perspectives on American Sign Language research*, edited by L. Friedman, 57–107. New York: Academic Press.

O'Malley, P. (1975). *The grammatical function of indexic reference in American Sign Language*. Research, Development and Demonstration Center in Education of the Handicapped, University of Minnesota, Minneapolis. Unpublished manuscript.

Padden, C. (1983). *Interaction of morphology and syntax in American Sign Language*. Ph.D. diss., University of California, San Diego.

Petitto, L. (1983). *From gestures to symbol: the relationship between form and meaning in the acquisition of personal pronouns in American Sign Language*. Ed.D. diss., Harvard University.

Stockwell, R., Schachter, P., and Partee, B. H. (1973). *The major syntactic structures of English*. New York: Holt, Rinehart, and Winston.

Wilbur, R. (1979). *American Sign Language and sign systems*. Baltimore, MD: University Park Press.

# Parameters for Questions: Evidence from wh-Movement in ASL

Diane Lillo-Martin

In this paper I will present some data on the formation of wh-questions in American Sign Language (ASL). The data show that wh-movement in ASL exhibits a different pattern from wh-movement in English and other languages. I make several generalizations about wh-movement possibilities in ASL, and indicate where further data are necessary. I then go on to suggest two possible theoretical analyses of these data within the Government and Binding framework (Chomsky, 1981, 1986a, b, and others). This framework makes claims about the nature of language in terms of a system of Universal Grammar, which includes abstract principles that hold for all languages and parameters by which language differences are captured. If the theory of Universal Grammar accurately describes linguistic universals, they should be tested with data from signed languages. Thus, the theory of universal grammar can be informed by sign language data. Furthermore, sign language researchers can use the technical tools from such theories to help account for generalizations observed across a variety of languages.

## EVIDENCE FROM FOUR SPOKEN LANGUAGES

This section presents data from Chinese, French, English, and Italian, that has been used to motivate several parameters for questions. The next section presents data from ASL relevant to these proposals.

### Chinese

In English, wh-questions appear with a wh-word at the beginning of the sentence; thus, it is said that wh-movement is a syntactic operation in English. However, in Chinese, wh-phrases do not move in the syntax, as illustrated in sentence 1.

(1) ni    kanjian-le    shei?
    you see-ASP      who
    'Who$_i$ did you see $t_i$?'

Huang (1982) argues that, although Chinese does not display syntactic wh-movement, it does have wh-movement at the level of logical form, LF. In this way, the position of the wh-word at LF indicates its scope. As evidence for this proposal, Huang notes that the wh-element that is left *in situ* in syntax still has the scope that it would have if it were moved. Sentences 2a and 2b (Huang's 162, 163, p. 254) illustrate the scope-bearing property of wh-words in Chinese.

(2) a. [Zhangsan wen wo [shei mai-le   shu ]]
        John        ask I   who  buy-ASP book
        'John asked [me] who$_i$ $t_i$ bought books.'

   b. [Zhangsan xiangxin [shei mai-le   shu ]]
        John        believe   who  buy-ASP book
        'Who$_i$ does John believe $t_i$ bought books?'

As Huang explains, "The only surface difference among these sentences is in the choice of the matrix verb. . . . As the translation shows, the single difference in the choice of the verb is responsible for the fact that [2a] must be interpreted as a statement taking an indirect question, [and 2b] must be interpreted as a direct question" (1982, 254). Thus, the LF representations for English and Chinese both show that the question word has scope over the rest of the clause. The LF representation of sentence 1 is then as given in example 3.

(3) [$_{CP}$ shei$_i$ [$_{IP}$ ni kanjian-le $t_i$]]

Huang proposes to account for the difference between English and Chinese wh-questions by saying that there is a parameter associated with Move-α: by this parameter languages can choose whether wh-movement occurs in the syntax (English) or at LF (Chinese).[1]

### French

Although movement of wh-words is sometimes observed in French syntax, this movement is optional, as the examples in 4 show.

(4) a. Qui as-tu vu?
   b. Tu as vu qui?
      'Who$_i$ did you see $t_i$?'
      (Lasnik & Saito, 1987)

This perhaps presents evidence for another parameter related to wh-movement: whether syntactic movement is obligatory when possible (English) or optional (French).[2]

### English

In English, extraction of a wh-element out of an embedded clause is, in general, totally acceptable, as illustrated in sentence 5.

(5) [$_{CP}$ Who$_i$ did John tell Mary [$_{CP}$ $t'_i$ Bill saw $t_i$?]]

This type of extraction is commonly analyzed as movement of the embedded wh-question word to the front of the embedded clause and subsequent movement to the front of the matrix clause. Each movement leaves a trace, indicated by co-indexed "*t*s." English wh-movement is constrained, however, by the principle of subjacency, which states that such movement cannot cross more than one "barrier." For English, NP and IP can be considered barriers (for more on the notion of barrier, see below; for more on the barriers in English see Chomsky, 1986b; Grimshaw, 1986).[3] In sentence 5 no single movement crosses more than one bounding node. However, in sentence 6 the movement out of an NP violates subjacency; hence, the sentence is ungrammatical.

(6) *$[_{CP}$ Who$_i$ do you believe $[_{NP}$ the claim that $[_{IP}$ Bill saw $t_i$ ]]]?

### *Italian*

Rizzi (1982) examines wh-movement in Italian, and concludes that in Italian, NP and CP are bounding nodes, although IP is not. This is based on data that show that extraction out of a wh-island is possible in Italian. An example is given in 7.

(7) Tuo fratello, a cui mi domando che storie abbiano
     raccontato, era molto preoccupato.
     'Your brother, to whom I wonder which stories they
     told, was very troubled."

Rizzi thus concludes that there is a parameter associated with subjacency, namely, the choice of bounding nodes. English has NP and IP, and Italian has NP and CP.[4]

Thus, we observe three parameters for questions: (1) whether wh-movement occurs in the syntax or at LF; (2) whether syntactic wh-movement is obligatory or optional when possible; and (3) which nodes are barriers (bounding nodes) for subjacency. Let us now turn to the data from ASL, and see how it bears on these parameters.

## EVIDENCE FROM ASL

In American Sign Language, some wh-movement does take place in the syntax. This is illustrated in example 8.*

$$\overline{\qquad\qquad\text{whq}\qquad\qquad}$$
(8) a. $_a$WHAT$_i$ $_b$MARY EAT $t_i$?
     'What$_i$ did Mary eat $t_i$?'

---

*The following notation is used in the ASL examples:

   SIGN    Signs are written as uppercase English glosses with approximately the same meaning as the ASL sign.

   $_a$SIGN$_b$   Subscripts are used to indicate spatial relations. All nouns are marked with a subscript to indicate the locus with which they are associated (see Lillo-Martin and Klima, 1986). Verbs that are inflected for agreement are marked with a subscript at the beginning to indicate subject agreement, and/or a subscript at the end to indicate object agreement.

   $\dfrac{\text{whq}}{\text{SIGN}}$   Grammatical facial gestures are noted with a line drawn over the signs that occur concurrently with the facial gesture. "whq" on such a line indicates the wh-question facial gesture; "*t*" indicates the topic facial gesture.

<u>          whq        </u>
b. $_a$WHO$_i$ $_b$JOHN LIKE $t_i$?
   'Who$_i$ does John like $t_i$?'

<u>                         whq   </u>
c. $_a$WHO$_i$ $_b$JOHN $_b$TELL$_a$ $t_i$ $_c$BILL 'LIKE' $_d$MARY?
   'Who$_i$ did John tell $t_i$ that Bill has a crush on Mary?'

However, wh-words are often found *in situ*, as illustrated in example 9.

<u>             whq     </u>
(9) a. $_a$MARY $_a$SEE$_b$ $_b$WHO?
     'Who$_i$ did Mary see $t_i$?'

<u>           whq    </u>
b. $_a$SALLY LOVE $_b$WHO?
   'Who$_i$ does Sally love $t_i$?'

<u>                       whq  </u>
c. $_a$BILL $_a$TELL$_b$ $_b$WHO $_c$JOHN 'LIKE' $_d$MARY?
   'Who$_i$ did Bill tell $t_i$ that John has a crush on Mary?'

Apparently, wh-words can always be left *in situ*. Alternatively, a strategy is employed that involves two sentences, as illustrated in sentence 10.

<u>                       whq  </u>
(10) $_a$BILL FEEL $_b$JOHN 'LIKE' $_c$SOMEONE. $_c$WHO $_c$PRONOUN?
    'Who$_i$ does Bill think John has a crush on $t_i$?'

In some sentences, a wh-word can be found at the right, as illustrated in sentence 11.

<u>                  whq  </u>
(11) $_a$WHO $_b$JOHN 'LIKE' $_a$WHO?
    'Who$_i$ does John have a crush on $t_i$?'

I believe the wh-words found at the right are best analyzed as a copy of the left wh-word, rather than a right COMP, though I will not provide any arguments for this hypothesis here.

The situations in which wh-words *can* move are, however, limited. The proper generalization seems to be that in most cases, a wh-word can be moved only if it is in the matrix sentence. Wh-words are generally not fronted out of embedded clauses. This is illustrated in example 12.[5]

<u>                       whq  </u>
(12) a. *$_a$WHO$_i$ $_b$BILL FEEL $_c$JOHN 'LIKE' $t_i$?

<u>                     whq  </u>
   b. *$_b$BILL FEEL $_a$WHO$_i$ $_c$JOHN 'LIKE' $t_i$?

<u>                     whq  </u>
   c. $_b$BILL FEEL $_c$JOHN 'LIKE' $_a$WHO?
     'Who$_i$ does Bill think John has a crush on $t_i$?'

The same pattern of results can be found in adjunct wh-questions, as illustrated in examples 13 and 14.

whq

(13) a. WHY$_i$ $_a$BILL $_a$LEAVE $t_i$?

whq

    b. $_a$BILL $_a$LEAVE WHY?
      'Why$_i$ did Bill leave $t_i$?'

whq

(14) WHY $_a$BILL FEEL $_b$JOHN $_b$LEAVE?
    *'Why$_i$ does Bill think John left $t_i$?'
    'Why$_i$ does Bill think $t_i$ John left?'

Single-clause adjunct questions (13) can have the wh-word fronted or *in situ*. An adjunct wh-word at the beginning of a multi-clause sentence (14) can be interpreted only as questioning the matrix; it cannot have an interpretation in which the wh-word has been fronted out of the embedded clause. These data indicate that in adjuncts as well as arguments, a wh-word can remain *in situ* or can be fronted in a matrix clause, but cannot be fronted out of an embedded clause.

In general, a wh-word from an embedded clause also cannot simply move to the beginning of the embedded clause, as illustrated in example 12b above. However, as should be expected, wh-movement within an embedded clause under a matrix verb like WONDER is allowed (in fact, required), as illustrated in sentence 15.

whq

(15) $_a$JOHN WONDER $_b$WHO$_i$ $_c$BILL 'LIKE' $t_i$.
    'John wonders who$_i$ Bill has a crush on $t_i$.'

This shows that ASL has embedded questions; furthermore, the matrix verbs that select for embedded questions are limited as in English (for example, WONDER, ASK, KNOW-WELL).

As sentence 15 indicates, scope arguments can be used to show that even though in many cases ASL does not show syntactic wh-movement, it, like Chinese, does have wh-movement at LF. For example, the scope difference between sentences 16a and 16b is the same as the difference in English, giving evidence that WHO moves to have scope over the entire sentence in 16b but not 16a. Notice that in ASL, this scope difference is also reflected in the scope of the facial gestures accompanying the signs.

whq

(16) a. $_a$JOHN $_a$ASK$_1$ $_b$WHO $_b$BUY $_c$BOOK.
      'John asked (me) who$_i$ $t_i$ bought the book.'

whq

    b. $_a$BILL THINK $_b$WHO $_b$SEE$_c$ $_c$MARY?
      'Who$_i$ does Bill think $t_i$ saw Mary?'

In sentence 16a, the wh-word WHO has scope only over the lower clause, while in 16b, WHO has scope over the entire sentence, as indicated in the translation.

As Huang argues, a natural description of these facts is to assume that in LF, wh-movement takes place, raising the wh-words so that they appear in the proper COMP, c-commanding the segments of the sentences over which they have scope.

Following Huang again, we can see evidence that subjacency does not apply at LF in ASL, just as in Chinese. Examples 17 and 18 show that a wh-word can remain *in situ* in an island in syntax. The LF movement of these wh-words would violate subjacency if that principle applied at LF.

(17) a.                                            whq
        $*_a$WHO$_i$ $_b$JOHN WONDER $_c$WHO LOVE $t_i$?

    b.                                  whq
        $_a$JOHN WONDER $_b$WHO LOVE $_c$WHO?
        'Who$_i$ does John wonder who$_j$ $t_j$ loves $t_i$?'

(18) a.                                              whq
        $*_a$WHO$_i$ $_b$JOHN $_b$KISS$_c$ $_c$SALLY BEFORE $t_i$ $_a$LEFT?

    b.                                      whq
        $_a$JOHN $_a$KISS$_b$ $_b$SALLY BEFORE $_c$WHO $_c$LEFT?
        'Who$_i$ did John kiss Sally before $t_i$ left?'

The generalizations that can be made to describe the facts illustrated above include: (1) wh-movement in ASL can occur in the syntax; but (2) syntactic movement is optional; and (3) syntactic wh-movement in ASL is constrained by something stricter than subjacency in English or Italian. These first two generalizations fit in with the first two parameters discussed above with relation to data from Chinese, French, and English. However, neither the English setting nor the Italian setting on the third parameter can account for the ASL facts in generalization 3. How can these facts be accounted for within a principles-and-parameters theory as described above?

## ANALYSES

I will present two possible accounts for these facts and related ones within the Government and Binding theory, approaching the question raised by generalization 3. Is there an additional parameterization of subjacency that can be used to account for ASL?

In earlier analyses of subjacency, the barriers (bounding nodes) relevant for each language were merely stipulated: NP and S were the bounding nodes for English, and NP and S′ were the bounding nodes for Italian. Within this framework, the right results for ASL could come from stipulating that NP, S, and S′ are all bounding nodes for ASL (along with some additional assumptions about the relevant derivations). However, current approaches try to motivate the bounding nodes through the theory of barriers. Although this makes the analysis of ASL more complex, it is important to try to advance the theory in this way.

The definitions for barriers and subjacency proposed by Lasnik and Saito (in preparation) are given in propositions 19 and 20.

(19) γ is a barrier for β if
    (i) γ is a maximal projection,
    (ii) γ is not an A-binder
    (iii) γ is not L-marked, and
    (iv) γ dominates β

(20) β is subjacent to α if for every γ,
    γ a barrier for β,
    the maximal projection immediately dominating γ dominates α

To account for the ASL data described above, we could parameterize the definition of barriers given in definition 19 and say that for ASL, (iii) is not relevant. Condition (iii) excuses complement CPs from barrierhood, since they are L-marked.[6] However, if (iii) does not apply in ASL, then complement CPs will be barriers, since with this parameterization whether γ is L-marked won't make a difference as to whether it is a barrier. It is also necessary to stipulate that VP is never a barrier. Otherwise, extraction of an object in a single-clause sentence would not even be available. This is part of Lasnik and Saito's framework, and they discuss several parts of the theory from which it might follow.

With this stipulation, movement will never be allowed out of embedded clauses in ASL. This analysis is illustrated in example 21, for the sentences in 12a and 14. WHO can move to the SPEC of the embedded COMP, because this movement crosses one barrier (IP), and the landing site is within the maximal projection immediately dominating IP. But then WHO would have to cross the barrier CP and go beyond the maximal projection immediately dominating CP (that is, VP), in order to land in the matrix SPEC of COMP.[7] Hence, the movement is ruled out.

(21) a. $*[_{CP}$ WHO$_i$ $[_{IP}$BILL FEEL $[_{CP}$ $t'_i$ $[_{IP}$JOHN 'LIKE' $t_i]]]]$       whq

b. $*[_{CP}$ WHY$_i$ $[_{IP}$BILL FEEL $[_{CP}$ $t'_i$ $[_{IP}$JOHN 'LEFT' $t'_i]]]]$       whq

Notice that if this analysis is correct, it makes a prediction regarding the relative status of sentences 21a and 21b. Sentence 21a is only a subjacency violation, since the trace of movement can meet the ECP by being properly governed by the verb SEE. But sentence 21b is also an ECP violation, since the trace of movement of the adjunct WHY is not properly governed. Following reports that subjacency violations are usually more mild than ECP violations, sentence 21b should be somewhat less acceptable than 21a. Here the facts are unclear to me.

If this parameterization is the appropriate way to account for the differences in syntactic wh-movement between ASL and English, the question of learnability should be addressed. Notice that if a signing child mistakenly assumes that ASL has the English setting on this parameter, he has no positive evidence to tell him that this is not so. On the other hand, if a child assumes the ASL setting first, positive evidence in the form of grammatical long-distance extraction informs a child learning an

English-type language to change the parameter setting. As long as the facts in generalization 3 are kept distinct from the facts in generalizations 1 and 2 and (b), this parameter is a case where the subset principle (Berwick, 1985; following Dell, 1981) will apply, since only short extraction is allowed with the ASL setting, but short and long extraction are both available with the English setting.

However, there is no motivation for this parameterization apart from the facts discussed above. If part (iii) of sentence 19 can be parameterized, why cannot parts (i), (ii), and (iv)? Perhaps some or all of these are parameterized, but no proposals have been made to this effect as far as I am aware. Let me pursue another possible method of accounting for the ASL data.

Various authors have proposed filters that produce the effect that [+ WH] elements must be found in [+ WH] COMPs, and cannot be in [− WH] COMPs, at various levels (for example, Lasnik and Saito, 1984). Tiedeman (1987) extends this notion as in proposition 22.

> (22) An element marked [αF] for any given feature, F,
>      cannot land on a landing site marked [−αF].

Tiedeman's proposal opens the door to a second possible analysis for the ASL data. Under this analysis, the definition of barriers can be left as given in proposition 19, but ASL will differ from English in that for ASL, all verbs that select sentential complements subcategorize for [− WH] complements. Since [+ WH] elements cannot land even on a [− WH] SPEC of COMP, this prohibits long-distance movement, as illustrated in sentence 23. WHO could not land in the embedded SPEC of COMP, which is [− WH]. But since the embedded IP is a barrier, WHO has to land in CP. Movement all the way to the matrix violates subjacency.

$$(23)\quad *[_{CP}\ \text{WHO}_i\ [_{IP}\text{BILL FEEL}\ [_{CP}\ [_{IP}\text{JOHN 'LIKE'}\ t_i]]]]$$

Under this account, there still is no independent reason for claiming that ASL has no bridge verbs. However, independent facts about other constructions can be examined for corroborating evidence. If, for various constructions in addition to wh-questions, there is evidence that ASL complements are marked [− WH], then this supports this analysis.

The learnability question can again be raised. If children believe that all verbs select complements unmarked for [WH], then a child learning ASL has no positive evidence that ASL verbs select [− WH] complements; hence unmarked for [WH] cannot be the initial choice. However, notice that children need to learn the [WH] selection of verbs anyway, since even in English, some verbs select [± WH], and others select complements unmarked for [WH]. Notice also that this account places language variation in the lexicon, where languages are most distinct. This is in line with the lexical parameterization hypothesis (Wexler and Manzini, 1987).

Both of these accounts handle the island and adjunct facts reported above. In addition, data from other kinds of $\overline{\text{A}}$ movement can be handled by both of these accounts, with additional reasonable assumptions. First consider topicalization. Example 24 shows that topicalization is also subject to the same boundedness restrictions as wh-movement.[8]

(24) a. $\overline{\text{MARY}}^{\,t}_i$, $_b$JOHN 'LIKE' $t_i$.

   $_a$MARY$_i$, $_b$JOHN 'LIKE' $t_i$.
   'Mary$_i$, John has a crush on $t_i$.'

b. *$_a\overline{\text{MARY}}^{\,t}_i$, $_b$BILL FEEL $_c$JOHN 'LIKE' $t_i$.
   'Mary$_i$, Bill thinks John has a crush on $t_i$.'

Following Lasnik and Saito, topicalization can be analyzed as adjunction, but this movement needs to go through the embedded COMP. Example 25a shows that the barriers analysis extends straightforwardly to these cases. Example 25b shows that the features analysis does too, if we assume (following Lasnik and Saito) that topicalized elements are marked [ + TOP].[9]

(25) a. *[$_{CP}$ [$_{IP}\overline{\text{MARY}}^{\,t}_i$ [$_{IP}$BILL FEEL [$_{CP}$ $t'_i$ [$_{IP}$JOHN 'LIKE' $t_i$ ]]]]]

b. *[$_{CP}$ [$_{IP}\overline{\text{MARY}}^{\,t}_i$ [$_{IP}$BILL FEEL [$_{CP}$ [$_{IP}$JOHN 'LIKE' $t_i$ ]]]]]
   $-$ TOP

One possible test between these two analyses would be to check movement out of NP or PP. If such movement were ungrammatical, then the barriers approach would be more appropriate, since the NP and PP would be $X^{max}$'s, which would count as barriers. However, if the sentences were acceptable, the features account would be better, since under this account NP and PP would not count as barriers.

The problem that confronts us is that movement out of NP or PP is perhaps ruled out on separate grounds. There is a dearth of real prepositions in ASL (see, for example, Fischer, 1987), and complex NP structures are similarly hard to find. I have not been able to elicit the appropriate sentences, and thus must leave this issue for future research.

However, the ASL data can also provide some support for Lasnik and Saito's analysis of topicalization. In sentences 26a and 26b we see that topicalization and wh-elements can occur in the same clause.

(26) a. $_a\overline{\text{MARY}}^{\,t}_i$, $_b\overline{\text{WHO}}^{\,whq}$ $_b$SEE$_a$ $t_i$?

   $_a$MARY$_i$, $_b$WHO $_b$SEE$_a$ $t_i$?
   'Mary$_i$, who$_j$ $t_j$ saw $t_i$?'

b. $_a\overline{\text{MARY}}^{\,t}_i$, $t_i$ $_a$SEE$_b$ $_b\overline{\text{WHO}}^{\,whq}$?

   $_a$MARY$_i$, $t_i$ $_a$SEE$_b$ $_b$WHO?
   'Mary$_i$, who$_j$ $t_i$ saw $t_j$?'

Lasnik and Saito allow topicalized elements in COMP in the matrix clause, even though topicalized elements can also be adjoined. The analysis of sentences 26a and b will then have the topicalized element in COMP, and the wh-elements *in situ*. However, sentences 27a and 27b show that while a wh-element is in SPEC of COMP, no topicalized element can be adjoined to IP.

$$\overline{\text{whq}} \underline{\qquad} t(\underline{\quad}\text{whq})$$

(27) a. $*_a\text{WHO}_i \; _b\text{MARY}_j, \; t_i \; _a\text{SEE}_b \; t_j$?

      'Who$_i$, Mary$_j$, $t_i$ saw $t_j$?'

$$\overline{\text{whq}} \underline{\qquad} t(\underline{\quad}\text{whq})$$

b. $*_a\text{WHO}_i \; _b\text{MARY}_j, \; t_j \; _b\text{SEE}_a \; t_i$?

      'Who$_i$, Mary$_j$, $t_j$ saw $t_i$?'

The reason that the sentences in 27 are out is that the subject trace is not properly governed. In sentence 27a, WHO is too far away to govern its trace (since there are two IP barriers between them). In 27b, MARY cannot properly govern its trace since it is not an $X^0$.

## CONCLUSIONS

In conclusion, data from ASL taken with data from other languages indicates that wh-movement is constrained by at least three parameters: (1) whether Move-$\alpha$ affects wh-phrases in the syntax or at LF; (2) whether wh-movement is obligatory when possible or optional; (3) the restrictions on how far wh-phrases can move, which might be stated as a parameterization of the definition of barriers, or as the features specified by lexical items taking sentential complements. This supports these parameters as part of Universal Grammar, and the inclusion of signed languages within the range of languages studied to determine the possible parameters within the theory of Universal Grammar. Although more work is necessary to determine the full range of parameters for questions, this paper demonstrates the importance of evidence from ASL.

## NOTES

This research was supported in part by a grant from the Research Foundation at the University of Connecticut; in part by NINCDS grant #NS18010 to Dr. Vicki Hanson at Haskins Laboratories; and in part by National Science Foundation Grant #BNS81-11479 to Dr. Ursula Bellugi at the Salk Institute for Biological Studies. Robyne Tiedeman and I are currently expanding this work and integrating it into a much larger study with additional data from a number of languages; I would like to thank him and Howard Lasnik for their helpful comments on this work. I would also like to thank Dennis Schemenauer, Maureen O'Grady, Lucinda O'Grady, June McMahon, and Leo Lalime for primary ASL data.

1. Even for those languages that have wh-movement in the syntax (for example, English), there is evidence for LF wh-movement in certain structures. For example, in English multiple wh-questions, one wh-word is left *in situ*, as illustrated in example (i).

    (i)  Who bought what?

    Although the object wh-word "what" is left *in situ*, the same scope arguments can be applied to argue that the LF representation of (i) is as given in (ii).

    (ii)  [$_{CP}$ who$_i$ [$_{CP}$ what$_j$ [$_{IP}$ $t_i$ bought $t_j$]]]

2. Apparently there is some division among French dialects regarding the status of sentences like 4b. Although in some dialects such questions can be only echo questions, in others they are reported as optional variants of the questions with moved wh-words.

3. Although many of the studies I am citing used earlier terminology such as "bounding nodes" rather than "barriers," S rather than IP, and S' rather than CP, I will translate these terms into the currently proposed notions for the sake of consistency. Occasionally, details (which are irrelevant for the present discussion) differ.

4. Current research indicates that the English/Italian subjacency difference may be more subtle. Some English speakers seem to accept the Italian value on this parameter, and some Italian speakers seem to have the English value. This indicates that the parameter perhaps describes different dialects rather than different languages. I will, however, continue to refer to these two settings as "English" and "Italian."

5. For some signers, examples like 12c are unacceptable. These signers produce multiclause wh-questions using two sentences, as in example 10. This option is also available to signers who accept example 12c. Throughout the paper, I will be discussing the judgments of signers who accept 12c.

6. $\alpha$ L-marks $\beta$ iff $\alpha$ is a lexical category that $\theta$-governs $\beta$.

7. Note that, although in Chomsky's (1986a) theory of barriers, adjunction to VP is available, this is not a way out of a subjacency violation in Lasnik and Saito's account.

8. Note that it has generally been assumed that ASL allows long-distance topicalization (for example, Padden 1983), as illustrated in (i). However, I claim that the sentences with apparent long-distance movement are actually best analyzed as left dislocation, with a resumptive pronoun (overt or null) in the place of the moved element; see (ii). See Lillo-Martin (1986a, b) for arguments that there is a null resumptive pronoun in sentences like (i), as well as an overt resumptive pronoun in (ii).

             _____t

(i) $_a$MOTHER, $_f$PRONOUN HOPE $_b$SISTER SUCCEED $_b$PERSUADE$_a$
    ($_a$pro) $_a$TAKE-UP $_c$EXERCISE CLASS.
    'Mother$_i$, I hope my sister manages to persuade
    (her)$_i$ to take an exercise class.' (Padden, 1983)

             _____t

(ii) $_a$MOTHER, $_f$PRONOUN HOPE $_b$SISTER SUCCEED $_b$PERSUADE$_a$
    *($_a$PRONOUN) EAT $_c$COOKIE.
    'Mother$_i$, I hope my sister manages to persuade
    her$_i$ to eat a cookie.'

9. It would probably be desirable to collapse the features for [± WH] and [± TOP]. In current work I am pursuing this possibility.

# REFERENCES

Berwick, R. (1985). *The acquisition of syntactic knowledge*. Cambridge, MA: MIT Press.

Chomsky, N. (1981). *Lectures on government and binding*. Dordrecht: Foris.

———. (1986a). *Barriers*. Cambridge, MA: MIT Press.

———. (1986b). *Knowledge of language: Its nature, origin, and use*. New York: Praeger Press.

Dell, F. (1981). On the learnability of optional phonological rules. *Linguistic Inquiry* 12:31–37.

Fischer, S. (1987). The head parameter in American Sign Language. Paper presented at the Fourth International Conference on Sign Language Research, 15–19 July, Lappeenranta, Finland.

Grimshaw, J. (1986). Subjacency and S/S' parameter. *Linguistic Inquiry* 17:364–69.

Huang, C. T. J. (1982). Logical relations in Chinese and the theory of grammar. Ph.D. diss., MIT.

Lasnik, H., and Saito, M. (1984). On the nature of proper government. *Linguistic Inquiry* 15:235–90.

———, and Saito, M. (in preparation). *Move α*. Cambridge, MA: MIT Press.

Lillo-Martin, D. (1986a). Parameter setting: Evidence from use, acquisition, and breakdown in American Sign Language. Ph.D. diss., University of California, San Diego.

―――. (1986b). Two kinds of null arguments in American Sign Language. *Natural Language and Linguistic Theory* 4:415–44.

Lillo-Martin, D., and Klima, E. (1986). Pointing out differences: ASL pronouns in syntactic theory. Paper presented at the Conference on Theoretical Issues in Sign Language Research, I, 13–16 June, Rochester, New York.

Padden, C. (1983). Interaction of morphology and syntax in American Sign Language. Ph.D. diss., University of California, San Diego.

Rizzi, L. (1982). *Issues in Italian syntax*. Dordrecht: Foris.

Tiedeman, R. (1987). WH-questions, parametric variation, and the ECP. University of Connecticut Working Papers in Linguistics, vol. 1, 116–42.

Wexler, K., and Manzini, R. (1987). Parameters and learnability in binding theory. In *Parameter Setting*, edited by T. Roeper and E. Williams, 41–76. Dordrecht: Reidel.

# ASL Relative Clauses
# and Their Interaction with
# Null Categories

Dana Miller

In his 1977 dissertation, Liddell asserts that most restrictive relative clauses in ASL are best described as being internally headed. That is, the following English sentence:

(1)
           _____r

RECENTLY DOG CHASE CAT COME HOME

'The dog which recently chased the cat came home.'[1]

would have the structure noted in figure 1.

Similarly constructed relative clauses occur in several unrelated languages. Gorbet (1973) analyzes internally headed relative clauses (IHRCs) in Diegueño, Hale and Platero (1974) identify this construction in Navajo, and Williamson (1987) in Lakhota, to name a few.

Cole (1987) argues, however, that IHRCs are, in fact, not internally headed. Instead, he proposes that they have phonologically null heads in S-structure, which are co-indexed with an NP in the modifying clause, as illustrated in figure 2.

This reanalysis is motivated by the distribution of internally headed relative clauses across languages; that is, IHRCs occur only in OV (object-verb) languages, in languages with null anaphora, and in languages that have left-branching relative clauses. Although ASL is considered by most to be an SVO language, it does have null anaphora, and its relative clauses are typically left-branching.

In addition, Cole (1987) points out that his reanalysis introduces structures (as illustrated in figures 3 and 4) that are consistent with Langacker's (1969) and Ross's (1969) theory that "an anaphor cannot both precede and command its antecedent" (in Cole, 1987, 283). (Langacker states that A is said to command B if the first S node above A dominates B, that is, it is possible to trace down the tree from the S node to B. For example, in figure 1—NPb commands NPa, but NPa does not command NPb.)

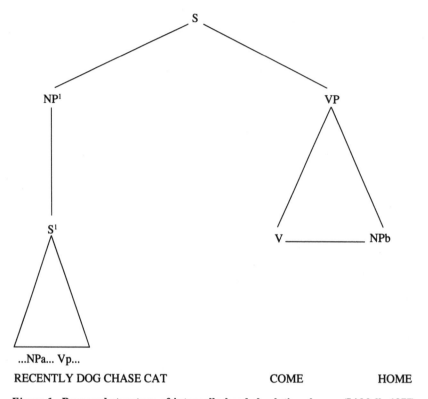

*Figure 1.* **Proposed structure of internally headed relative clauses (Liddell, 1977).**

If we examine the structures in figures 3 and 4, we see that both left-branching structures (figures 3a and 3b) predict grammatical relative clauses, that is, with a null argument in either the main clause heading the relative, or in the relative clause with an external lexical head. In figure 3a the null argument commands but does not precede its antecedent, and in figure 3b the null argument precedes but does not command its antecedent.

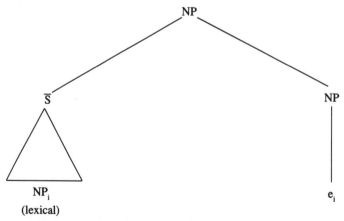

*Figure 2.* **Proposed structure of internally headed relative clauses (Cole, 1987, 278).**

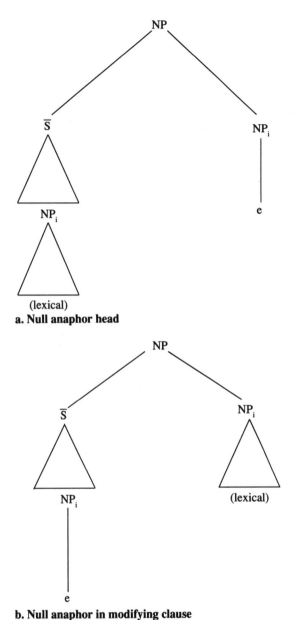

a. Null anaphor head

b. Null anaphor in modifying clause

*Figure 3.* Left-branching relative clause (head on right) (Cole, 1987, 284).

The situation is different in right-branching structures. In figure 4a the empty category both precedes and commands its antecedent; thus, it is predicted to be ill-formed. On the other hand, in figure 4b, the lexical head precedes and commands the null category and is predicted to be grammatical.

This paper provides evidence to support this alternative analysis of internally headed relative clauses in ASL. I propose that the sentential position of the null

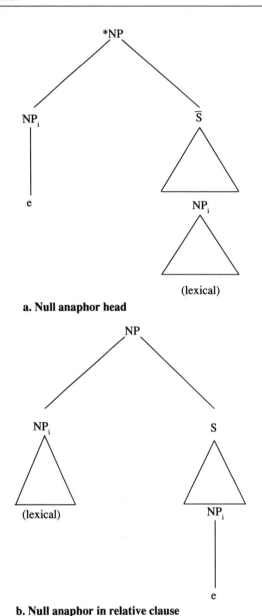

**a. Null anaphor head**

**b. Null anaphor in relative clause**

*Figure 4*. **Right-branching relative clause (head on left) (Cole, 1987, 285).**

element with regard to the relative clause predicts the predominance of ASL relative clauses in sentence-initial positions, and their lack of frequency in sentence-final positions. Furthermore, the fact that ASL has three verb types that differ in the positions of null categories they permit is crucial in accounting for this distribution. This generalization is not captured by previous analyses of internally headed relative clauses.

## EVIDENCE OF THE EXISTENCE
## OF RELATIVE CLAUSES IN ASL

The identification of relative clauses in ASL is a recent (and disputed) phenomenon. Thompson (1977) claims that there is no subordination in ASL, and Coulter (1981) suggests that ASL has restrictive clauses, but these clauses are very similar to ASL topics, and appear to be conjoined—not embedded. Coulter states that "this construction is different enough from the prototypical structure of a relative clause that it could reasonably be considered to be a different construction entirely" (1981, 17).

Both Coulter (1981) and Liddell (1977, 1978) agree that these "relative clauses" have nonmanual signals that mark them. Restrictive relative clauses are pointed to by a brow raise, slight backward head tilt, and a raising and tensing of the upper lip. A similar signal (with all but the raising and tensing of the upper lip) marks a topicalized constituent.

For instance, in sentence 1, the relative clause begins at RECENTLY and ends at CAT.

Coulter (1981) claims that this type of construction is better analyzed as two adjacent clauses, with the subject of the second sentence deleted because it is understood. Liddell (1978), however, claims that this sentence contains a relative clause followed by the main clause. He provides photographs to illustrate the difference between the above sentence and two adjacent sentences, or one with two conjoined clauses and no relative clause (p. 71). In the latter case, the appropriate facial expressions fail to accompany the first clause (a fact that Coulter does not regard as relevant in his treatment of relative clauses as conjoined). In addition, there is a difference in continuity between the two sentences. In the sentence with the two independent clauses, there is a brief relaxation of the hands between the clauses that is not present in a sentence with a restrictive relative clause and main clause.

To further illustrate the point that there are, in fact, relative clauses in ASL, Tweney and Liddell (1977) conducted sentence perception tests, in which signers were shown sentences masked with visual "noise." Although the individual signs were often difficult to recognize, the sentences with relative clauses (which were marked with the nonmanual "r" signal) were always properly identified as being relative clauses.

Liddell (1977) was also interested in whether relative clauses occur naturally in stories (and not only when signers are asked to translate an English sentence with a relative clause). To investigate this, he gave signers a short story to read in which information about the three main characters was very limited. The characters were introduced as one man, another man, and the next man—no names were given. When the signers were asked to retell these stories, the most convenient way to refer to the characters was with relative clauses. Liddell found that signers either assigned each character a number to which they later referred, or used NPs with restrictive relative clauses. (In ASL, nonrestrictive relatives appear as adjacent or conjoined clauses with no "r" marking—thus, in effect, ASL does not have nonrestrictive relative clauses.)

Finally, Liddell (1977) notes grammatical differences between conjoined sentences and those with relative clauses. While a conjoined sentence is grammatical with the addition of "but" between the clauses, the addition of "but" between the relative clause and main clause in ungrammatical:

(2)         [RECENTLY DOG CHASE CAT] BUT [NOT-YET COME HOME]

'The dog recently chased the cat but hasn't come home.'

_____r

(3)         *[RECENTLY DOG CHASE CAT] BUT [NOT-YET COME HOME]

'The dog which recently chased the cat but hasn't come home.'

## NULL CATEGORIES IN ASL

Lillo-Martin (1986) suggests that there are two types of empty categories in ASL. One type arises from a process similar to one that occurs in pro-drop languages like Spanish and Italian. In these languages, we find examples like:

(4)         Soy estudiante.              'I am a student.'

where the pronoun is dropped.

Lillo-Martin points out that, "in most . . . . [pro-drop] languages, there is a connection between the presence of rich overt agreement morphology and the possibility for pro-drop . . . . Furthermore, in many languages with agreement other than subject agreement, such as object agreement or prepositional agreement, these positions may also be left null" (1986, 62).

With ASL "inflecting" verbs, we find null pronominals in both subject and object positions. The verbs are marked for agreement in several ways. (Please note that my account represents a considerable simplification.)

NPs are assigned indices or loci in the signing space, and the relation of the verb to these NPs (that is, the verb's agreement markers) are reflected by movement from one NP locus to another. An NP may receive its index by signing it and then following it by pointing the index finger to some unassigned locus. Alternatively, the NP may be signed, and then followed by an inflecting verb at an unassigned locus in the signing space. That locus is then associated with the particular NP. In both cases, once a locus (index) is assigned to a particular NP, further reference to it can be made by movement of the verb to or from that position without the use of a pronoun (as in pro-drop), or by the use of a co-indexed pronoun. [Kegl (1987) points out that HIT-type verbs not only involve movement from the source to the goal locations and contact with the latter, but also verbs of this class have two associated pronominal proclitics that exhibit spatial agreement with NPs in the sentence or discourse.]

The analyses of Lillo-Martin (1986) and Kegl (1987) differ considerably in the structures they propose for verbs; however, they converge on the classification of null categories present in ASL. Kegl suggests that there are

> three processes which effect the distribution of empty categories and empty argument positions: Topic Np Deletion, Pro-Drop and Case Absorption. . . .[The verbs LIKE, GIVE, and HIT] are transitive, but their agreement patterns and the possible positions in which arguments can occur differ. LIKE agrees only with its subject and allows an NP (with which it does not agree) to occupy object position. GIVE agrees with both its subject and object and also allows an NP in object position. The third verb,

. . . HIT, behaves like GIVE with respect to agreement, but prohibits the presence of an NP in object position. (1987, 150–51)

In Kegl's notation, the above verb types have the syntactic patterns illustrated in figure 5. It is important to note that verbs like GIVE and HIT have subscripts both before and after the verb. LIKE, on the other hand, has no subscript following it, but rather a full NP.

The second type of empty category mentioned earlier occurs with LIKE-type verbs. These result from topic-NP deletion and exhibit a subject-object asymmetry; that is, a subject pronoun may be truly null, having no co-indexed discourse topic, while the object pronoun (or category) must be bound to a previously mentioned discourse topic. Kegl notes, however, that the empty category in subject position may have a source other than topic NP deletion, that is, pro-drop. "This is likely since all verbs agree with their subjects and all subject positions allow null pronouns" (1987, 158).

The third category of verbs are those like HIT, which do not allow postverbal NPs. This is the result of a clitic that follows the verb and absorbs the case it assigns. For some signers, however, this class of verbs is collapsed with the GIVE class; thus, they can have postverbal NPs.

## NULL CATEGORIES AND THEIR RELATION
## TO RELATIVE CLAUSES

As I stated earlier, Cole's reanalysis of internally headed relative clauses as having null external heads provides a plausible derivation of this type of relative clause construction. This interacts in an advantageous manner with the ASL verb classes and null categories.

Cole (1987) suggests that both internally headed relative clauses (IHRCs) and externally headed relative clauses (EHRCs) can be described by *one* structure, which varies only as to the lexical content of the NP head and the position of the head in relation to the relative clause, as in figures 3a and 3b, and 4a and 4b. Liddell (1977),

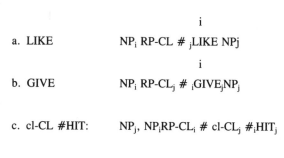

a. LIKE $\qquad$ NP$_i$ RP-CL # $_j$LIKE NPj

b. GIVE $\qquad$ NP$_i$ RP-CL$_j$ # $_i$GIVE$_j$NP$_j$

c. cl-CL #HIT: $\qquad$ NP$_j$, NP$_i$RP-CL$_i$ # cl-CL$_j$ #$_i$HIT$_j$

Key:
cl-CL: classifier clitic
RP-CL: role-prominence clitic

***Figure 5.*** **Syntactic patterns of three ASL verb classes (Kegl, 1987, 150).**

on the other hand, proposes that externally headed relative clauses are derived from internally headed relative clauses by a transformation that promotes the external head, as illustrated in figure 6.

Liddell also considers this structure to be advantageous over one that proposes an external NP head and a coreferential NP head, with deletion under identity of the relevant NP (depending on whether the relative clause is internally headed or externally headed). "The difficulty stems from the deletion of the external head. The external NP bears all the primacy conditions (i.e., it both precedes and commands the internal NP) and should not be deletable on the basis of identity with the internal NP" (1977, 261). This can be seen in figure 7.

Cole argues against analyses like Liddell's (1977) based on the distribution of internally headed relative clauses cross-linguistically. He suggests that, "these relative clauses are found in languages having left-branching rather than (or in addition to) right-branching NP structure. . . . This limitation on IHRCs is predicted if a) IHRCs have structure [figure 8a and not figure 8b or 8c], and anaphors are restricted in their distribution . . . based on [the principle] by Langacker (1969) and Ross (1969)" (1987, 282–83).

To see whether Cole's (1987) Anaphoric-Head Hypothesis better characterizes ASL relative clauses, we need to examine the distribution of sentence-initial and sentence-final relative clauses. On this point, both Liddell (1977) and Coulter (1981) concur: the preferred position for the ASL relative clause is sentence initial. Furthermore, Liddell states that sentence-final relative clauses are usually externally headed.

Liddell attributes the preference of ASL sentence-initial relative clauses to the fact that "old information tends to be mentioned first" (1977, 228). Coulter adds, "The reason for this is not entirely clear" (1981, 12). He states that it may be due to their function, and possibly to their historical origin. With regard to Coulter's latter point, Cole (1987) points out that internally headed relative clauses occur most frequently in OV languages, which was true of early ASL.

If Cole's theory is correct, the fact that most ASL relative clauses are sentence initial is not surprising. If a relative clause with a lexical head were to follow a null head in the main clause (as a sentence-final IHRC would), the sentence would violate

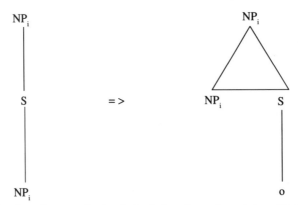

*Figure 6.* **Derivation of externally headed relative clause from internally headed relative clause (Liddell, 1977, 262).**

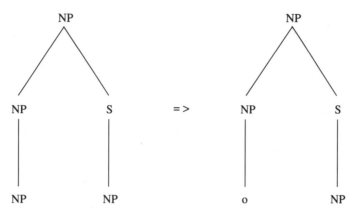

*Figure 7.* Alternate derivation of internally headed relative clause (Liddell, 1977, 261).

Langacker's (1969) and Ross's (1969) principle, as figure 4a illustrates. On the other hand, a sentence-initial IHRC with an internal lexical head would be grammatical, as illustrated in figure 3a.

Furthermore, if we consider the point that Kegl makes that "all verbs agree with their subjects and all subject positions allow null pronouns" (1987, 158), internally headed relative clauses in initial position with null pronoun heads following them should be constrained only by pragmatic considerations specific to ASL.[2]

The situation is different, however, when we look at sentence-final relative clauses whose antecedent is the object of the matrix clause. According to Cole's theory, we should not find relative clauses with antecedents in the positions in ASL where the object of the verb cannot be lexical, if that position precedes and commands a co-indexed lexical NP in the embedded relative clause (as in figure 4a). This is precisely what we note with HIT-type verbs, which cannot have lexical NPs as objects. Thus, Cole's theory predicts that we would not find sentences like 5, 6, and 7 in ASL, that is, with the lexical NP internal to the sentence final relative clause. Liddell

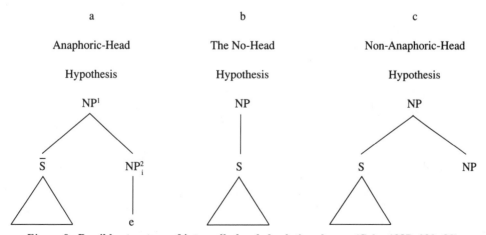

*Figure 8.* Possible structure of internally headed relative clauses (Cole, 1987, 282–83).

agrees with Cole when he points out that "there is a strong tendency . . . for the external head to appear when the relative clause follows the verb" (1977, 162). Thus, the following sentences are predicted to be ill-formed:

(5)    I hit the girl you hit.        *PRO1 HIT$_i$ GIRL$_i$ YOU HIT$_i$

(6)    I hit the girl you like.       *PRO1 HIT$_i$ GIRL$_i$ YOU LIKE PRO$_i$

(7)    I hit the girl you insulted.   *PRO1 HIT$_i$ YOU INSULTED GIRL$_i$

In addition, for other verb classes, we would not expect to find either overt or null pronominals preceding the lexical NPs (with which they are co-indexed), if these NPs are in an embedded clause that follows the main clause.[3] This situation occurs when an internally headed relative clause follows the verb, and it leads to a violation of Langacker's (1969) and Ross's (1969) theory.

As might be expected, examples of sentence-initial relative clauses are more prevalent in the literature. My informant, who is a deaf ASL signer of deaf parents, agreed that sentences of this type, 'The dog which recently chased the cat came home' are fine. However, when asked for judgments on sentences with sentence-final relative clauses, while he understood and accepted them, he instead offered versions with conjoined clauses.

In another task, he was presented with two English stories, aimed at eliciting relative clauses. After he read each one, he was asked to sign it.[4] In doing this, he used only one relative clause, a sentence-initial externally headed relative clause, 8:

(8)   INDEX$_{10}$ ONE GIRL HE$_j$ NEVER LIKED $_j$LIKED, ALWAYS CL#$_j$KICKING$_{10}$.

'That one girl whom he disliked was always kicking him.'

I was more successful at eliciting relative clauses, however, when I asked my informant to translate English sentences into ASL based on the characters in one of the stories. I also asked him to translate sentences that I wrote with the intention of comparing the use of sentence-final relative clauses with the three different transitive verb types.[5] I presented these in all possible combinations in both the main clause and the relative clause. I chose relative clauses that modified the direct object of the main verb. In addition, I wanted to use a minimum of relative pronouns. Thus, in most instances the "empty category" or "missing constituent" was the object of the verb in the relative clause. This configuration allows omission of the relative pronoun. I also included sentences from Liddell (1977). These were presented without a context or story.

Of the sixteen sentences I asked my informant to translate, he returned seven sentences with relative clauses.

(9)   BETH NEVER ₁LIKED THAT GIRLⱼ HER BROTHER AND SISTER
      ALWAYS INSULTEDⱼ.

'Beth disliked the girl her brother and sister always insulted.'

(10)  ₁DISLIKE THAT GIRL ₂INSULTⱼ.

'I dislike the girl you insulted.'

(11)  LOUISE ₁LIKE THAT GIRL WENT OFF WITH MARY.

'Louise likes the girl who went away with Mary.'

(12)  ₁ASK BOYⱼ TO ⱼGIVE₁ DOGₖ THAT INDEXₘ URSALA
      ALWAYS ₘKICKEDₖ.[6]

'I asked him to give me the dog that Ursala kicked.'

(13)  I ₁BUYⱼ DOG THAT ⱼKICKₖ CAT.

'I bought the dog that kicked the cat.'

(14)  O ⱼLOVES ⱼHIT(redup) ONE GIRL, INDEX₁₀ BOY ALWAYS
      INSULT ALL GIRLS.

'One girl loves to repeatedly hit someone, the boy that always
insults all the girls.'

(15)  SAMⱼ CL₁HIT₁, THAT₁ GIRL NAMED MARY ALWAYS ₁KICKⱼ.

'Sam hit someone, that girl named Mary that always kicked him.'

'Sam hit a girl named Mary who always kicked him.'

It is interesting to note that the only sentence-final relative clauses I elicited
were translations, that is, sentences elicited when the informant was given an English
sentence with a relative clause in it and asked to sign it. This may reflect the fact
that it is difficult to construct sentence-final relative clauses in ASL, especially when
the NP head is the object of the matrix verb and the direct object in the relative
clause. In order for the speaker to avoid a violation of the null-anaphor theory, there
cannot be a null category in the main clause if it precedes the lexical NP it is co-
indexed with in the embedded clause.

As mentioned earlier, I predicted that relative clauses would be used most freely
with LIKE-type verbs in the main clause. In fact, the results confirm this. Half of
the sentences with relative clauses were of this verb class.

Because my informant rarely used the relative clause facial gesture, I was
concerned that I would have problems determining whether the relative clauses were
internally or externally headed. In sentences 9, 10, and 11 (those with the verb LIKE),
there was no problem identifying the NPs as being external to the relative clause. In
sentences 12 and 13, the complementizer ''that'' appears to be the head of the relative

clause, leaving the lexical NP in the main clause. Thus, the informant avoided the ungrammatical structure we saw in figure 4a earlier.

Finally, I predicted that relative clauses after verbs of the HIT-class would be ungrammatical, because these verbs do not allow a lexical NP in object position. This class is collapsed with the GIVE class for many ASL speakers. My prediction seems to be borne out for my informant. However, if you examine sentence 14, you'll note that the postverbal NP is the subject, that is, the verb has been fronted. The speaker pauses and then continues. Thus, the object is actually outside of the sentence and *it* heads the relative clause. We have the same situation in sentence 15. This may be a strategy to avoid a violation of the null-anaphor theory, as a null pronominal in the object position of the main clause would no longer command this lexical NP.

In the remainder of the sentences, my informant avoided relative clauses. Instead he used sentences with conjoined clauses, or he used two separate sentences.

I can only hypothesize that because several constructions with sentence-final relative clause result in ungrammatical sentences, speakers employ strategies to avoid the situation where a null category may precede and command a lexical NP. This is consistent with predictions based on Cole's (1987) Anaphoric-Head Hypothesis.

## CONCLUSION

I argue in this paper that Cole's analysis of IHRCs provides a plausible explanation for the distribution of relative clauses in ASL; that is, "internally headed relative clauses are not in fact internally headed, but . . . have phonologically null heads which, being some kind of pronominal, are coindexed with an NP in the modifying clause" (1987, 278). While competing theories (Coulter, 1981; Liddell, 1977, 1978) describe possible structures of relative clauses in ASL, they cannot explain the predominance of sentence-initial relative clauses. The examination of the interaction of verbal classes and their null categories with possible relative-clause positions illustrates that Cole's (1987) Anaphoric-Head Hypothesis successfully predicts the distribution of relative clauses in ASL.

## NOTES

I would like to thank Judy Kegl for her assistance in my work with the informant as well as for her patience and wisdom.

1. The notation I am using is the following:
   - Uppercase English glosses represent signs with approximately the same meaning as the English word.
   - Relative clauses are indicated by a line above the constituent followed by ''r.''
   - Topicalized constituents also have a line, but are followed by a ''t.''
   - Agreement markings on the verb in the object position (without an overt pronominal) are glossed (- his/his) for third-person singular, for example.

2. Coulter (1981) uses this latter point as one of his arguments against the analysis of ASL relative clauses as being embedded. He states that in ASL, ''the characterizing function of the relative

clause must be relevant to the sense of the main clause . . . and the head of a relative clause . . . must be both definite and nongeneric", (p. 9).

His other arguments against the analysis of relative clauses as subordinate clauses include the fact that "there need be no shared NP" (p. 9). He offers the following example (pp. 11–12):

```
                                      r
```

REMEMBER ROOMMATE BUY CAR, NOW NOT + HAVE-TO BICYCLE COMMUTE

'Remember (my) roommate bought a car (?), now (I) don't have to commute by bicycle.'

Coulter (1981) states that, "although the 'relative clause' here is relevant to the main clause, in that it describes a situation which enabled the event described in the main clause to take place, it does not modify any NP in the main clause" (pp. 11–12). In this case, I think he misidentifies the relative clause. It seems to me that a better translation would be: 'Remember my roommate who bought a car, now I don't have to commute by bicycle.'

3. Please note that with inflecting verbs like GIVE, a pronominal is not required to fill the gap in a relative clause or that left by a topicalized constituent, but with LIKE-type verbs, an overt pronoun is required (when the gap is deeply embedded). The following examples from Lillo-Martin (1986, 69) illustrate this point. (KNOW is a plain verb, that is, it belongs to the LIKE class.)

```
              t
```

$_a$THAT MAN, $_b$DAVID SAY $_c$MICHELE FINISH $_c$GIVE$_a$ BOOK.

'That man, David said Michele already gave a book to (-him).'

```
              t
```

$_a$THAT $_a$MAN, $_b$DAVID SAY $_c$MICHELE DON'T-KNOW $_a$PRONOUN.

```
              t
```

*$_a$THAT $_a$MAN, $_b$DAVID SAY $_c$MICHELE DON'T-KNOW$_e$.

'That man$_i$, David said Michele doesn't know him$_i$.'

4. This is one of the stories the informant was asked to sign: "Little Sam doesn't like girls very much. He's always fighting with the ones in his building. There's one girl who he just dislikes. Some of them he insults a lot. He loves to hit one girl, but there's one he seems to like. Sam's sisters Mary, Louise, and Beth are not much better than Sam."

5. These are the sentences the informant was asked to sign.

   1. Mary kicks the girl Sam hits.
   2. Louise hits the girl Sam dislikes.
   3. Beth kicks the girls Sam insults.
   4. Sam dislikes the girl Mary likes.
   5. He also dislikes the girl Louise hits.
   6. Beth dislikes the girls his brother and sisters insult.
   7. Sam insults the girls Beth dislikes.
   8. Sam likes the girl Louise went (away) with.
   9. Louise likes the girl who went (away) with Mary.
   10. Beth likes the girl Louise likes.
   11. I forced the boy who ate my hamburger to give me a dollar.

12. I fed the dog that bit the cat.
13. The dog which chased the cat barked.
14. I asked him to give me the dog that Ursula kicked.
15. I bought the dog that bit the cat.
16. I bought the cat the dog bit.

Sentences 11 through 16 appeared in Liddell (1977). The numbering of the sentences in the body of the paper does not always correspond to the numbering in the note, as my informant did not sign every sentence I presented him with, and sometimes produced sentences similar, but not identical to, those I asked him to sign. For example, he signed sentence 10 (in the paper) when I asked him to sign sentence 7 (in the note).

6. Liddell (1977) discusses three ASL signs, which he refers to as THAT$_a$, THAT$_b$, and THAT$_c$. THAT$_a$ appears to be more than an optional wh-word that can be used to indicate the lexical head of the relative clause:

$$\underline{\hspace{6cm}}^r$$

PRO.1 FORCE [BOY EAT POSS.1 HAMBURGER]s GIVE [X:PRO.1] ONE-DOLLAR

$$\underline{\hspace{6cm}}^r$$

PRO.1 FORCE [BOY THAT$_a$ EAT POSS.1 HAMBURGER] GIVE
[S:PRO.1] 1-DOLLAR

'I forced the boy who ate my hamburger to give me a dollar.'

(from Liddell, 1977, p. 231)

Liddell states the first sentence, which does not have an instance of THAT$_a$, could be misinterpreted, despite the nonmanual signal r, as meaning 'I forced the boy to eat my hamburger. . . .'

THAT$_b$ and THAT$_c$ are used differently than THAT$_a$—they usually appear after sentence-final relative clauses. Furthermore, while THAT$_b$ seems to be part of the relative clause, THAT$_c$ occurs after the relative clause, as an independent clause. They can both be translated as, 'that's the one' (Liddell, 1977).

Coulter (1981) adds that THAT$_c$ can be inflected to agree with the noun it is referring to:

i = intensifier                           $\underline{\hspace{3cm}}^i$ nod

nod = affirmation                 $\underline{\hspace{3cm}}^r \underline{\hspace{1.5cm}}$

JOHN KICK DOGj, CHASE CAT, THATj

'John kicked the dog, that chased the cat, that's (the one).'

(p. 12)

# REFERENCES

Cole, P. (1987). The structure of internally headed relative clauses. *Natural Language and Linguistic Theory* 3:277–302.

Coulter, G. (1981). A conjoined analysis of American Sign Language relative clauses. University of Rochester, Rochester, NY. Unpublished manuscript.

Gorbet, L. (1973). How to tell a head when you see one: disambiguation in Diegueño relative clauses. *Linguistic Notes from La Jolla* 5:63–82.

Hale, K., and Platero, P. (1974). Aspects of Navajo anaphora: Relativization and pronominalization. *Dine bizaad nanil iih (Navajo Language Review)* 1:9–28.

Kegl, J. (1987). Coreference relations in American Sign Language. In *Studies in the Acquisition of Anaphor*, vol. 2, edited by B. Lust, 135–70. Dordrecht: Reidel.

Langacker, R. W. (1969). On pronominalization and the chain of command. In *Modern studies in English*, edited by D. A. Reibel and S. A. Schane, 160–86. Englewood Cliffs, NJ: Prentice-Hall.

Liddell, S. K. (1977). An investigation into the syntactic structure of American Sign Language. Ph.D. diss., University of California, San Diego.

———. (1978). Introduction to relative clauses in American Sign Language. In *Understanding language through sign language research*, edited by P. Siple, 59–90. New York: Academic Press.

Lillo-Martin, D. C. (1986). Parameter setting: evidence from use, acquisition, and breakdown in American Sign Language. Ph.D. diss., University of California, San Diego.

Ross, J. R. (1969). On the cyclic nature of English pronominalization. In *Modern studies in English*, edited by D. A. Reibel and S. A. Schane, 187–200. Englewood Cliffs, NJ: Prentice-Hall.

Thompson, H. (1977). The lack of subordination in American Sign Language. In *On the other hand: New perspectives on American Sign Language*, edited by L. Friedman, 181–96. New York: Academic Press.

Tweney, R., and Liddell, S. K. (1977). The perception of grammatical boundaries in ASL. Bowling Green State University and the Salk Institute. Unpublished manuscript.

Williamson, J. (1987). An indefiniteness restriction for relative clauses in Lakhota. In *On the representation of (in)definiteness*, edited by E. Reuland and A. ter Neulen, 168–90. Cambridge: MIT Press.

# Is ASL like Diegueño or Diegueño like ASL? A Study of Internally Headed Relative Clauses in ASL

Josep M. Fontana

In *American Sign Language Syntax* (1980), Scott K. Liddell argues that ASL has "internally headed relative clauses" (IHRCs) comparable to the structures proposed in Gorbet (1974) to describe restrictive relatives in Diegueño. The same analysis has been proposed by others to account for similar constructions occurring in a significant number of genetically unrelated languages (see Hale and Platero, 1974 for Navajo; Cole, 1982 for Ancash Quechua; and Williamson, 1987 for Lakhota). In a recent article, Cole (1987) advances an alternative analysis of these constructions arguing that IHRCs are not really internally headed but instead have phonologically null external heads in S-structure, which are co-indexed with an NP in the modifying clause. Cole provides convincing evidence showing that the nominal considered the head in previous analyses of IHRCs cannot be interpreted as such in any structural sense.

Whether they posit internal or external heads, all previous attempts to analyze IHRCs assume that these constructions involve a restrictive relative clause, which is by definition in a position of structural subordination in relation to the main clause. The findings reported in this paper, however, suggest that such an approach does not appropriately describe the type of construction known as "internally headed relative clause."[1] Rather, I will argue that the application of the term "relative clause" to these structures is pertinent only insofar as the relation between the main clause and the modifying clause is characterized in terms of semantic or pragmatic dependence rather than subordination of a syntactic type. The results of this investigation indicate that IHRCs are best described as patterns of two adjoined constituents organized in terms of TOPIC-COMMENT structures of the kind discussed in Gundel (1986) and Ochs-Keenan and Schieffelin (1976). More specifically, I argue that IHRCs are similar to left-dislocation structures (LD). In addition to providing an acceptable account from the perspective of their syntactic description, the suggested analysis captures some interesting generalizations about IHRCs that cannot otherwise be captured.

The approach proposed in this paper provides a satisfactory explanation for some puzzling attributes of ASL relatives, for instance: the modifying clause almost invariably occurs in sentence-initial position; the modified element—or, rather, the asserted element according to our analysis—must be a nongeneric, definite NP; and the two clauses involved need not even share a coreferential NP as long as the statement of the second clause is relevant to the theme in the preceding clause.

## THE UNDERLYING PROBLEM: DO INTERNALLY HEADED RELATIVES REALLY EXIST?

### Relativization in American Sign Language

One of the major achievements in Liddell's (1980) work is his finding that nonmanual expressions are essential for an understanding of the structure of ASL utterances. With respect to the topic under discussion, Liddell's basic claim is that certain facial expressions that are produced simultaneously with certain sequences of manual signs mark these strings as restrictive relative clauses.

According to Liddell, this type of nonmanual sign is clearly distinguished from other similar facial expressions and has a single, specific function. In particular, he argues that markers of relativization are characterized by brow raise, head tilted back, and upper lip raised. This characteristic facial expression is symbolized by ''r'' in his transcriptions of ASL data. Thus, the sequence RECENTLY DOG CHASED CAT in example 1, which is produced coterminously with this distinctive nonmanual signal, would form a restrictive relative clause: 'the dog which recently chased the cat' (1980, 136).

(1)
$$\overline{\qquad\qquad\qquad\qquad\qquad}^{\;r}$$
RECENTLY DOG CHASE CAT COME HOME
'The dog which recently chased the cat came home.'

According to Liddell, restrictive relative clauses in ASL are best described as being internally headed—as proposed by Gorbet (1973) for Diegueño—and they have an underlying structure as shown in figure 1.

The structural description that Gorbet proposes for Diegueño relatives is presented in figures 2 and 3 (note that Diegueño is a language with OV [object-verb] order).

### Arguments for External, Null Heads of IHRCs

The validity of such structural descriptions, however, is questioned in Cole (1987). As evidence against positing the existence of an internal head in this type of construction, Cole provides the following example from Ancash Quechua,[2] example 1 in his article, reproduced here as example 2.

As Cole points out, *bestya-ta* cannot be construed as the syntactic head of the relative clause, but rather, must be considered a constituent of the subordinate clause.

(2)  [NP  nuna  **bestya-ta**      ranti-shqa-n]    alli
          man   horse-ACC      buy-PERFECT-3   good

     bestya-m               ka-rqo-n.
     horse-EVIDENTIAL    be-PAST-3


'The horse the man bought was a good horse'.

The main reason, he argues, is the appearance of the accusative case marker "-ta." This is appropriate only if *bestya* is the subordinate direct object, but not if it were the head of an NP that happens to be the subject of the sentence. Hence, he concludes, "bestya-ta in [example 2] is not the (S-structure) head, but, rather a constituent of the modifying clause" (1987, 281).

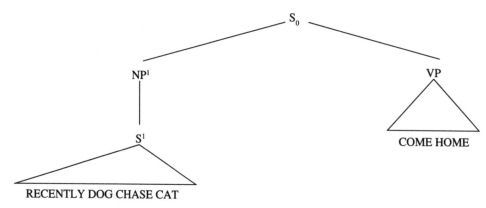

*Figure 1*. **Proposed structure of IHRCs in ASL (from Liddell, 1980).**

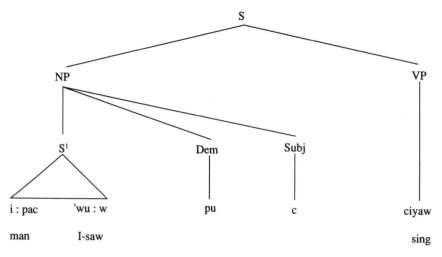

'The man I saw sang.'

*Figure 2*. **Internally headed relative clause in Diegueño (from Gobert, 1974).**

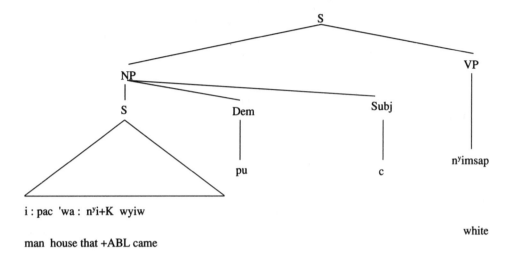

i : pac 'wa : nʸi+K  wyiw

man  house that +ABL came

white

'The house that the man came from was white.'

*Figure 3.* **Internally headed relative clause in Dieguéño (from Gorbet, 1974).**

As an alternative analysis of this construction, Cole (1987) proposes that IHRCs have phonologically null heads at S-structure. This phonologically null head is co-indexed with an NP within the modifying clause that is interpreted as the head. The structural description that he assigns to example 2 is shown in figure 4.

Since the main lines of the argument in favor of this hypothesis are to be found in Cole (1987), I can omit a detailed account of his proposal. Here, I will simply adopt his analysis and extend it to ASL. In this respect, one of the key arguments in Cole's proposal of S-structures like that in figure 4 for IHRCs is that only the structure in figure 4 and not in figures 1 or 2 could explain the significant restrictions on the distribution of IHRCs cross-linguistically.

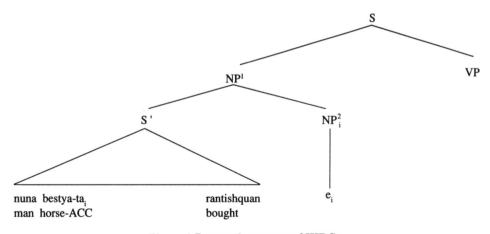

nuna  bestya-ta$_i$           rantishquan        e$_i$
man  horse-ACC              bought

*Figure 4.* **Proposed structure of IHRCs.**

Some authors have argued that IHRCs are found only in OV languages (for example, Gorbet, 1977; Keenan, 1978). In Cole's view this pattern follows directly from the fact that OV languages can exhibit left-branching syntactic structures in NPs, that is, the head occurs as the right-most constituent of the phrase. If the distribution of anaphors, he continues, is governed by the principle due to Langacker (1969) and Ross (1969) that states that an anaphor cannot both precede and command its antecedent, then the structure in figure 4, but not the structure in figure 5, is possible.

In other words, assuming that the essential feature of IHRCs is that they are structures headed by a null anaphoric element, the principle just stated explains why this type of construction is found only in languages characterized by an OV order.[3]

It should be apparent, however, that the advancement of a similar proposal for ASL will encounter significant difficulties. First, although this has been a highly controversial subject in the past, the latest research shows that ASL is better described as having a basic SVO order. Thus, if we accept Cole's proposal of a phonologically null pronominal functioning as a head of the relative clause, ASL "relative" clauses such as figure 1 would be expected to have structures like figure 6.

Clearly, independently of which anaphora condition we take to be correct, either the principle above or Reinhart's (1976)—an anaphor cannot command its antecedent—the structure in figure 6 is predicted to be ungrammatical, since the anaphoric element both precedes and commands its antecedent.

The problem, however, turns out to be not that ASL is an exception among languages with IHRCs but rather that structures like that in figure 4 fail to capture appropriate generalizations for those languages.[4] In the following section, I propose an alternative analysis of this construction in ASL. This analysis is not only consistent with the characteristic phrase structure of ASL, but it also helps to explain certain properties of this type of expression that would go otherwise unexplained.

I then go on to argue that such an analysis makes the correct predictions about this type of structure in other languages as well. In particular, I show that the same structural description proposed here to describe ASL IHRCs can account for similar constructions found in Diegueño, Lakhota, and Quechua. The analysis of IHRCs in ASL that this paper argues for is very similar to Cole's (1987) in that it also requires the construal of a null anaphoric element as a crucial component. However, it becomes

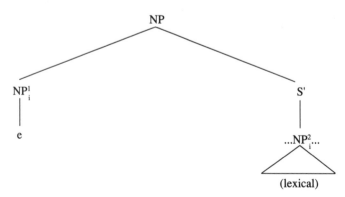

*Figure 5.* **Right-branching structure with null-anaphor head.**

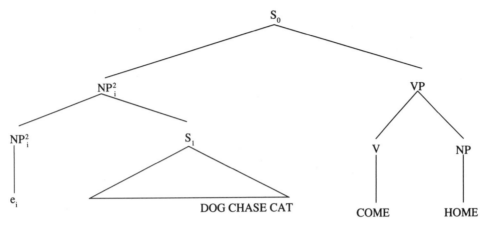

*Figure 6.* **Right-branching structure in ASL.**

clear that the nature of the empty category assumed here is substantially different from that proposed in Cole (1987).

## IHRCs AS TOPIC-COMMENT STRUCTURES

### *What Syntax Can Tell Us about Discourse and What Discourse Can Tell Us about Syntax*

The postulation of a phonologically null NP occurring between the restrictive clause and the main verb is independently motivated by the structural properties of ASL. As Shepard-Kegl (1985) and Lillo-Martin (1986) argue, this language can be posited to have the same type of empty category that is found in the so-called pro-drop languages such as Spanish or Italian, the pronominal "pro." In ASL, NPs are frequently assigned spatial indexes by making the sign corresponding to a given NP at some arbitrary locus and then either pointing in that direction or by looking at that spatial point while signing it.

From then on, pronominal reference is made by indicating the loci associated with the intended referents. Subsequently, the different arguments of the verbs are individualized by the movement of the verb in relation to the different points in space. Thus, in a conversation where the NP 'John' has been previously established at spatial location "i," the sentence 'John chased a cat' will be likely to have the following realization:

(3)     $pro_i$ $_i$CHASED CAT

That is, the signer does not make the handshape for "John" but simply initiates the signing of the verb CHASE at location "i." Hence, it is reasonable to argue that this spatially expressed system of verbal agreement generates a series of inflectional markers that function exactly as if an overt pronoun were present (see Lillo-Martin, 1986 for a detailed account).

Having introduced these new considerations in our discussion of ASL relative clauses, we are now ready to view constructions like example 1 from a completely new perspective. Thus, a reformulation of the transcription in figure 1 that uncovers the structural features discussed above would be as shown in example 4.

$$\overline{\text{r}}$$

(4) s1 [RECENTLY DOG$_i$ CHASE CAT]    s2 [pro $_i$COME  HOME]

The underlying structure that at first sight would seem more appropriate for this example is shown in figure 7.

### Topic-Comment Structures in ASL

However, this is obviously not the whole story. For one thing, if we accept the analysis illustrated in figure 7 in its present form, we are forced to conclude that both clauses correspond to two independent predications. Yet it should be obvious that examples like 1, which are informationally equivalent to the English gloss assigned by Liddell, contain only one focus of information. Furthermore, this structural description fails to provide a satisfactory explanation of the role of the nonmanual signs marked as "r" in Liddell's notation.

In order to find a plausible explanation for this apparent contradiction, we may consider the observations made by a number of authors about the important role that discourse factors play in the overall organization of ASL. Let us review some remarks about the similarities between ASL restricting clauses and ASL topics found in the literature.

Coulter (1981) argues that the facial expressions that mark relatives and topics in ASL are almost identical. Topics lack the raised upper lip, but have the raised eyebrows and lifted chin.[5] Still more relevant is the observation that topics and IHRCs are both initial, nonasserted constituents that must be followed by an assertion (Coulter, 1981, 17).

From a functional perspective it is clear that the strings marked with "r" in Liddell's notation share many of the properties that typically characterize "topic-hood." Chafe (1976), for instance, defines the functional role of topics as follows: "What the topics appear to do is limit the applicability of the main predication to a certain restricted domain. . . . The topic sets a spatial, temporal, or individual frame-

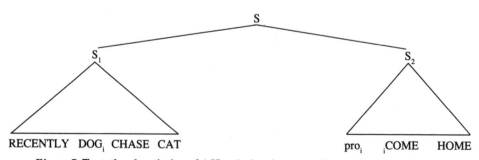

*Figure 7.* **Tentative description of ASL relatives in terms of coordinated structures.**

work within which the main predication holds" (p. 50). From this standpoint, it should be apparent that the concept "relativization" could be reformulated by extending it beyond its syntactic centered attributes. With a slight modification, however, Liddell's claim that nonmanual signs play a fundamental role in ASL relatives can still be shown to be a very valuable point. I argue that the basic function of the facial expression is to indicate the major constituent boundary between the referent establishing clause (topic NP) and the main predication in constructions that can be characterized in terms of TOPIC-COMMENT structures.

The consideration of ASL relative clauses in these terms has a number of obvious advantages. For instance, restrictive clauses in ASL almost invariably occur in sentence-initial position. This follows naturally if we interpret IHRCs as some kind of topic entities, that is, clauses whose only function is to restrict the set of possible referents about which the predication of the following clause holds.[6] Furthermore, it can be shown that IHRCs in ASL strongly resemble typical cases of TOPIC-COMMENT structures investigated in various languages (see Gundel [1986] for an extensive treatment of this subject).

Ochs-Keenan and Schieffelin (1976), for instance, define "left-dislocation" in English as structures with the format "referent + proposition" or "referent + background proposition + main proposition".[7] According to these authors, the fundamental discourse function of left-dislocated structures is to bring "a referent into the foreground of the listener's consciousness" (1976, 242). That is, they make a referent that was not the current "topic" into the "center of attention" of the communicative interaction between the interlocutors. Ochs-Keenan and Schieffelin (1976) observe that "typically, the initial referent is some entity known to or knowable by the hearer from the non-verbal context of the utterance or from some prior background experience. In other words, it is some entity that the hearer can identify or recognize" (p. 242).

Also relevant is their observation that these constructions frequently involve the use of a certain type of verb as a common strategy for bringing a referent into the discourse. They refer to these verbs as "locating verbs" and cite among them "look at," "consider," "know," and "remember." It is now much easier to understand the remark made by Liddell that relative clauses in ASL "may also be introduced by signs like REMEMBER" (1980, 145).

Following the analysis suggested here, the function of REMEMBER in examples like 5 from Liddell's book (his example 26) are no longer problematic.

(5)  [REMEMBER CAT DOG BITE] s ] NP  RUN-AWAY
'[Remember] the cat the dog bit, [it] ran away.'

The possible complications pointed out by Liddell with respect to the status of REMEMBER as a main-clause verb or as a part of the relative clause thus find a straightforward explanation. Contra Liddell, there is no need to claim that this verb is not a real verb but "some sort of relativizer" because "it still has some semantic content (i.e., remembering) in addition to its syntactic relativizing function" (1980, 145).

Furthermore, the interpretation of the restrictive clauses as topic elements also appears to make all the right predictions in a number of related areas. Li and Thompson (1976) and Gundel (1986), for instance, note that although a subject can be either definite or indefinite, one of the primary characteristics of topics is that they must be definite.[8] This is precisely the case in ASL where the NPs traditionally interpreted as the heads of the relatives must be definite. As noted by Coulter (1981), sentences such as example 6 (example 8 in his article) are not found in ASL:

<pre>
       *  _____   r
(6)       PERSON COOK MEAT,   SHAKE PEPPER TOO MUCH.
</pre>

Coulter argues that example 6 is uninterpretable unless the addressee knows which person cooked the meat. According to Coulter (1981), the use of restrictive clauses like the one in example 6 is appropriate only if the purpose of the utterance is to identify which person cooked the meat, and then to make some comment about that person (p. 11).[9]

In addition, the existence of sentences such as example 7 (Coulter, 1981, example 12) also has a straightforward explanation under the proposed analysis.

<pre>
        _____   r
(7)    REMEMBER ROOMMATE BUY CAR,  NOW NOT+HAVE-TO BICYCLE
       COMMUTE.
</pre>

> 'Remember (my) roommate bought a car (?), now (I) don't have to commute by bicycle.'

Example 7 contains a clause with the same facial expression that Liddell claims marks relative clauses. However, this clause does not modify any NP in the "main" clause. Only if we interpret the marked clause as a topic of some kind can we explain why it need not have a selectional relation with the verb in the following clause. Subjects, but not topics, are by necessity arguments of the predicative constituent. Under the structural description that would correspond to the analysis suggested here, only "pro" is selected by the verb in the comment clause as its subject, not the whole topic clause (see figure 9 for details). As example 7 shows, the two clauses in this type of ASL constructions need not share a co-indexed NP as long as the statement of the second clause is relevant to the theme in the preceding clause.

Given these considerations concerning the syntax and discourse of IHRCs in ASL, it should be apparent that they are better described as similar to left dislocation (LD) rather than relativization proper. Although the literature on the subject is not very explicit in this respect, LDs have been assumed to have structures along the lines of figure 8. The main aspect that this structure attempts to reflect is that the

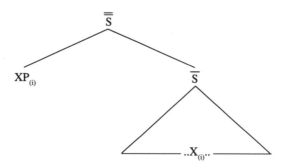

***Figure 8.* Left-dislocated structure.**

element marked as XP is adjoined to $\bar{S}$ rather than a part of the same constituent structure. No movement transformation is involved in relating XP to any of the elements under S.

One of the typical properties of LDs (which distinguishes them from similar topic-comment structures, for example, TOPICALIZATION, or from relative clauses) is that they frequently involve the presence of a personal pronoun in the predicative clause that is coreferential with the left-dislocated NP. However, like the ASL examples discussed above, the left-dislocated constituent and the clause need not share a coreferential element as long as the appropriate pragmatic or semantic relationships hold between the leftmost NP and the clause under S'.

Thus, in the following examples of LD in English, we find instances of each one of these cases. Given the appropriate contexts, both the expressions in examples 8 and 9 are possible.

(8)     a. That man I met in Spain, he is my husband now.
        b. As for the blankets, I don't think we will need them tonight.

(9)     a. Those paintings we saw this morning, I'll never be able to understand abstract art.
        b. As for the blankets, I don't think it's going to be cold tonight.

Given these considerations, the sort of adjustments needed by figure 7 should be apparent. I will propose that ASL "relatives" have an underlying structure as in figure 9.[10] The crucial aspect to note here is that this analysis assumes no embedding of the element typically characterized in previous analyses of IHRCs as the restrictive relative clause. That is, the left-most NP is not an argument of the verb in the main predication (or comment clause).

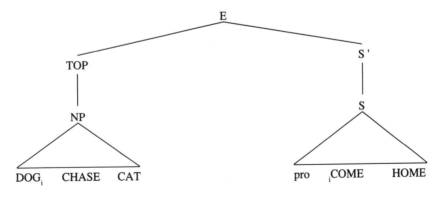

'The dog that chased the cat, it came home.'

*Figure 9.* **Proposed structure of internally headed relative clauses in ASL.**

# IS ASL LIKE DIEGUEÑO OR DIEGUEÑO
# LIKE ASL?

## *Demography of Pronominals in IHRCs: Some Ignored Individuals*

Let us now test whether the analysis proposed here for ASL can be generalized to include IHRCs in other languages. If this is the case, it will be worthwhile to pursue this line of investigation. To this end, I analyze instances of this construction found in Diegueño (Gorbet, 1974), in Lakhota (Williamson, 1987), and in Quechua (Cole, 1987). [For some observations on Navajo, see Fontana (1989).]

The first step is to show that IHRCs in these languages share the attributes of ASL that made the structure in figure 9 a plausible alternative description in the discussion above. One of the essential features of the kind of structures proposed here is the possibility of positing the existence of a pronominal in the comment clause that can be co-indexed with an antecedent in the restrictive clause. Owing to its anaphoric nature, this element inherits the referential properties of the expression in the leftmost NP, and hence the predication holds only for that specific referent.

Returning to the Diegueño examples, figure 2 is repeated here as figure 10, we can show that the construal of a category behaving exactly as "pro" behaves in ASL is also motivated in this language. According to Gorbet (1974), Diegueño distinguishes the clauses "i:pac 'wu:w" and "i:pac 'wa: nʸi+k wyiw," which he assumes are embedded clauses, from the same strings with purely sentential status, by the addition of the demonstrative morpheme PU. Thus, when PU is present, the structural description of the string changes as in example 10:

(10)    a.  i : pac 'wu:w                    [I saw the man] s

        b.  i : pac 'wu:w pu               [ [The man I saw] s ] NP

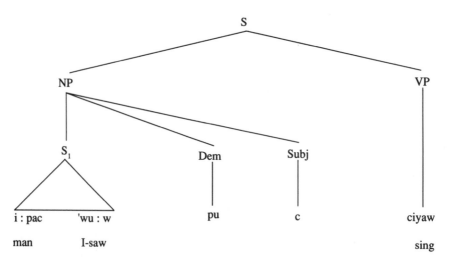

'The man I saw sang.'

*Figure 10.* **Internally headed relative clause in Diegueño (from Gobert, 1974).**

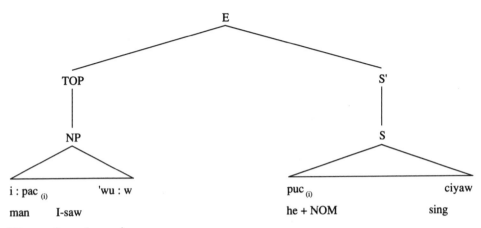

'The man I saw, he sang'

*Figure 11.* **Proposed structure of Diegueño IHRCs.**

Gorbet goes on to argue that the resulting constituent after the attachment of PU is licensed as a subject by the addition of the case morpheme, C, which marks the whole string as nominative. However, a close examination of Diegueño grammar, in light of our observations about ASL above, provides a simpler explanation for the otherwise puzzling use of PU in these constructions.

True personal pronouns in Diegueño exist only for the first and second person. However, the demonstrative PU, apart from occurring as a determiner, is commonly used as a third-person personal pronoun (see Langdon [1970] for a complete description of the pronominal system of Diegueño). In figure 10, and also in figure 3, we see the occurrence of a pronominal element PU that happens to be morphologically marked by C as nominative. Thus, the same role filled by "pro" in ASL is filled in Diegueño by an element that is phonologically realized in S-structure and that bears clear formal marks of its grammatical role. The alternative structural description for figure 10 is then figure 11:

This analysis predicts that in all IHRCs we must be able to posit the existence of a pronominal element that may be a phonologically realized expression as PU in the Diegueño figure 11 or a null argument of the type "pro" as in the ASL figure 9. Examples 11 and 12 (4a and 9a in Williamson, 1987) show that our predictions also hold for Lakhota. Independently of the structural description assumed by Williamson, we can see in example 11 the occurrence of a pronoun, *he*, with zero morphological marking (singular), which has an antecedent (*owiza*, "quilt") in the clause-initial NP. Likewise, in example 12, we find another pronoun, this time marked for plural, that is coreferential with *wiya*, "women." Both of these pronouns occur after a definite article, *ki*, which marks the preceding NP as a definite expression.

(11)  [NP$_i$ [s Mary [owiza wa]$_i$ kage] ki] he   ophewathu
       Mary quilt   a    make the Dem I-buy

      'I bought the quilt that Mary made.'

(12)  [[Wiya   eya   owiza ki   kaga pi] ki] hena cheya pi
       Women some quilt the made P1 the those cry   P1

      'The women who made the quilt cried.'

Notice that the determiner *ki* behaves very similarly to those particles found in other languages marking a word or a string of words as the topic of the construction (for example Japanese *wa*).

The assumption that IHRCs in Lakhota have the structures proposed here provides, in addition, a straightforward explanation for some of the scope facts observed by Williamson (1987). She notes that example 13 (her 19a), which she claims contains a negative indefinite NP embedded in a relative clause, is ungrammatical. In example 14 (her 20a), where the NP is a plain indefinite, the expression becomes grammatical in Lakhota.[11]

(13)   *[[Tuweni u    pi sni] ki] hena iyokipi pi
     no one    come P1 Neg Det those happy  P1

'*Those such that not any came are happy.'

(14)   [[Tuwa   (eya) u    pi sni ki  hena iyokipi pi
     someone some come P1 Neg the those happy  P1

'Those who didn't come are happy.'

Notice that if we assume that IHRCs in Lakhota have similar structures to those proposed in figure 9, more appropriate glosses for examples 13 and 14 would be:

(15)   'No one came, those are happy'

(16)   'Some people that didn't come, those are happy'

Given that it is uncontroversial that anaphoric elements cannot have antecedent expressions that have no referents, the pattern of grammaticality shown by examples 13 and 14 follows straightforwardly. The pronoun *hena* in the comment clause of example 13 would be co-indexed with *tuweni* "no one", which obviously has no possible referential interpretation.

With respect to Imbabura and Ancash Quechua, the confirmation of our predictions is provided by Cole himself in example 10 of his article, given here as example 17. The parentheses indicate the optionality cf the enclosed elements.

(17)   (ñuka) mishki-ta    randi-rka-ni.  (ñuka) (chay-ta)
     (I)     candy-ACC  buy-PAST-1  I     that-ACC

     miku-rka-ni.
     eat-PAST-1

     'I bought candy. I ate it.'

Immediately after providing this example, Cole adds that in Quechua subject and object pronouns can be omitted under discourse conditions similar to those in which pronouns are used in English (1987, 282). Thus Quechua permits null anaphora, which is consistent with the following alternative analysis of figure 4.

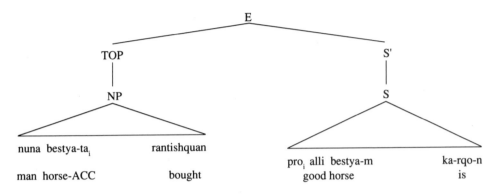

'The horse that the man bought, it's a good horse.'

*Figure 12.* **Proposed structure of IHRCs in Quechua.**

### The Simplicity Factor

As discussed in the preceding sections, previous analyses of IHRCs do not provide a satisfactory account of certain characteristic attributes of these structures in ASL, either from a formal or a discourse perspective. In addition, the two approaches represented here by figures 1 and 4 crucially fail to explain the presence in the surface structure of Diegueño and Lakhota IHRCs of pronominal elements whose grammatical role is made obvious by their syntactic distribution and by their overt morphological marking. Furthermore, I argue that analyses like the one proposed here are also to be preferred on theory-internal grounds.

Both figures 1 and 4 require the incorporation of additional machinery to allow for a plausible account of how the interpretive rules of the semantic component apply to render the meaning of the sentences. I have already mentioned the problems observed by Cole (1987) regarding the possible conflicts in the interpretation of certain nominals as heads of the IHRCs in languages where case is overtly marked morphologically.

In relation to $\theta$-theory, none of the analyses fares very well. On the one hand, in structures like figure 1, the so-called head would be assigned both the $\theta$-role corresponding to the position of the higher NP in the argument structure of the matrix verb and the $\theta$-role corresponding to its position in the argument structure of the verb in the embedded clause. Such an analysis clearly involves a violation of the $\theta$-criterion of Government and Binding theory as reproduced below.

(16)   $\theta$-Criterion (slightly simplified): Every NP must be taken as the argument of some predicate; furthermore, it must be so taken at most once. Or: Every chain must receive one and only one $\theta$-role.

On the other hand, Cole (1987, 300) summarizes the essential points in his proposal: "(1) IHRC have at S-structure phonologically null heads which are coindexed with a nominal inside the modifying clause that is interpreted as the head; and (2) at LF the nominal interpreted as the head has been raised from the modifying clause into head position" (1987, 300).

According to Cole, the structure of IHRCs at LF would have forms that resemble figure 13.

Given the uncontroversial assumption that the moved element must form a chain with the co-indexed trace that head raising leaves inside the embedded clause, the resulting chain would receive two different θ-roles: one assigned by the verb in the embedded clause, and one assigned by the matrix verb. As determined by the projection principle, the θ-criterion holds at D-structure, S-structure, and LF. Hence, if Cole's analysis is accepted, the structures that we obtain after head raising has applied would also result in violation of the θ-criterion.

There is an obvious way to circumvent this problem. We can assume that the verb in the matrix clause assigns the θ-role not to the head but rather to the NP containing it. This, however, forces us to accept the following awkward situation: at LF, the θ-role assigned to the higher NP is different from that of its head.

The main problem posed by Cole's analysis, however, comes in relation to the status of the empty category that he proposes as the head of IHRCs. Cole says of it only that it is "some kind of pronominal," exceedingly vague as a definition. First, the ad hoc character of this category becomes apparent if we bear in mind that it lacks the independent motivation that led to the postulation of null arguments in other NP positions.

The closest type of anaphoric element that comes to mind is the null pronominal that has been proposed for the so-called pro-drop parameter. Rizzi (1982), for instance, assumes that the null element in subject position of pro-drop languages is a trace. Jaeggli (1982) claims that this empty category is a PRO. Chomsky (1982), on the other hand, proposed that this null category is a "pro," that is, unlike PRO, this element can be governed, but it need not be properly governed.

However, even if we can get around the complications involved in licensing any of these categories to occur in the structural position of the head of a relative clause, we still face a major problem. Given that Cole's analysis crucially requires IHRCs to undergo a rule of head raising,[11] independent of which type of null category this element is assumed to be, the following observation holds: the node in the head NP position must be capable of receiving the lexical material after head raising has applied. It logically follows that the null anaphora referred to by Cole cannot be posited to be a trace, PRO, or "pro," for these categories are not viable sites to receive displaced lexical elements. Hence, the possibilities of finding an acceptable definition for this category become dramatically restricted.

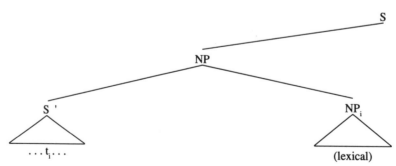

*Figure 13.* **Proposed LF structure of IHRCs (from Cole, 1987).**

# CONCLUSION: UNSOLVED PROBLEMS

In this paper I show that the consideration of IHRCs as types of topic-comment expressions similar to LDs can capture generalizations about this type of construction that eluded previous analyses. Structures like 9 have the additional advantage of providing a less problematic syntactic description of IHRCs without resorting to unmotivated stipulations. Since in the analysis proposed here, the left-most NP is by definition not an argument of the sentence containing the main predication, the problems discussed in the previous section simply do not arise. Note that the solution to the problem of whether we should posit external or internal heads for the NPs containing clausal constructions does not fundamentally affect the adequacy of structures like in figure 9 to describe IHRCs. As things stand, I can see no advantages of analyses like in figure 1 over those like in figure 4 as far as the internal structures they assume for the NPs previously interpreted as containing the restrictive relative clauses. Hence, the proposal advanced in this paper will, for the moment, remain neutral in this respect.

In conclusion, it should be noted that some important questions about the nature of IHRCs in oral languages still remain to be answered. For instance, in ASL we have seen that the anaphoric element of the comment-clause is linked to the referent introduced by the topic-clause by signing the verb at the previously specified location. However, in languages like Quechua, where no such formal marking is available, the different strategies employed by speakers to solve possible conflicts in reference must still be accounted for.

Furthermore, if it is the case that IHRCs have structures like the ones proposed here, we would expect that oral languages will have distinctive intonational contours marking the boundaries between topic NP and main predication in the way facial expressions do in ASL. These and other problems, however, remain empirical questions to be solved by a detailed study of these languages in a natural setting.

# NOTES

This paper has benefited greatly from criticisms, suggestions, and observations by Jack Hoeksema, Anthony Kroch, Judy Kegl, Ellen Prince, Joseph DeChicchis, Beatrice Santorini, and Megan Moser. Needless to say, the responsibility for all shortcomings is totally mine.

1. For ease of exposition, I will continue to refer to these constructions as internally headed relative clauses or IHRCs, despite the claim advanced here that they are not in fact relative clauses in a strict sense.
2. Ancash Quechua has been often cited—together with Diegueño—as a paradigm case of a language with internally headed relative clauses.
3. Note, however, that Cole's line of argumentation is forced to stipulate that the choice between the principle stated and Reinhart's (1968) condition on anaphora (that is, an anaphor cannot command its antecedent) is a parameter in regard to which languages may differ, since there are languages that have left-branching NP structures that do not have IHRCs.
4. In fact, it is worth noting that ASL would not be the only exception to Cole's generalization. As observed by Lehman (1984, 117), Dagbani, a Niger-Congo language of the Gur subgroup whose basic word order is SVO, also has IHRCs.
5. If we consider that what Liddell and other authors have recognized as topics are fronted NPs, it is not difficult to see why this barely distinguishable variation might not be so essential after

all. It is reasonable to suppose that this light lip raising may stem from very trivial physical or mechanical factors. The signer, when extending the marking of topichood to a longer sequence of signs, must exercise an additional effort to maintain the facial expression coterminous with the marked string. Such strain would be manifested in a slight raising of the lip, which is not noticeable when the marked element is a single sign. Of course, this is just a hypothesis. A considerably more detailed study is needed in order to ascertain any claim about the correlation between length of the marked string and shape of the facial expression.

6. It is very significant in this respect that when the supposedly relative clause is not in initial position it is frequently followed by a demonstrative, as in the following example extracted without modification from Liddell (1980): PRO.1 BUY [[DOG THATa BITE CAT]$^g$THATc]$_{NP}$. This example could be paraphrased as: 'I bought, (you know) that dog that bit a cat?, that one,' where the referent of the demonstrative is interpreted from the spatial location of the signing, which makes it coreferential with the NP DOG by its being signed at the same locus.

7. These authors redefine the concept of "left dislocation" to include constructions that technically would not be considered as such. However, the crucial point they try to convey in this article is that in the structures that they label 'left dislocation' (which also include instances of left dislocation proper), referents and propositions are linked pragmatically rather than syntactically.

8. Reinhart (1981), however, has argued that such a claim is not valid. As we will see, there are some examples of IHRC languages, specifically Lakhota, that do not seem to have this restriction.

9. Notice, in addition, that elements construed as heads of ASL relatives are always indexed to a specific location, whereas indefinite NPs are just signed but are not indexed in the same fashion. Indexing, then, could be considered as a formal mark of definiteness in ASL.

10. The higher node "E" stands for "expression" (as in Banfield, 1973). The proposed structure is only a first attempt to formalize the relations that hold between the two distinct components. The point of the representation in example 9 is to express that the string marked with "r" in Liddell's notation is not to be interpreted as a predication, but rather as some device used to restrict the set of possible referents about which the predication of the clause, under S', holds.

11. To be fair, one has to admit that scope facts in Lakhota involve more complexities than just those presented in examples 13 and 14.

12. One of the arguments offered by Cole to support the existence of a rule of head raising is related to the fact that Quechua also has headed relative clauses. If both headed and null-headed relative clauses have the same semantic interpretation, the question arises whether they require separate interpretive rules. Cole argues that this problem is amenable to a natural solution under his analysis since both types of relatives would have identical structure at LF after a rule of head raising converts IHRCs into lexically headed relatives. He then adds that possible problems concerning government of empty positions are avoided if we assume that in Quechua ECP applies only at LF after head raising has applied.

# REFERENCES

Banfield, A. (1973). Narrative style and the grammar of direct and indirect speech. *Foundations of Language* 10:1–39.

Chafe, W. F. (1976). Givenness, contrastiveness, definiteness, subjects, topics and point of view. In *Subject and topic*, edited by Ch. N. Li, 25–55. New York: Academic Press.

Chomsky, N. (1982). *Some concepts and consequences of the theory of government and binding*. Cambridge: MIT Press.

Cole, P. (1987). The structure of internally headed relative clauses. *Natural Language and Linguistic Theory* 5:277–302.

Coulter, G. R. (1981). A conjoined analysis of American Sign Language relative clauses. University of Rochester, Rochester, NY. Unpublished manuscript.

Fontana, J. M. (1989). On the structure of so-called "Internally headed" relative clauses. *The Penn Review of Linguistics.* University of Pennsylvania.

Gorbet, L. (1973). How to tell a head when you see one: Disambiguation in Diegueño relative clauses. *Linguistic Notes from La Jolla* 5:63–82.

———. (1974). Relativization and complementation in Diegueño: Noun phrases as nouns. Ph.D. diss., University of California, San Diego.

———. (1977). Headless relatives in the Southwest: Are they related? *Proceedings of the Berkeley Linguistic Society* 3:270–78.

Gundel, J. K. (1986). Universals of topic-comment structure. In *Language typology and language universals,* edited by E. Moravcsik et al., 209–42. Amsterdam: J. Benjamins.

Hale, K., and Platero, P. (1974). Aspects of Navajo anaphora: relativization and pronominalization. *Diné Bizaad Nánil'iih (Navajo Language Review)* 1:9–28.

Huang, C-T. J. (1984). On the distribution and reference of empty pronouns. *Linguistic Inquiry* 15:531–74.

Jaeggli, O. (1982). *Topics in romance syntax.* Dordrecht: Foris.

Keenan, E. (1978). Relative clauses in the languages of the world. University of California at Los Angeles. Unpublished manuscript.

Langacker, R. (1969). On pronominalization and the chain of command. In *Modern studies in English,* edited by D. Reibel and S. Schane, 160–86. Englewood Cliffs, NJ: Prentice-Hall.

Langdon, M. (1970). *A grammar of Diegueño, the Mesa Grande dialect.* Berkeley: University of California Press.

Lehman, Ch. (1984). *Der Relativsatz.* Tübingen, Gunter Narr Verlag.

Li, Ch. N., and Thompson, S. A. (1976). Subject and topic: A new typology of language. In *Subject and Topic,* edited by Li, Ch. N., 459–89. New York: Academic Press.

Liddell, S. K. (1980). *American Sign Language syntax.* The Hague: Mouton.

Lillo-Martin, D. (1986). Two kinds of null arguments in American Sign Language. *Natural Language and Linguistic Theory* 4:415–44.

Ochs-Keenan, E., and Schieffelin, B. (1976). Foregrounding referents: A reconsideration of left dislocation in discourse. *Berkeley Linguistic Society,* 2:240–57.

Reinhart, T. (1976). *The syntactic domain of anaphora.* Ph.D. diss., MIT.

Rizzi, L. (1982). *Issues in Italian syntax.* Dordrecht: Foris.

Ross, J. R. (1969). On the cyclic nature of English pronominalization. In *Modern Studies in English,* edited by D. Reibel and S. Schane, 187–200. Englewood Cliffs, NJ: Prentice-Hall.

Shepard-Kegl, J. (1985). *Locative relations in American Sign Language word formation, syntax and discourse.* Ph.D. diss., MIT.

Williamson, J. (1987). An indefiniteness restriction for relative clauses in Lakhota. In *On the representation of (in)definiteness,* edited by E. Reuland and A. ter Meulen, 168–90. Cambridge: MIT Press.

# PART

# IV

# SOCIOLINGUISTICS

# The Emerging Deaf Community in
# the Dominican Republic: An
# Ethnographic Study

Barbara Gerner de Garcia

This study of the deaf community in the Dominican Republic is a preliminary ethnographic study. It is the result of qualitative research undertaken over the course of five years, 1983 to 1987. Approximately eight months were spent in the community. All observations involved members of the deaf community in Santo Domingo, the capital city of the country. The community includes around 100 adults who live in the capital and many more who are isolated within the capital itself and in outlying areas. There is also a much smaller organized community of about twenty-five deaf adults in the second largest city, Santiago.

Data for this study were obtained through participant observation, notes, and interviews. Visits were made to the deaf club, to the deaf church, to a night school for deaf adults, to a theater group rehearsing and performing in a national festival, and to the homes of deaf people and hearing people active in the deaf community. Some videotaping was done in order to collect data on Dominican Sign Language (DRSL).

I entered into the community without problems. The Dominican deaf community looks to the American deaf community as a model. Americans interested in deaf people are seen as a resource and are enthusiastically received. Communication with Americans is generally possible because the lexical base for DRSL is borrowed from ASL. My fluency in Spanish, family ties to the country through marriage, and growing up with a deaf brother were all helpful.

My informants included members of the Dominican deaf community, hearing Dominicans who work with the deaf, and a missionary couple that consisted of a deaf Bolivian pastor and his American wife.

To my knowledge, there has not been any study of this community. These deaf people cooperated with me in the hope that it would bring them recognition in the world's deaf community. Without their help and cooperation and that of hearing people active in their community, this study would not have been possible.

259

# AN EMERGING DEAF COMMUNITY

All societies have deaf members, but not all deaf people organize themselves in the same ways. The American deaf community is by far the most organized in the world. It has evolved a distinct language, culture, and supporting institutions. The deaf communities of the developing world offer a contrast to the highly organized U.S. community.

Working primarily in the Caribbean, the anthropologist William Washabaugh has described three types of deaf communities: isolated, developing, and diglossic (1981). Isolated deaf communities have been identified in the Amazon of Brazil (Fereira-Brito, 1985), the Caribbean island of Providence (Washabaugh, 1979, 1981, 1986), and Mayan Mexico (Shuman, 1980). In such communities, deaf people are accepted but often ignored. They do not group together, but rather usually live isolated from one another. Providence Island, for example, is an isolated deaf community with a high incidence of hereditary deafness. The deaf inhabitants are scattered over the tiny island and have limited contact with one another. They range widely in age. There have been enough deaf people over a number of generations to have created a sign language, which is used by both deaf and the hearing islanders. However, the hearing islanders tend to communicate with the deaf islanders only when necessary, and the deaf population is excluded from the real life of the island (Washabaugh, 1986).

Diglossic deaf communities are heavily influenced by the dominant language of the hearing community. Washabaugh (1981) labels the U.S. deaf community as diglossic because its members recognize the advantage of moving between two codes, their language and the language of the powerful. Diglossia implies there is a need for the minority language speakers to move between languages and to devalue their vernacular.

The third type of deaf community is the developing deaf community. According to Washabaugh (1981), a characteristic of a developing deaf community is a lack of a consistent tradition of deaf education. This lack of a consistent educational system may prevent deaf people from devaluing their own sign language, because there is apparently a relationship between educating deaf people and leading them to devalue their vernacular. The deaf population of Grand Cayman Island, located in the Caribbean south of Cuba, for example has been educated either in Jamaica, the United States, or more recently on the island. There is an indigenous sign language due to a high incidence of hereditary deafness, and a two-handed fingerspelling system that is distinct from both the British and American alphabets. Many of the old Caymanian signs are similar to Providence Island signs, despite a distance of hundreds of miles of ocean. This is probably due both to borrowings (islanders did make their livings on the sea and had contact) and to cultural similarities (Washabaugh, 1979). Deaf Caymanians have been exposed to Jamaican Sign Language, which seems to be related to British Sign Language and to ASL.

The Dominican Republic, a Spanish-speaking country of almost 7 million, shares the Caribbean island of Hispaniola with Haiti. There is a sizable deaf population in the capital city of Santo Domingo (population 1,400,000), as well as in the second-largest city, Santiago (population, 285,000). Deaf people are found in all parts of this island, which is about the size of Vermont and New Hampshire, 18,816 square miles (*World Almanac*, 1988).

Like Grand Cayman Island the Dominican Republic did not have universal free education for deaf children until twenty years ago. Less than ten years after deaf children were brought together in the first national school for the deaf in the capital city, missionaries coming from Puerto Rico introduced a form of sign language using American signs. This lexicon became the major influence on Dominican Sign Language (DRSL), but the national school system for the deaf does not use sign language. In the early 1980s, the use of total communication was considered, but subsequent upheavals in the national school have prevented its implementation. The deaf community of the Dominican Republic appears then to share several of the characteristics of developing deaf communities. The nation lacked the means of educating deaf children until recently, and deaf people are still proud of their use of sign language.

The emerging deaf community in the Dominican Republic is made up entirely of young adults between the ages of fifteen and about thirty. They are the first products of the national school. The community is just beginning to become cohesive. In the early 1980s, an Association for the Deaf was founded, which is the focus of the deaf community. The lack of older members is reported to be due to the previous isolation of deaf people. One of the goals of the young deaf people is to find these older isolated deaf people and bring them into the community.

## EDUCATION OF THE DEAF

In the Dominican Republic, the literacy rate is between 68 percent (*Information Please Almanac*, 1988) and 77 percent (*World Almanac*, 1988). Before there was a national school for the deaf in the Dominican Republic, parents who had the economic means sent their deaf children to Puerto Rico or the United States to be educated. There were also a few deaf children who were educated in regular schools. Probably many deaf children were kept at home and not sent to school, a practice that continues today. Deaf girls are less likely than boys to be sent to school, and many are not allowed out of the house alone. This tradition is reflected by the limited participation of adult deaf women in the deaf club, where men outnumber women more than two to one. Cultural attitudes toward women as well as toward deafness are responsible for the lack of involvement of women.

In the 1960s a group of parents formed La Asociacion Pro-Educacion de los Sordosmudos, Inc., and sought financial help from philanthropists and businesses to establish a national school for the deaf. La Escuela Nacional de los Sordosmudos was established in Santo Domingo in 1967. A few years after the founding of the school, it moved to larger facilities. The government has no role in the education of the deaf in the country and the private sector still is the source of funding.

The school currently has an enrollment of about five hundred pupils. The national school also has nine satellite schools throughout the country. In total, the system serves about eight hundred deaf students from preschool through age twenty-one. Recruitment is done mostly through word of mouth, television, and the press.

Students attend school for a half-day. They go for four hours in either the morning or afternoon. Older students are provided with vocational training in traditional areas such as printing, sewing, shoe repair, or hairdressing. There is a night school for deaf adults aged fourteen and older where students work to gain a high school diploma.

Education in the school is oral. In the early 1980s an attempt was made to change to a total communications approach, or simultaneous oral Spanish and signs, but this was not implemented due to a teacher's strike in the fall of 1985 that resulted in the firing of the director of the school and all but one teacher. The school is now staffed by teachers with no training in deaf education. Some of the teachers are only high school graduates, the minimum requirement for teaching in many Latin American countries. This development halted the transition to the use of sign language in the school.

In addition to the national schools, private schools for the deaf are now available. There is a private oral school in Santo Domingo. Some preschool children are serviced in small classes in private clinics, and some of the teachers who previously worked at the national school have set up a school.

There is no postsecondary education for deaf people in the Dominican Republic. Only three deaf adults have been known to go on for education beyond high school. These three have done so without accommodations for their deafness and with virtually no resources. Given the economic realities and the lack of possibilities for able-bodied adults with university educations, there is little incentive in this context for deaf people to struggle for postsecondary training.[1]

The preparation of teachers of the deaf faces a number of difficulties in the Dominican Republic. La Universidad de Pedro Henriquez (UNPHU) is a private university with a training program for teachers of the deaf. The program was established in the 1970s with the help of a South American educator of the deaf. According to a graduate, the program was initially a comprehensive program that produced well-trained teachers. But by the 1980s it was failing to attract students due to high tuition costs and limited opportunities for teachers of the deaf. With low enrollment, the program was unable to maintain its quality and now its future is tenuous (Dionny Recio, personal communication, 3 August 1986).

There are no deaf adults working in the national school, which is not surprising given the current state of deaf education. During the teacher's strike, the American missionary previously mentioned was asked to teach classes, but her deaf husband volunteered and was turned down. Although the president of the deaf club recently was working in a private preschool class for deaf children as an assistant, this is the first time a deaf person has been involved in the education of deaf children in the Dominican Republic. The low educational achievement of the majority of deaf adults in the country is likely to keep them out of the classrooms as teachers of the deaf.

## A DESCRIPTION OF THE DEAF COMMUNITY

The deaf club in the capital city of Santo Domingo is the only one in the country. It was set up in 1982 as an outgrowth of a club for young deaf people set up by the Asociacion Pro-Educacion. As the deaf students completed their education, they realized the need for their own association run for and by deaf people. They have a president and officers whom they elect every four years. They held elections for the second time in 1986. There are approximately 130 members, including several members from the city of Santiago, in the interior of the country. Most weekends, about a third of the members come to the club.

There are virtually no older deaf people in the deaf club. Obviously there are older deaf people in the Dominican Republic, but before there was a school for the deaf to bring them together, deaf people grew up in isolation from one another. The incidence of hereditary deafness is low and the vast majority of deaf people are the only deaf members of their families.

A current goal of the deaf club is to become completely autonomous. It is housed in the facilities of the Asociacion Pro-Educacion and is limited to a few set hours on Saturday afternoon and Sunday morning for activities (there is at least one regular meeting place in a park where deaf men congregate during the week). The deaf club would like to find another building that would allow members flexibility and independence. They hope that the government may give them space. Sports activities are currently sponsored by the school for the deaf. Economic limitations prevent their participation in the World Games for the Deaf.

Gallaudet University sent a group to Santo Domingo in 1986 to meet with the officials of the deaf club. A teacher of the deaf from Santo Domingo was the liaison. She had spent a month in Washington in the spring of 1986 as a participant in a program for Latin American teachers of the deaf. She was the second Dominican educator to participate in this program. As liaison, she has been working with the deaf club to follow up on the recommendations made by the group from Gallaudet.

The organization of the deaf club needed to be improved in order to be stronger and more self-sufficient. The club was advised to hold regular meetings to discuss and develop club policy. It was told to set up bylaws and to keep careful notes of all proceedings. The Gallaudet team recommended that elected officers be responsible for guiding the members to establish goals and plan their implementation.

A major obstacle to the deaf club's becoming an independent organization run for and by deaf people is the deaf members' lack of confidence in their own abilities. However, some of the members are beginning to view themselves as capable people. They are learning the need to help themselves rather than to depend on the philanthropy of others (hearing people). They have set up a dues-paying system to provide much needed seed money to initiate some planned projects. Most members pay about $.50 a month, and those with jobs voluntarily pay more. This is a tremendous move forward, given the tradition of charity that has supported the education of deaf Dominicans.

The altruism of the hearing majority toward the deaf community is a form of control based on paternalism. Harlan Lane (1987) named paternalism as the chief villain in deaf education. Paternalism is insidious because although it claims to be based on altruistic motives, its real motive is control. Based on his experiences in Africa, Lane draws parallels between the paternalism of the colonizer toward the colonized and the paternalism of the hearing world toward the deaf. This relationship is perpetuated when deaf people accept their inferior status. The danger also exists of the deaf population of the underdeveloped world's looking to the developed world, especially the United States, for leadership in their struggle for change. In looking for change to come from the outside, they continue to be dependent on the paternalism of others.

The greatest influence on the Dominican deaf community in organizing itself has been from the outside. Missionaries, contact with Gallaudet, and deaf Dominicans who have lived in the United States have all influenced the formation of the community. The neighboring island of Puerto Rico has a large deaf community that is more organized than the Dominican community. When a group of about twenty-five Puerto Rican deaf people visited Santo Domingo, the contrast was apparent. Many of the Puerto Ricans had been educated on the mainland United States. This is common because Puerto Rico lacks educational opportunities, and the citizens of Puerto Rico can travel freely back and forth to the United States and can reside there. The Puerto Rican group included a Gallaudet student and an older American deaf man who had moved to Puerto Rico to help deaf people there. In the group were two older deaf people, aged about fifty-five or sixty. They had never been to school, and they used home signs to communicate. Members of their group interpreted for them. It was encouraging to see the participation despite language differences. The Puerto Rican group was an example to the Dominican deaf community as to how they could accommodate older deaf Dominicans.

## THE ROLE OF MISSIONARIES

Since its inception, deaf education has been linked to the saving of souls. During the Middle Ages, the first teacher of the deaf, the Spanish priest Pedro Ponce de Leon, taught his deaf pupils to speak because he believed that their lack of speech would condemn them eternally (Hoemann, 1981). Saint Paul had said that "faith comes through hearing" (Lane, 1984), which linked the ability to hear with being saved. When the Abbé de l'Epée began teaching deaf children in the 1760s in France, he believed he would save himself by saving their souls. It was Epée who put the natural sign language of the deaf to work to teach the faith. He taught deaf children to read in order to be able to teach them Christian doctrine (Lane, 1984). Thomas Gallaudet, who traveled to Europe to seek help in setting up the first permanent school for the deaf in America, was a minister.

Woodward succinctly states the historical goal of deaf education in his title *How You Gonna Get to Heaven if You Can't Talk to Jesus?* Educators of the deaf have been described as having a religious-like missionary zeal (Woodward, 1982). This is most likely a result of the evolution of deaf education from religious education. Learning to read (and for some to speak) was a by-product of saving deaf souls.

Missionaries have been a major influence on the deaf community in the Dominican Republic. A signed language based on the lexicon of ASL and oral Spanish was brought by missionaries from Puerto Rico in the 1970s. Missionaries also set up a summer Bible camp in the interior of the country, which brought together young deaf people from all over the island. This is what helped the deaf community organize itself beyond the capital city and link up with the group in Santiago.

In 1985 a deaf Bolivian minister and his hearing American wife set up a ministry for the deaf community in Santo Domingo. They had spent the two previous years in Puerto Rico and prior to that had set up a mission school for the deaf in Bolivia, which was the first to use sign language. The minister had himself learned ASL from American missionaries as a child in Bolivia. He received further training in the United States.

This couple ran religious services and Bible classes. They taught ASL to deaf and hearing church members. They encouraged the use of native signs and believed it was better to learn signs from deaf people than from books. The Dominican deaf community, isolated and neglected previously, was receptive to their efforts. Although the Bolivian minister and his wife left in the winter of 1987, and their replacements had not arrived by the summer of 1987, some deaf people are continuing to meet on Saturday afternoons at the same time and place they had met with the Bolivian minister. He did enable them to have their own church, and he gave them enough guidance to continue on their own.

However, a different denomination of missionaries filled the void. These missionaries are hearing and American, and they seem to have much less respect for the deaf community. They tell the Dominicans that their signs are wrong. They run their services on Sundays at the same hours that the deaf club meets, and they send church members to the deaf club to try and get the deaf people to drop what they are doing and come to church. In their newsletter of August 1987, these newly arrived missionaries describe their mission by opening with a quote from Isaiah: ''And in that time, the deaf will hear the words of the book.'' They go on to say that the Americans have arrived in Santo Domingo and with the help of a minister of unspecified Latin origin, are teaching sign language to deaf Dominicans and to hearing people who will be missionaries for them.

The missionaries' influence on this deaf community has been both positive and negative. After the deaf club the church seems to be the next most important organization for deaf people in the Dominican Republic. Teaching sign language to hearing people has helped eliminate some of the deaf Dominicans' isolation, but to what extent is it being used by hearing people to control deaf people? The use of ASL has an impact on the attitudes toward indigenous sign language and may lead to its demise.

## THE RIGHTS OF DEAF PEOPLE

Deaf people in the Dominican Republic are denied rights that American deaf people take for granted. The most basic right, the right to an education, is granted only through the charity of others. There are no government-sponsored schools for deaf children. No community or welfare services, social security, food programs, rehabilitation services, or interpreters are available for the deaf community.

There are no guarantees of equal employment opportunities. In a nation that suffers from massive unemployment and underemployment, deaf people are lucky to have any jobs at all. By their own estimates, only about 25 percent of the deaf community is employed. The deaf minister put the estimates at a lower 15 percent. Deaf people say they have little hope for getting jobs. There is so much competition for jobs that deaf adults say they are ignored. Their perception of the hopelessness of the situation leads to what the missionaries describe as a self-defeating attitude and a loss of motivation to seek employment. This attitude is not limited to deaf people, but seems to be prevalent among the poorer classes. The powerlessness of the poor prevents them from envisioning a future that they can control. Many deaf people talk about emigrating to the United States and quite a few do illegally enter the United States. Since the basis of the U.S. immigration law is to allow immigration of people who will contribute to society, not be ''burdens'' (Sloan, 1987), there are more restrictions on the immigration of the disabled to the United States.

Deaf people also say that their families will take care of them, so that they don't really have to work. A prevalent attitude is that handicapped people can't work to support themselves or lead independent lives. Deaf people tell of being exploited in jobs because they are deaf. A number of the men who worked in a local printing shop were paid only 10 percent of the minimum wage. When they eventually realized that they were being taken advantage of, they quit. They state that it is often the case that the alternative to unemployment is exploitation.

Some of the deaf people in the Dominican Republic have used their vocational training to get jobs. A few of the deaf women work as hairdressers. A family with four deaf children runs a printing business. Several men work in photo studios, a business found on every corner in the capital. One deaf man who was trained in computer programming at a private university (without the help of interpreters, note-takers, etc.) works for the government utility company. Deaf people say the few who are working get jobs through family ties, connections, and a lot of determination.

Deaf people are not allowed to get drivers' licenses for either cars or motor-cycles. Many ride motor scooters without licenses. The deaf visitors from Puerto Rico urged the Dominicans to fight for the right to get drivers' licenses, since this goal is within the reach of the Dominican deaf community.

Communication is not particularly easy for anyone in the Dominican Republic. In a country with a population of approximately 6,785,000, there are only 175,000 or so telephones (*World Almanac*, 1988). Before the widespread availability of TTYs in the United States, deaf people spent a lot of time driving around to see one another (Jacobs, 1974). Because there are so few phones, Dominican society doesn't depend on them. Everyone travels to see each other without making any prior arrangement. But in the Dominican Republic there are no telecommunication devices like those used by deaf people in the United States and other countries.

Since the mail in the Dominican Republic is extremely unreliable, Dominican deaf people can't depend on the mail for reaching people. Invitations, etc., must be made and accepted face-to-face by most deaf and hearing people in this society. In the capital, with a population of over 1.4 million (1986 estimates from *World Almanac*, 1988), there are only about 150 mail carriers. A strike by the overworked carriers in 1984 did not help improve the situation and the service now is less reliable than ever.

## MARRIAGE PATTERNS IN THE DEAF COMMUNITY

Most deaf people in the United States marry deaf people, and about 10 percent of deaf children have deaf parents (Baker and Cokely, 1980). Endogamous marriages in the U.S. deaf community have been at a rate of between 85 percent and 95 percent since the turn of the century (Markowicz and Woodward, 1982). At the end of the nineteenth century, Alexander Graham Bell argued against marriages between deaf individuals, and he also argued against bringing large numbers of deaf children together in residential schools. He believed that residential schools would contribute to intermarriage and lead to a race of congenitally deaf people (Groce, 1985).

But Edward Fay's 1898 study of family deafness found that only 9.7 percent of deaf couples have deaf children. Furthermore, residential schools and sign language were not exclusively responsible for endogamous marriages, as many deaf marriages involved partners who had been educated in different schools—residential and day, oral and manual (Lane, 1984).

Until very recently, the isolation of deaf people in the Dominican Republic meant that marriage between deaf people was unknown. Despite this, there is still a significant number of deaf children being born. This refutes Bell's claim that banning deaf intermarriage would reduce the incidence of deafness. Because there was no school for the deaf until 1967, or any other means of bringing deaf people together, deaf people married hearing people if they married at all. For this reason, there are no known cases of deaf children of deaf parents in the Dominican Republic. Even in 1986, there were fewer than ten deaf married couples in Santo Domingo. About half of them had children, all born hearing. When asked if they would prefer to have a hearing child or a deaf child, those with children all expressed a preference for hearing children. As reasons for their response, they cited the lack of resources for deaf people and not wanting their children to suffer as they had as a deaf person in their society. The respondents did not think that the ease of raising a deaf child as a deaf parent was a good enough reason to wish their children to be deaf. Perhaps they felt that wanting to parent a deaf child because it would be easier or more fulfilling would be a selfish attitude.

There is some hereditary deafness in the Dominican Republic. There may be a higher incidence of deafness in the western town of Barahona (population 49,100 in 1981). In the capital of Santo Domingo, there is a family with four deaf children (the family that runs the printing business). Both parents are hearing, and they have a total of eight children. Informants also report a family in Santiago with several deaf children and hearing parents. These apparently are both cases of marriages between hearing people carrying genes for deafness. As intermarriage between deaf people increases, there will very likely be some deaf children born to these couples. The incidence of deaf children born to deaf parents is about 10 percent in the United States, but it remains to be seen what the occurrence will be in the Dominican Republic.

## COMMUNITY IDENTITY

The Dominican deaf community is in the process of forging its identity. The U.S. deaf community identifies its members according to the criteria of attitudinal deafness (that is, whether a person identifies him or herself as a member of the deaf community and is accepted by that community [Baker and Cokely, 1980]). According to Baker and Cokely (1980), there are four avenues to membership in the U.S. deaf community: loss of hearing, ability to affect community through political involvement, use of ASL, and participation in social activities in the community. To some degree, these criteria are important in the Dominican deaf community, but they are not as highly developed.

Hearing loss was the initial impetus for the Dominican young adults to organize themselves. Also central to their common identity is their use of a sign language. There are a number of deaf people in the community who succeeded in oral education, but have learned sign language in order to be part of the deaf community. Many orally educated deaf adults in the United States learn to sign for the same reason (Jacobs, 1974).

Natural languages have considerable variation (Wilbur, 1987). Although everyone signs at the deaf club, there is considerable variation in the use of signs. Wilbur (1987) states that wide variation exists in ASL due to factors such as age and educational background of signer, geography (signs vary from place to place), and the setting of the signed exchange.

In the deaf club, some of the variation is extreme. There are four deaf siblings (previously mentioned) who use many home signs and indigenous signs. The youngest brother, in his late teens, acts as the interpreter for his brother and two sisters. He may be more fluent in DRSL because he spends more time at the club than his sisters, and he went to school at a much younger age than his brother. This gave him more opportunity to communicate with deaf people outside of his family.

The role of the "speaker" in the deaf club is to reinterpret all proceedings of club business meetings. He uses mime, indigenous signs, and explanations to assure that as many people as possible participate.

Until recently, the club retained the name of its parent organization La Asociacion Pro-Educacion de los Sordosmudos, including the term "deaf-mute." The Dominicans were urged to drop the term "mute" by the Puerto Rican deaf visitors, as it has a negative connotation. "Mute" seems to imply an inability to express oneself (Freeman, Carbon, and Boese, 1981). Over the past five years, the use of the term "mudo" (mute) has become more infrequent. The club is now in the process of adopting the name La Asociacion de Sordos Dominicanos (Association of Dominican Deaf). However, the public's use of "mute" is likely to persevere for many years. It is still the custom to refer to deaf children and adults as "mudos" (mutes). In families, the deaf child's name is not used. Instead, the deaf family member is referred to as "el mudo" (the mute). This may also be the custom in rural Puerto Rico, where handicapped people are known by their disability (C. Collazo, November 1987, personal communication).

## DEVELOPING VERSUS DIGLOSSIC DEAF COMMUNITIES

The term "diglossia" was first used by Ferguson in 1959 to describe societies that use one or more languages or varieties of a language. In addition to the primary dialects, there might exist a very different, superimposed variety, used perhaps for written literature and usually learned through formal education. Ferguson characterizes the separation of languages as usually assigning one as a (H)igh language and the other as a (L)ow language relative to the functions and status of those languages. Fishman (1972) expands the notion to include "functionally differentiated language varieties of any kind."

When two languages are in contact, one frequently has more prestige. The prestigious language is the language of the majority. Associated with that prestige is power. There are very few situations in the world where attitudes toward two or more contact languages are equally positive. In most contact situations, the language of the minority is described as having no world value, unproductive, lacking a written grammar, and limited in the ability to express abstract concepts. Users of the minority language are considered uneducated, less cultured, and low class (Grosjean, 1982).

Washabaugh (1981) finds the original definition of diglossia by Ferguson to be inadequate. Furthermore, he argues that the concept of diglossia has now been overextended. Washabaugh prefers to talk about two types of diglossia: (1) ritual diglossia, such as the exaltation of a language such as classical Arabic and (2) political diglossia, which promotes a second language because of the status and power that that language represents. Thus, Washabaugh describes deaf communities that become literate in the majority language and model their sign language on it, as being politically diglossic. Associated with the higher status of the majority language—the language of the hearing community—is a devaluation of the vernacular sign language.

This devaluation of the signed vernacular of the deaf community is furthered if the sign language is proscribed (Washabaugh, 1981). The status of ASL in the United States today has increased tremendously in the past decade due to research that finds it to be a rule-governed language with all the structure of an oral language (Grosjean, 1982). Yet despite this increased prestige, the use of ASL in deaf education is still virtually proscribed (Woodward, 1988).

Many of the young Dominican deaf recount experiences in school when any signing or use of gestures was punished. However, they do not display contempt for sign language nor any notion that it is inferior to spoken language. This lack of contempt is a characteristic of developing deaf communities (Washabaugh, 1981).

If there is a diglossia in the Dominican Republic, it may be developing for the use of indigenous signs versus ASL signs. Indigenous signs exist, but they are difficult to collect. This is likely due to their lower status, and to the nationalities and hearing status of those collecting signs. In two years' residence, the missionary couple collected only a few dozen signs. It is likely that some signs act as a way of maintaining ethnic identity in the deaf community and are not readily shared with outsiders (Woodward, 1979). Deaf informants also stated that they do not use many indigenous signs with foreigners because they would not understand them.

I frequently observed that indigenous signs were referred to as the "wrong" signs and ASL signs as the "right" signs. This is likely the result of foreign influence. Deaf Dominicans report that their indigenous signs have been corrected by the latest group of missionaries, who offered the ASL sign as the right sign. This interference has resulted in more status being given to ASL signs than to indigenous signs.

## DOMINICAN SIGN LANGUAGE (DRSL)

The missionaries' importation of manually encoded Spanish using the ASL lexicon roughly parallels the arrival of French Sign Language (FSL) in early nineteenth century America. FSL was brought to the United States by Laurent Clerc, a deaf Frenchman who came to teach at the first permanent school for the deaf in America. Woodward (1980) claims that FSL creolized with existing sign languages to create ASL. After the national school brought deaf children together in the Dominican Republic, indigenous signs arose. Sign languages are created whenever there exists what Washabaugh calls a "linguistically critical mass," that is, enough deaf people to evolve a code. Families with several deaf children can provide such a situation.

The deaf Dominicans view sign language as something that was brought in from the outside—a gift of the missionaries. The sign language they were using as children in school was very likely immature, and they probably did not think of it as a formed sign language. Thus, the perception that sign language was brought from Puerto Rico is a result of a lack of identity for the indigenous sign language whose evolution was interrupted by the arrival of imported sign language.

A goal of the association is to publish a sign language dictionary for the Dominican Republic. Such a project is important, but difficult to carry out. A dictionary would enable more hearing people to learn the language of deaf people. Because it would be a product of deaf people, it would raise their status. But difficulties arise related to the contents of the dictionary. Some in the deaf community see the dictionary as a means of preserving and giving status to indigenous signs. Others believe the dictionary should include all signs used in the community—both borrowed from ASL and indigenous. Given the lower status of indigenous signs, care would have to be taken to elicit and include them.

Before the missionary couple came in 1984, the Dominicans learned some signs through the book *Curso Basico*, the Spanish version of T. J. O'Rourke's *A Basic Course in Manual Communication* (1979). This book was brought from Puerto Rico and contributed to the lexical borrowings from ASL.

The Dominican deaf community is in its first generation and is just beginning to organize itself. DRSL is a new sign language with indigenous and foreign influences. The community is a developing deaf community that is on its way to becoming a diglossic deaf community. It remains to be seen what course this process takes.

In the Caribbean, especially in any country with a history of U.S. influence, the spread of ASL appears to occur in several ways. First, it may be introduced through missionaries. In the case of the Dominican Republic, a deaf missionary transmitted the ASL he had learned in Bolivia from missionaries. The Peace Corps recruits volunteers to work with the deaf, and in countries such as Honduras they publish sign language dictionaries that are based on ASL signs (personal communication, Joan Wattman, March 1983). Although the Peace Corps is a pervasive presence in the Dominican Republic, it is not working with the deaf community. Second, ASL may be brought to a country by native teachers who go to the United States to participate in teacher training in the area of deafness. Two Dominican educators have participated in month-long seminars run by Gallaudet University in Washington, D.C., for Latin American educators of the deaf. Third, deaf children and young deaf people may go to the United States for education. This is not common now in the Dominican Republic, as there is a national school for the deaf and most people lack the financial means to travel to the United States. Thus there is not much influence at this point from returning deaf Dominicans. Although those who emigrate do return, their visits are only occasional, and the cases of those returning to live is limited to possibly only one person. The fourth means of ingress is through visiting Americans who know ASL. They usually come for short periods of time, such as the group that came from Gallaudet. The fifth means of entry is through the introduction of sign language books and other materials from the United States.

### Use of Borrowed Features in DRSL

Some variations in sign language are due to the influence of the spoken language environment in which the sign language exists. In the United States, the use of features of ASL and English in sign language result in the occurrence of what has been labeled "Pidgin Sign English" (PSE) (Wilbur, 1987). Woodward (1973) describes characteristics of PSE as including fingerspelling of articles such as "a," "an," "the"; the use of sign TRUE/REALLY for the copula; the use of invented signs; the use of copula plus verb for the progressive tense; and the use of FINISH for perfective aspect of verb.[2]

I did not observe the use of articles borrowed from oral Spanish, or the copula among deaf Dominican signers. More "Spanish-like" signing would be characterized by use of linear sentence structure and word order that conforms to oral Spanish. Manual codes for English use many of the lexical items from ASL and grammatical and morphological structures borrowed from English. This attempt to represent English in a visual-manual mode is perhaps a result of the higher status of English. It is characteristic of the diglossia attributed to the American deaf community by Washabaugh (1981).

The influence of English also results in signs that are formed using a handshape that is equivalent to the first letter of the English word it purports to represent. New signs may be created in ASL, in part, by using a hand configuration referring to the first letter of the English word and by maintaining the movement and place of articulation of the sign (Klima and Bellugi, 1980). For example, the ASL sign for PARENTS, a compound consisting of the signs MOTHER-FATHER, is signed more and more with a P handshape instead of the 5 handshape used to articulate both the signs MOTHER and FATHER. In this case, the meaning of parents (mother and father) is lost when the initialization occurs.

Apart from the influence of manual codes for English, ASL does have a number of signs that are always initialized. For example, the days of the week, except for Sunday, use initial letters. This initialization could be a borrowing from FSL, as in FSL, the days of the week are initialized. Greek Sign Language (GSL), a more recently evolved European sign language, has very few initialized signs. However, in Greek Sign Language, the signs for the days of the week appear to have been borrowed from FSL and then changed. In fact, GSL still retains two initialized signs for the days of the week (Kourbetis. 1986).

In DRSL, initialized signs for the days of the week are used except for Sunday. ASL does not use an initialized sign for Sunday either. There is an indigenous sign for Sunday in DRSL that is being replaced by the ASL sign. In DRSL, initialization occurs when signers borrow the sign from ASL (see table 1).

In DRSL three of the days of the week (Monday [*lunes*], Thursday [*jueves*], and Friday [*viernes*]) have changed the initialization to conform with Spanish. Saturday (*sabado*) did not have to change. Tuesday (*martes*) uses the English initialization. This seems to be evidence that the initialization was borrowed from ASL and is changing to conform with Spanish. Wednesday (*miercoles*) seems to be in the

*Table 1.* **A Comparison of ASL and DRSL Handshapes Representing the Days of the Week**

| English | ASL handshape | Spanish | DRSL handshape |
| --- | --- | --- | --- |
| Monday | M | lunes | L |
| Tuesday | T | martes | T |
| Wednesday | W | miercoles | M or W |
| Thursday | H | jueves | J |
| Friday | F | viernes | V |
| Saturday | S | sabado | S |

*Table 2.* **Initialized ASL and DRSL Signs of English–Spanish Cognates**

| English | Spanish | ASL/DRSL handshape |
|---------|---------|--------------------|
| idea | idea | I |
| association | asociacion | A |
| perfect | perfecto | P |
| north | norte | N |
| south | sur | S |
| permission | permiso | P |
| language | lenguaje | L |
| law | ley | L |

process of making the transformation; it is signed with either M or W. This process can be expected to continue to change to reflect Spanish.

Because English has Latin roots, many of its words are similar to spoken Spanish. Words that have similar forms and meaning are called cognates. Cognates are historically related to words in another language (Baker and Cokely, 1980). Some of the words that have initialized signs in ASL are cognates of Spanish words. In DRSL, some of these cognates retain the initialization (see table 2).

There are other signs that are initialized in ASL that begin with different letters in Spanish. Some of these signs are initialized in DRSL to conform with the Spanish spelling. For example, the signs for family members are initialized in both ASL and DRSL. In ASL, AUNT is signed with an A handshape and in DRSL, it is signed with a T handshape to conform with the Spanish word *tia*.

There are cases of initialized signs that have been borrowed from English into DRSL without any change. It is possible that the hand configurations are perceived as handshapes instead of initial letters. Some of these signs are also in the process of changing and some signers use the ASL initialized sign while others change the initialization to conform to Spanish (see table 3).

## CONCLUSION

The deaf community in the Dominican Republic has been using sign language for only about ten years. They have acquired the lexicon of ASL through very restricted input and are creating a sign language, DRSL, based on indigenous signs and ASL. Because of lack of models of a target language they are being forced to create a structure or a grammar for their language (Bickerton, 1981; Goodhart, 1984). They

*Table 3.* **Initialized DRSL Signs Borrowed from English/ASL**

| English | Spanish | ASL handshape | DRSL handshape |
|---------|---------|---------------|----------------|
| water | agua | W | W |
| lazy | haragan | L | L |
| ready | listo | R | R |
| world | mundo | W | W |
| live | vivir | L | L or V |
| church | iglesia | C | C or I |

have acquired the ASL that they do have through limited contact with fluent ASL signers, contact with hearing users of varying forms of ASL/PSE, and sign language books.

This description of the Dominican deaf community, although a preliminary study, does offer an example of another developing deaf community. As this community grows in number, in age, and in experience, it will provide insights into the processes and issues involved as deaf people create social structures to support a deaf community.

## NOTES

1. The term "able-bodied" is used here because deafness is generally seen in the Dominican Republic as a disability and deaf people are regarded as unable to work. Some deaf people who are working report that they got their jobs through "connections."
2. The three studies prior to 1988 that purport to describe PSE are based either on no data (Woodward, 1973; Woodward and Markowicz, 1979) or on data that are not interactive and do not reflect the sociolinguistic reality of the language contact situation. In their study of language contact in the American deaf community, Lucas and Valli (1987, 1989) reexamine the outcome of language contact in the deaf community and propose the term "contact signing" as more appropriate than PSE, both for linguistic and sociolinguistic reasons.

## REFERENCES

Baker, C., and Cokely, D. (1980). *American sign language: A teachers' resource text on grammar and culture*. Silver Spring, MD: T. J. Publishers.

Bickerton, D. (1981). *Roots of language*. Ann Arbor, MI: Karoma Publishers.

Fay, E. A. (1898). *Marriage of the deaf in America*. Washington, DC: Volta Bureau.

Fereira-Brito, L. F. (1985). Similarities and differences in two Brazilian sign languages. *Sign Language Studies* 42:45–56.

Ferguson, C. (1959). Diglossia. In *Language in culture and society*, edited by D. Hymes, 429–39. New York: Harper and Row.

Fishman, J. (1972). *An introduction to sociolinguistics*. Newbury, MA: Newbury House.

Freeman, R., Carbine, C., and Boese, R. (1981). *Can't your child hear?*. Austin, TX: Pro-Ed.

Gerner de Garcia, B. (1988). Dominican Sign Language. Boston University. Unpublished raw data.

Goodhart, W. (1984). *Morphological complexity: ASL and the acquisition of sign language in deaf children*. Ph.D. diss., Boston University.

Groce, N. (1985). *Everybody there spoke sign language*. Cambridge: Harvard University Press.

Grosjean, F. (1982). *Life with two languages*. Cambridge: Harvard University Press.

Hoemann, H. (1981). *The sign language of Brazil*. New York: Mill Neck Foundation.

Hoffman, M., ed. (1988). *World almanac*. New York: Phorus Books.

*Information Please*. (1988). Boston: Houghton Mifflin.

Jacobs, L. (1974). *A deaf adult speaks out*. Washington, DC: Gallaudet University Press.

Klima, E., and Bellugi, U. (1980). *The signs of language*. Cambridge: Harvard University Press.

Kourbetis, V. (1986). Greek Sign Language. Boston University, Center for Deafness and Communication. Unpublished manuscript.

Lane, H. (1984). *When the mind hears*. New York: Random House.

———. (1987). *Paternalism and the third world*. Symposium conducted at Northeastern University, Boston, October.

Markowicz, H. (1982). Language and the maintenance of ethnic boundaries in the deaf community. In *How you gonna get to heaven if you can't talk to Jesus?*, edited by J. Woodward, 3–9. Silver Spring, MD: T. J. Publishers.

O'Rourke, T. (1979). *Curso basico*. Silver Spring, MD: National Association of the Deaf.

Quigley, S. and Frisna, R. (1961). *Institutionalization and psychoeducational development in deaf children*. New York: Council on Exceptional Children.

Shuman, M. (1980). The sound of silence in Nohya: a preliminary account of the sign language used by the deaf in a Maya community in Yucatan. *Language Science* 2:144–73.

Sloan, I. (1987). *Law of immigration and entry to the U.S. of America*. New York: Ocean Publishers.

Stuckless, R., and Birch, J. (1966). The influence of early manual communication on the linguistic development of deaf children. *American Annals of the Deaf* 106:436–80.

Washabaugh, W. (1980). The manufacturing of a language. *Sign Language Studies* 29:291–329.

———. (1981). The deaf of Grand Cayman Island. *Sign Language Studies* 31:111–33.

———. (1986). *Five fingers for survival*. Ann Arbor, MI: Karoma.

Wilbur, R. (1987). *American sign language: Linguistics and applied dimensions*. Boston: College Hill.

Woodward, J. (1973). Some characteristics of Pidgin Sign English. *Sign Language Studies* 3:39–46.

———. (1978). Historical bases of American Sign Language. In *Understanding language through sign language research*, edited by P. Siple, 333–48. New York: Academic Press.

———. (1979). *The signs of sexual behavior*. Silver Spring, MD: T. J. Publishers.

———. (1982). Beliefs about and attitudes towards deaf people and sign language on Providence Island. In *How you gonna get to heaven if you can't talk to Jesus?*, edited by J. Woodward, 51–74. Silver Spring, MD: T. J. Publishers.

———, Allen, T., Schildroth, A. (1988). Linguistic and cultural role models for hearing-impaired children in elementary school programs. In *Language, learning, and deafness*, edited by M. Strong, 184–91. New York: Cambridge University Press.

# Dialectal Flexibility in Sign Language in Africa

Robert Serpell, Mackenzie Mbewe

This paper is organized in four parts. Part one outlines our theoretical perspective on language and communication in general, and more specifically on sociolinguistic parameters of language planning. Part two provides a brief description of Zambia in terms of its geographical, demographic, cultural, and linguistic situation. In part three, we discuss the historical development of sign language in Zambia and draw some comparisons with a selection of other cultural areas within and outside Africa. In part four, we conclude with a preliminary exploration of some policy implications of our analysis.

## THEORETICAL PERSPECTIVE

### The Nature of Language

Our discussion of theoretical issues in sign language research in Zambia is premised on the following orientation toward the nature of language as a means of communication. We conceive of language not as an impartial container for the transmission of information, but as an actively negotiated set of intersubjective understandings with systematic characteristics that are not only semiotic (or semantic) and grammatical (phonological, morphological, and syntactic) but also pragmatic. Whereas a great deal of the linguistic research published about sign language in recent years has focused on the morphophonological and syntactic dimensions of linguistic analysis, our concerns in the present study are primarily with the semiotic and pragmatic dimensions.

Sign language, like spoken language, can be classified in terms of several types of language variety: the most general term is perhaps "code," but this term has been the subject of controversy in view of its potentially mystifying connotations. The notion of "code-switching," developed by Gumperz (1971, 1982) in conjunction with the notion of social stratification of speech varieties following the work of Ferguson (1959) and Fishman (1966), has drawn attention to the versatility of most

275

speakers in a multilingual society in deploying the multiple linguistic resources in their repertoire for pragmatic purposes. At the same time, however, the resistance of certain aspects of observed usage to attempts to classify them in terms of compartmentalized codes has forced a recognition of the fluidity of language in such communities.

The notion of an "idiolect" recognizes that the linguistic usage of each individual speaker (or signer) has unique characteristics that are tolerated by his or her audience and indeed used by them as a basis for discriminating his or her utterances from those of others. A "dialect," on the other hand, specifies a distinctive subset of usage features shared by speakers who also share some other social characteristics such as geographical residence (a local dialect), ethnicity (a tribal dialect), class membership, etc.

Finally, we must consider the notion of "register." As Halliday (1975, 126) puts it, "In any social context, certain semantic resources are characteristically employed; certain sets of options are, as it were, 'at risk' in a given semiotic environment. These define the register." A competent member of a speech (or sign) community is expected to understand and deploy such aspects of what Gregory (1967) calls "diatypic variation." Attempts to characterize this dimension in terms of switching between High- and Low-status codes have proved to be an oversimplification, leading Gumperz to advance the notion of "metaphorical" code-switching. Other analysts suggest that we need a completely different, more subtly differentiated taxonomy (for example, Pride, 1983).

An earlier generation of descriptive linguistic studies documented a wide range of ways in which languages in contact interpenetrate each other, particularly at the level of the lexicon in the form of so-called borrowing. Moreover, diachronic studies show that what is initially construed as a foreign intrusion often becomes incorporated within the standard usage of a later generation, and its exogenous origins are often either forgotten or at least cease to be perceived as socially or culturally problematic. Thus, the fluid, multiple repertoire of a contemporary multilingual community may well represent a transitional state within a process of gradual language change.

### Sociolinguistic Parameters of Language Planning

Public and official attempts to plan and manage the process of language change are often informed by a conceptualization of language form and usage that is quite remote from the realities exposed by sociolinguistic studies. Those cases of centralized language planning that have been historically documented tend to be characterized by prescriptive standardization, compartmentalization, and at least an implicit bias toward social stratification (Das Gupta, 1968; Rubin and Jernudd, 1971; Kashoki, 1973; Serpell, 1978, 1980).

A full discussion of the merits and disadvantages of this kind of approach to language would require a discussion of its philosophical underpinnings. Habermas (1978), for instance, in an influential analysis, has drawn attention to the distinction between the technical, hermeneutical, and emancipatory interests of the social sciences and has argued persuasively that an exclusive emphasis on their technical contribution to public decision making can often lead to the covert, if not unconscious, imposition of political values by an elite on the rest of society without any consultation.

## *Diglossias*

The term "diglossia" was coined by Ferguson (1959) to characterize a speech community in which two distinct language varieties coexist in such a way that all members of the community are fluent in both varieties but deploy them in systematically different types of social situation. The main dimension of contrast emphasized by Ferguson is prestige, with the (H)igh variety being reserved for formal, public usage and the (L)ow variety being used as a vehicle for the expression of informal, and generally private topics. Fishman (1967) extends this analysis to the description of the speech communities of former colonies in the Third World, arguing that the language of the former colonial power tends to take on many of the functions of a (H)igh code, while the indigenous languages are reserved mainly for the functions of a (L)ow code. A close analysis of prevailing usage in Zambia, however, reveals that the correspondence is not complete in all respects (Serpell, 1980). Moreover it is far from clear, even in Ferguson's original analysis, that the L-code is consistently devalued. As the "language of hearth and home," for instance, it tends to have a privileged status with respect to the communication of personal intimacy.

A similar ambivalence is described by Stokoe (1970) in his exploratory account of sign language diglossia in the deaf culture of the United States, with ASL on the one hand recognized as "indigenous" and hence authentic, while on the other hand often giving way to signed English for communication in high-prestige, public situations where the power of nonnative signers is felt.

Washabaugh has urged a distinction between two types of diglossia: ritual diglossia and political diglossia, the former involving "the exaltation of a language, but not directly of the people who use it," while "in political diglossia a second language is promoted, in a community, not because of the esteem accorded to it, but because of the status of its native speakers." He thus likens the prestige attached in some deaf communities to "spoken language or a sign language modeled on it" to the prestige attached to English or French relative to Creole in the mainstream, hearing cultures of many Caribbean-island societies. In extreme cases, in such politically diglossic deaf communities, "vernacular sign languages" come to be regarded "as unsystematic assemblages of gesticulations and facial contortions" (1981, 117–118).

Such politically biased value judgments make the assessment of local sign language dialects and idiolects very problematic in Third World countries, where many deaf people have grown up in virtual isolation from other deaf people and where a series of enthusiastic advocates of different systems of deaf education have tended to "feed different communicative systems to the deaf and spice them with negative attitudes toward all other systems but their own" (Washabaugh, 1981, 130). Washabaugh suggests that the developing deaf communities in such societies have an important opportunity to avoid the tragic self-devaluation characteristics of more settled, politically diglossic deaf communities. On the other hand, he warns that the pattern of educational eclecticism that they are experiencing "leaves behind its own rough wake through which the deaf must navigate" (1981, 132).

## THE SITUATION OF THE DEAF IN ZAMBIA

### *Geographical Features*

Zambia is a landlocked country in central Africa, lying between latitudes 8 and 18 degrees south of the equator and between longitudes 22 and 34 degrees east of the

Greenwich meridian. It is surrounded at its borders, clockwise, by Tanzania to the northeast, Malawi, Mozambique, Zimbabwe, Botswana, Namibia, Angola, and Zaire. In extent Zambia is 753,000 square kilometers (291,000 square miles)—about the size of Texas in the United States, or greater than the combined area of France, Belgium, the Netherlands, and Switzerland in Europe.

### Demographic Features

The overwhelming majority of the people of Zambia are Africans of Bantu origin, but Asians of Indian origin, Europeans, and people of mixed descent constitute small minority communities. English is the official language for commerce, education, science and technology, and diplomatic intercourse. Ten major indigenous languages are spoken, all from the same Bantu group (Kashoki, 1978). Ici-Bemba, Ci-Nyanja, Ci-Tonga, and Si-Lozi are the most widely spoken of these languages. The distribution of the major language groups in rural areas is shown on the map (fig. 1). Ici-Bemba is also very widely used as a *lingua franca* in the towns of the copperbelt, while Ci-Nyanja is the major *lingua franca* of the capital city of Lusaka. In this multilingual society, most individuals can claim fluency in two or three languages (Mytton and Kashoki, 1978), and the interaction between different languages in every day spoken usage tends to be characterized by a high degree of fluidity, especially in urban areas (Serpell, 1978, 1980).

The overall population density is low (about eight persons per square kilometer), but it is very unevenly distributed. About half of the Zambian population live in small modern cities and towns, and the rest live in widely scattered villages whose economy centers on subsistence agriculture. Since 1950 the population has been increasing at an annual growth rate between 2.5 and 3.5 percent, from 2.4 million to 5.7 million in 1980, and is currently (1988) estimated at 7.0 million.

Table 1 illustrates an increasing trend toward urbanization since Zambia gained political independence in 1964. Table 2 illustrates the population growth at approximate ten-year intervals. As a result of its escalating rate of population growth, Zambia's population comprises a very high proportion of young people, more than half aged less than fifteen years.

### Prevalence Data

The census tally of hearing-impaired persons in the Zambian population is generally open to doubt for a variety of reasons. First, a hearing impairment is invisible. Second, the enumerators are inconsistent in their coverage of households. Third, experience suggests that parents may hide their hearing-impaired children, either from the fear that their children may be taken away, or from a sense of shame about their parenthood to such children.

The United Nations has proposed a formula for estimating prevalence of hearing impaired in developing countries of 20 in every 10,000 people. Applying this in Zambia would yield an estimate of fourteen thousand, but such estimates, based on prevalence rates in industrialized countries are very unreliable in Third World countries like Zambia, where medical services cannot reach everyone, where no systematic research has been done on the epidemiology of hearing impairment, and where precise assessment of hearing loss is rarely (indeed scarcely ever) done. The Zambia National Campaign to Reach Disabled Children (Nabuzoka, 1986), which contacted less than

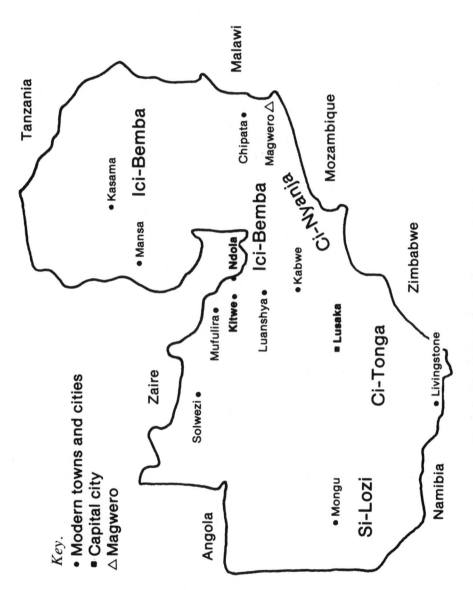

*Figure 1.* Distribution of major languages in Zambia.

*Table 1.* **Urban–Rural Population Distribution**
(in millions)

| Census Year | 1963 | 1969 | 1974 | 1980 |
|---|---|---|---|---|
| Urban percentage | 20.5 | 29.4 | 35.6 | 43.0 |
| Rural percentage | 79.5 | 70.6 | 64.4 | 57.0 |
| | 100.0 | 100.0 | 100.0 | 100.0 |

*Source.* Adapted from Mbewe (1984, 15). Reconstructed from the official census data for selected years (Zambia Government, 1973, 1979, and 1982).

two-thirds of its target families in 1982, identified over eight hundred children aged from five to fifteen years with significant hearing and/or speech disabilities. About half of these children were not enrolled in school; a similar number were attending regular primary schools; and about two hundred were enrolled in special classes with teachers who had received specialized training for education of deaf students. In the absence of reliable data, clinicians report that the major known causes of deafness in Zambia are measles, meningitis, and otitis media.

### Effects of Hearing Impairment

A hearing impairment alters the social and psychological patterns of a person's life: monitoring the environment becomes relatively difficult; social relationships are disturbed when parents and other siblings find it difficult to relate to a child or adult who cannot hear and talk like them; psychological identification and feelings of belonging and socialization are disturbed. In adulthood, the focus of social relationships and identification shifts from hearing people to others having hearing loss. In the long run, most deaf people are isolated from the mainstream of society.

### The Role of School

School remains the major alternative community that can restore hearing-impaired persons to the mainstream and help them understand that they are a unique cultural group in spite of their altered cultural circumstances.

Residential special schools, in particular, afford unique opportunities for the emergence and development of a deaf culture. Such schools are characterized by mutual support networks and autonomous communication systems. At school, the deaf use sign language extensively to express ideas with their hands; they learn to speech-read words spoken to them; they learn to read and write in a language of the majority hearing people; and they learn to use fingerspelling to represent letters of the alphabet.

*Table 2.* **Population Growth in Zambia**
(in millions)

| Census Year | 1950 | 1960 | 1969 | 1980 |
|---|---|---|---|---|
| Population | 2.4 | 3.2 | 4.1 | 5.7 |

*Source.* Zambia Government census of population reports for selected years.

These communication systems coexist as a fluid repertoire in deaf communities, and they help the deaf to communicate fluently with each other in peer groups. Jones (1986, 9–10) makes the following observations about the role of school. First, an ability to communicate fluently and therefore to make relationships and share group and individual roles in school allows deaf people to build a good self-image or self-esteem. Second, the socialization process (the learning of attitudes and roles, the building of emotions and feelings together with the learning of language) is attained through social interaction, much of it in groups. Third, the elements of the culture in which a person is brought up are communicated, directly or indirectly, through language—the sign language of the deaf included.

Besides being a vehicle of socialization and cultural transmission, sign language is used by the hearing impaired to establish identity and solidarity and to fight for civil rights. As in many other countries, the deaf people of Zambia have had to struggle for recognition as a community with their own unique concerns. Sign language has been an important symbol of cultural identity, and it has served to unify those who have access to it and to demonstrate to the hearing community that deaf people have a capacity to communicate that the hearing community typically underestimates. For this reason the documentation of what constitutes sign language, as distinct from an unsophisticated set of gestures, and of what varieties are currently in use in the region, as well as the formulation of a strategy for its promotion and development is of great cultural and political importance.

## SIGN LANGUAGE IN ZAMBIA

The amount and quality of sign vocabulary that deaf persons are able to develop or acquire depends on the cultural environment they live in. Deaf persons living in isolation from other deaf people but surrounded by hearing persons tend to develop few signs for their "active" sign language vocabulary. This is because the hearing community makes little systematic use of signs in social interaction with them, and hence provides little stimulation or discriminative feedback to promote the elaboration of a full-fledged vocabulary. Kair (1988) describes this type of isolation as the norm for most deaf people in Tanzania, and scattered reports from other African countries confirm that a similar situation prevails in many parts of the continent.

Deaf persons living in deaf communities tend by contrast to develop a relatively rich "active" sign language vocabulary because they are always refining their sign language, inventing and adding new signs to their basic active sign vocabulary. This type of deaf community typically comes into existence only in such settings as special schools, colleges, or large industrial establishments with a relatively large population of deaf persons.

### Similarities in Signs

Deaf persons living in isolation within the same cultural enclave encompassed by Zambia and the immediately adjacent regions of neighboring states (notably Malawi, Tanzania, and Zaire) often develop identical signs for certain phenomena, perhaps based on paralinguistic gestures common to the cultures of the region. For example, an illiterate deaf man, John M. (fifty-two years old) in the Luapula Valley of northern Zambia signs as follows:

| MAN/FATHER | Stroke bearded chin |
| --- | --- |
| SIT | Shoulders and folded arms sunk in resting position |
| WOMAN/ MOTHER | Touch both sides of chest with hand extended downward to represent sagging breasts |
| SEARCH | Open hands beating about in the air |

Isolated deaf adults in other parts of Zambia sign in a similar way for the same phenomena, though they have never been in contact with one another.

### Differences in Signs

Other signs used by isolated deaf persons living within the same cultural enclave differ in ways which can be related to variations in technology use, the level at which actors are involved, or differences in experience of the various social groups.

**Technology.** In northern Zambia most people drink beer from a container by using a copper or aluminum conduit (tube) or a hollow riverbank reed. Accordingly, deaf persons in northern Zambia sign for beer as an imaginary copper tube held up to the lips between the thumb and the index finger, complemented by sucking action with the mouth. In eastern Zambia, on the other hand, men normally drink beer from a container with their lips. Here the deaf sign for beer as an imaginary beer container held in both hands, shaken in circular plane, then brought to the lips for a sip.

**The Actor's Level of Involvement.** This may create differences in signing for the same phenomenon. For example, Zambian women pick vegetables with their hands. Deaf women accordingly sign VEGETABLES as a clenched fist with only the thumb and index finger pinching and plucking imaginary vegetables.

Deaf children in residential schools, however, have developed a different sign at the eating stage where they initially get involved as follows: A fist hand with only the thumb and index finger picks up an imaginary tangle of cooked vegetables, shakes off excess loose bits, then puts it into the mouth.

**Differences in Experience.** For instance, the difference in fishing experience among various social groups in part explains the different signs for fish.

Some fishermen hold freshly caught live fish by the gills, and the fish flaps to free itself. Thus a sign for fish used by many deaf persons, whether fishermen themselves or only observers, becomes an open hand, palm up, flapping in the air supported at the wrist by the grip of the other hand. But some deaf men catch fish with a fishing line. Their sign for fish is therefore the action of pulling the hooked fish out of the water. Other deaf people who have only observed fish swimming in a river or aquatic tank have developed a sign for fish based on its movement: an open vertical hand wriggling and waving like the movement of a fish in water. Yet another group of deaf people who deal in dry gutted fish have developed the following sign for fish: the vertical palms in PRAYER position are swung apart like opening a book.

### Planned Language Development: Steps Toward a National Sign Language

Two main types of development have been responsible for the gradual evolution of what may perhaps be called the beginnings of a Zambian national sign language from various idiolects and dialects described above: refinement of the different signs and their acceptance into the basic sign language; and cross-cultural borrowing.

**Refinement.** Although differences in form exist within the same cultural enclave, much as they do across cultural boundaries, in the second author's experience, culturally differing deaf persons, either while entering into casual conversation or while in the process of establishing a more lasting comradeship, often attempt to reach a compromise. First, they explain to each other the etymological origin of the signs. Second, they adopt the most appealing sign. Adoption of such a sign depends on its cultural, practical, or artistic appeal to the deaf people concerned.

The development of the first, refined Zambian local sign language started at the Magwero School for the Deaf in eastern Zambia in the 1950s. Deaf children were picked up by missionaries from the neighborhood of Magwero Mission station on both sides of the Zambia/Malawi border. While resident at Magwero, deaf children pooled their knowledge of signing, refined their signs, and established the means of communication for the deaf community that was created when the mission opened Magwero School for the Deaf in 1955.

**Cross-Cultural Borrowing.** Africa has had cultural contacts with the outside world for a long time. The most recent phase of contact followed the entry into Africa by European expeditionists, traders, and Christian missionaries in the eighteenth and nineteenth centuries. Among the Christian missionaries that came to Africa, the Dutch Reformed Church missionaries founded the first schools for the blind and for the deaf at Magwero in eastern Zambia, in the years 1905 and 1955 respectively.

At that time, European educators were fervent advocates of an oral system of education for the deaf. Speech was upheld as incontestably superior to sign at most international congresses held in Europe. In this context, the Dutch missionary teachers of the deaf cannot be said to have brought the knowledge of sign language to the deaf in Zambia. Zambian Sign Language was developed and refined by the deaf pupils themselves.

In the teaching situation the missionary teachers of the deaf insisted on the use of the oral system or method, while in casework and counseling situations they found it expedient to learn Zambian Sign Language from their deaf pupils. They added only the two-hand manual alphabet, which was currently in use in European special schools. This kind of cross-cultural borrowing was not actively encouraged through cultural exchange programs until after political independence by most African countries in the second half of the twentieth century, particularly during the 1960s.

Following political independence (which Zambia achieved from Britain in 1964), nongovernmental organizations (NGOs) and African governments embarked on programs of providing special education provision for the deaf. These programs have been closely tied to bilateral "foreign aid" under which personnel from a particular European country come to Africa as technical advisors, while African professionals go to Europe for specialist training. In the case of Zambians, these overseas trained professionals went as far as Scotland (at Moray House College of Education); England and Wales (at Manchester, Birmingham, London, and Cardiff universities); Netherlands (at St. Michael's); Ireland (at Dublin University); the United States (at Gallaudet University); Denmark; and more recently in Finland at the University of Jyvaskyla.

One consequence of these exchanges has been the transfer to particular African countries of the particular sign languages used for educational purposes in the "aid-donor" countries such as Denmark, Finland, France, Norway, Sweden, the United Kingdom, and the United States. Tanzania, for example, in recent years has experienced on a piecemeal basis no less than five different national sign languages brought by "foreign aid" personnel from Denmark, Finland, Sweden, West Germany, and the United States, while Zambia has so far been exposed to only one foreign sign language, namely American Sign Language.

The consequences of such uncoordinated intrusions from various foreign languages are initially somewhat chaotic. But it should not be forgotten that there is unity and strength in diversity. The many foreign sign languages that have contributed elements to the current beginnings of a Tanzanian sign language might one day make it richer and more widely intelligible throughout the region than Zambian Sign Language, with its more restricted source of borrowing from only ASL. This speculation is inspired by the experience of Ki-Swahili in East Africa, particularly in Tanzania. By communicating in Ki-Swahili—a language born out of diction borrowed from many different languages in the context of the regional Arab slave trade—Tanzanians have become more united and have come to understand each other as Taifa Stars (the national football team), as dock workers, as Ujaama villagers, and so on, while those local languages that could claim a greater degree of indigenous authenticity have come to be seen as secondary in Tanzanian society.

### Policy Issues for Sign Language Development in Zambia

The encounter with a multiplicity of foreign sign languages has prompted some African countries to embark on a program of rediscovery of the roots of their local sign languages. In Zambia, in August of 1982, a national conference was held on the theme of "basic education for the deaf in Zambia" (Mbewe and Serpell, 1982). One of the resolutions adopted was that an effort should be made to document and publicize the main elements of Zambian Sign Language as used among deaf Zambians. This was construed as a first step toward standardization of Zambian Sign Language. Similar steps have been taken in other African countries including Ethiopia, Kenya, and Zimbabwe.[1]

Arising from the Zambian conference resolution, a survey was conducted and a preliminary handbook has been published (Bwalya, 1985) which is destined to form the basis of future work on the development of sign language suitable for both local and national purposes. Issues still to be confronted in this language development work include the following.

How should lexical diversity be handled? Should a core of national vocabulary be defined, and other lexical variants be treated as local dialects? If so, what would be the criteria for deciding that a dialectal variant has become so popular that it now qualifies for inclusion in the core of the national sign language? Alternatively, should all the local variants documented at this initial stage of formal documentation of local usage be included in the national lexicon?

Should pragmatic/social differentiation be planned? A truly national sign language need not necessarily be used for all social purposes and in all social situations. Thus in spoken language usage in Zambia, English (an exogenous language, and ironically the language of the former colonial power) is often used for strictly national functions in preference to any of the indigenous languages on the grounds that it is politically more "impartial" than any of the latter. Yet for a narrower definition of "local" purposes, such as an agricultural show, a traditional festival, or even a political rally in a rural district or a low-income urban housing area, one of the indigenous languages with strong local currency is typically preferred as expressing greater social solidarity. Now if the preferred pattern of sign usage in a particular residential community such as a school for the deaf differs in certain respects from the officially approved national sign language, should it be regarded as "deviant" and "unacceptable," or should the planners of sign language development in Zambia recognize from the outset that such variation is a normal and desirable way of expressing such subtle differences as national versus local community allegiances?

At what stage should second- or third-language training in sign be offered?

Which sign languages should be selected for this, given the state of development of other sign languages on the continent?

Which of Zambia's spoken languages should be favored in the incorporation of fingerspelled elements?

How important is it to study local grammatical as distinct from lexical forms?

Can it be taken for granted that word order, inflections and patterns of morphological structure will sort themselves out as the language develops, or should planners try to influence this evolutionary process?

## CONCLUSION

Sociolinguistic studies of spoken languages have documented the prevalence of individual multilingualism and of dialectal fluidity in African cities. Yet educational policy has generally failed to accommodate these phenomena. In the case of special education of the deaf, many of the same psychological, sociological, and logistical problems tend to recur writ large.

One of the sad legacies of the European experience has been that until quite recently many educators in Africa—even if they are not outright oralists—have been reluctant to acknowledge the supreme educational importance of signs, the natural language of the deaf, in the design and implementation of their education. Yet sign language has many outstanding merits as a medium of education: (1) Sign language transcends subnational (for example, tribal) languages in Africa and smothers ethnic differences that sometimes ignite and intensify fierce interethnic fighting; (2) Sign language helps the deaf at school to become socialized and to become competent members of society; (3) Sign language imbues the deaf with a strong awareness of their cultural identity and their civil rights.

Where language changes are centrally planned there is likely to arise a tendency to prescribe standards with a bias toward social stratification, and this can often lead to the covert imposition of political values by the planning elite on the rest of society.

In the field of special education, especially in countries with small populations and very limited infrastructure, economies of scale place a high premium on supranational, regional institutional development. If specialist teachers of the deaf in several different countries are to receive their training at a single regional center, there is an obvious logistical attraction in the idea of promoting a single sign language for the region as a whole.

In practice, however, planning for special education in African countries has been sharply fragmented across nations, and even within nations has been marked by minimal coordination and frequent abrupt discontinuities. The beginnings of a quite gratuitous political diglossia have, in the main, been encouraged by African scholars returning from overseas training and by bilateral foreign aid personnel working in Africa as technical advisors.

The transfer to African countries of multiple foreign sign languages creates transitory but intrusive chaos, which may stabilize and crystallize into a new, richer, and widely intelligible sign language with the passage of time. But it also causes the near death of indigenous sign language idiolects and dialects as most deaf people want to learn and use spoken/written language and the sign language modeled on it. Furthermore, in attempting to rediscover the roots of the indigenous sign languages researchers often seem to be prone to, sometimes unconsciously, imposing their personal values. Thus a researcher may encourage the development of an indigenous sign language and at the same time infiltrate and contaminate the indigenous language with signs from another sign language experience.

Against this complex background, the prevailing eclectic and flexible attitude toward sign language forms favored by most indigenous deaf people in Africa appears to constitute a healthy survival strategy.

## NOTE

1. Examples of preliminary compilations of local/national signs for these countries were presented and discussed at the East African Sign Language Seminar at Arusha, Tanzania, 29 August to 10 September 1988. See also Ndurumo (1988).

## REFERENCES

Bwalya, A. L., ed. (1985). *Zambian Sign Language*. Lusaka: Curriculum Development Centre.

Das Gupta, J. (1968). Language diversity and national development. In *Language problems of developing nations*, edited by J. A. Fishman et al., 17–26. New York: Wiley.

Ferguson, C. A. (1959). Diglossia. *Word* 15:325–40.

Fishman, J. A. (1966). Bilingualism with and without diglossia; diglossia with and without bilingualism. *Journal of Social Issues* 23:29–38.

Gumperz, J. J. (1971). *Language in social groups*. Stanford, CA: Stanford University Press.

———. (1982). *Discourse strategies*. London: Methuen.

Gregory, M. (1967). Aspects of varieties differentiation. *Journal of Linguistics* 3:177–98.

Habermas, J. (1978). *Knowledge and human interests*. London: Heinemann.

Halliday, M. A. K. (1975). *Learning how to mean: Explorations in the development of language*. London: Arnold.

Jones, K. (1986). The social-psychological needs of deaf people. In *Beyond Hobson's choice: The appraisal of methods of teaching language to deaf children*, edited by G. Montgomery, 8–12. Edinburgh: Scottish Workshop Publications.

Kair, D. (1988). My two years working with the deaf in Tanzania: A reflection. Paper presented at the East African Sign Language Seminar, August–September 1988, Arusha, Tanzania.

Kashoki, M. E. (1973). Language: A blue-print for national integration. *Bulletin of the Zambia Language Group* 2:19–45.

Kashoki, M. E. (1978). The language situation in Zambia. In *Language in Zamiba*, edited by S. Ohannessian, and M. E. Kashoki, 9–46. London: International African Institute.

Mbewe, M. S. (1984). Integration in special education for the hearing impaired in Zambia. B. Phil. Ed. diss., Birmingham University.

———, and Serpell, R., eds. (1983). Basic education for the deaf in Zambia. Report of the national conference held in Lusaka, August 1982, Lusaka, University of Zambia.

Myklebust, H. R. (1964). *The psychology of deafness*, 2d ed. New York: Grune and Stratton.

Mytton, G., and Kashoki, M. E. (1978). Multilingualism. In *Language in Zambia*, edited by S. Ohannessian and M. E. Kashoki, 35–46. London: International African Institute.

Nabuzoka, D., ed. (1986). Reaching disabled children: a compilation of reports on the Zambia National Campaign to Reach Disabled Children, 1981–1985. Lusaka: Institute for African Studies. Unpublished manuscript.

Ndurumo, M. M. (1988). Development and implementation of sign language in Kenya. In *Proceedings of the Tenth World Congress of the Federation of the Deaf*, vol. 2, edited by R. Ojala, 443–46. Espoo, Finland: Finnish Association of the Deaf.

Pride, J. B., ed. (1983). *New Englishes*. Rowley, MA: Newbury House.

Rubin, J., and Jernudd, B. H. (1971). *Can language be planned? Sociolinguistic theory and practice for developing nations*. Honolulu: Hawaii University Press.

Serpell, R. (1978). Learning to say it better: A challenge for Zambian education. In *Language and Education in Zambia*. Communication 14, edited by L. N. Omondi and Y. T. Simukoko, 29–57. Lusaka: Institute for African Studies.

———. (1980). Linguistic flexibility in urban Zambian children. In *Studies in child language and multilingualism*, edited by V. Teller and S. J. White, 97–119 [Special issue]. *Annals of the New York Academy of Sciences* 345.

Stokoe, W. (1970). Sign language diglossia. *Studies in Linguistics* 21:27–41.

Washabaugh, W. (1981). The deaf of Grand Cayman, British West Indies. *Sign Language Studies* 31:117–33.

Zambia Government. (1973). *Census of population and housing 1969*. Final Report, vol. 1: Total Zambia. Lusaka: Central Statistical Office.

———. (1979). *The 1974 sample census of population, Republic of Zambia*. Second Report: Results and interim projections of population, 1974–84. Lusaka: Central Statistical Office.

———. (1982). *Monthly digest of statistics*. Lusaka: Central Statistical Office.

# ASL, English, and Contact Signing

Ceil Lucas, Clayton Valli

Woodward (1973) and Woodward and Markowicz (1975) claimed that the signing that results from language contact in the American deaf community is a pidgin resulting from deaf-hearing interaction. Indeed, there does exist a kind of signing that results from the contact between ASL and English, and that exhibits features of both languages. This paper is part of an on-going study of language contact in the deaf community and the specific objectives of this paper are (1) to describe the data-collection methodology used to induce switching between ASL and this contact signing;[1] (2) to provide an overview of the language use that occurred during the data collection; and (3) to describe the sociolinguistic factors that sometimes correlate with the production of signing that is other than ASL. The linguistic features of contact signing are discussed at length in Lucas and Valli (1989).

The preliminary evidence suggests that the outcome of language contact in the American deaf community is unique, and quite different than anything that has been described to date in spoken language communities. The objective, then, is reexamination as a way of getting at an accurate characterization of this unique and complex phenomenon.

It seems that the first step in understanding language contact in the deaf community is to have an understanding of the enormous complexity of that contact in terms of participant characteristics and varieties of language available to those participants in a contact situation. For example, in terms of participant characteristics, it is clearly not enough simply to distinguish deaf individuals from hearing individuals. Participants in a contact situation may be deaf ASL/English bilinguals who attended a residential school at an early age (entering, say, at age three or four) and learned ASL as a first language from other children and were taught some form of English, usually from hearing teachers who did not sign natively;[2] they may be deaf individuals who were mainstreamed at an early age and learned to sign, be it ASL or Signed English or both, relatively late; they may be the hearing children of deaf parents, again ASL/English bilinguals who learned ASL at home natively; they may be hearing individuals who learned ASL or some variety of Signed English relatively late in life. Participants in a language contact situation may also include hearing individuals who are English monolinguals and do not sign, as well as deaf ASL monolinguals with a minimal command of English in any form. Similarly, the varieties of language available to participants in a contact situation range from ASL to spoken English or Signed English, and to a variety of codes for English that have been implemented in educational settings. The participants in any given language-contact situation will have been exposed to some or all of the above, and may display a wide range of skills in all or some. Finally, it is crucial to understand that the participants in such a language contact situation have both a vocal channel and a visual channel available, and the latter includes both manual and nonmanual grammatical signals. That is, the participants in such a language contact situation have hands, mouth, and face available for the encoding of linguistic messages.

In this regard, it is important to bear in mind the parallels between language contact in spoken language communities and language contact in the deaf community. With spoken languages, two language communities may be in contact but there may not actually be many bilingual individuals in those communities. The linguistic outcome of language contact in that situation is different from the linguistic outcome of the interaction of bilingual individuals. In turn, the interaction of bilingual individuals who share the same native language is apt to be different from the interaction of bilinguals who have different native languages—comparing, say, two French-English Canadian bilinguals who both have French as a first language, as opposed to two French-English Canadian bilinguals, one of whom claims French as a first language and one of whom claims English as a first language. Code switching may occur in both of these situations, but the reasons for it and the linguistic form it takes may be quite different. And this is all in contrast, finally, with the interaction of a bilingual speaker with a monolingual speaker, be that interaction in the second language of the bilingual (and the native language of the monolingual), or vice versa—the case, say, of a Spanish-English bilingual interacting with a monolingual English speaker. If the bilingual's first language is Spanish and the interaction is in English, the linguistic outcome of the interaction can probably be predicted to be different from interaction in Spanish with the monolingual who is in the earliest stages of learning Spanish.

There exist parallels for all of these situations in the deaf community, and as explained earlier, participants' characteristics may vary widely among language-contact situations. The following is a partial outline of possible language contact situations in the American deaf community, according to participant characteristics:

- deaf bilinguals with hearing bilinguals,
- deaf bilinguals with deaf bilinguals,
- deaf bilinguals with hearing spoken-English monolinguals,
- hearing bilinguals with deaf English signers,
- deaf bilinguals with deaf English signers,
- deaf English signers with hearing spoken-English monolinguals,
- deaf English signers with hearing bilinguals,
- deaf English signers with deaf ASL monolinguals,
- deaf bilinguals with deaf ASL monolinguals,
- deaf ASL monolinguals with hearing bilinguals.

## DEFINITIONS

Several issues arise from this outline. One concerns the problematic and relative concept of bilingualism. As in spoken-language situations, participants in language contact situations in the deaf community display a range of competence both in ASL and in English, and in the latter, both in forms of English-like signing and in written English. For the purposes of the present study, bilingualism is defined in demographic terms: deaf bilinguals are individuals who learned ASL natively, either from their parents or at an early age from their peers in residential-school settings, and who have been exposed to spoken and written English all their lives, beginning with the school system and continuing in their adulthood in the working world and through interaction with native English speakers. For this study, hearing bilinguals are native English speakers who learned to sign as adults, both through formal instruction and through interaction with deaf people, and who, while not being native ASL signers, do not use manual codes for English either. Specific sign use in the study will be discussed later. Again, it is crucial to recognize the range of competence in hearing bilinguals, such that the linguistic outcome of interaction between the hearing child of deaf parents (hence, possibly, a native user of ASL) with a deaf bilingual might be quite different from that of a deaf bilingual with a hearing bilingual who, while competent, learned as an adult.

Informal observation and anecdotal evidence suggest that the distinction between deaf people and hearing people is also an important variable in the outcome of language contact in the American deaf community. Deaf individuals may sign quite differently with other deaf individuals than with hearing individuals and may initiate an interaction in one language and radically switch when the fact that an interlocutor is hearing is revealed. For example, it has been observed that a deaf native ASL user may initiate an interaction with another individual whom he believes to be deaf or whose audiological status has not been clarified. The latter participant may well be a near-native user of ASL. However, when the latter is found to be hearing, it would not be unusual for the deaf participant to automatically switch "away from ASL" to a more English form of signing. The distinction between deaf people and hearing people clearly plays a central role in language contact in this particular community, and has been carefully attended to in this study.

One might predict that the different contact situations listed in the outline would yield to different linguistic outcomes, all of them of interest. For example, there is a lot of informal observational evidence that when speaking English with no deaf individuals present, hearing bilinguals occasionally code switch into ASL and code mix English and ASL features. Another outcome is seen when, in interaction with hearing individuals who do not sign at all, a deaf bilingual who does not use his voice in interaction with other deaf people or with hearing people who sign may opt to use spoken English in combination with gestures. Similarly, there is informal observational evidence that in interacting with hearing individuals who are in the early stages of learning to sign, deaf native ASL users may use a form of "foreigner talk." Finally, the outcome of language contact between native signers of different sign languages (for example, ASL and Italian Sign Language) may have unique characteristics. There is anecdotal and casual observational evidence for the existence of all of the language contact situations listed. What is required at this point is carefully collected videotaped and ethnographic data, and critical descriptive analyses.

This paper focuses on the outcome of language contact in the first situation in the outline: deaf bilinguals with hearing bilinguals. The reason for choosing this focus is that characterizations of language contact in the American deaf community have thus far been limited to this focus, to the interaction between deaf people and hearing people, and this interaction contact has been characterized as producing a kind of pidgin. As stated earlier, one of the objectives of this study is to reexamine this characterization, in part through another objective of the study, that is, a preliminary description of the lexical, morphological, and syntactic features of language production resulting for the interaction of deaf and hearing people. There are suggestions in the literature that the outcome of the interaction of deaf bilinguals with other deaf bilinguals may sometimes be a language variety other than ASL. The present study has collected considerable data of such interaction. However, a detailed linguistic analysis of the deaf-deaf variety, and a comparison of that variety with the hearing-deaf variety will be reserved for future study.

## THE OUTCOME OF LANGUAGE CONTACT

Given the variety of participant characteristics and varieties of language available, it should not be surprising that the linguistic outcome of language contact is something that cannot be strictly described as ASL or as a signed representation of English. The issue is not that contact signing occurs, or what to call it, but rather how to characterize it. This contact signing has been characterized as "an interface between deaf signers and hearing speakers" (Fischer, 1978, 314) and has been labeled "Pidgin Sign English" (PSE) by Woodward (1972, 1973). Three studies have investigated the linguistic characteristics of PSE: Woodward (1973), Woodward and Markowicz (1975), and Reilly and McIntire (1980). Woodward states that "sometimes people sign something that seems to be a pidginized version of English. The syntactic order is primarily English, but inflections have been reduced in redundancy, and there is a mixture of American Sign Language and English structure" (1973, 17). He further states that "these characteristics point up some close similarities between PSE and other pidgins. In most pidgins, articles are deleted; the copula is usually uninflected; inflections such as English plural are lost and most derivations are lost, just as they are in PSE. Perfective aspect in pidgins is often expressed through *finish* or a similar verb like *done*" (1973, 42).

Woodward (1973) and Markowicz (1975) provide a description of some of the linguistic characteristics of PSE. Their inventory of features includes articles, plurality, copula, aspect, agent-beneficiary directionality, negative incorporation, and number incorporation, and they also discuss PSE phonology, specifically, handshapes, location, and movement.

Reilly and McIntire define PSE as "a form of signing used by many hearing people for interacting with deaf people and thus is a commonly encountered dialect of ASL" (1980, 151). They point out that "although PSE has been classified as a pidgin language, it differs from most pidgins in important ways. . . . Syntactically, PSE does not appear as many other pidgins. Because it does make use of a number of English grammatical devices for creating complex sentences, it has access to a wider range of grammatical constructions than do most pidgins" (1980, 152).

The PSE label has been very widely adopted and the analogy with spoken-language pidgin situations and language contact in general has been extended to include the idea of diglossic variation along a continuum. The suggestion that Ferguson's concept of diglossia might be applicable to the deaf community was first made by Stokoe (1969). By the low (L) variety, Stokoe intends ASL, and as he states, "the H ('superposed' or 'high') variety is English. However, this English is a form most unfamiliar to usual linguistic scrutiny. It is not spoken but uttered in 'words' which are fingerspelled or signed'' (1969, 23). As Lee points out, ''the concept of a sign language 'continuum' linking the H and L varieties . . . has become quite popular. This continuum represents a scale of all the varieties of ASL and English produced by both deaf and hearing signers. These varieties imperceptibly grade into ASL on the extreme and English on the other'' (1982, 131). It has been claimed that a number of varieties exist along the continuum, and it is some complex of these varieties that the label PSE has been said to identify.

A notable problem with earlier descriptions concerns the lack of data or the problems with the data used to back up claims about the linguistic and sociolinguistic nature of the signing being described. Neither in Woodward (1973) nor in Woodward and Markowicz (1975) is there any description of the sample that serves as the source for the list of features proposed for PSE. Woodward has indicated (personal communication, 1988) that the description of PSE was based in part on the sample from his dissertation: 140 individuals, ranging in age from thirteen to fifty-five, with 9 black signers and 131 white signers. However, these data are still problematic as the basis for a description of language contact, because the data were elicited by a hearing researcher on a one-on-one basis with the use of a questionnaire, and were not interactional, and the signers providing these data range from deaf native ASL signers to hearing nonnative signers, making it virtually impossible to separate out features of the language produced that are a function of language contact from features that are a function of second-language acquisition.

For example, Woodward and Markowicz claim that the ASL rule of negative incorporation may occur in PSE, but that ''deaf signers use more negative incorporation than hearing signers'' (1975, 18). This may indeed be true, but it might also reflect a difference in language competence (that is, native signers knowing and competently using a rule that nonnative signers may be in the process of learning), rather than a language contact between hearing and deaf signers. It would seem that deaf-language production and hearing-language production in a language contact situation would necessarily be different by virtue of differences in language-acquisition backgrounds and that the features of contact signing (PSE) could not be described based on data that combine native and nonnative signer's productions, and that are not interactional.

Researchers have certainly been aware of the need to separate native and nonnative production, and in fact, Lee reports that ''Stokoe (personal communication) suggests that there may in fact be two PSE continua: a $PSE_d$ produced by deaf signers and a $PSE_h$ produced by hearing signers. $PSE_d$ is likely to have more ASL grammatical structures and to omit English inflections. $PSE_h$ tends to have greater English influence and rarely approaches the ASL extreme of the continuum'' (1982, 131).

The need for separation, then, has been recognized, but this need is not reflected in the actual descriptions of PSE that have been advanced. Thus, Reilly and McIntire (1980) base their description of the differences between PSE and ASL on videotapes of a children's story as signed by four consultants. Three of these consultants are hearing. Two have deaf parents and two of the three hearing consultants did not sign in childhood. The instructions for different versions of the story were given in ASL, or ''in PSE and spoken English simultaneously . . . or interpreted, i.e., signed as they were being read aloud by the investigator'' (p. 155).

Although there is greater awareness of the need to control for the variable of signer skill, and although the description of PSE is based on videotaped data, the same problem of separating the consequences of language contact from the consequences of second language learning arises. In their conclusions, Reilly and McIntire observe that "it seems that there is a gradation from structures that are more obvious to the language learner (classifiers and directional verbs) to those that are more and more subtle (sustained signs and facial and other non-manual behaviors). This gradation is reflected in differential usage by different signers" (1980, 183). Once again, we encounter the "apples and oranges" dilemma resulting from descriptions of PSE based on the sign production of signers with differing competence and ages of acquisition. Furthermore, data collection in analogous spoken-language situations do not typically yield naturalistic data, and accordingly, it is not clear that the data upon which Reilly and McIntire's description of PSE are based bear any resemblance to the language production in a natural-language contact situation.

It seems clear that any study that proposes to describe the linguistic outcome of language contact in the American deaf community should at the very least take its departure from data collected in naturalistic interactional settings that reflect language contact situations as closely as possible. It does not seem unfair to say that studies claiming to describe the linguistic outcome of language contact in the American deaf community to date may not reflect the actual situation, due to either a lack of data or problematic data. Due to the problems presented by the data in the studies to date, any characterizations of language contact in the American deaf community—pidginization, foreigner talk, learner's grammars, a diglossic continuum—demand reexamination.

## THE PRESENT STUDY

In light of the enormous complexity of language contact in the American deaf community and of the problems inherent in earlier studies attempting to describe the situation, we focused on only one particular type of interaction. The major goals of the present study are (1) to provide a preliminary description of deaf bilinguals interacting with hearing bilinguals, and (2) to base that description on carefully collected data that reflects natural interaction as closely as possible.

To this end, we formed six dyads of informants. All of the twelve informants, with one exception, rated themselves as very skilled in ASL, and all twelve rated themselves as skilled in English. Of the twelve informants, nine were born deaf, one was born hard of hearing and is now deaf, and two were born hearing and became deaf at fifteen months and three years, respectively. Five of the twelve came from deaf families, and of the remaining seven, five attended residential schools for the deaf and learned ASL at an early age. One informant learned ASL from other deaf students in a mainstream program (see table 1 for a summary). Considering the family and educational background of all but one of the informants, their self-evaluations of their language skills are accurate: they are bilinguals who learned ASL either natively from their parents or at a very early age from peers (all but one in a residential school setting), and they have had exposure to and contact with English all their lives. The data from one informant who did not learn ASL until age twenty-one (born deaf, hearing family) was excluded from the analysis, and in fact, the videotapes for this informant reveal minimal use of ASL. The dyads were composed as follows:

The participants in dyads 1 and 2 share similar backgrounds, as do the participants in dyads 4, 5, and 6. Dyad 3 was deliberately "mixed," consisting of one individual born deaf in a deaf family, and one born deaf in a hearing family and

*Table 1.* **Composition of Dyads**

| Dyad | Characteristics of Participant A | Characteristics of Participant B |
|------|----------------------------------|----------------------------------|
| 1 | Deaf family, born deaf, residential school | Deaf family, deaf at fifteen months, public school |
| 2 | Deaf family, born deaf, deaf day school | Deaf family, born hard of hearing, now profoundly deaf, deaf day school |
| 3 | Deaf family, born deaf, residential school | Hearing family, born deaf, residential school |
| 4 | Hearing family, born deaf, residential school | Hearing family, deaf at age three, residential school |
| 5 | Hearing family, born deaf, residential school | Hearing family, born deaf, mainstream program |
| 6 | Hearing family, deaf at age three, residential school | Hearing family, born deaf, learned ASL at age twenty-one, public school |

having attended residential school. In dyads 1, 3, and 6, the participants did not know each other; in dyads 2, 4, and 5, they did.

In the first part of the data collection, the videocameras were present, but at no point were the technicians visible. The sign production of the six dyads was videotaped during interaction first with a deaf researcher who signed ASL, then with a hearing researcher who produced English-like signing and used her voice while she signed, and finally alone with each other. The whole interview experience began with exclusive contact with the deaf researcher.

The interview consisted of a discussion of several broad topics of general interest to members of the deaf community. Four statements were presented and participants were asked if they agreed or disagreed, and why.[3] It was hypothesized that (1) the situation with the deaf researcher might induce ASL, but that the relative formality of the situation and the presence of a stranger may preclude it; (2) the situation with the hearing researcher would induce a shift away from ASL to contact signing; and (3) the third situation—the informants alone with each other—would elicit ASL. The structure of the interviews in terms of relative formality and informality is summarized in table 2.

The structure of the interviews has strong parallels with Edwards's research design for studying British Black English. A major concern in that study was that the methodology be improved "so as to ensure that this corpus authentically reflects the range of individual and situational variation which exists within the black community" (1986, 9). Edwards recognized the obvious need for the Black interviewers to gain access to vernacular speech. She assumed that the presence of a sympathetic young Black interviewer, that is, of a peer, would guarantee the use of the vernacular among the informants, but "our observation made it clear that many young black people use Patois only in in-group conversation, so that the presence of any other person, even the young Black fieldworker, would be enough to inhibit Patois usage.

*Table 2.* **Interview Structure**

| Interview Situation | Formal | Informal |
|---|---|---|
| With deaf interviewer | + | |
| Dyad alone | | + |
| With hearing interviewer | + | |
| Dyad alone | | + |
| With deaf interviewer | + | |

The obvious solution was to create a situation in which the young people were left alone'' (p. 17).

As in the Edwards study, participants in the present study were left alone twice and asked to continue discussing the topics introduced by the interviewer. In the first instance, the deaf interviewer was told that he had an emergency phone call that required him to leave. After an eight-to-ten-minute period, the hearing researcher arrived and explained that she would be taking the deaf researcher's place. The interview continued and the hearing researcher then left to check on the deaf researcher. The dyad was again left alone until the return of the deaf researcher.

Following the completion of the interview, the participants were told that there had in fact been no emergency, and were given the reason for the deaf researcher's departure. The participants viewed portions of the tapes and discussed the purpose of the research with the researchers. All the participants were glad to be told that the ''emergency'' was false, and they accepted it as part of the data-collection procedure.

Based on a preliminary examination of the data, some interesting observations can be made about the overall pattern of language use during the interviews.

## LANGUAGE USE DURING THE INTERVIEWS

Based on the assessment by a deaf native ASL user, the overall pattern of language use during the interviews is summarized in table 3.[4]

The information in table 3 should be read as follows: In the first dyad, participant A used ASL under all conditions; A's language use is in contrast with B's, who used contact signing and Signed English with the deaf interviewer, contact signing with A, and Signed English with the hearing interviewer. And so on, for all six dyads. As can be seen from this summary, some participants start out with one kind of signing in a particular condition, and then change to another kind of signing within the same condition. Participant B in dyad 5, for example, produced contact signing with the deaf interviewer. When alone with Participant A, B produced ASL, and then produced contact signing again when the hearing interviewer appeared. When the hearing interviewer left A and B alone, B continued to produce contact signing for a while, and then produced ASL. B continued to produce ASL upon the return of the deaf interviewer, and did so until the end of the interview.

There are several interesting observations that can be made based on table 3. As predicted, nine of the twelve informants produced a form of signing that was ''other than ASL'' with the hearing interviewer—either contact signing or Signed

*Table 3.* Language Use During the Interviews

| | Dyad | | | | | | | | | | | |
| | 1 | | 2 | | 3 | | 4 | | 5 | | 6 | |
| Situation | Part. A | Part. B | Part. A | Part. B | Part. A | Part. B | Part. A | Part. B | Part. A | Part. B | Part. A | Part. B |
| With deaf interviewer | ASL | C.S./S.E. | ASL | ASL/C.S. | ASL/C.S. | C.S. | ASL | S.E. | ASL | C.S. | ASL | C.S. |
| Dyad alone | ASL | C.S. | ASL | ASL | ASL/C.S. | ASL/C.S. | ASL | C.S. | ASL | ASL | C.S. | C.S. |
| With hearing interviewer | ASL | S.E. | ASL/C.S. | C.S. | C.S. | S.E. | ASL | C.S. | C.S. | C.S. | C.S. | C.S. |
| Dyad alone | ASL | C.S. | ASL | ASL | ASL/C.S. | ASL/C.S. | ASL | C.S. | C.S./ASL | C.S./ASL | C.S./ASL | C.S./ASL |
| With deaf interviewer | ASL | C.S. | ASL | ASL/C.S. | ASL/C.S. | ASL/C.S. | ASL | C.S. | ASL | ASL | ASL | C.S. |

*Key.* Part. = participant; C.S. = contact signing; S.E. = Signed English

English with voice. In some cases, the informants produced ASL with the deaf interviewer and alone with each other, as might be expected. However, some unexpected results emerged. Three informants used ASL with the hearing interviewer, in spite of a widely held belief that deaf native signers automatically switch away from ASL in the presence of a nonnative signer. Furthermore, two of the informants (1A and 4A) used ASL consistently in all of the situations. One might predict that both of these informants come from deaf families; however, 4A is from a hearing family. Another unexpected result was the production of contact signing both with the deaf interviewer and when the informants were left alone. The deaf interviewer consistently signed ASL, and though it was predicted that the informants would produce ASL both in this situation and when left alone, that was not the case. Indeed, in one case, an informant produced Signed English with the deaf interviewer. These results are particularly interesting given another widely held belief that deaf native signers will consistently sign ASL with each other if no hearing people are present. The observations on the overall pattern of language use during the interviews can be summarized as follows:

- Some informants used contact signing or Signed English with the hearing interviewer, as expected; others used ASL throughout.
- ASL was used with the hearing interviewer by some informants, but not others.
- Contact signing was produced with the deaf interviewer and when the informants were alone.
- ASL was used not only by deaf informants from deaf families but also deaf informants from hearing families.

These observations appear to challenge the traditional perspective on language contact in the American deaf community. For example, it has always been assumed that contact signing (known as PSE) appears in deaf-hearing interaction, for obvious reasons—chiefly, that the hearing person might not understand ASL. An extreme position has held that the very purpose of contact signing is to prevent hearing people from learning ASL (Woodward and Markowicz, 1975, 12). More measured approaches simply describe contact signing as the product of deaf-hearing interaction. Little has been said, however, about the use of contact signing in exclusively deaf settings. While comprehension might explain the occurrence of contact signing in deaf-hearing interaction, it is clearly not an issue in portions of the interviews described here, as all participants are native or near-native signers and in some instances sign ASL with each other. The choice to use contact signing with other deaf ASL natives, then, appears to be motivated by sociolinguistic factors. These factors include the formality of the interview situation (along with the presence of videotape equipment), and a participant's lack of familiarity in some cases with both the interviewer and the other informant. The videotaped data also clearly present counterevidence to the claims that deaf people never or rarely sign ASL in the presence of hearing people, as two of the informants chose to sign ASL throughout the interview. We suggest that this choice is motivated by other sociolinguistic factors such as the desire to establish one's identity as a bona fide member of the deaf cultural group, a desire that may supersede considerations of formality or lack of familiarity. Different sociolinguistic factors motivate the language choices of different individuals. This is further illustrated by the use within a given interview situation of a different kind of signing by each informant. Figure 1 provides a more graphic summary of informant language use within the interviews.

Three distinct patterns emerge from figure 1. One pattern, as seen with dyads 1 and 4, consists of the two informants using distinctly different kinds of signing, and never overlapping with each other. For example, in dyad 1, informant 1A consistently used ASL throughout the interview, even though 1B started out with contact signing and Signed English, then moved first to contact signing, then to Signed English, and then back to contact signing. Similarly, in dyad 4, 4A consistently used ASL, while 4B started out with Signed English and then consistently used contact signing. Neither 1B nor 4B ever approached the use of ASL during the interview. The first pattern, then, is that one informant's signing during the interview is consistently distinct from the other.

In dyads 2 and 6, we see a second pattern, in which the informants use different kinds of signing during the first part of the interview, with the deaf interviewer, but when left alone, use the same kind of signing. In dyad 2, informant 2A continued with ASL, and 2B switched to ASL; in dyad 6, informant 6B continued with contact signing, and 6A switched to contact signing. In dyad 6, the informants used the same kind of signing and switched in the same way toward ASL when left alone, and then signed quite differently with the deaf interviewer. In dyad 2, the informants did not sign in exactly the same way, but they did shift in the same direction. Also interesting in both dyads is the fact that despite shifting during the interview, each informant signed the same way with the deaf interviewer at the end of the interview as at the beginning.

The third pattern is seen in dyads 3 and 5, in which the informants begin the interview with different kinds of signing. One informant then shifted toward the other, and then both informants either used the same kind of signing for the rest of the interview (dyad 5), or used the same kind of signing, then shifted in the same direction, and then used the same kind of signing again (dyad 3).

The question arises as to what accounts for the use of different kinds of signing by individual informants within the interviews. Switching that seems to be motivated by the presence of a hearing person can be seen in these data: seven of the twelve informants switched from ASL signing or ASL signing with some contact signing features to contact signing or Signed English with voice in the presence of the hearing interviewer. Of the remaining five informants, two consistently signed ASL in all situations; the other three produced contact signing when the hearing interviewer arrived and continued doing so with the hearing interviewer. Five of the twelve informants are from deaf families, and it is very interesting to note that four of those five are among those who switched in the presence of the hearing interviewer. Of the five informants who did not switch with the hearing interviewer, only one was from a deaf family.

Signing behavior with hearing people, however, does not explain the occurrence of contact signing with the deaf interviewer or when the informants are alone. The occurrence of contact signing in the latter situations can be accounted for by several factors, such as the formality of the interview situation and the lack of familiarity of the informants with the deaf interviewer.

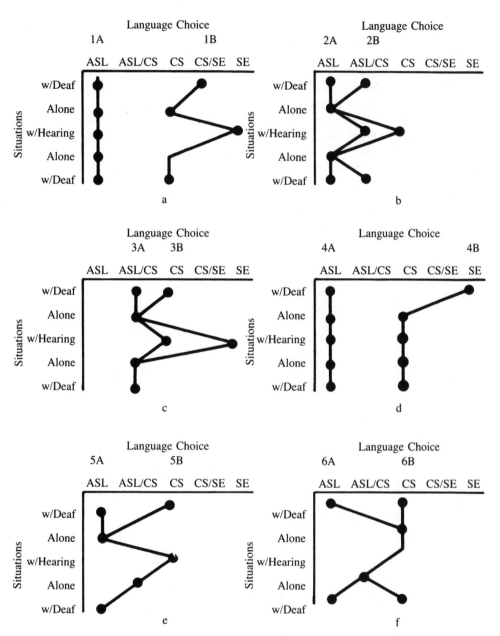

*Figure 1.* **Patterns of language choice: (a) dyad 1; (b) dyad 2; (c) dyad 3; (d) dyad 4; (e) dyad 5; (f) dyad 6.**

Attitudes concerning the kind of signing that is appropriate in different situations have long been noticed and described. Indeed, it was these language attitudes and the concomitant language choices that prompted Stokoe's 1969 description of the language situation in the deaf community as "diglossic," that is, ASL strictly for some situations and a more English-like signing strictly for others, with no overlap.

The characterization of the language situation in the deaf community as diglossic has been reexamined by Lee, who states that although "there is indeed variation [in the deaf community], . . . code-switching and style shifting rather than diglossia appear to be the norm" (1982, 127). Three of Ferguson's nine criteria are linguistic (lexicon, phonology, and grammar), and six are described by Lee as sociolinguistic (literary heritage, standardization, prestige, stability, acquisition, and function), and she observes, "I have found none of the nine characteristics actually consistent with diglossia, at least in some parts of the linguistic community" (1982, 147).

Although it is not clear at this point what the roles of code switching and style shifting are in the deaf community, it is clear from Lee's reexamination and from these data that the situation is not strictly diglossic. Clearly some of the informants in this study saw ASL as inappropriate for any part of the interview. Specifically, informants 1B and 4B never used ASL. Other informants saw ASL as appropriate only when left alone with no interviewer present. In each one of the six dyads, a shift occurred when the deaf interviewer left and the informants were left alone, and it is striking that whenever the signing of one informant shifted toward the signing of another, it was, with one exception, a shift from contact signing or Signed English, to or toward ASL. That is, informants 1A, 2A, 3A, 4A, and 5A used ASL with the deaf interviewer at the beginning of the interview, and informants 1B, 2B, 3B, 4B, and 5B used contact signing or Signed English. When the deaf interviewer left, the latter informants switched to or toward ASL. The one exception was informant 6A, who signed ASL with the deaf interviewer and then switched to contact signing when left alone with 6B, who also produced contact signing. This may have occurred because, of the twelve informants, 6B was the only one who learned ASL relatively late. 6A may have switched to contact signing in an attempt to accommodate 6B. The fact that ASL was seen as appropriate only when the interviewers were absent is further supported by the fact that two of the informants (2B and 6B) switched away from ASL to contact signing when the deaf interviewer reappeared at the end of the interview. Any attempt, however, to claim that there is evidence here for a diglossic situation is quickly thwarted by the language use of informants who used ASL in all of the interview situations, with no apparent regard for formality, familiarity, or audiological status of interlocutor.

The patterns seen in figure 1 provide an illustration of Giles' (1977) theory of accommodation in linguistic behavior (Valli, 1988). Such accommodation may take the form of convergence, nonconvergence, or divergence. With convergence, the speaker will choose a language variety that seems to fit the needs of the person being talked to. Under some conditions, however, a speaker may diverge to disassociate himself from the listeners and/or to emphasize his loyalty to his group. Nonconvergence occurs when one speaker does not move away from another, but simply continues using a variety that differs from other speakers. Figure 1 provides examples of all three. In dyad 1, for example, Participant 1B converges with 1A when the dyad is left alone. 1B then converges with the hearing interviewer, while 1A provides an example of nonconvergence with the hearing interviewer by continuing to use ASL as he has all along. In all the dyads except 6, the B participants converge toward the A participants, toward ASL. As was mentioned before, in dyad 6, 6A may converge toward 6B because 6B learned sign language relatively late and may not be comfortable using ASL.

A major goal of this chapter was to describe the sociolinguistic conditions that accompany the production of signing that is other than ASL, signing that has been labeled PSE. It has been claimed that this kind of signing occurs in the presence of hearing people, either for reasons of comprehension or to deny them access to ASL. However, the videotaped data in this study clearly demonstrate that this contact signing is produced among deaf native ASL signers in the absence of hearing people. The sociolinguistic factors that motivate this production appear to include the relative formality of the interview situation and the lack of familiarity with other interlocutors. There is clear evidence that contact signing is considered more appropriate than ASL in some situations. Furthermore, an examination of the conditions of language contact situations in the deaf community reveals that from a sociolinguistic standpoint, these situations are not at all analogous to the sociolinguistic conditions that give rise to spoken-language pidgins.

It is clear that not all language contact situations result in pidginization. Grosjean provides a succinct summary of this issue: "The usual outcome of bilingualism . . . is a return to monolingualism: this may take the form of maintenance of the group's second language and the disappearance of the first language (often referred to as mother-tongue displacement of language shift); or the evolution to a new language through processes of pidginization and creolization" (1982, 38). In a review of the state of the art in interlinguistics, Muysken (1984) lists several possibilities for a language contact situation: a third language, dialect shift, foreign accent, code switching, relexification, code mixing, and foreigner talk. Furthermore, there has been continuous and vigorous debate concerning the fundamental nature of pidgins and pidginization at least since Hall's pioneering work in the 1960s. Participants in the debate include DeCamp (1971), Alleyne (1971), Whinnom (1971), Bickerton (1975, 1977), Samarin (1971), Ferguson and De Bose (1977), Todd (1974), Kay and Sankoff (1974), Rickford (1981), Bickerton (1981, 1984), Sankoff (1984), and Mühlhäusler (1986). However, there appears to exist a basic convergence of opinions concerning the unique nature of pidginization as having at its inception a very particular set of sociolinguistic circumstances. As Barbag-Stoll states:

> The fundamental condition for the occurrence of pidginization is a contact situation involving two or more different languages. This should by no means imply, however, that any contact of two or more languages will result in hybridization. If the source languages are closely related, the output product is more likely to be a dialect, as the prevailing process will be substitution rather than simplification. If the spread of the source language is symmetrical when it is learnt through formal means, it is likely to result in bilingualism. Whether the output is a pidgin or a standard language depends on the degree of availability of target models and the extent to which they are exposed to the learners. If the standard language models are easily accessible and if the nature of the contact situation is such that the speaker interacts mostly with native speakers of the target language, he is most likely to learn the non-pidginized version of it. However, if the target language is spoken mainly with non-native speakers and the target models are rare, the output will most probably be pidgin. (1983, 24)

Barbag-Stoll stresses the availability of target models and the extent to which learners are exposed to them as central to the pidginization process. Hall (1962) stresses the fact that the language in question was not native to any of its users. De Camp defines a pidgin as ''a contact vernacular, normally not the native language of any of its speakers. It is used in trading or in any situation requiring communication between persons who do not speak each other's native languages'' (1971, 15). De Camp goes on to say that pidgins are characterized by limited vocabularies, elimination of many grammatical devices such as number and gender, and a drastic reduction of redundant features, but cautions against equating this reduction with simplification. Bickerton (1975) states that at the inception of the pidgin-creole cycle, future pidgin speakers already had established grammars of their own, and, in fact, were often multilingual. They were confronted by the grammar of the superstrate language and then removed both from their own language communities and from the target superstrate language. In later work, he characterizes pidginization as ''second-language learning with restricted input'' (1977, 49), and states:

> We can conclude that pidginization is a process that begins by the speaker using his native tongue and relexifying first only a few key words; that, in the earliest stages, even the few superstrate words will be thoroughly rephonologized to accord with substrate sound system and phonotactics; that subsequently, more superstrate lexicon will be acquired but may still be rephonologized to varying degrees and will be, for the most part, slotted into syntactic surface structures drawn from the substrate; that even substrate syntax will be particially retained, and will alternate, apparently unpredictably, with structures imported from the superstrate. (1977, 54)

Pidginization, then, is clearly the result of a unique kind of language contact, and the key elements in understanding the pidginization process appear to be the relative access to the target model, the lack of a mutually intelligible language among interlocutors, an immediate need for communication, and interruption of access to one's native language.

What is striking is that although one result of language contact in the American deaf community has been labeled ''Pidgin Sign English,'' the sociolinguistic situation in this community does not coincide with the ''classic'' pidgin situation or with any of the key elements. Let us assume, for example, that English is considered the superstrate language in the deaf community. Clearly it is the native language of hearing users of contact signing. However, even deaf native ASL signers, for whom English may not be a native language, still have extensive exposure to and contact with English, in various forms, first in educational settings and later in their adult lives through employment, interaction with hearing people, and through print and broadcast media. This exposure to and contact with English is accompanied by ongoing ASL interaction with other native signers. The result for such native ASL signers in American society is a maintained bilingualism. And, as was outlined earlier, there are many different kinds of contact situations occurring in the deaf community, depending on participant characteristics.

We see parallels with Whinnom's (1971) description of ''cocoliche,'' the Spanish spoken by Italian immigrants in Argentina (but not spoken by Argentines). One reason for the occurrence of cocoliche is the resistance to fully integrating into the Spanish-speaking community. This leads one to speculate about a signer's choice of contact signing, for example, over strict Signed English. Furthermore, because cocoliche represents a form of second-language learning, Whinnom points out that the speech of no two individual cocoliche speakers can ever be quite identical. This has clear parallels with the diversity of educational backgrounds of individuals in the deaf community and what, as a consequence, they bring with them to a contact situation. However, Whinnom also points out that with cocoliche, the pressures of formal language instruction do not play a role, and this represents a difference from the deaf community, as we cannot discount the role of English in contact signing as a result of its role in the educational system.

The present study describes some of the sociolinguistic outcomes of language contact in the deaf community and reveals the situation to be considerably more complex than earlier descriptions indicate. Lucas and Valli (1989) describe the linguistic outcome of language contact and provide a detailed contrast of the features of contact signing with those of spoken-language pidgins and of Signed English.[5] One interesting and perhaps ironic fact about the linguistic outcome is the occurrence of English structural features in contact signing, features that do *not* include the invented signs that are part of the manual codes for English that have been implemented in the educational system. One part of the irony lies in the fact that there is considerable use in the educational system of these manual codes, and it would not be unreasonable to predict that elements of these codes would occur in bilingual contact situations. However, very little evidence of those codes was found in the data. Another part of the irony has to do with the generally negative reception that these codes have received from members of the deaf community (Baker and Cokely, 1980). It should be clear from the present study that resistance to invented codes for English should not be mistaken for resistance to English per se, as the indigenous, natural signing that occurs as a result of the contact between bilinguals has many English features. Clearly the social stigma about invented systems does not preclude the occurrence of English features. The crucial difference is the difference between an invented representation of a language imposed on its users, and a naturally occurring form of language observed not only in deaf-hearing interaction, but also in the interaction of deaf native ASL users with one another.

Some final speculation about the future of language contact in the deaf community: In this study, we have described the occurrence of contact signing in situations where ASL might be predicted (that is, between deaf individuals who are native ASL users). We have suggested that the occurrence of "other than ASL" can be accounted for by a variety of sociolinguistic factors, including lack of familiarity between participants or formality of the situation. Clearly, the choice of "other than ASL" is being made in some situations; "other than ASL" is clearly seen as more appropriate in some situations. If this were not so, native ASL users who choose ASL in some situations would use it in situations where they now choose "other than ASL." By way of conclusion, we suggest, as have other researchers (for example, Stokoe, 1969), that the choice of "other than ASL" and the view that ASL is not appropriate for some situations are the direct results of a sociolinguistic situation in which ASL has been ignored and devalued, and in which the focus has traditionally been on the instruction and use of English. We suggest that, as ASL becomes more highly valued and becomes formally and fully recognized and used as a legitimate tool for communication in any situation, that the outcome of language contact in the American deaf community will change noticeably.

# NOTES

We are grateful to Scott Liddell, Walt Wolfram, and Bob Johnson for providing very detailed and valuable feedback on this paper. This paper is a preliminary version of a chapter that appears in C. Lucas (ed.), (1989), *The Sociolinguistics of the deaf community*. San Diego, CA: Academic Press.

1. Based on a preliminary examination of the linguistic and sociolinguistic data, we are reluctant at this point to call the contact signing that we have observed a "variety" or a "dialect," that is, a discrete and consistent linguistic system. The absence of such labels in the present study is conscious. Bob Johnson (personal communication) has observed that, due to the wide variety of language skills and backgrounds and educational backgrounds that signers bring with them to language contact situations, the best way to describe the outcome of language contact in the American deaf community may be as a collection of individual grammars. Further description of our data will shed light on his observation.

2. At this point, evidence for the occurrence of signed or spoken English in the home, along with ASL, is largely anecdotal. For example, a Gallaudet undergraduate whose parents are deaf and who signs ASL as a first language remarked, in a class journal, "At first when I was born, my parents thought I was hearing due to a *very* little hearing loss. Afraid that I may have poor speech and English skills, they decided to use Straight English and their voices whenever talking to me." The same student remarks that her parents went back to using ASL. And another student states, "I was introduced to ASL since I'm the daughter of deaf parents and the fifth deaf generation. When SEE [Signing Exact English, a manual code for English] was emphasized in the 70s, my mama decided to learn SEE and placed me in a mainstream program where SEE was strongly used." Both of these comments imply the use of some form of English signing by native ASL signers in the home with their children. Furthermore, Woodward observes that "it has been estimated that 10–20 percent of the deaf population has deaf parents. A tiny proportion of these parents are highly educated and have native English competence. In this tiny minority of the deaf, PSE [Pidgin Sign English, Woodward's term for the outcome of language contact in the deaf community] may be learned with ASL from infancy" (1973c, 44). However, sociolinguistic and ethnographic data to support comments and observations such as these are nonexistent.

3. The four statements introduced for discussion were as follows: (1) Someone in a public place (airport, restaurant) discovers that you're deaf and wants to help you. That is acceptable. Agree or disagree? (2) The hearing children of deaf people are members of the deaf culture. Agree or disagree? (3) Gallaudet University should have a deaf president. Agree or disagree? (4) Mainstreaming is better than residential schools. Agree or disagree?

4. At this stage of the study, assessment of the signing on the tapes (that is, ASL versus other-than-ASL versus Signed English) is based on the judgment of the researchers. ASL and other-than-ASL was judged by a deaf native signer; Signed English consistently included the use of voice and hence included input from the hearing researcher. The final analysis, however, will not be limited to the judgment of the researchers. The second part of the data collection will consist of having native signers view each tape at least twice and indicate by pushing a button when switches away from ASL or back to ASL take place. These native-signer júdges will be asked to characterize the language production between the switch points, and it is this production that will form the basis for the eventual description of contact signing. The entire methodology was first designed and employed by Robert E. Johnson, Scott Lidell, Carol Erting, and Dave Knight in a pilot project entitled "Sign Language and Variation in Context" (SLAVIC, 1984), sponsored by the Gallaudet Research Institute. The database will eventually include the signing production of twenty individuals, twelve white and eight black. The sign production of the black informants reflects their interaction with black interviewers (hearing and deaf) and white interviewers (hearing and deaf).

5. That the linguistic outcome of contact between ASL and English does not seem best described as a pidgin was observed accurately by Cokely (1983), who reviews the preconditions defined by other researchers for the emergence of a pidgin (e.g. Ferguson and DeBose, 1977), describes the ASL–English contact situation, and states that

> "this situation, then, can be described as one in which members of the Deaf community communicate with hearing people in a foreigner talk register of ASL, and members of the hearing community communicate with Deaf people in a foreigner talk register of English" (1983, 11). He goes on to state that "the ASL–English contact situation does not, in fact, result in the emergence of a pidgin. Although the process of pidginization may be detected in the ASL–English situation, the preconditions for the development of a pidgin language are not adequately met. Instead the variation along the ASL–English continuum of varieties or registers can be accounted for by the dynamic interplay of foreigner talk, judgments of proficiency, and learners' attempts to master the target language—whether this is ASL for hearing users or English for Deaf users" (1983, 20).

There is an apparent difficulty with Cokely's characterization of language contact in the deaf community. Consider a possible analogy with spoken-language contact situations. In the contact between a native speaker of Italian, for example, and a nonnative speaker of Italian, it would be quite strange to expect that the "foreigner talk" variety of Italian used by the native speaker would include any elements of the nonnative speaker's first language. More likely would be that the foreigner-talk variety would simply be a modified version of Italian. The variety of signing that the deaf native-ASL signer uses with many hearing people, however, would seem to include at least some features of English, and thus would not seem to qualify strictly as foreigner talk. This is also the case for the variety of signing that hearing people may use with deaf people. Woodward (1985) describes Cokely's observations as "challenging to Woodward's (1973) analysis of the varieties between ASL and English as pidgin language." Woodward contends that by 1980, however, the notion that varieties referred to by "PSE" as a discrete pidgin had already been abandoned, and cites his own 1980 work to support this contention: "While it is true that PSE is different from pure ASL and from pure English, it is not a separate language. There is no way in the world to define where PSE begins and ends" (1985, 19). Bochner and Albertini address the issue of PSE within the context of language acquisition and correctly observe that it is difficult to draw a clear parallel between spoken language pidgins and PSE. They go on to state that "a pidgin may be developing in North America schools and workplaces among users of mutually unintelligible sign systems" (1988, 13). However, their claims are not data based. They observe that "objective and detailed descriptions of the structure and function of signing being used in these situations would clarify the picture" (1988, 14). To fully understand the preliminary inventory of contact signing features in these data, and to get a clearer understanding of what kind of linguistic phenomenon this is, it is useful to compare it to (a) inventories of the features of English-based spoken language pidgins, to which contact signing has been compared, and (b) the features of other kinds of signing such as Signed English, which by its nature is English-based. These comparisons appear in Lucas and Valli (1989).

# REFERENCES

Alleyne, M. C. (1971). Acculturation and the cultural matrix of creolization. In *Pidginization and creolization of languages*, edited by D. Hymes, 169–86. New York: Cambridge University Press.

Barbag-Stoll, A. (1983). *Social and linguistic history of Nigerian Pidgin English.* Tubingen: Stauffenberg-Verlag.

Bickerton, D. (1975). *The dynamics of a creole system.* London: Oxford University Press.

―――. (1977). Pidginization and creolization. Language acquisition and language universals. In *Pidgin and creole linguistics,* edited by A. Valdman, 49–69. Bloomington: Indiana University Press.

―――. (1981). *Roots of language.* Ann Arbor, MI: Karoma Publishers.

―――. (1984). *The role of demographics in the origin of Creoles.* Paper presented at NWAVE XIII, October, Philadelphia.

Bochner, J. H., and Albertini, J. A. (1988). Language varieties in the deaf population and their acquisition by children and adults. In *Language learning and deafness,* edited by M. Strong, 3–48. Oxford: Blackwell.

Cokely, D. (1983). When is a pidgin not a pidgin? An alternative analysis of the ASL–English contact situation. *Sign Language Studies* 38:1–24.

DeCamp, D. (1971). The study of pidgin and creole languages. In *Pidginization and creolization of languages,* edited by D. Hymes, 13–39. New York: Cambridge University Press.

Edwards, V. (1986). *Language in a black community.* San Diego, CA: College Hill Press.

Ferguson, C., and De Bose, C. (1977). Simplified registers, broken language and pidginization. In *Pidgin and creole linguistics,* edited by A. Valdman, 99–125. Bloomington: Indiana University Press.

Fischer, S. (1978). Sign language and creoles. In *Understanding language through sign language research,* edited by P. Siple, 309–31. New York: Academic Press.

Giles, H. (1977). *Language, ethnicity, and intergroup relations.* London: Academic Press.

Grosjean, F. (1982). *Life with two languages.* Cambridge, MA: Harvard University Press.

Hall, R. A. (1962). The life-cycle of pidgin languages. *Festschrift de Groot. Lingua* 11:151–56.

Kay, P., and Sankoff, G. (1974). A language-universals approach to pidgins and creoles. In *Pidgins and creoles: Current trends and prospects,* edited by D. DeCamp and I. Hancock, 67–72. Washington, DC: Georgetown University Press.

Lee, D. M. (1982). Are there really signs of diglossia? Reexamining the situation. *Sign Language Studies* 35:127–52.

Lucas, C., and Valli, C. (1989). Language contact in the American deaf community. In *The sociolinguistics of the deaf community,* edited by C. Lucas. San Diego, CA: Academic Press.

Mühlhäusler, P. (1986). *Pidgin and creole linguistics.* Oxford: Blackwell.

Muysken, P. (1984). The state of the art in interlinguistics. *Revue Québecoise de linguistique* 14:49–76.

Reilly, J., and McIntire, M. (1980). American Sign Language and Pidgin Sign English: What's the difference? *Sign Language Studies* 27:151–92.

Rickford, J. R. (1981). A variable rule for a creole continuum. In *Variation ommibus,* edited by D. Sankoff and H. Cedergren, 201–8. Alberta: Linguistic Research.

Samarin, W. J. (1971). Salient and substantive pidginization. In *Pidginization and creolization of languages,* edited by D. Hymes, 117–40. New York: Cambridge University Press.

Sankoff, G. (1984). Creoles and universal grammar: The unmarked case. Colloquium presented at the annual meeting of the Linguistic Society of America, December, Baltimore, MD.

Stokoe, W. C. (1969). Sign language diglossia. *Studies in Linguistics* 21:27–41.

Todd, L. (1974). *Pidgins and creoles.* London: Routledge and Kegan Paul.

Valli, C. (1988). Language choice: Convergence and divergence. Gallaudet University, Washington, DC. Unpublished manuscript.

Whinnom, K. (1971). Linguistic hybridization and the "special case" of Pidgins and Creoles. In *Pidginization and creolization of languages,* edited by D. Hymes, 91–115. New York: Cambridge University Press.

Woodward, J. C. (1972). Implicational lects on the deaf diglossic continuum. Ph.D. diss., Georgetown University.

———. (1973). Some characteristics of Pidgin Sign English. *Sign Language Studies* 3:39–46.

———, and Markowicz, H. (1975). Some handy new ideas on pidgins and creoles: Pidgin sign languages. Paper presented at the Conference on Pidgin and Creole Languages, Honolulu, Hawaii.

———. (1985). Sociolinguistic variation involving American Sign Language. Gallaudet University, Washington, DC. Unpublished manuscript.

# Linguistic Transference and Interference: Interpreting Between English and ASL

Jeffrey Davis

Research suggests that interlingual transference—for example, code-switching, code-mixing, and lexical borrowing—typically characterize conversational style in bilingual communities (Gumperz and Hernandez-Chavez, 1971; Gumperz, 1976; DiPietro, 1978; Poplack, 1980; Poplack, Wheeler, and Westwood, 1987). The fact that there has been prolonged and intensive contact between ASL and English has resulted in linguistic outcomes similar to those found in other bilingual communities. These outcomes are shaped by factors unique to the ASL-English contact situation (for example, linguistic channel availability and manner of language acquisition).[1]

The complexity of the ASL–English contact situation in terms of participant characteristics and varieties of language used by these participants has only begun to be systematically described (Lucas, 1989; Lucas and Valli, 1989; Davis, 1987, and 1989). Interpreting between ASL and English has significant implications for signed language interpreters, who function at the point of interface of both languages and cultures. The interpreting field is an excellent arena for the study of language contact phenomena, but has heretofore been neglected by researchers.

Code-switching and code-mixing, for example, have been identified as devices for elucidation and interpretation (Kachru, 1978; Davis, 1989). Code-switching and code-mixing may be viewed as a liability or an asset in interpretation—the former being the case when the switch or mix is sporadic and unsignaled (interference), the latter as a linguistic strategy used to avoid vagueness and ambiguity (transference).

The questions to be addressed in this paper are these: How do interpreters visually or manually represent source language forms (English) in the target language output (ASL)? What is the nature and the structure of the interpreters' representations of English forms in the visual-manual modality of ASL? When can interlingual transfer between ASL and English be considered code-switching, code-mixing, or lexical borrowing? I analyze English to ASL interpreting data for examples of interlingual transference and interference in the target language (ASL) output. I make a distinction between interlingual transference and interference. Transference happens when interpreters encode English forms in the ASL output, as opposed to interpreting them.

When interpreters encode English forms visually, they mark them in very systematic ways. This is a strategy that disambiguates and elucidates discontinuities between ASL and English. Interference, on the other hand, occurs when the encoding of English forms in the ASL output interferes with the propositional content of the message. Encoded English forms that are sporadic and unsignaled appear to be a form of interference.

## ENGLISH-TO-ASL INTERPRETING[2]

In the case of English-to-ASL interpreting, English is the source language and ASL is the target language. Interpretation is a process whereby the source language message is immediately changed into the target language. Interpretation requires comprehension of the source-language input, immediate discarding of words from the source language, analysis of the source message for meaning, and restructuring the source message into the target language output (Seleskovitch, 1978). This endeavor is more difficult when the two languages involved are structurally divergent, as would be the case, for example, with English and Russian, Finnish and Spanish, and English and ASL. English-to-ASL interpretation involves not only two structurally different languages, but different linguistic modalities as well (aural/oral versus visual/gestural). If the situation weren't complex enough, it is exacerbated by the fact that one language has traditionally enjoyed greater status and wider use than the other. That is, English (the majority language) has heretofore been the primary language used in deaf education and is held to be the language needed for purposes of upward mobility. ASL (the minority language) has traditionally been relegated to use in informal settings and used primarily for intragroup activities.

## ASL AND ENGLISH BILINGUALISM

The ASL–English contact situation is parallel to cases of societal bilingualism—that is, one language enjoys greater prestige and wider use than the other. In language contact situations where there is uneven situational and functional allocation of the languages, the result is typically different configurations of bilingualism—that is, dominance in the majority language, balanced bilingualism, or dominance in the minority language (Mougeon, Beniak, and Valois, 1985). Grosjean points out that "most bilinguals use their languages for different purposes and in different situations, and hence 'balanced' bilinguals, those who are equally fluent in both languages, are probably the exception and not the norm" (1982, 235). At the societal level, then, the U.S. deaf community can be best described as multilingual, since ASL, English, English-based signing, and contact signing[3] are used to varying degrees. Individual deaf Americans are also likely to be bilingual—that is, most members of the community use signed, written, or even spoken English in addition to ASL.[4]

A unique characteristic of interpreting in an ASL–English contact situation, then, is that the deaf audience who are the consumers of English to ASL interpretation usually exhibit some degree of bilingual proficiency. In other words, while interpreting into the target language (ASL), the interpreter may assume that the deaf audience has some written or even spoken proficiency in the source language (English). The audience, of course, may not always be bilingual. There are situations where the deaf consumer(s) may be ASL monolingual and expect a different interpreting output (that is, ASL with minimal transference from English). When the deaf audience is bilingual, however, the interpreter may sometimes encode spoken English words or phrases in the visual mode, as opposed to interpreting them. That is, in some instances, English words or phrases can be fingerspelled; a visual representation of English syntax can be given in the sign modality; or ASL signs can be accompanied by the mouthing of English words. In the present study, I am interested in describing when interlingual transference from English to ASL is patterned and rule governed, as opposed to random and sporadic (that is, interference).

## DEFINITIONS

Linguistic transference results from prolonged language contact. Code-switching, code-mixing, and lexical borrowing are the most common forms of transfer found among bilingual communities of the world (Poplack, 1980; Sankoff and Poplack, 1981; Mougen, Beniak, and Valois, 1985). Code-switching is the broader term used to refer to any stretch or portion of discourse where there is alternation between two languages. In other words, in code-switching there is a complete switch to the other language, including switching the phonology and morphology. According to this definition, "code-switching" can be used to refer only to cases where someone signing ASL stops and starts speaking English, or vice versa.

Code-switching, however, is usually extended to include switches from ASL signing to English-based signing—that is, switching within modality (Lee, 1983). Switches that are motivated by a change in the speech event or situation have been referred to as "situational code-switching" (Gumperz, 1976). When bilinguals switch for stylistic or rhetorical purposes, this is referred to as "conversational code-switching" (Gumperz and Hernandez-Chavez, 1971). Lee (1983) finds that, depending on the topic, situation, and participants, a signer may switch from ASL signing to signing that is more like English (that is, situational code-switching). At other times, usually for stylistic purposes or as a rhetorical device, an ASL signer may manually encode an English word or phrase in the visual mode (that is, conversational code-switching). The research done by Lee (1983) supports the notion that the types of code-switching found in bilingual and multilingual hearing communities are also evident in the signing of bilinguals in the multilingual deaf community.

Code-mixing, on the other hand, is much more difficult to distinguish. In code-mixing, "pieces" of one language are used while a speaker is basically using another language. The language used predominantly is the base or primary language, and the language from which the pieces originate is the source language. There is debate in the literature about the appropriate use of the code-mixing and code-switching labels. The debate arises out of how to differentiate switches within sentences (intrasentential) from switches at or between sentence boundaries (intersentential). Some researchers argue that the term "code-mixing" rather than "code-switching" should be used to refer to intrasentential phenomena—for example, switches occurring within a sentence, clause, or constituent (Kachru, 1978; Sridhar and Sridhar, 1980; Bokamba, 1985).

Lucas and Valli (in press) discuss how code-mixing is used by deaf individuals in the ASL–English contact situation and distinguish it from cases of code-mixing described for spoken language situations:

> Mixing within components, while possible, is necessarily sequential—that is, it seems impossible to produce two phonological events from two different spoken languages simultaneously. However, in the contact signing described here, in which a signer produces ASL lexical items on the hands, and simultaneous mouthing of the corresponding English lexical items, the result seems to be simultaneous production of two separate codes.

"Code-mixing" is used in this paper to describe the interpreters' simultaneous mouthing of English words while signing ASL.

Lexical borrowing is different from code-switching and code-mixing (Poplack, Sankoff, and Miller, 1987). In the case of lexical borrowing, words from one language are used repeatedly in another language until they eventually become indistinguishable from the native vocabulary. That is, the borrowed lexical item becomes assimilated into the borrowing language. The borrowed form gets used longitudinally across speakers until it takes on the phonological and morphological characteristics of the borrowing language. In contrast to established loan words, "nonce borrowings" are words that do not have frequent or widespread use in the borrowing language (Weinreich, 1953; Sankoff, Poplack, and Vanniarajan, 1986). They may be used only in one context by one speaker. Similar to established loan words, however, nonce borrowings share the phonological and morphological characteristics of the borrowing language.

"Linguistic interference" is the transfer of rules from one language to another. This is in contrast to the interlingual transfer of material from the source language while the rules of the base language are maintained—that is, "transference" (Mougeon, Beniak, and Valois, 1985). In spoken-language interpreting, for example, if a monolingual English audience were depending on an interpreter to understand the lecture of a visiting Russian scholar and the interpreter used an occasional Russian word or sentence construction, this use might be considered a form of interference. In the case of signed-language interpreting, the inappropriate use of English mouthing during ASL interpretation could be considered a form of interference. For example, the interpreter might use English mouthing where ASL nonmanual markers are needed (for example, adverbials). Glossing of ASL signs during ASL to English interpretation would also be a form of interference. If the ASL verb GO-TO is reduplicated, for example, an interpreter might incorrectly interpret "go, go, go," rather than the appropriate English translation—"to frequent."

Since sign language interpreters are usually required to interpret simultaneously between spoken English and ASL—two structurally different languages—some interference between the languages can be expected. Unfortunately, it is notoriously difficult to ferret out factors that contribute to interference—for example, difficulty of the topic, lack of linguistic proficiency in one of the languages by the interpreter, simultaneously versus consecutively interpreting the message, etc.

It is conceivable that the interpreter's lack of ASL proficiency can significantly contribute to linguistic interference. For example, an interpreter who learned ASL as a second language might be more likely to use idiosyncratic grammatical constructions. In order to separate outcomes of language contact that may be the result of second-language acquisition (that is, if the interpreter learned ASL as a second language and uses idiosyncratic grammatical constructions—interference) from outcomes of language contact (that is, regular and rule-governed linguistic behavior like code-switching and lexical borrowing), the data used in this study are from interpreters whose native language is ASL. Since the interpreters are interpreting into their native language (ASL), I assume that interference from English is minimal. I will systematically describe how interpreters "flag" a switch from ASL to English-based signing, or simultaneously mark an ASL sign with English mouthing.

## THE DATABASE[5]

Sign Media, Inc. (1985) has produced and marketed a videotape entitled *Interpreter Models: English to ASL (lectures)*. I examined the interpreting performance of the two ASL interpreting models presented in this tape because it is specifically designed to present models of English-to-ASL interpretation.[6] For the purposes of this study, I transcribed the first spoken English lecture and simultaneous ASL interpretations. The topic of this lecture was radio and television measurement services—for example, Arbitron and Neilson. These measurement services determine which radio and television programs consumers are listening to or watching.

  I transcribed the spoken English using conventional orthography, and transcribed the interpreted ASL into gloss form including information about the use of ASL grammatical features—nonmanual behaviors, use of space, indexing, and mouthing. This resulted in three sets of transcriptions: the spoken English and both ASL interpretations. Two hearing graduate assistants verified the English transcriptions, and two deaf native ASL consultants and one interpreter consultant verified the transcriptions of the ASL interpreting. All transcriptions, verifications, and analyses were done using videoequipment that allows forward and backward slow-motion viewing and full stop with minimal distortion. Following verification of the transcripts, the spoken English text was matched with the interpreted ASL.

  I then analyzed the data to determine if and when the interpreters were using code-mixing, code-switching, or lexical borrowing. There are at least three major ways in which English words or phrases are represented in the visual modality during ASL interpreting: (1) pronounced mouthing of English words (without voicing) while simultaneously signing ASL, (2) prefacing or following an ASL sign with a fingerspelled word; (3) marking or flagging a fingerspelled word or the signed representation of an English word or phrase with certain ASL lexical items—for example, the index marker, the demonstrative, quotation markers, etc. Each of these categories will be discussed along with examples from the data. I will also discuss how the visual representation and flagging of English may or may not be code-switching, code-mixing, and/or lexical borrowing.

### *Mouthing English Words While Simultaneously Signing ASL*

Because of the differences in linguistic modality (visual-gestural versus aural-oral), interlingual transference between spoken English and ASL is of a different nature than between two spoken languages. Because of the constraints to the auditory channel imposed by deafness, vocalization is not used to convey linguistic meaning in ASL. The mouth, on the other hand, because it is highly visible, is sometimes used to convey linguistic meaning (for example, adverbials). Because the mouth is sometimes available, one salient characteristic of intensive language contact between ASL and English is that the mouth is sometimes used to visually represent certain English words. This appears to be a type of simultaneous code-mixing that occurs rather than sequential switching from one language to another. In this system, the features of both languages are produced simultaneously. Over time, many of the mouthed English words are no longer recognizable as English, and in many cases, native ASL users may not even recognize the mouthing as a phonological remnant from English. The interpreters' mouthing is included in the present data corpus through the use of forward and backward slow-motion and full-stop videoequipment, and through verification by the deaf consultants.

In the following examples, the spoken English input is given first, followed by the ASL interpretation. The level of transcription shown above the glosses of the ASL signs is the interpreters' use of mouthing. The following diacritics are used: *ENG* ↑ indicates the clear use of English mouthing; *ENG* ↓ means that there was reduced English mouthing; *ASL MOUTH* refers to the use of adverbials (for example, MM, TH, PAH, CHA, etc.) A switch from English mouthing to ASL mouthing, or vice versa, is indicated with //. In the case of reduced English mouthing, the part of the gloss that gets mouthed is marked with double underlines. Finally, the symbol # preceding the example indicates fingerspelling, the + symbol indicates sign reduplication, and * means that the sign is articulated emphatically.

The following examples show how the interpreters simultaneously use English mouthing, reduced English mouthing, and ASL mouthing across the interpreted ASL text:

> (1a) Spoken English input: . . . lots of people have heard about Neilson television rating services which is on the television side of the fence and we are a, ah, kind of share that market in terms of providing measurement data for the television services. But in radio, Arbitron is the "major book."

ENG ↓             //ENG ↑     //ASL MOUTH//

(1b) Interpreter 1: MANY PEOPLE KNOW NAME#NEILSON, FOCUS

ENG ↑      //      //ASL MOUTH      //ENG ↑   ENG ↑

#T.V. + +, (left space) POSS-PL, (shift to right space) THAT#ARBITRON,

         ENG ↑      // //ASL MOUTH     //

#NEILSON (shifts back to left space)#TV + +, HAVE SHARE PL-POSS

     //ENG ↓      //      //ENG ↑   //

(hesitates) BUSINESS (shift back to right space)#RADIO (left indexic marker),

//ASL MOUTH//   ENG ↑      //ASL MOUTH

REALLY#ARBITRON TOP

        ASL MOUTH     //ENG ↓         //ASL MOUTH//   ENG ↓

(1c) Interpreter 3: UNDERSTAND, PEOPLE-INDEXIC-PL, FAMOUS KNOW

       //ENG ↑           //ASL MOUTH//

NAME WHICH,#ANIELSON (interpreter self corrects) THAT (right indexic

    ENG ↑     //ASL MOUTH         //ENG ↑   //   ENG ↓

marker)#NEILSON, STRONG CONNECTION#TV + +, FAMOUS SAME-AS

//ENG ↑          //ENG ↓     //ASL MOUTH//ENG ↑          //ENG ↓

#ARBITRON SAME-AS FOCUS#TV + + + + MEASURE PEOPLE WATCH,

//ASL MOUTH                                              //ENG ↑

HOW-MANY SO-FORTH, UNDERSTAND + + FOCUS RADIO (left indexic

//ENG ↓

marker), #ARBITRON *STRONG

(2a) Spoken English input: So you listen to it in the morning as you're getting up, then you go out in your car and the drive times as they refer to them, are the major times that people listen in the United States to the radio, is when they're driving to work, and when they're coming home.

ASL MOUTH //ENG ↓                          //ASL MOUTH          //ENG ↓

(2b) Interpreter 1: WELL, MORNING GET-UP LISTEN-TO +, OUT CAR,

//ASL MOUTH      //ENG ↑     //ENG ↓                        //ASL MOUTH

DRIVE-TO   CALL   DRIVE-TO   (hesitates)   TIME,   THAT,   DRIVE-TO,

//ENG ↓        //ASL MOUTH               //ENG ↓        //ASL MOUTH

MOST-TIME TEND-TO DRIVE-TO WORK, #BACK HOME DRIVE-TO LISTEN-

//ENG ↑

TO RADIO

ENG ↓                          //ASL MOUTH          //ENG ↓ //ASL MOUTH

(2c) Interpreter 2: GET-UP MORNING LISTEN, GET-IN CAR DRIVE

//ENG ↑ "called"                ENG ↑                //ASL MOUTH          //

QUOTATION   MARKERS   D-R-I-V-E   T-I-M-E   QUOTATION   MARKERS

ENG ↑              //ASL MOUTH  //ENG ↑ //ASL MOUTH  //ENG ↓        //ASL MOUTH  //ENG ↓

THAT, DURING TIME DRIVE THAT WHEW IMPORTANT FOR RADIO

//ASL MOUTH                                          //ENG ↑  //

BECAUSE PEOPLE TEND-TO DRIVE-FROM-HERE-TO-THERE + + WORK

ASL MOUTH

COMMUTE LISTEN-TO

From analysis of these data, there appears to be a range of mouthing in the ASL interpreting data. In what is perhaps best described as code-mixing, English words are sometimes clearly visible on the mouth—for example, nouns, question words, numbers, lists, and fingerspelled words. At the other extreme, most mouthing in ASL is no longer seen as representing ENGLISH (for example, the mouthing that accompanies the ASL signs LATE, HAVE, and FINISH). In the latter examples, English words appear to have been borrowed into ASL by way of mouthing and

ASL mouthing ⟵————— reduced English ⟵————— English mouthing
e.g., adverbials                                  e.g., nouns
        verbs                                              q-words
        modals                                            numbers
                                                              lists
                                                              fingerspelling

⟵————————
Toward lexification

*Figure 1.* **A range of mouthing during ASL interpretation.**

subsequently lexicalized into ASL. Further research is needed in order to elucidate these processes. There are cases where the use of mouthing can be accurately described in terms of code-mixing. In other instances, the use of reduced English mouthing may be best described as a form of lexical borrowing; other times, mouthing appears strictly a feature of ASL—as is the case with adverbial markers that bear no synchronic or diachronic relation to English.

### ASL Signs Prefaced or Followed by a Fingerspelled Word

Fingerspelling is a system for representing the English alphabet manually by varying handshapes. It is used primarily to represent proper nouns and English terms that do not have ASL lexical equivalents. Fingerspelling is usually articulated in the space between the face and dominant shoulder and the palm orientation is toward the addressee. Clearly, fingerspelling forms an integral part of ASL (as opposed to being a part of English). In contrast to single ASL signs, which usually involve one or two handshapes, fingerspelling a word often involves many different handshapes.

Battison suggests that borrowing lexical items from English via fingerspelling and restructuring them phonologically and sometimes morphologically is an active process in ASL. Fingerspelled words, which are structurally different from ASL signs, are restructured systematically to fit the formational patterns of ASL. Some of the systematic changes a fingerspelled word undergoes in this process are deletion of handshape letters, dissimilation of handshapes and assimilation of the number of fingers involved, location changes, movement additions and orientation changes, and semantic restructuring of the signs. The lexical items that result from this process have been referred to as "fingerspelled loan signs" (Battison, 1978, 218–19).

It can be argued, however, that the fingerspelling of English words is not lexical borrowing in the literal sense (Liddell and Lucas, personal communication). That is, in the lexical borrowing that takes place between spoken languages, a lexical item, a form-meaning pairing in one language, is borrowed into another language. When this happens, there are typically phonological and/or semantic adjustments that make the form-meaning relationship in the borrowing language different from the source language. For example, the French lexical item *croissant* ([kwasō]) was borrowed into English and is now pronounced [krowsant].

This process is not exactly what takes place in the ASL–English situation. For example, the orthographic representation of the English word "date" occurs as a fingerspelled lexical item in ASL, consisting of a sequence of four ASL morphemes, D-A-T-E. In spoken-language borrowing situations, a relationship exists between the phonologies of two languages, but the relationship here is between the orthographic system used for representing one language (English), and the phonological system of another, ASL. Furthermore, the relationship between the phonologies of the spoken languages is one of "borrowing"—one language borrows the sounds of another—and the result is a loan. At no point, however, can the relationship between English orthography and ASL phonology be characterized as borrowing. ASL morphemes are never borrowed from the orthographic English event; they are simply used to represent the orthographic event.

A fingerspelled word, then, can never technically be described as English. Fingerspelling, by its very nature, is an ASL phonological event. In a pattern similar to lexical borrowing, however, a fingerspelled word may get used repeatedly and eventually become lexicalized into ASL. In other words, a fingerspelled word begins to undergo systematic phonological, morphological, and semantic changes like those described by Battison (1978). Fingerspelled words that undergo the process of lexicalization may eventually become an integral part of the ASL lexicon. This usually happens when the fingerspelled word gets used longitudinally across speakers, but lexicalization is also evident when words get fingerspelled repeatedly in a single context.

The interpreters in this study use fingerspelling in the following ways: lexicalized fingerspelled signs, which have been lexicalized into ASL through the processes described earlier; nonce fingerspelling, which are context and topic specific, but follow the pattern of lexicalization already described; and full fingerspelling, wherein each letter of the word is clearly represented. Some examples from the data are:

Lexicalized fingerspelled signs used by Interpreter 1:

| #WHAT | #DATE |
| #TV | #CAR |
| #SPORTS | #IF |
| #CARTOONS | #BACK |
| #DO-DO | #NEWS |
| #HOBBY | #CO |
| #US | |

Lexicalized fingerspelled loan signs used by Interpreter 2:

| #BOYS (2-handed) | #SHOW |
| #OR | #BUSY (2-handed) |
| #CO | #WHAT |
| #SPORTS | #NEWS |
| #TV | #ALL |

Some fingerspelled signs are used like nonce events. In these data, these nonce events typically start out as examples of full fingerspelling (that is, produced in the area typically used for fingerspelling, with all handshapes represented, and with palm orientation away from the signer). Examples include: #RADIO, #ARBITRON, and #NEILSON. These words are context and topic specific. Both interpreters, following repeated use by the speaker, start treating these words like ASL lexical items as opposed to fingerspelled representations of English orthographic events. For example, there is deletion and/or assimilation of the number of handshape letters involved during the production of these repeated fingerspelled words.

Sometimes the interpreters preface or follow an ASL sign with a fingerspelled word. For example:

(3) Spoken English input: public affairs Interpreter 1: <u>DISCUSS</u> #<u>PUBLIC AF-FAIRS</u>

(4) Spoken English input: cartoons Interpreter 1: <u>FUNNY</u> #<u>CARTOONS</u>

(5) Spoken English input: billboards Interpreter 2: #<u>BILLBOARDS</u> <u>OPEN C-CL</u>

(6) Spoken English input: drive times Interpreter 2: <u>QUOTATION MARKERS</u>, #<u>DRIVE TIMES</u>, <u>QUOTATION MARKERS</u>, <u>THAT</u> <u>DRIVE-TO THAT</u>

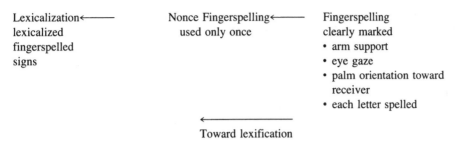

*Figure 2.* **A range of fingerspelling in ASL interpreting.**

In these cases it appears that an English word gets fingerspelled because there is no lexical counterpart for that word in ASL. The fingerspelled word often gets flagged with an ASL lexical marker (for example, a classifier predicate, demonstrative pronoun, or quotation mark). Other times, the interpreter chooses to tag an ASL sign with the fingerspelled representation of the English word used by the speaker (examples 3 and 4). From the preliminary analysis of these data, there appears to be a range of fingerspelling being used.

Fingerspelling, then, gets marked in very patterned ways by the interpreters. For example, mouthing of the English gloss accompanies all fingerspelled words—even lexicalized fingerspelled signs. Indexing, eye gaze, and support of the active arm with the passive hand also marks the fingerspelling used. In their use of fingerspelling, the interpreters appear to follow a pattern of movement toward lexification of fingerspelled signs into the structure of ASL.

In sum, it appears that fingerspelling serves a variety of purposes in ASL. Personal communication with deaf consultants indicates that ASL signers sometimes use fingerspelling for stylistic purposes. For example, an ASL signer may opt to fingerspell a word rather than sign the ASL equivalent. An ASL sign may be prefaced or followed with a fingerspelled representation of that sign. What is also evident in these examples is the simultaneous use of two phonologies—an ASL representation of an English orthographic event that is accompanied by English mouthing. The processes involved in fingerspelling need further elucidation before accurate labels can be attached, although it is suggested that ''fingerspelled representation'' may characterize the phenomenon more accurately than ''fingerspelled loan sign'' or ''lexical borrowing.''

### Marking or Flagging a Fingerspelled or Signed English Form with ASL Lexical Items

In this category, we find English forms that are visually represented and flagged in very specific ways. Consider the following:

(7a) Spoken English input: A lot of parents, young parents, use television as a babysitter.

ENG ↓                            //ENG ↑

(7b) Interpreter I: MANY MOTHER-FATHER YOUNG, FINE #TV + +,

//ASL MOUTH       //ENG ↑   //    ASL MOUTH

TAKE-ADVANTAGE-OF, BABY TAKE-CARE-OF, SO-TO-SPEAK

In example 7, the interpreter marks the speaker's metaphoric use of the television as a babysitter with the ASL sign SO-TO-SPEAK. This sign is similar to the one for QUOTATION MARKERS, except that the former is done lower and more rapidly in sign space. In the following example, the QUOTATION MARKERS sign and the demonstrative THAT is used:

(8a) Spoken English input: Then you go out in your car and the drive times as they refer to them . . .

(8b) Interpreter 2: GET-IN CAR, DRIVE-TO, QUOTATION MARKERS, #DRIVE-TIMES, QUOTATION MARKERS, THAT DRIVE-TO THAT

(8c) Interpreter 1: OUT CAR, DRIVE-TO, CALL DRIVE (hesitates) TIME, THAT DRIVE-TO

Interpreter 2 fingerspells 'drive times' and marks it before and after it is spelled with QUOTATIONS. It is as though the interpreter is setting this form off as a lexical item that is not ASL. Interpreter 1 prefaces DRIVE TIME with the labeling sign CALL, hesitates, then marks it with the demonstrative followed by what 'drive times' means—that is, DRIVE-TO. Interpreter 2 also incorporates the use of the demonstrative.

## SUMMARY AND CONCLUSIONS

In this paper I describe how interpreters sometimes encode spoken English words or phrases visually. For example, an interpreter can fingerspell the orthographic representation of an English word or can give a visual representation of English syntax in the sign modality. Other times, an interpreter accompanies ASL signs by the simultaneous mouthing of English words. I have discussed the possibility that these visual representations of English qualify as code-switching, code-mixing, and lexical borrowing.

The results of intensive contact between two structurally different languages like ASL and English is extremely complex and points to a need for modification of the terms traditionally used to characterize language contact phenomena. For example, according to the literal definition of "code-switching," there needs to be a complete switch to another language, including a switch to the phonology. According to this definition, a "true" switch could only occur if an ASL signer stopped signing and began speaking English (or any other language for that matter). In order to understand the underlying linguistic and sociolinguistic processes involved in code-switching, the literal definition must be extended to include a switch from ASL to English-based signing, that is, switching within modality.

The term "code-mixing" should not be loosely applied either. It does not imply that the two contact languages are thrown together in a random and ungoverned fashion. In the form of the simultaneous use of English mouthing and ASL, code-mixing appears to be highly rule-governed. This is demonstrated by the fact that both native ASL interpreters use it in very similar ways. Code-switching and code-mixing must also be distinguished from interference (which is often a result of inadequate second language acquisition) and lexical borrowings (which are commonly used even among monolinguals).

These data exhibit the movement toward lexification within the target language (ASL). The manual representation of English forms visually is primarily an intra-sentential phenomenon. That is, the interpreters' representation of English in the visual-gestural modality is restricted to single or double lexical items within what otherwise is an ASL text. That English mouthing sometimes marks the ASL inter-preting output has to do with the cross-modality nature of the ASL–English contact situation—that is, visual-gestural and oral-aural. Because deafness closes the auditory channel to linguistic input, vocalization is not used for linguistic encoding purposes in ASL. But because the mouth is highly visible, it is used to convey linguistic meaning (for example, adverbials). One of the characteristics of intensive contact between ASL and English, then, is that the mouth may sometimes be used to represent certain English words visually. In the vast majority of cases, the interpreters do not mouth what they hear. Rather, they gloss by way of mouthing, what is on their hands. This appears to be a type of simultaneous code-mixing, rather than a sequential switch from one language to another.

Since both native ASL interpreters in this study produce mouthing in similar ways, the use of mouthing seems patterned. English mouthing marks fingerspelled words and most lexicalized fingerspelling; is used for emphasis; and marks lists, numbers, and question words. The deaf consultants agreed that both interpreters used mouthing appropriate to ASL. In fact, it was only through slow-motion viewing that the native ASL signers recognized some of the mouthing as being pronounced English. Both consultants felt that deaf signers use mouthing in much the same way as did the interpreters. This paper proposes that there exists a range of mouthing in ASL. At one extreme, English words are clearly mouthed; at the other, mouthing is no longer seen as representing English. It appears that some English words are borrowed by way of mouthing and subsequently lexicalized into ASL (that is, native ASL signers see the use of mouthing as a part of ASL).

The use of fingerspelling also appears to follow a pattern toward lexification into ASL. The interpreters in this study sometimes represent an English word or phrase through fingerspelling because there is no translation equivalent for that word in ASL. Other times, a multimeaning ASL sign is tagged or prefaced with a finger-spelled English word. In such cases, the fingerspelled word is flagged in very specific ways—for example, mouthing, eye gaze, indexing, labeling, quotation markers, palm orientation, and so forth. When a fingerspelled word gets used repeatedly in a single context, it begins to be lexicalized in ASL according to patterns similar to those found with lexicalized fingerspelled signs.

The degree to which there is interlingual transference during English to ASL interpretation appears to be determined by the participants, topic, and setting. In many interpreting situations, the deaf audience has some degree of written or spoken proficiency in the source language (English). In a sense, the interpretation is needed not because the deaf audience members don't understand English, but because they cannot hear it. Based on the assumption that the audience may be bilingual, the interpreter has the option of encoding some spoken English words in the visual mode. The mouthing and fingerspelling of English words by the interpreters in this study appears to be not sporadic or unsignaled, but rather patterned and rule governed. It serves to disambiguate and elucidate the interpreted message.

# NOTES

1. Linguistic channel availability means that the oral channel, more specifically the mouth, when not otherwise being used for ASL grammatical purposes (for example, adverbials), may be available to encode English. Manner of language acquisition refers to the fact that for the majority of deaf individuals, ASL is acquired from deaf peers and/or in the residential school setting, as opposed to from parents.
2. ASL interpreting is to be distinguished from signed language transliterating—that is, changing an English message from one form of English to another. The goal of transliteration is to produce a morpheme to morpheme correspondence between spoken English and sign language. In a broad sense, this is a visual representation of English. The transliterator attempts to render spoken English in a visually accessible form. Depending on the topic and context, and if no qualified ASL interpreter is otherwise available, a deaf individual fluent in English may sometimes request transliteration.
3. Lucas & Valli (this volume) describe contact signing which results from the contact between ASL and English, and which exhibits features of both languages.
4. In the case of the deaf community, the lack of bilingual proficiency for some deaf individuals seems exacerbated by the lack of bilingual education for deaf children, the inability of most families to use ASL with their deaf children, and the barrier deafness imposes to spoken English input via the auditory channel.
5. Davis (in process) has collected interpreting data in a controlled study of signed language interpreters, and is in the process of analyzing these data for examples of code-switching, code-mixing, and lexical borrowing. In that study, four interpreters (two native and two non-native ASL signers) were filmed simultaneously interpreting a spoken English lecture. Comparing the ASL interpreting of native and non-native ASL interpreters can perhaps further our understanding of linguistic transference as a strategy among bilinguals and interpreters, and linguistic interference as faulty second language learning or as instances of processing errors.
6. There are two interpreted lectures on the tape produced by Sign Media, Inc. (1985). The tape first shows one of the spoken English lectures, followed by the two ASL interpretations of that lecture, then both interpreters and lecturer are shown simultaneously. This is the format for both lectures. The source language was English and the target language ASL (see, for example, Interpreter Models: English to ASL [lectures], Sign Media, Inc. 1985).

# REFERENCES

Battison, R. (1978). *Lexical borrowing in American Sign Language*. Silver Spring, MD: Linstock Press.

Bokamba, E. G. (1985). Code-mixing, language variation and linguistic theory: Evidence from Bantu languages. Paper presented at the Sixteenth Conference on African Linguistics, Yale University.

———. (1987). The nature and structure of sign language variation in the United States deaf community. Doctoral comprehensive paper, University of New Mexico, Albuquerque.

Davis, J. E. (1989). Distinguishing language contact phenomena in ASL interpretation. In *The sociolinguistics of the deaf community*, edited by C. Lucas, San Diego, CA: Academic Press.

———. (in process). Interpreting in a language contact situation: The case of English to ASL interpretation. Ph.D. diss., University of New Mexico, Albuquerque.

DiPietro, R. J. (1978). Code-switching as a verbal strategy among bilinguals. In *Aspects of bilingualism*, edited by M. Paradis, 275–82. Columbia, SC: Hornbean Press.

Grosjean, Francois. (1982). *Life with two languages*. Cambridge, MA: Harvard University Press.

Gumperz, J. J. (1976). The sociolinguistic significance of conversational code-switching. In *Papers on language and context*. Working Papers of the Language Behavior Research Laboratory, no. 46. Berkeley, CA: University of California.

———, and Hernandez-Chavez, E. (1971). Bilingualism, bidialectalism, and classroom interaction. In *Language in social groups: Essays by John J. Gumperz*, edited by A. S. Anwar, 311–39. Stanford, CA: Stanford University Press.

Kachru, B. B. (1978). Code-mixing as a communicative strategy in India. In *International dimensions of bilingual education*, edited by J. Alatis, 107–24. Washington, DC: Georgetown University Press.

Lee, D. M. 1983. Sources and aspects of code-switching in the signing of a deaf adult and her interlocutors. Ph.D. diss., University of Texas, Austin.

Lucas, C. (1989). "Introduction." In *The sociolinguistics of the deaf community*, edited by C. Lucas. San Diego, CA: Academic Press.

———, and Valli, C. (1989). Language contact in the American deaf community. In *The sociolinguistics of the deaf community*, edited by C. Lucas. San Diego, CA: Academic Press.

Mougeon, R., Beniak, E., and Valois, D. (1985). *Issues in the study of language contact: Evidence from Ontarian French*. Toronto: Centre for Franco-Ontarian Studies.

Poplack, S. (1980). "Sometimes I'll start a sentence in Spanish y termino en español": Toward a typology of code-switching. *Linguistics* 18:581–618.

———, Sankoff, D., and Miller, C. (1987). *The social correlates and linguistic consequences of lexical borrowing and assimilation*. Social Sciences and Humanities Research Council of Canada, March 1987 Report.

———, Wheeler, S., and Westwood, A. (1987). Distinguishing language contact phenomena: Evidence from Finnish-English bilingualism. In *Proceedings of the VI International Conference on Nordic and General Linguistics*, edited by P. Lilius et al., 33–56. Helsinki: University of Helsinki Press.

Sankoff, D., and Poplack, S. (1981). A formal grammar for code-switching. *Papers in Linguistics* 14:3–46.

———, Poplack, S., and Vanniarajan, S. (1986). The case of the nonce loan in Tamil. Centre de recherches mathématiques. Technical report 1348. University of Montreal.

Seleskovitch, D. (1978). *Interpreting for international conferences*. Washington, DC: Penn and Booth.

Sign Media Inc. (1985). *Interpreting models of English to ASL (Lectures)*. Commercial videotape produced by Sign Media, Inc., 817 Silver Spring Ave., Suite 206, Silver Spring, MD.

Sridhar, S., and Sridhar, K. (1980). The syntax and psycholinguistics of bilingual code-mixing. *Canadian Journal of Psychology* 34:407–16.

Thelander, S. (1976). Code-switching or code-mixing? *Linguistics* 183:103–23.

Weinreich, U. (1953). *Languages in contact*. The Hague: Mouton.

# PART

# V

# LANGUAGE
# ACQUISITION AND
# PSYCHOLINGUISTICS

# Types of Instructional Input as Predictors of Reading Achievement for Hearing-Impaired Students

## Barbara Luetke-Stahlman

Paramount in discussing reading problems and deafness are two well-documented points: hearing-impaired children do not acquire language in an age-appropriate manner (King and Quigley, 1985; McAnnlly, Rose, and Quigley, 1987; Moores, 1987; Quigley and Paul, 1984) and deficits in language abilities are related causally to reading problems (Perfetti and Hogaboam, 1985; Vellutino, 1979). King and Quigley (1985) note that it is not unusual for hearing-impaired students to begin the task of reading without the knowledge base, cognitive or linguistic skills, or comprehension of English figurative language needed to process written material. It is predictable that such students will not read on grade level.

Furth (1966) and Trybus and Karchmer (1977) study large groups of hearing-impaired youth using standardized reading tests and find that the average reading ability is fourth-grade level. Furth finds that only 8 percent of his sample of 5,370 subjects could read above this level. Conrad (1979) analyzes the results of hearing-impaired students' ability to read as tested by a standardized test and discerns that sixteen-year-old hearing-impaired students read at the same level as 10-year-old hearing students. Using a cloze procedure rather than a standard test format, Moores (1967) and O'Neill (1973) both conclude that hearing-impaired students score lower than hearing students on reading achievement tests and that average reading ability of hearing-impaired is about fourth-grade level.

King and Quigley (1985) attribute the finding that hearing-impaired students generally seem to plateau at the third- or fourth-grade level to the change in emphasis of reading about this time. That is, prior to third grade, texts and tests emphasize word analysis and vocabulary. Beyond third grade, materials and tests require use of prior knowledge to infer meanings that are not stated explicitly in the text.

Some educators believe that the mode of communication used to teach reading to a hearing-impaired child can influence his/her reading ability. Two studies investigate the reading abilities of students exposed to the oral-only mode of instruction compared to students exposed to other methods. Rogers, Leslie, Clarke, Booth, and Horvath (1978) report that oral-only subjects perform higher on vocabulary and reading comprehension than their counterparts exposed to simultaneous communication. Lane and Baker (1974) study a select group of readers at the Central Institute for the Deaf, a private school in the Midwest, and find that these students score higher than those studied by Furth (1966). The reader is reminded also, that given the times in which these studies occurred, it is unlikely that any of the students in the nonoral group had been exposed to a sign system used in a complete and consistent manner for any length of time. In a more recent study (Geers and Moog, 1987), 100 orally trained, upper-middle-class, hearing-impaired students were tested using the Stanford Achievement Test and found to have an eighth-grade reading level.

In the 1970s, several systems were invented for use with hearing-impaired students. Approximately two-thirds of the programs for hearing-impaired students now use some form of these systems (Woodward, Allen, and Schildroth, 1985). The systems are based on the assumption that manually coding the English language for hearing-impaired students will make it easier to learn and, thereby, improve literacy abilities. With the systems in use for over a decade, it is possible now to study the possible advantage to using an input that closely corresponds to the form and content of spoken English compared to those that do not.

Several inventors or proponents of the various sign systems have conducted at least one study that attempts to demonstrate the advantage of a specific input (Bornstein et al., 1980; Gustason, 1981; Raffin, Davis, and Gilman, 1978; Washburn, 1983). However, no study concludes that any one method of simultaneous communication positively affects academic advancement, as compared to other languages or systems. During the period of popularity of simultaneous communication systems, Allen (1986) analyzed data from two norming projects for hearing-impaired students to ascertain if levels of reading achievement had changed from 1974 (before sign systems were prevalent) to 1983. His study finds little gain relative to that achieved by hearing peers. The hope that signing English for instructional purposes would enhance the literacy achievement of hearing-impaired students seemingly has not been realized. In fact, at state conferences for the deaf in two consecutive years, keynote speakers (Frank Bowe, chair of the National Commission on Deafness, and Steven Quigley, noted researcher in deaf education) claimed that total communication had not proven to be the panacea expected.

In addition to the variable of input used, Ogden (1979) completed a follow-up to the Lane and Baker study using CID (oral-only) students and documented the importance of socioeconomic status. He finds the CID students to be a socioeconomic elite group. Brasel and Quigley (1977) also find socioeconomic status to be related to the reading and English language development of hearing-impaired students.

The variable of methods and material, which could serve to further differentiate programs, has been studied only via survey studies. Several studies conclude that the methods used to teach reading to hearing-impaired students are identical to those used with hearing students (Clarke, Rogers, and Booth, 1982; LaSasso, 1978). LaSasso (1978) finds that there are four basic approaches used to teach hearing-impaired students: the language experience approach is the most popular (84 percent), followed by the use of basal readers (74 percent), the use of individualized library books (42 percent), and programmed instruction (36 percent). (Teachers could indicate more than one choice.)

The purpose of this study is to investigate the reading abilities of a large number of hearing-impaired students exposed to variants of simultaneous communication as instructional input while controlling for variables that have been shown to affect reading achievement. The hypothesis is that students exposed to inputs that were a language or were an invented system designed to correspond closely to the form and content of spoken English (for example, oral English only, Cued Speech, Seeing Essential English, Signing Exact English, American Sign Language) would score higher on reading tests than students exposed to inputs that did not as closely represent spoken English (for example, Signed/Manual English and Pidgin Sign English).

## METHODS

### Subjects

A large number of hearing-impaired students (n = 176) participated in the study. These children were of normal intelligence, five to twelve years of age, had no additional handicapping conditions that interfered with learning other than impaired hearing, and had been enrolled in their school program for at least three years. Information about the sex, minority status, socioeconomic status, and hearing acuity of the subjects appears in table 1.

Subjects represented programs using various instructional inputs. There were twenty-seven subjects exposed to oral-only input, five subjects exposed to Cued Speech (Cornett, 1967), twenty subjects exposed to Seeing Essential English (Anthony, 1971), thirty-eight subjects exposed to Signing Exact English (Gustason, Pfetzing, and Zawolkow, 1975), fifty-three subjects exposed to Signed/Manual English (Bornstein and Saulnier, 1980; Washington State School for the Deaf, 1972), twenty-one subjects exposed to Pidgin Signed English (PSE), and twelve subjects who used ASL.

Seventy-five percent of the subjects using ASL were hearing-impaired children of at least one deaf parent, judged to be users of ASL by an ASL-using deaf teacher employed at the school, and had lived at residential schools for at least three years. Although these students were not taught English literacy via ASL (Woodward, Allen, and Schildroth, 1985), research and practice from the field of hearing bilingual education (reviewed in Luetke-Stahlman, 1983) would predict that hearing-impaired

*Table 1.* **Characteristics of Subjects**

| Subjects | Group A n = 109 | Group B n = 91 |
|---|---|---|
| Male | 41% | 41% |
| Female | 58% | 58% |
| Minority | 12 | 27 |
| | 11% | 35% |
| Anglo | 102 | 50 |
| | 90% | 65% |
| Middle class | 75% | 91% |
| Aided PTA | 53 (25 S.D.) | 47 (22 S.D.) |
| Unaided PTA | 92 (21 S.D.) | 47 (18 S.D.) |

students with an age-appropriate first-language base in ASL could achieve English literacy more successfully than hearing-impaired peers who did not have an age-appropriate language base in English.

Subjects were divided into two primary groups of learners: those exposed to input that had the potential to represent a complete language or system (labeled "Group A") and those exposed to input that incompletely and inconsistently represented English (labeled "Group B"). Group A subjects were those exposed to oral-only English, Cued Speech, Seeing Essential English (SEE-1), Signing Exact English (SEE-2), and ASL. Group B subjects were those exposed to Signed/Manual English and PSE.

### Instruments

Date of birth, age at time of testing, aided and unaided audiometric information, and home-environment survey data were collected for each subject. Videotaped language samples and questionnaires concerning sign use were obtained from at least two teachers in each program using signed instructional input (see Moeller and Luetke-Stahlman, in press, for procedural information).

Surveys regarding reading were collected from all programs used in the study. Question 1 of the survey asked teachers to indicate the types of materials used to teach reading, question 2 asked how new and difficult vocabulary was taught, and question 3 asked about procedures used to test story comprehension.

A literacy battery adapted from Moeller and McConkey (1983) consisting of seven tests was administered to each subject. The two reading measures were the Passage Comprehension Test (Woodcock-Johnson Psychoeducational Battery, 1982) and the Johns Sight Word List for third graders (Johns, 1978).

The Passage Comprehension Test consists of twenty-six items. Four of the initial items provide the subject with a picture clue and a sentence to read that is missing one word. Subjects read the material provided and supplied the target word (see table 2). In later items, there is no pictorial context supplied, and the reader has to use his/her linguistic knowledge of the passage to be able to complete it. The tester uses a provided answer key that lists correct and incorrect responses.

The Johns Sight Word List for third graders is a list of typed words. Subjects read each word and say and/or sign it. A short comprehension question is asked of the subject in those situations in which the student cannot be understood or there is suspicion that the student is sounding out the word without comprehension of its meaning (for example, "Can you tell me where a conductor works?").

### Procedure

In most cases I tested or supervised student teachers testing the subjects. A school professional (for example, speech and language pathologist, head teacher) tested two groups of oral-only subjects, two groups of subjects exposed to SEE-1, and the subjects exposed to cued speech. All subjects were tested in the language or system used in their school program (that is, signed/manual English subjects were tested in SE/ME, PSE students in PSE, and ASL students in PSE or SE/ME).

Each subject was tested individually in a familiar room at the school of attendance. Testing lasted approximately thirty minutes per subject.

**Table 2.** **Items from the Passage Comprehension Test**

The soup _____ hot.

A clock tells us what _____ it is.

When you go to the library, there are many _____ to look at and read.

Reptile eggs look a lot like bird eggs. Some are almost perfectly _____ like ping-pong balls; others are oblong.

The enclosed folder gives you complete details on our Home Mortgage protection plan. Please _____ it carefully; it can be of great importance to you.

Our teacher's announcement that we were going to have an assembly was always greeted with joyous excitement. Give us anything _____ arithmetic.

## Analysis

To determine whether subjects exposed to input that had the potential to represent a complete language or system scored higher on two reading tests than students exposed to an incomplete input, I used an analysis-of-covariance procedure. Various inputs served as independent variables, and the two reading tests served as dependent variables. Age and hearing acuity were manipulated as covariates.

Frequency counts and percentages were calculated to determine whether the complete and incomplete groups differed with regard to reading-curriculum and home-linguistic-environment factors. Analysis of variance was used to determine significant differences among items of these surveys.

Percentages of voiced mean-length-utterance (MLU), signed MLU, voice-to-sign ratio, and semantic intactness (Moeller and Luetke-Stahlman, in press) were used to analyze teachers' language samples and to verify the Group A/Group B distinction.

Finally, analysis of covariance was used to compare each instructional input with every other instructional input, disregarding the prior categorization of "corresponding" and "not corresponding" groupings. The Newman-Kuels procedure allowed a determination of which groups of subjects exposed to specific inputs scored higher on the literacy battery than other groups of subjects.

## RESULTS

Group A and Group B subjects were similar in many ways (see table 1). The ratio of males to females was about equal for each group throughout the series of analyses. More parents of Group B subjects judged themselves to be middle and lower class than parents of Group A subjects. In two comparisons more Group A subjects judged themselves to be upper-middle class (a 20 percent difference in replies was indicated when 10-to-12-year-olds and subjects with profound unaided losses were compared).

The minority status of the subjects appears in table 3 for the series of analyses. Group B subjects included more minority students than Group A. For these reasons, Anglo-only data was analyzed for all comparisons of interested (See Luetke-Stahlman, submitted).

Results of the analysis of covariance comparing Group A subjects' means on the reading tests with those of Group B subjects were that there was no significant difference in the means of the scores of the two groups of subjects for the Johns Sight Word Test. Group A subjects scored higher on the Passage Comprehension test when both aided and unaided acuity were covaried in conjunction with age (see tables 4 and 5, below). Group A subjects answered correctly approximately eleven questions and Group B subjects approximately seven questions (when age and aided acuity were covaried, eight questions). There was a significant difference in the means of the Group A subjects compared to the Group B subjects also when only Anglo subjects were utilized for the analysis. Group A subjects answered correctly approximately eleven questions and Group B subjects eight questions (when age and aided acuity were covaried, nine questions). Passage Comprehension Test means (unaided acuity covaried) were significant again for Group A when four-to-six-year-old subjects were compared to their Group B counterparts (Group A mean = 5; Group B mean = 2); when seven-to-nine-year-old, Group A subjects were compared to their Group B counterparts (Group A mean = 10; Group B mean = 6); and when ten-to-twelve-year-old Group A subjects were compared to their Group B counterparts (Group A mean = 13; Group B mean = 10). When Group A subjects with severe unaided losses were compared to Group B subjects in this category, the. Group A subjects scored significantly higher on the Passage Comprehension Test (Group A mean = 13; Group B mean = 7). Group A subjects with unaided losses categorized as profoundly deaf scored higher on the Passage Comprehension Test than did Group B subjects in this category (Group A mean = 11; Group B mean = 8). Comparisons for the Passage Comprehension Test are displayed in figure 1.

Table 6 provides the means of the raw scores of Group A and Group B subjects on the Passage Comprehension Test. A comparison of the grade equivalent mean score for each analysis to those listed in the test manual for hearing children is graphed

***Table 3.* Minority Status**

| Subjects | | Group A | Group B |
|---|---|---|---|
| All subjects: | Minority | 12   (11%) | 27 (35%) |
| | Anglo | 102   (90%) | 50 (65%) |
| 4 to 6 years: | Minority | | |
| 7 to 9 years: | Minority | 7   (14%) | 8 (26%) |
| | Anglo | 42   (85%) | 23 (74%) |
| 10 to 12 years: | Minority | 2   (5%) | 9 (30%) |
| | Anglo | 36   (95%) | 21 (70%) |
| Severe loss: | Minority | 0   (0%) | 5 (27%) |
| | Anglo | 19 (100%) | 13 (72%) |
| Profound loss: | Minority | 6   (8%) | 16 (37%) |
| | Anglo | 68   (92%) | 27 (63%) |

*Table 4.* **Group A vs. Group B Controlling for Age and Unaided Acuity**

| | Group A | Group B | | | | | | | | |
|---|---|---|---|---|---|---|---|---|---|---|
| Male | 40.8% | 41.6% | | | | | | | | |
| Female | 59.2% | 58.4% | | | | | | | | |
| Middle Class | 75.7% | 90.6% | | | | | | | | |

| | Sum of | | | | | N | | X | | |
|---|---|---|---|---|---|---|---|---|---|---|
| Covariates | Squares | df | MS | F | P | A | B | A | | B |
| Unaided loss | .67 | 1 | .67 | .03 | .856 | 104 | 74 | 98.5 (19.7) | | 91.6 (26.4) |
| Age | 55.65 | 1 | 55.65 | 81.9 | .001 | 104 | 74 | 9.1 (2.4) | | 9.4 (2.0) |
| Passage Comprehension Test | 665.1 | 1 | 655.1 | 32.2 | $p < .001$ | 104 | 74 | 10.7 (6.1) | | 7.3 (4.5) |

in figure 2. The mean scores of the two younger sets of Group A subjects equated those of hearing peers. However, ten-to-twelve-year-old Group A students did not average scores above the fourth-grade level.

Differences in reading performance were also apparent when the means of subjects' scores were analyzed by specific inputs without *a priori* categorization. As can be seen in table 7, when the data from Anglo-only subjects with severe and profound unaided acuity was analyzed, the subjects exposed to SEE-2 outscored all other groups. Students exposed to SEE-1 and oral English outscored subjects exposed to PSE and SE/ME.

### Reading-Curriculum Results

Reading-curriculum comparisons revealed a high degree of similarity among programs. All programs used basal readers, teacher-made materials, and library books to teach reading skills. New and difficult vocabulary was taught in isolation and drills. All programs promoted both a process (prediction, main idea, compare/contrast, networking, etc.) and a product approach (find the right answer in the test, complete questions on worksheets, etc.) There was a significant difference ($p < .03$) between Group A and Group B in regard to the use of a product approach to teach story comprehension. All Group B programs used this approach, but only 43 percent of the Group A programs indicated such use.

*Table 5.* **Group A vs. Group B Controlling for Age and Aided Acuity**

| | Group A | Group B | | | | | | | | |
|---|---|---|---|---|---|---|---|---|---|---|
| Male | 40.8% | 41.6% | | | | | | | | |
| Female | 59.2% | 58.4% | | | | | | | | |
| Middle Class | 75.7% | 90.6% | | | | | | | | |

| | Sum of | | | | | N | | X | | |
|---|---|---|---|---|---|---|---|---|---|---|
| Covariates | Squares | df | MS | F | P | A | B | A | | B |
| Aided loss | 8.8 | 1 | 8.8 | .42 | .518 | 92 | 53 | 52.5 (24.8) | | 47.1 (22.3) |
| Age | 1614.7 | 1 | 1614.7 | 77.2 | $p < .001$ | 92 | 53 | 9.1 (2.4) | | 9.4 (2.0) |
| Passage Comprehension Test | 521.1 | 1 | 521.1 | 24.9 | $p < .001$ | 92 | 53 | 10.7 (6.1) | | 7.3 (4.5) |

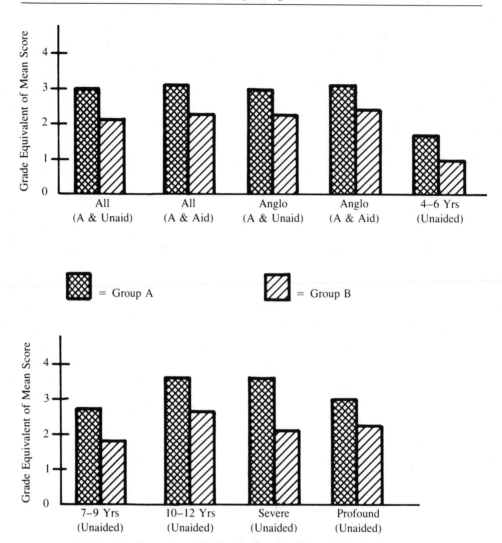

***Figure 1.*** **Results for Group A and B for the Passage Comprehension Test on all analyses of significance.**

### Teacher-Language-Sample Results

Results of the analysis of videotaped language samples (Luetke-Stahlman, in press) confirmed that Group A signers encoded significantly more form and meaning in the signed portion of their utterances than did Group B signers. The sign-to-voice ratio (see Moeller and Luetke-Stahlman [in press] for a detailed explanation of calculation) for twenty-five Group A teachers was 89 percent, compared to 70 percent for Group B teachers. Group A teachers were able to encode 90 percent of their spoken meanings in the signed portion of their utterances (based on a taxonomy adapted from Bloom and Lahey [1978]) compared to 58 percent for Group B ($p < .03$). Interjudge reliability ratios for the transcribing and coding of the samples was between 88 percent and 90 percent.

*Table 6.* **Passage Comprehension Test Grade and Age Equivalents**

| | Group A | | | | Group B | | | |
| Comparison Reference | Passage Comprehension Raw Score (SD) | Grade Equivalent | Age Equivalent | Mean Age | Passage Comprehension Raw Score | Grade Equivalent | Age Equivalent | Mean Age |
|---|---|---|---|---|---|---|---|---|
| Table 1 | 10.7 (6.1) | 3.0 | 8-8 | 9.1 | 7.3 (4.5) | 2.1 | 7-5 | 9.4 |
| Table 2 | 10.7 (6.1) | 3.0 | 8-8 | 9.1 | 7.3 (4.5) | 2.1 | 7-5 | 9.4 |
| Table 3 | 10.9 (6.1) | 3.0 | 8-8 | 9.1 | 8.0 (4.9) | 2.2 | 7-8 | 9.4 |
| Table 4 | 10.9 (6.1) | 3.0 | 8-8 | 9.1 | 8.0 (4.9) | 2.2 | 7-8 | 9.4 |
| Table 5 | 4.8 (2.9) | 1.7 | 6-10 | 5.0 | 1.9 (2.0) | 1.0 | 5-10 | 5.0 |
| Table 6 | 9.6 (5.9) | 2.7 | 8-3 | 8.0 | 6.3 (3.9) | 1.8 | 7-1 | 8.0 |
| Table 7 | 12.5 (4.2) | 3.6 | 9-5 | 11.0 | 9.6 (4.1) | 2.7 | 8-3 | 11.0 |
| Table 8 | 12.9 (7.6) | 3.6 | 9-5 | 9.8 | 6.5 (4.7) | 2.1 | 7-5 | 8.4 |
| Table 9 | 10.8 (5.7) | 3.0 | 8-8 | 9.2 | 8.0 (5.0) | 2.2 | 7-8 | 9.6 |

## DISCUSSION

Results of this study indicate that students exposed to instructional inputs that are a language or are systems in which an attempt is made to complete code English score higher on one of two selected tests of reading than do students exposed to input in

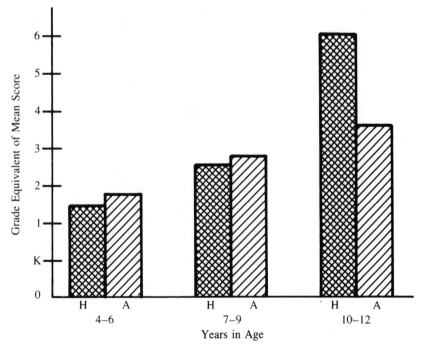

*Key.* H = hearing
A = Group A

*Figure 2.* **Complete group comparisons to hearing peers for reading comprehension.**
*Source.* **McGrew and Woodcock, 1985.**

***Table 7.*** **Significance ($p < .05$) between Languages and Systems Comparing Anglo Subjects with Unaided Severe and Profound Losses[1]**

|  | SEE-2 $n = 26$ | SEE-1 $n = 16$ | Oral English $n = 22$ | PSE $n = 17$ |  |
| --- | --- | --- | --- | --- | --- |
| Oral English | Passage Comp.* |  |  |  |  |
| SEE-1 | Passage Comp.* |  |  |  |  |
| SEE-2 |  |  |  |  |  |
| SE/ME $n = 23$ | Passage Comp.* | Passage Comp.* | Passage Comp.* | Passage Comp.* |  |
| PSE | Passage Comp.* | Passage Comp.* | Passage Comp.* |  | Northwest Syntax Screening Test |
| ASL $n = 12$ | Passage Comp.* | Passage Comp.* | Passage Comp.* |  |  |

[1]Vertically listed inputs are significant over horizontally listed inputs
*Significant also when *all* subjects were compared with age and unaided hearing acuity covaried

which teachers do not attempt to correspond closely to spoken English. Young deaf students exposed to languages or systems that are presented in a consistent and complete manner score only slightly below their hearing, age-equivalent peers (i.e., four-to-six-year-olds and seven-to-nine-year-olds).

The Passage Comprehension Test, a cloze test that provides more pictorial and contextual support than the Johns Sight Word List, proves to be a useful tool in delineating groups of learners. Overall, Group A learners functioned at the third-grade level and Group B learners at the second-grade level on the test according to norms utilizing hearing children. Given that reading task requirements become more difficult after third grade, it would be important to study students longitudinally in both groups to ascertain if the effect of exposure to oral English, ASL, SEE-1 and SEE-2 would continue to have a positive advantage for older students.

Subjects exposed to SEE-2 scored significantly higher on the Passage Comprehension Test compared to subjects exposed to other instrumental inputs. Subjects exposed to SEE-1 and oral English performed about equally well on this text compared to the other groups. Subjects exposed to Signed/Manual English and Pidgin Signed English evidenced the lowest scores. However, the PSE group scored significantly higher than the SE/ME group on the Passage Comprehension Test. The group of subjects using ASL had the lowest number of subjects, included some children who did not have deaf parents, and included subjects who were not exposed to their first language, ASL, in the classroom. These students had significantly lower scores on the Passage Comprehension Test than did subjects exposed to oral English, SEE-1, and SEE-2.

This study involved a large number of hearing-impaired subjects attending public, private, and residential schools. It controlled for age, aided, and unaided hearing loss. In addition, the sex and socioeconomic status of subjects did not favor any group that consistently scored higher on the Passage Comprehension Test. Educators should take note of these results and strive to provide a consistent, complete, and comprehensible language input to students while maintaining educational options for all hearing-impaired students.

# REFERENCES

Allen, T. (1986). A study of the achievement patterns of H.I. Students: 1974–1983. In *Deaf children in America*, edited by A. Schildroth and M. Karchmer, 161–206. San Diego: College Hill Press.

Anthony, D. (1971). *Seeing Essential English*, vols. 1 and 2. Anaheim, CA: Educational Services Division.

Bornstein, H., and Saulnier, K. (1980). Signed English: A brief follow-up to the first evaluation. *American Annals of the Deaf* 126:69–72.

Brasel, K., and Quigley, S. (1977). The influence of certain language and communication environments in early childhood on the development of language in deaf individuals. *Journal of Speech and Hearing Research* 20:95–107.

Clarke, B., Rogers, W., and Booth, J. (1982). How hearing impaired children learn to read: Theoretical and practical issues. *Volta Review* 84:57–69.

Conrad, R. (1979). *The deaf school child*. London: Harper and Row.

Cornett, R. (1967). Cued speech. *American Annals of the Deaf* 112:3–13.

Furth, H. G. (1966). A comparison of reading test norms of deaf and hearing children. *American Annals of the Deaf* 111:461–62.

Geers, A., and Moog, J. (1987). Factors predictive of the development of reading and writing skills in the cogenitally deaf: Report of the oral sample. St. Louis, MO: Central Institute for the Deaf.

Gustason, G. (1981). Does Signing Exact English work? *Teaching English to the Deaf* 7. Washington, DC: Gallaudet College, Department of English.

———, Pfetzing, D., and Zawolkow, E. (1974). The rationale of SEE. *Deaf American* (September): 5–6.

Johns, J. (1978). Johns Sight Word List for third grade. Northern Illinois University, DeKalb, IL, 60115-2854. Unpublished paper.

King, C., and Quigley, S. (1985). *Reading and deafness*. San Diego, CA: College-Hill Press.

Lane, H., and Baker, D. (1974). Reading achievement of the deaf: Another look. *Volta Review* 76:489–99.

LaSasso, C. (1978). National survey of materials and procedures used to teach reading to hearing impaired children. *American Annals of the Deaf* 23:22–30.

Luetke-Stahlman, B. (submitted). Two instructional communication modes used with Anglo hearing-impaired students: The link to literacy. *Journal of Hearing Disorders*.

———. (in press). A description of the form and content of four sign systems used in classrooms of hearing-impaired students in the United States. *American Annals of the Deaf*.

———. (1983). Applying bilingual models in classrooms for the hearing-impaired. *American Annals of the Deaf* 128:21–29.

McAnally, P., Rose, S., and Quigley, S. (1987). *Language learning practices with deaf children*. Boston: Little Brown.

Moeller, M. P., and Luetke-Stahlman, B. (in press). Parents' use of Signing Exact English: A descriptive analysis. *Journal of Speech and Hearing Disorders*.

Moeller, M., and McConkey, A. (1983). Evaluation of the hearing impaired infant: What constitutes progress. Paper presented at the annual meeting of the American Speech-Language-Hearing Association, 18–21 November, Cincinnati, Ohio.

Moores, D. F. (1987). *Educating the deaf: Psychology, principles, and practices*. Boston: Houghton Mifflin.

———. (1967). Applications of "cloze" procedures to the assessment of psycholinguistic abilities of the deaf. Ph.D. diss., University of Illinois, Urbana-Champaign.

Ogden, D. (1979). Experiences and attitudes of oral deaf adults regarding oralism. Ph.D. diss., University of Illinois, Urbana-Champaign.

O'Neill, M. (1973). The receptive language competence of deaf children in the use of base-structure rules of transformational generative grammar. Ph.D. diss., University of Pittsburgh.

Perfetti, C., and Hogaboam, T. (1975). The relationship between single word decoding and reading comprehension skill. *Journal of Educational Psychology* 67:461–69.

Quigley, S., and Paul, P. (1984). *Language and deafness.* San Diego: College-Hill Press.

Raffin, M., Davis, J., and Gilman, L. (1978). Comprehension of inflectional morphemes by deaf children exposed to a visual English sign system. *Journal of Speech and Hearing Disorders* 21:387–400.

Rogers, W., Leslie, P., Clarke, B., Booth, J., and Horvath, A. (1978). Academic achievements of hearing impaired students: Comparison among selected sub-populations. *British Columbia Journal of Special Education* 2:183–213.

Trybus, R., and Karchmer, M. (1977). School achievement scores of hearing impaired children: National data on achievement status and growth patterns. *American Annals of the Deaf Directory of Programs and Services* 122:62–69.

Vellutino, F. (1979). *Dyslexia: Theory and research.* Cambridge, MA: MIT Press.

Washburn, A. (1983). SEE-1: The development and use of a sign system over two decades. *Teaching English to deaf and second-language students* 2. Washington, DC: Gallaudet College, Department of English.

Washington State School for the Deaf. (1972). *An introduction to manual English.* Vancouver: Author.

*Woodcock-Johnson psychoeducational battery.* (1982). Hingham, MA: Teaching Resources Company.

Woodward, J., Allen, T., and Schildroth, A. (1985). Teacher and deaf students: On ethnography of classroom communication. In *Proceedings of the first annual meeting of the Pacific linguistic conference*, edited by S. Delancy and R. S. Tomlin, 479–93. Eugene, OR: University of Oregon.

# Lexical Acquisition in Sign and Speech: Evidence from a Longitudinal Study of Infants in Deaf Families

## Jennifer Ackerman, Jim Kyle, Bencie Woll, Mark Ezra

Although there has been considerable interest in the development of children's language in the English-speaking world, there has been only a very limited amount of work on acquisition in special populations. When such work has been done, it has often been on opportunity groups who have been discovered at a time when language growth is underway in the general population. Such a group is children in deaf families. We know a great deal about their development at school, and sometimes we have been able to track back to the time when they come into contact with services, around two to three years old. There have been some studies of their progress in speech (Gregory and Mogford, 1981), and many others in sign (e.g., Klima and Bellugi, 1979, and Schlesinger and Meadow, 1972). However, children in deaf families remain an elusive group for many simple reasons. Deaf people who are sign users are about 1 in 2,000 of the population and are less likely to marry than hearing people (Kyle and Allsop, 1982). As a result, there are few children available to study. When we further narrow the population by asking for deaf children in these deaf families, the sample becomes even smaller. In the United Kingdom, we estimate that a deaf child is born into a deaf family only once in 40,000 live births.

Our work with the deaf community gave us contact with a number of young married deaf couples, a number of whom had children at about the same period of time. Our contacts led us into a study of the emergence of sign language in children in deaf families. Because we knew the families before the children were born, in a number of cases we were able to begin to film the children from a very early age. We now have an overlapping record of the development of a group of children from the first few months until the age of three. Having said that, what we have to report today is still "in its infancy." Major problems of analysis remain to be solved and there is a considerable amount of data that is still to be encoded.

## RECENT REPORTS

Our earlier work on this data concentrated on the first year of life and considered the problems that in theory must exist for a deaf mother in creating joint reference for a child. In lab recordings, we discovered major differences between deaf and hearing mothers in the language they use with their children (Kyle, Woll, and Ackerman, 1987). Deaf mothers mix speech and sign even when the child is deaf, but within this system there are patterns that seem to correspond to the developmental phase of the child. As the child moves from a primitive proto-conversation stage of interest in the face to an object-oriented interest, a deaf mother begins to use more sign. She begins to adopt more specific attentional strategies. She talks and signs less than a hearing mother talks. She names objects more and repeats more. She questions less.

When we examine specific attentional tasks (Kyle, Ackerman, and Woll, 1988), we find that a deaf mother adopts a pattern to direct her child's attention. She refers to objects before pointing, and she does not talk or sign while she points. She works with the child's eye gaze and will not engage in a game until the child looks at her. In comparison, a hearing mother does not refer to objects before pointing. She uses other devices like ''What's that?'' and then answers the question herself as the child's eye gaze rests on the object. In this way, the language of a hearing mother is overlaid on the joint reference. A deaf mother's comments precede or follow the child's visual attention. When we have looked at the deaf children in hearing families in the second year of life, they seem to lack the discipline of attention that is developed in the child in the deaf family in this first year. Our question now is: ''What happens in the second year?''

## THE PROJECT

We are currently studying thirteen children from deaf families and twelve from hearing families. Of the thirteen children in deaf families, five are deaf and eight are hearing. They have been recorded from the age of a few months until they were three. Three have not yet reached the age of three years. Eight of the hearing families have hearing children and were recorded from a few months until one year old. The other four deaf children have been added to our study in the last few months and their data are not yet ready for analysis because they are still in the first year. The children are recorded twice a month in the first year and then once a month until they are three years old. The recordings alternate between home and lab recordings, and we will describe only the home recordings here.

The home recordings are done in two segments: the first involves asking the mother to demonstrate any new developments in the child since the last filming and then to play with a set of toys (we use two books, simple jigsaw puzzles, and some building blocks with pictures on the sides—the toys are varied with the child's age). The second part involves filming for five prearranged but random time slots of five minutes duration in a two-hour period. During this time the deaf researcher carries the camera around following the child as if the filming were continuous. Until the end of the session, mother and child are not informed just which sections are filmed. In this way we hope to achieve more natural behavior. It is true that mothers tend to carry out their normal routine rather than sit with the child.

## Data Analysis

We must emphasize that our data analysis is still at an early stage. This is because not all of our children have reached three years of age, and because we have begun to add deaf children from hearing families. There are two sources of data for us to draw on: the reports of the mothers on the child's sign development and the filmed sequences of interaction. We will concentrate on the period from the emergence of the reported first sign and look at data during the second year of life. Our questions are: How early and in what way do signs develop in children in deaf families? How do these relate to the gestures reported among hearing children? (See, e.g., Volterra, 1983; Caselli, 1987; and Acredolo & Goodwyn, 1988.)

## Mothers' Reports

We have found it difficult to get our mothers to use written forms, but we have collected data each month of home filming on the observed "new language" that the child has developed. The interpretation of what a sign is has been left to the mothers. This encourages only the reporting of sign/gestures that the mothers believe to be communicative. One can argue that a more rigorous diary study would limit the reporting to more manageable data, but we believe that the mothers are less constrained in this way. We have since managed to classify the responses.

As might be expected, there is considerable variation in the children in both type and age of reported signs. Our reports are taken from three deaf children in deaf families (one boy and two girls) and from five hearing children in deaf families (two boys and three girls).

Excluding reports of BYE-BYE, which frequently came early, the first reported signs were at 11.0 months for deaf children and at 11.4 months for hearing children. The boys' signs came later, at an average of 12.3 months; the girls' signs were reported at 10.6 months. Bonvillian, Orlansky, and Novack (1983) point out the difficulty of dealing with the first word and suggest that the first ten words/signs is a more useful measure. Table 1 compares their data and ours with the figures provided by Nelson (1973). Our deaf children are closer to Nelson, mainly due to the effect of one boy who was extremely slow to reach ten signs (that is, 21 months).

It is questionable whether evaluating onset of signing is a useful way to consider deaf and hearing children. Volterra (1986) argues strongly that one needs to consider gestural development in hearing children to make meaningful comparisons. A recent study by Acredolo and Goodwyn (1988) is very helpful in this respect. Their longitudinal diary study of the development of symbolic gesturing allows exactly this more direct comparison. Acredolo & Goodwyn (1988) exclude five conventional

*Table 1.* **Average Age to Reach Ten Words/Signs**

| Study Group | Average Age |
| --- | --- |
| Nelson (1973): words (hearing children) | 15.1 months |
| Bonvillian et al (1983): signs (hearing children) | 13.2 months |
| Reported data: signs (deaf children) | 15.3 months |
| signs (hearing children) | 13.0 months |

gesture categories of pointing to comment, pointing to request, "yes" and "no" as replies, and waving for "bye-bye." They focus on five categories: object signs, requests, attributes, replies, and events.

We have applied these categories to the mothers' reports in a preliminary analysis. As one might expect, many of the reported signs by our deaf mothers are very similar to the gestures described by the hearing mothers. This increases the problem of discriminating between sign and gesture. Acredolo and Goodwyn (1988) report the first object gesture at 15.59 months, but our deaf mothers report them rather earlier (11.33 months for deaf children and 11.4 months for hearing children— though these are often signs like MAMA and DADA). Attribute gestures (such as "hot" and "all gone" seem to occur around the same time in both reports: 15.27 months in Acredolo and Goodwyn (1988) and 15 months for deaf children and 14.2 months for hearing children.

Examining the first twenty-five signs reported by our deaf mothers, we find that object signs are generally the most used category ranging between 64 percent and 88 percent of the signs reported. This is the result that Nelson and Lucariello (1985) claim to be common in hearing children's development of spoken language. Interestingly, Gregory and Mogford's (1981) study of older children indicates that deaf children are likely to have fewer of these object names in their spoken vocabulary than hearing children. What our reports seem to imply is that this result is confined to the spoken vocabulary; our children seem to be using a similar number of object names in sign to that reported in hearing children.

A general observation on the development of these initial signs is that they seem to arise in the context of direct tuition by deaf mothers. Certainly our results on deaf mothers' different interaction style seems to support this (Kyle, Woll, and Ackerman, 1987; Kyle, Ackerman, and Woll, 1987). In Acredolo and Goodwyn's study, only 32 percent of action gestures were seen to arise within interactive routines. How this might apply to deaf families can be considered in relation to the data collected in our study.

### Home Filming

The recordings collected during the visits to the deaf families now constitute a large corpus of diverse data. There is still a great deal to be done before this is fully processed and so only a subset will be used here. In addition, we are currently looking at sequences where mother and child are engaged in interaction for at least 1.5 minutes. This means that the recordings involve cooperative activity between mother and child, and this mostly focuses on book reading and play with blocks. As part of a general examination of speech and sign development and the situations in which it arises, we have developed a coding system that takes into account not only the child's utterance but also the preceding activity by the mother. We will first consider the distribution of mothers' modeling (M), soliciting of the child's utterances (SOL) and of the spontaneous productions of the child (SP).

Both the solicit and model can occur in a number of ways: signed, spoken, gestured, with deictic gesture or with some combination. We need to know the extent to which the mother seems to set up the child's learning by offering a direct model for the child. When we take the definition of model to mean the immediately preceding utterance, then we find that modeling is not the most common feature of interaction.

Mothers typically attempt to elicit the signs from their children and then reinforce with an appropriate version of the sign (table 2).

Dealing with all the interactions in this part of the data, we find that the greater number of interactions are spontaneous on the child's part and that a minority (less than 25 percent) occur in the context of modeling. Acredolo and Goodwyn (1988) claim only 32 percent of their symbolic object gestures were acquired within an interactive routine. This finding implies a great deal more active tuition on the part of the deaf mothers.

Deaf mothers also seem to use the solicit category slightly more in the second part of the second year. It occurs in 27 percent and 36 percent (hearing and deaf children respectively) up to age 1.5, and then 36 percent and 52 percent between 1.6 and 1.11. The most typical example of this type of interaction is of the form, "What's this?" or POINT . . . WHAT?

## LOOKING AT LEXICAL ACQUISITION

The main point of concern for studies like this, and the point that makes almost all lexical analysis problematic, is the difficulty of distinguishing between sign and symbolic gesture. The various definitions available are unsatisfactory. For a signal to be a sign or word, Volterra and Caselli (1985) suggest, "(a) the signal has been used (at least once) to refer to a referent not present in the immediate environment; and (b) the signal has been used with various communicative intentions (i.e., more than one)."

Goldin-Meadow and Mylander (1985), studying deaf children in hearing families, decide that a communicative gesture must meet both criteria: "(a) the motion must be directed to another individual . . . and (b) the gesture must not be a direct motor act on the partner or on some relevant object." This definition allows them to deal with deictic gestures and with characterizing signs. They then go on to try to provide some guidelines for glossing characterizing signs.

In fact, neither definition, nor comparable ones for words, is particularly helpful since it is unlikely that periodic video recordings can allow us to adequately meet Volterra and Caselli's requirement that a sign be used in a range of settings for different exemplars of the same class. The weaker aspect that it be used for items not present does not help, since reference to objects not visible may occur in the context of request in a routine and the same instances arise in hearing children. And

*Table 2.* **Maternal Approach to Interaction (percentage occurrence in samples from five children aged 1:0 to 1:11)**

|  | Hearing children | | Deaf children | |
|---|---|---|---|---|
|  | **SOL** | **SP** | **SOL** | **SP** |
|  | 25 | 52 | 41 | 44 |
|  | 38 | 31 | 53 | 38 |
|  |  |  | 43 | 51 |
|  | 33 | 42 | 46 | 44 |

SOL = Solicit
SP   = Spontaneous

that, perhaps, is the crux of the matter. Acredolo and Goodwyn (1988), in their definition of gestures in hearing children, include the same elements as Volterra and Caselli (1985): the gesture has to appear repeatedly in the same form and has to be generalized beyond the specific situation in which it was acquired.

The question becomes simpler: Are we dealing with a proliferation of object signs or a series of symbolic object gestures? Are these simply analogous to the problems in determining words? The signs we have reported in our mothers' study share many characteristics with the gestures listed by Acredolo and Goodwyn (1988), and if we take away the early emergence of name signs such as MAMA or DADA, the dates of emergence of the different classes look similar. In the examples in table 3, the predominant sign type is object names and attributes or characterizing gestures. Perhaps to understand this we need to take on Nelson and Lucariello's (1985) view: "The assumption here is that during the first half of the second year the event representation remains unanalysed in terms of specific concepts of objects, actions and actors. It is only during the second half of the second year, in general, that discrete concepts are differentiated from the whole. We believe that this explains the prelexical period of word use followed by lexical (denotational) uses in the latter half of the second year" (p. 80). Such a change would allow us to incorporate both signs and meaningful symbolic gestures (and words) into our data without being concerned about their ultimate status (assuming we keep to the minimum levels of definition suggested by the authors above). In addition it would explain the increase in solicit behavior in the mothers in the second half of the first year: the game of naming is becoming more interesting for the child and the mother has less need to model.

Since the main topic of the paper is the extent of the child's development of a lexicon, it is appropriate to turn to the considerations for sign development. We are not yet at the stage of providing the lexical details that we had hoped for in preparing our abstract. The analysis is proving more complex than expected. All we can do is provide some direct access to the data being considered. Table 3 has three extracts of a deaf girl and her deaf mother at ages 1.3, 1.6, and 1.9. We can see the change in the interaction and the move from mother leading to child leading. The lexical development appears to be visible even in this limited data. We see only single signs up to 1.6, and these occur in very clearcut routines designed to elicit sign. However, in the 1.6 recording, the child overgeneralizes the sign CAR to "coach" or "bus" and the mother explains. By 1.9 the child is producing multi-element utterances and is leading the interaction. Such a development is as predicted by Volterra (1986). It seems to support the notion that much of the early development of sign is similar to that of spoken language.

## CONCLUSION

In this paper we have only skimmed the surface of the issues for the study of sign language acquisition. We believe that many of the patterns of interaction among deaf mothers and their children at this age are similar to those of hearing mothers, with perhaps some preponderance of solicit behavior. This in turn may lead to an earlier appearance of a range of sign/gestures. These sign/gestures are probably best dealt with as prelexical. They fit more with the types found by Acredolo and Goodwyn (1988) for hearing children.

**Table 3.** The Shift in Children's Use of Sign from Prelexical to Syntactic (1.3 to 1.9)

| Mother | Daughter | Comments |
|---|---|---|
| *1.3: Play Routine Involving Naming of Items on a Play Cube* | | |
| POINT WHAT THAT?<br>'That . . . what's that?' | | |
| | "tree" | Only interpretable in context, as it is incompletely formed in the wrong location. |
| TREE | | Mother repeats response offering correct sign. |
| POINT, WHAT POINT<br>'A tree! What's that?' | "car" | |

This early interaction is characterized by the routine, and the child appears to respond in her turn rather than having any clear idea of the lexical use of the sign.

*1.06: Play Routine (as above)*

| Mother | Daughter | Comments |
|---|---|---|
| POINT?<br>'What's that?' | | |
| | TREE | With correct handshape and speech sound, now recognizable. |
| TREE!<br>'Yes, a tree!' {shows cube} | | |
| | CAR | |
| CAR!<br>'Yes, a car!' {shows cube} | | |
| | CAR | Here the child overgeneralizes and the mother corrects. It seems the child is now attaching labels to items as in the lexical stage. |
| BUS, BIG BUS, CAR SMALL, POINT BUS BIG<br>'It's a bus, a big bus, a car is small, that's a big bus.' | | |

Here the child has made great progress and is an active participant in the naming routine. She is able to manipulate the labels and is actively making judgments.

*1.9: Mother and child looking at some books*

| Mother | Daughter | Comments |
|---|---|---|
| DOLL POINT WHAT?<br>'A doll, what is it?' | | |
| | DOLLY<br>HAIR-WASH | [child sign] |
| WHO WASH-HAIR WHO?<br>'Who's washing hair?' | | |
| | DOLLY | |
| GIRL DOLL | | |
| | DOLLY | |
| DOLL, WHO WASH-HAIR?<br>'A doll, who is washing hair?' | | |
| | WHERE J? PLAY J<br>"Where's Julie? Play with Julie." | |
| JULIE PLAY? | | |
| | HOME<br>"She's at home." | |
| HOME | | |
| | JULIE PLAY, JULIE PLAY | |

Here the child is entering into conversation and is actually leading. She introduces two new topics generated from the book, first the doll with the hair wash, and second that she can play with Julie.

These extracts from the same child signing in BSL show the extent of development over this short period of six months in the second year and indicate the relative sophistication of a deaf child of this age.

Although we suggest that these sign/gestures seem to appear earlier in deaf children, we do not consider that this means that sign language develops earlier than spoken language in hearing children. However, the differences in mother-child interaction (in the first year of life), which we have already reported, would seem to create more opportunity for certain types of symbolic gesturing to appear and for the deaf mother this would be a salient feature of interaction. It is easy to see how this might lead to the belief in earlier acquisition of sign language. However, the precise status of sign/gesture distinction in the deaf child's development remains to be completely established.

## NOTE

This research was supported by a grant from the Economic and Social Research Council of the United Kingdom.

## REFERENCES

Acredolo, L., and Goodwyn, S. (1988). Symbolic gesturing in normal infants. *Child Development* 59:450–66.

Bonvillian, J., Orlansky, M. D., and Novack, L. L. (1983). Early sign language acquisition and its relation to cognitive and motor development. In *Language in sign*, edited by J. G. Kyle and B. Woll, 116–25, London: Croom Helm.

Caselli, M. C. (1987). From communication to language: deaf and hearing children's development compared. *Sign Language Studies* 39:113–44.

Goldin-Meadow, S., and Mylander, C. (1985). Gestural communication in deaf children. *Monograph of the Society for Research in Child Development* 207:49.

Gregory, S., and Mogford, K. (1981). Early language development in deaf children. In *Perspectives on BSL and deafness*, edited by B. Woll, J. G. Kyle, and M. Deuchar, 218–37. London: Croom Helm.

Klima, E., and Bellugi, U. (1979). *The signs of language*. Cambridge, MA: Harvard University Press.

Kyle, J. G., and Allsop, L. (1982). *Deaf people and the community*. Final report to Nuffield Foundation. Bristol: School of Education.

Kyle, J. G., Woll, B., and Ackerman, J. (1987). A pragmatic analysis of deaf mother–infant interaction. *ISLA Monographs* 1.

Kyle, J. G., Ackerman, J., and Woll, B. (1987). Signing for infants: Deaf mothers using BSL in the early stages of development. Paper presented at International Symposium on Sign Language Research, 15–19 July, Lappeenranta, Finland.

Kyle, J. G., Ackerman, J., and Woll, B. (1988). Attention and belief: Deaf mothers communicating with their infants. In *Proceedings of child language seminar*, edited by G. Collis and V. Lewis. Warwick: Warwick University.

Nelson, K. (1973). Structure and strategy in learning to talk. *Monograph of the Society for Research in Child Development* 38.

———, and Lucariello, J. (1985). The development of meaning in first words. In *Children's single word speech*, edited by M. D. Barrett, 59–86. London: Wiley.

Schlesinger, H., and Meadow, K. P. (1972). *Sound and sign: Childhood deafness and mental health*. Berkeley: University of California Press.

Volterra, V. (1983). Gestures, signs and words at two years. In *Language in sign*, edited by J. G. Kyle and B. Woll, 109–15, London: Croom Helm.

————. (1986). What sign language research can teach us about language acquisition. In *Signs of life*, edited by B. Tervoort, 158–63. Amsterdam: Dutch Foundation for the Deaf and Hearing-Impaired Child.

————, and Caselli, M. C. (1985). From gestures and vocalizations to signs and words. In *SLR 83—Sign language research—Proceedings of the third international symposium on sign language research*, edited by W. C. Stokoe and V. Volterra, 1–9. Silver Spring, MD: Linstok Press.

# A Psycholinguistic Approach to Categorizing Handshapes in American Sign Language: Is [A_s] an Allophone of /A/?

Anthony Moy

Even though linguistic studies on American Sign Language (ASL) began some thirty years ago a consensus on a phonological analysis has yet to materialize. Stokoe, Casterline, and Croneberg (1965) made the first attempt at a phonemic analysis of ASL, and it was important for at least four reasons: (1) it showed that ASL signs, which previously had been viewed as mimetic, imitative, and lacking any structure, have a formational organization analogous—although not identical—to the phonological structure of spoken languages; (2) it introduced a notational system that for the first time allowed signs to be represented more or less phonemically; (3) it was based on fairly traditional American descriptivist grounds—emphasis was on obtaining the most economical phonemic analysis based on contrast and distinctiveness, rather than on systems of rules and underlying representations; and (4) it presumed that signs should be analyzed as the simultaneous rather than sequential realization of phonemes, as in spoken languages.

The first result has withstood the test of time, and subsequent research has deepened our understanding of the structural properties of ASL showing that the iconic properties of signs, which are superficially most apparent, mask their internal organization. For instance, before Stokoe et al., signs were thought to be composed of just about any kind of movement of the hands, with no limits on possible handshapes. This work showed that assumption to be false: ASL signs can be described with a closed set of handshape, movement, and location primes (phonemes).

The status of the other three points is less certain. Stokoe's notation system is fairly widespread, although alternative systems have been proposed by, for example, Cohen, Namir, and Schlesinger (1977); Liddell (1984); and Liddell and Johnson (1986). There have also been other notation systems proposed whose application is not primarily linguistic, for example, Sutton Sign Writing. Furthermore, there have even been alternative proposals that the basic parameters along which signs should be analyzed need to be expanded to include palm orientation, contacting region, and hand arrangement (Battison, 1974; Klima and Bellugi, 1979). Whereas the other notation systems represent completely different ways of analyzing signs, these additional "minor" parameters are a refinement of Stokoe's analysis. Stokoe et al. had parceled out this information among the three basic parameters.

Another approach has been to accept Stokoe's analysis of parameters and the intrinsic simultaneous nature of signs, but to reject the specifics of his phonemic inventory. Friedman (1976) and Battison (1978) represent this approach. For example, Friedman uses the Stokoe notation system and accepts that an analysis of ASL must start with the simultaneous nature of sign formation; however, her inventory of handshape primes is significantly larger than that of Stokoe et al.: twenty-nine versus nineteen. This discrepancy seems to be due to differing goals: Stokoe et al. wanted the most economical, least redundant representation. Therefore, if two signs did not contrast with two handshapes, they were automatically collapsed as allophones. Friedman is more open to phonemicizing handshapes even if she cannot find minimal pairs. Thus, Stokoe et al. describe one phoneme /G/, which Friedman splits into $/G_1/$ and $/G_2/$. Also, Friedman has a large category of "loan phones"—handshapes "borrowed" from English (that is, the manual alphabet). These loan phones are rather rare distributionally, and Stokoe seems to ignore them because they are not intrinsically a part of ASL. Battison states but does not provide evidence that ASL has forty-five distinctive handshapes. Klima (1975) argues for forty handshapes.

Liddell (1984) proposes an alternative analysis that differs from the early Stokoe work in significant ways. First, he discards the notational system based on simultaneous phonemes. Despite its intuitive nature, the simultaneous analysis has several problems. Although functionally adequate for describing many signs, signs that change shape or location are notated somewhat awkwardly. Also, these changes, which are overlaid on the movement stream, are clearly sequential; they must occur in a certain order and their timing is critically linked to other nonmanual phenomena, especially facial markers, which are essential components of some signs. Using an autosegmental model, he argues that individual signs are composed of sequences of movements and holds in which each movement or hold has a separate configuration of handshape(s), orientation, and location, and with movements and holds forming a separate autosegmental tier capable of melodies. A major advantage of this approach is that it brings sign languages in line with spoken languages by emphasizing their common sequential organization. Previously, the fact that signs were analyzable only as simultaneous bundles made it extremely difficult to see the organizational parallels with spoken language.

Thus, paralleling the history of phonological work on spoken languages, phonological research on ASL has largely ignored psycholinguistic approaches and instead focuses on analyses recoverable from utterances alone, that is, "internal" evidence. In this experiment, I adapt the psychological task of concept formation (CF) to ASL to see if hypothesized allophones of sign phonemes are truly internalized and viewed by native speakers as "the same." In other words, is there external evidence (psychological) that might support proposed hypotheses on the phonological organization of ASL?

## THE ISSUE: PSYCHOLOGICAL REALITY OF /A/ HANDSHAPE ALLOPHONES

Specifically, I explore the proposed allophones of the handshape prime /A/. Stokoe et al. claim that /A/ has four allophones: [A], the handshape A in the manual alphabet;

[Å], which has the thumb extended ("thumbs up", "A-OK"); [A$_s$], which is the handshape S of the manual alphabet; and [A$_t$], which is the handshape T of the manual alphabet.[1] Friedman agrees with this analysis except she posits [A$_t$] as a separate phoneme, /T/. These handshapes share a common property, namely all fingers are adducted: the basic form is fistlike. They differ in the position of the thumb—adducted to the radial side of the first finger, [A]; adducted to the top of the second joint of the phalanges, [A$_s$]; abducted, [Å]. According to Stokoe, these handshapes are not distinctive. Distributionally, they never contrast, hence they are grouped together: "In American Sign Language these handshape differences are not used for significant contrast. Instead the users of ASL contrast the closed, fist-like, hand with other handshapes. Hands looking like the A, S, and T hands of fingerspelling (but in attitudes and actions that can not be used for fingerspelling) may be observed if a signer's activity is closely observed. These handshapes will be found to pattern, however, in allocheric [allophonic] ways" (1978, 45).

Furthermore, both Stokoe and Friedman claim some phonetic motivation for the distribution of [A] versus [A$_s$].[2] When contact is required on the side of the first finger, that is, where the thumb is for [A], "clearly it's easier to make this kind of side contact if the thumbs aren't in the way" (Friedman, 1977, 19). Furthermore "striking the forehead with the knuckle of the thumb can be painful—so that the sign STUPID is usually made with the closed hand in *A* configuration" (Stokoe, 1978, 45). But, as Friedman notes, there are signs that require this contact point yet do not have the [A$_s$] allophone. Of importance here is the grouping of [A] and [A$_s$] under /A/. Are they really allophones? Simply on distributional grounds and phonetic similarity, this is a plausible analysis. But there is reason to doubt this analysis because the A handshape and the S handshape are distinctive in fingerspelling. Although fingerspelling and signing are more or less independent systems, the fact that these handshapes are perceived by deaf people as clearly distinctive in finger-spelling might lead one to suspect that they are perceptually salient in signing as well, even if they never overtly contrast.

Another factor that comes into play here is the existence of fingerspelled loan words. ASL borrows lexical items from English via fingerspelling.[3] Usually such fingerspelled words undergo regular phonological processes that make the spelled items more signlike. For example, consider the loan sign #JOB. Unlike a purely fingerspelled J-O-B, #JOB has undergone several phonological changes: (1) certain letters can be deleted; (2) it is not spelled in the normal fingerspelling area (ipsilateral space in front of chest at about shoulder level); (3) there are handshape alterations from citation letters; (4) it can add movements that are not present in pure finger-spelling; (5) orientation of the handshape is altered from normal fingerspelling; (6) it can involve both hands (which happens only under special stylistic conditions or for emphasis in normal fingerspelling); and (7) it can be inflected like a normal sign (Battison, 1978). In other words, these loan words take on more qualities of signs and so occupy a half-world between pure signs and pure fingerspelling. Even if the A handshape and the S handshape do not contrast in signs, they do in fingerspelling and fingerspelled loan words, which do not neutralize the A versus S handshapes. One might speculate that it is important perceptually to maintain a distinction between A and S in signs as well.

To answer this question I ran a concept formation (CF) task on deaf subjects fluent in ASL. Jaeger states that "the basic assumption behind concept-formation experiments is that people have in their minds any number of concepts that can be brought to consciousness by presenting to them stimuli representing positive and negative instances of a concept, and training them to discriminate between the two'' (1980b, 244). Thus, in the case of allophones of /A/ I wanted to see if there is evidence for a phonemic category encompassing [A] and [A$_s$] that could be uncovered by a CF test.

There are two basic ways to structure a CF test. First, one can train subjects via positive and negative exemplars to respond to a certain target category, and then introduce test tokens to see whether or not they will include them in the target category. In this type of CF task, the basic metrics are whether the experimental tokens in question are included in the category and how many subjects do so (although it is possible to structure the task so that other information is rendered, for example, reaction times). An example of this type of CF task is Jaeger (1980b). Jaeger trained native English speakers to respond to the category /k/ by presenting them with various tokens of /k/ (except for the unaspirated [k] after /s/) and then tested to see if they include the unaspirated [k] after /s/ in this category.

Another approach is to train two matched groups to respond to two categories— a control category and a category including control plus test items—and then determine the number of successful trials to arrive at criterion for each group. If there is no significant difference between the two groups, then this is interpreted as evidence that the test items are in the same psychological category as the control items. If more trials are required to reach criterion for the control-plus-test-items category, then this indicates that the test items in some way are not grouped in the target category. The rationale here is that ''simple'' categories, for example, red objects, should require fewer trials to arrive at criterion than more ''complex'' categories, for example, red or round objects. This second approach is adopted here. The basic metrics are the number of trials necessary to arrive at criterion and the number of subjects in each group who reach criterion.

Thus, in the case of the proposed allophones of /A/, if Stokoe et al. and Friedman are right, then the number of trials to arrive at criterion with [A] and [Å] only should be the same as for the case when the target category is exemplified by [A], [Å], and [A$_s$]. This would indicate that [A$_s$] is grouped with the other phones as /A/.

It should be noted that one important difference between Stokoe et al. (1965) and this study may be in the conception of the phoneme. Although it is never explicitly stated, the theory of the phoneme in the Stokoe et al. study is paradigmatically descriptivist: phonemes are determined by contrast, phonetic similarity, and economy. But a more psychological conception of the phoneme seems to be present: ''However, examination of many pairs of similar signs for minimal contrast reveals that some of these points on the signer's body are not distinctly different (not tab *cheremes*) but occur in complementary distribution (thus are *allochers*, just as the English phoneme /p/ has an allophone with a puff of air in *pot* and an allophone without the puff in *spot*). To take an example from American Sign Language: the index finger of the dez hand [i.e., handshape] which looks like *g* or *d* of the manual alphabet brushes the tip of the nose (tab) in its action (sig) in the sign MOUSE. But when the sign is motion outward from near the same place, for instance in the sign SEE, *the signer and the viewer of the sign tend to think of the place as the signer's eyes*'' (1978, 41, emphasis added).

In any case, the conception of the phoneme I adopt is that of a psychological entity, not simply an analytical convenience. Basically, a phoneme constitutes a mental grouping, a perceptual category in which member allophones are viewed as "the same" in some sense of that word. If psychological considerations are irrelevant—as they are in the American descriptivist philosophy of science—then it is not clear what impact psycholinguistic considerations (such as this experiment) would have on a linguist's proposed phonemicization. But in its favor, even though the psychological conception of the phoneme may be philosophically anathema, it can be given empirical content through research paradigms such as CF.

# METHOD

The basic procedure for the trials-to-criterion CF test is first to administer a preliminary CF test on an unrelated category in order to sort subjects into two matched groups of equal ability. In this experiment as a pretest subjects were given a semantic category as a target: animals. The preliminary test consisted of thirty-five signs total. Criterion was set at thirteen consecutive correct responses. If subjects did not reach criterion and infer the correct category, they were dismissed and did not participate in the crucial CF tests. Of fifteen subjects tested, four failed to pass the preliminary CF test. By "matched," I mean that the average number of trials to criterion was the same for both groups. One group—the control—was then given a trials-to-criterion CF test in which the target category was exemplified by signs with [A] and [Å] handshapes; the experimental group was given a CF test where the target category was represented by [A], [Å], and [$A_s$] handshapes. Afterward, subjects were asked to name the category.

Relevant data come from four sources: (1) whether any subject reached criterion; (2) the number of trials to criterion; (3) ability to name the category; and (4) observations on their behavior and comments from subjects on strategies for guessing the category. No attempt was made to do an error analysis on responses.

All three CF tests consisted of randomized signs with 40 percent in the target category. The other 60 percent were selected randomly from several sign dictionaries and represent diverse formational types. Target signs had varying movement and location parameters with only handshape as a common trait. In the case of the control test, the target signs were equally divided between [A] and [Å]; in the experimental test, they were equally divided between the three hypothetical allophones. Both CF tests consisted of one hundred signs. Again criterion was taken to be thirteen consecutive correct responses.

Instructions were given in ASL, and both the instructions and the signs were presented by the experimenter. Unfortunately, due to time constraints I did not use videotape; this would have controlled the input to the subjects.

All fifteen subjects were deaf users of ASL. All either had deaf parents (three subjects) or had attended a residential school for the deaf (eleven subjects) except for one, who was included inadvertently. This subject attended schools for deaf in other countries and was later excluded from analysis. The purpose of limiting the test population to these two groups was to ensure that subjects had acquired ASL at a fairly early age. Also, I wanted to eliminate the population of users of manually coded forms of English (MCE). MCE differs from ASL in substantial ways even though both use the visual-manual channel for communication. In particular, MCE makes very high use of so-called initialized signs.

"Initialized signs" are signs that have been borrowed from ASL but in which the handshape has been changed to reflect the first letter of the English word for which the sign codes. For example, ASL has one sign glossed TRY that covers the same semantic territory as English "try," "strive," "attempt," "endeavor," "effort," etc. MCE codes these English words by using a T handshape for TRY, S handshape for STRIVE, A handshape for ATTEMPT, and E handshape for EFFORT. Subjects who use MCE as their primary communication system introduce at least two problems: (1) their control of ASL is unknown, and (2) they may have a heightened awareness of handshapes because of their importance in coding English words. Since the letters of the manual alphabet play an extremely important role in MCE, it would not be surprising if the handshape categories in these speakers strongly reflected the alphabet, that is, [A] and [A$_s$] would not be categorized together. Thus, these signers were excluded. Also, since I was investigating ASL, I wanted to exclude the influence of English as much as possible.

Subjects were seven females and eight males between the ages of twenty and twenty-nine years old except for one subject who was fifty-seven. They were recruited at Ohlone College in Fremont, California. The CF tests were administered "in the field," and they generally took about a half hour.

## RESULTS

Table 1 summarizes the results of the CF tests. For the pretest, the mean number of trials to criterion for the control group is 24.6; for the experimental group it is 23.2. Thus, although almost the same, the experimental group is slightly favored.

*Table 1.* **Summary of Concept-Formation Tests**

| Subject | Pretest Number of trials | Test Number of trials | Ranking |
|---|---|---|---|
| | *Control Group (A handshapes only)*[4] | | |
| #9 | 19 | 19 | 1.5 |
| #6 | 26 | 19 | 1.5 |
| #4 | 19 | 30 | 3 |
| #15 | 28 | 35 | 4 |
| #2 | 31 | never reached criterion | 8.5 |
| | av = 24.6 | | |
| | *Experimental Group (A and S handshapes)* | | |
| #1 | 35 | 57 | 5 |
| #5 | 18 | never reached criterion | 8.5 |
| #13 | 20 | " | 8.5 |
| #12 | 21 | " | 8.5 |
| #8 | 22 | " | 8.5 |
| #3 | 23 | " | 8.5 |
| | av = 23.17 | | |

Three statistical tests were performed on this data: Mann-Whitney test, T-test, and Chi-squared test. The Mann-Whitney test inspects the ranking of scores (rightmost column in table 1) to see whether there is any difference in the distribution of the two groups. Identical distribution supports the null hypothesis, that is, that subjects do not differ in their ability to discover the target category. This in turn suggests that [$A_s$] is correctly grouped under /A/. Since the critical value for ($n_1 = 6$, $n_2 = 5$) at the 0.05 level is 25, and U = 26.5 > 25, the results are significant (see table 2). They indicate that the probability that such a distribution is due to chance is less than 5 percent, and thus the null hypothesis must be rejected. Since the two groups respond differently to the two target categories, this suggests that [$A_s$] should not be grouped with [A] and [Å].

The T-test inspects the distribution of the two populations and computes the likelihood that the difference is due to chance, that is, that chance alone is responsible for the better performance of the control group. In computing the T-value, the score for subjects who did not reach criterion was arbitrarily set at 100, that is, the maximum number of trials. Thus, the T-test indicates that the probability that the difference in the distributions of the control and experimental scores is due to chance is extremely small, and the null hypothesis must be rejected (see table 3). However, the reliability of the T-test given is somewhat uncertain because of the small sample size. Hence, it is not the best indicator of the statistical significance of the data. Also, arbitrarily setting noncriterial scores to 100 masks the real values (assuming that it would have been possible to keep on testing for say, 150 or 200 trials without fatiguing subjects).

The last test is the Chi-squared. This test looks at the likelihood that the difference between the number of subjects that reach criterion in each group is due to chance. The results of the Chi-squared indicate that the difference between the control group and the experimental group in their ability to reach criterion is borderline significant (see table 4). Again, this suggests that the category with A and S handshapes is more complex than just A.

The evidence we have from the statistical analysis supports the conclusion that [$A_s$] cannot be grouped in the same category as [A] and [Å]. Fewer signers reach criterion when they must categorize them together, and those that succeed take significantly more trials to do so than the subjects exposed to [A] and [Å] only.

At the end of the test subjects were asked to name the category. Additionally, those that failed to reach criterion were again shown only the target signs and then asked to name the category. For the control group, every subject answered that the category was "signs with A" (while showing me the [A] handshape). In other words, they grouped [A] along with [Å]. When I pointed this out, they did not consider the difference important. That is, there is some evidence that [A] and [Å] are truly viewed as "the same" by ASL users. For the experimental group, the one subject who

*Table 2*. **Mann-Whitney Test Results**

Sum of ranks for control = 18.5
Sum of ranks for experimental = 47.5
$n_1 = 6$
$n_2 = 5$
U = 26.5
U' = 3.5

***Table 3*. T-Test Results**

Degrees of freedom = 10
T = 21.48
$p \ll 0.001$

reached criterion labeled the category "signs with A or S handshapes." Among the subjects not reaching criterion presented with the target tokens a second time, three said that the category was "signs with A or S handshapes." Finally, one subject in the experimental group mentioned that she had thought of handshapes and had hypothesized that it was A but was confused by the S shapes; she then gave up the handshape hypothesis and looked for some other category. Thus, subject comments suggest that [A$_s$] is not grouped with [A] and [Å], and that [A] and [Å] are perceived as "the same." (Of course, the latter claim needs to be confirmed by experiment such as a CF test.)

*Linguistic analysis*

## DISCUSSION

The evidence is promising that despite the lack of contrast, phonetic similarity, and economy-internal evidence, [A$_s$] should not be considered an allophone of the phoneme /A/ in ASL. However, there are several reasons to be cautious about this conclusion. First, the database is small. Ideally, I would have like to have tested at least twenty subjects who passed the pretest, but I simply was unable to recruit enough eligible subjects to participate within the two-week period in which I was testing, despite my best efforts.

Other potential problems concern the administering of the CF tests. I administered the test each time. The preferred method would have been to have videotaped the instructions and the test tokens and presented this, thus eliminating any variation in the presentation. This is particularly relevant to the instructions, for there was a wide variation in how I presented them. Some subjects grasped the task immediately, but others required more elaborate examples and explanations. I do not know to what extent this may have affected the results. Also, I translated the instructions into ASL. The optimal situation would have been to have asked a deaf, native signer to do the

***Table 4*. Chi-Squared Test Results**

|  | Reach criterion | Not reach criterion | Total |
|---|---|---|---|
| A handshape | Ob = 4 | Ob = 1 | 5 |
|  | Ex = 2.2727 | Ex = 2.7272 |  |
| A and S handshapes | Ob = 1 | Ob = 5 | 6 |
|  | Ex = 2.7272 | Ex = 3.2727 |  |
| Total | 5 | 6 | 11 |

*Note*. Degrees of freedom = 1
$X^2$ = 2.227 (including Yates correction factor)
$p < 0.10$

translation. At least a final check by a native signer would have ensured clarity. However, feedback from subjects was that the instructions were clear.

Two problems relate to design. First, on the CF test itself, 100 items is simply too many. I noticed signs of restlessness and of dying interest around the 50 to 60 mark. By that time, if subjects had not arrived at the correct category, they became disoriented and were unable to make any progress. Arbitrarily reducing the saturation point to, for example, 75, would affect the values from the T-test. However, given that the T-test is the least preferred of the statistical tests, this may be inconsequential.

Second, I noticed a problem in the transition from the pretest to the CF test proper. Since the target category for the pretest is a semantic category, some subjects seemed to continue to search for a semantic category in the CF test despite instructions not to do so and periodic reminders to ignore the meaning of the signs. If I were to do it over again, I would use a formational category for the pretest other than semantic. It would be easy to design a test using a movement prime or a location prime.

Regarding the grouping of [A] and [Å], one might ask whether there is some articulatory or visual reason to suggest this might be a universal category, or whether it is a language-specific fact, and that perhaps other sign languages exist that separate [A] and [Å] into different phonemes. I am unaware of any evidence for or against this speculation; however, there are two things to keep in mind: First, the thumb is a highly mobile articulator. Given the degrees of freedom of movement it has, I suggest that it is unlikely that [A] and [Å] would be universally grouped for motor-mechanical reasons. Furthermore, if the different position of the thumb in [A] and [$A_s$] does have a categorical difference, why not with [A] and [Å]? Second, there is some evidence that other sign languages that do have an A handshape, for example Chinese Sign Language (CSL), manifest phonetic differences in production at least as subtle as the position difference of the thumb:

> In a closer inspection of the videotaped Chinese sign FATHER used on the test, we noticed some fine distinctions that made us realize that a fist may not be just a fist. The Chinese sign FATHER was made with what seemed to be an odd closure. Whereas the ASL handshape in SECRET is relaxed, with fingers loosely curved as they close against the palm, in the CSL handshape in FATHER the fingers were folded over further onto the palm and were rigid, not curved. . . . We thought that the difference noted might be only a peculiarity of a single sign in a single rendition. But other signs of the chosen 30 made by one Chinese signer also have that handshape—namely, the Chinese signs FRIEND and TEACHER; when we examined them, we observed the same peculiarities. We also considered the possibility that the difference might be caused by something about that particular Chinese signer, perhaps the bone structure of his hand. But in tapes of the same signs made by five other Chinese deaf signers the observed differences from ASL occur consistently across signers. (Klima and Bellugi, 1979, 161–62)

If such phonetic detail is consistent in CSL yet different from ASL, it enhances the plausibility that the articulation of the thumb could also be a phonetic detail with cross-linguistic variation. Clearly, this is just speculation and fieldwork on other sign languages is necessary before we can come to any conclusions as to the intrinsic relation between [A] and [Å]. However, this evidence suggests that sign languages possess a level that is parallel to the fine phonetic detail of spoken languages, for example vowel length or voice-onset time, which cannot be ignored.

## SUMMARY

Previous analyses of the phonology of ASL have claimed that on the phonemic level the handshapes [A], [Å], and [$A_s$] can be grouped under the phoneme /A/. This conclusion was based on the lack of contrast between [$A_s$] and the other handshapes, their phonetic similarity, and reasons of economy or simplicity. This study utilizes the concept formation test to investigate the psychological reality of these claims. It is claimed that if [$A_s$] and the other allophones are in the same phonemic category, that this should be reflected in the number of trials to criterion in CF test where the target categories are A alone versus A and S, namely that there is no difference. On the contrary, if there is a difference—particularly if the category A and S requires more trials, that this difference is due to these handshape phones being in different phonemic categories.

The results show that deaf ASL users, when divided into two matched groups, take significantly more trials to reach criterion for the A and S handshapes than for the A handshapes alone. Also, significantly fewer signers reach criterion for A and S as compared to A. The Mann-Whitney test and T-test indicate that these results are statistically significant at the 0.05 level; the Chi-squared test indicates the results are significant at the 0.10 level. This allows us to tentatively conclude that [$A_s$] should not be grouped with [A] and [Å] under /A/, contrary to Stokoe et al. and Friedman.

This experiment demonstrates a paradigm for investigating the psychological reality of hypothesized phonological entities. Previous phonological analysis of ASL has depended on data from utterances—the distribution of phones—and other theoretical criteria such as phonetic similarity and simplicity. This model proposes instead that such phonological hypotheses must be and can be subject to empirical confirmation through psycholinguistic means. This study explores the application of the concept-formation test to a sign language, following the work of Jaeger (1980a, 1980b), with success, thus demonstrating its utility not only for exploring visual-gestural languages but also the general cognitive representation of language.

As a final note, let me suggest some further work that can be done on ASL using such techniques. First, the grouping of [A] and [Å] under /A/ should be confirmed, perhaps by CF test. We have preliminary evidence that suggests that signers view them as "the same." Second, the handshape T of the manual alphabet, [$A_t$], is also claimed to be an allophone of /A/ by Stokoe et al. (but not by Friedman). For the same reasons as for [$A_s$], this claim is suspect and should be investigated. Third, many signs do not have a static handshape throughout the entire sign: they start with one handshape and then change to another. It would be interesting to see how signs that, say, start with an A shape or end with an A shape but differ in their other segments are categorized. I purposely eliminated any such signs from this experiment because of their uncertain character. Are they grouped under /A/, or under the handshape of the other segment, or separately?

Fourth, concerning other parameters, the same paradigm can be applied. For example, Stokoe et al. claim that all signs that contact the trunk area of the body should be grouped under that location prime (symbolized as /[ ]/). This phoneme includes a diverse set of signs that range from contact at the top of the shoulders to contact at the hips. It also includes signs that have ipsilateral contact, contralateral contact, and ipsi- to contralateral contact (and vice versa). In this case, since handshapes are not involved, there is no independent reason to suspect that say, distinctions in fingerspelling would also be relevant to signs. But the wide area of the trunk—the distance from the shoulders to the hips—suggests that despite the lack of minimal pairs and any contrast, such locations might be better categorized as separate location primes in ASL if psychologically they are not grouped together. Again, this can be investigated by psycholinguistic means. Vision is often thought to possess more degrees of freedom (three-dimensional, nonlinear) than audition, and thus is thought of as capable of more discrimination. If it turns out to be true that phonetic locations are viewed as "the same," this would suggest in a rather spectacular way, I think, that the organization of vision-based languages truly parallels spoken languages on the level of phonetic detail and in how phonetically diverse entities are nevertheless mentally grouped together. Finally, comparative work on sign languages needs to be done to see whether they parallel spoken languages in the diverse ways in which phones are grouped phonemically as well as in the systematicity of phonetic detail. This too can be approached from an empirical, psycholinguistic paradigm rather than the well-worn path of analyses based primarily on internal evidence.

## NOTES

1. There is some ambiguity regarding Stokoe's intended analysis of [A] and [Å]. In Stokoe et al. (1965), [Å] is called an "allocher" (allophone) of /A/—for example, see p. 2 of their text— yet it is represented separately as A in the dictionary entries unlike the S and T allophones. However in Stokoe (1978), which is a revision of the 1965 text, [Å] is listed as a separate phoneme and is said to contrast with [A], but no examples are given. In any case, Friedman clearly states that [A] and [Å] are allophones of /A/.
2. I am aware of at least ten signs that do not fit their explanation: MYSELF, OURSELVES, ATTITUDE, TURTLE, SECRET, SUFFER, PATIENCE, AUDIOLOGY, DRAMA, AGGRESSIVE. These signs all have contact on the thumb side of [A]; their other parameters vary.
3. See Davis (this volume) for an extensive discussion of fingerspelling and the concept of borrowing in ASL.
4. Subjects #7, #11, and #14 did not reach criterion for the pretest; subject #10 did not satisfy the criteria for inclusion in this study.

## REFERENCES

Battison, R. (1974). Phonological deletion in American Sign Language. *Sign Language Studies* 5: 1–19.

———. (1978). *Lexical borrowing in American Sign Language*. Silver Spring, MD: Linstok Press.

Cohen, E., Namir, L., and Schlesinger, I. M. (1977). *A new dictionary of sign language*. The Hague: Mouton.

Friedman, L. A. (1976). Phonology of a soundless language: phonological structure of ASL. Ph.D. diss., University of California, Berkeley.

Jaeger, J. J. (1980a). Categorization in phonology: An experimental approach. Ph.D. diss., University of California, Berkeley.

———. (1980b). Testing the psychological reality of phonemes. *Language and Speech* 23: 233–53.

Klima, E. (1975). Sound and its absence in the linguistic symbol. In *The role of speech in language*, edited by J. Cavanaugh and J. Cutting, 249–70. Cambridge, MA: MIT Press.

Klima, E., and Bellugi, U. (1979). *The signs of language.* Cambridge, MA: Harvard University Press.

Liddell, S. K. (1984). THINK and BELIEVE: Sequentiality in American Sign Language. *Language* 60:372–99.

Stokoe, W. C. (1978). *Sign language structure.* Silver Spring, MD: Linstok Press.

Stokoe, W. C., Casterline, D. C., and Croneberg, C. G. (1965; rev. ed. 1976). *A dictionary of American Sign Language on linguistic principles.* Silver Spring, MD: Linstok Press.

# The Effects of Morphosyntactic Structure on the Acquisition of Classifier Predicates in ASL

Brenda S. Schick

One of the most notable aspects of the grammar of ASL is the productivity of multimorphemic classifier predicates. In comparison with English, ASL more closely resembles languages in which word order is relatively flexible and grammatical relations are represented by multimorphemic words, such as Navajo, Inuktitut (Eskimo), and Chipewyan (Baker, 1988; Denny, 1982). However, ASL diverges from these highly inflected spoken languages in terms of affixation, which in ASL takes the form of changes in handshape, movement of the hand/arm, and location of the sign articulation, none of which can be easily separated into "root" plus affixes (Schick, 1987; Supalla, 1982, 1986; Wilbur, 1987; Wilbur, Klima, and Bellugi, 1983). Within multimorphemic classifier predicates in ASL, three general categories exist in ASL (Schick, 1987; see McDonald, 1982; Supalla, 1982, 1986). These classifier types are differentiated by their morphosyntactic structure and function (for example, agentivity, locative relationships, grammatical relationships). This typology will be discussed in more detail below.

Because these predicates are, in part, iconically motivated, and because ASL is complex morphologically, the acquisition of ASL provides a unique opportunity to investigate the interaction of morphosyntactic structure and formational and representational complexity. Previous research on the acquisition of classifiers in spoken languages and ASL has been concerned with the child's ability to select an appropriate classifier morpheme, the handshape in the case of ASL (Gandour, Petty, Dardarananda, Dechongkit, and Mukngoen, 1984; Kantor, 1980; Matsumoto, 1984; Supalla, 1982). Because each morphological marker in ASL varies in meaning (for example, agentivity, spatial concepts, pronominal concepts), in the grammatical relation represented, and in its formal complexity, a primary hypothesis of this project was that children might acquire subsets of predicate morphology differentially. A secondary purpose was to attempt to define what constitutes semantic and structural complexity in a visual language in order to clarify factors that influence ease of acquisition. The current project is a comparative investigation of the acquisition of these classifier predicates in ASL. In the following section, each of the three categories of ASL classifier predicates, CLASS,[1] HANDLE, and SASS will be briefly described (see Schick [1987, in press] for a more extensive discussion).

## CLASS PREDICATES

In CLASS constructions, the noun referent is represented by a handshape that is an abstract semantic marker referring to prototypical categories of objects. Mandel (1977) describes the iconicity in this type of handshape as substitutive depiction because the handshape represents the substance of object, rather than outlining it, albeit in a highly abstract form. CLASS handshapes represent objects such as animate beings (PEOPLE) or land and water vehicles (VEHICLE). These categories are common in other classifier languages (Allan, 1977). Although some of the forms are highly animate, the resulting predicates are nonagentive. For example, when a predicate with a VEHICLE handshape moves, it is assumed that a human is in the vehicle although the form can also be used for a driverless car rolling down a hill. Some CLASS handshapes are shown in figure 1.

When a CLASS morpheme is combined with a movement root, the resulting predicate is an intransitive form representing the combination of the subject into the predicate construction, with the morphosyntactic structure, subject-verb. This type of predicate is typically used to express spatial relationships in which CLASS hand-

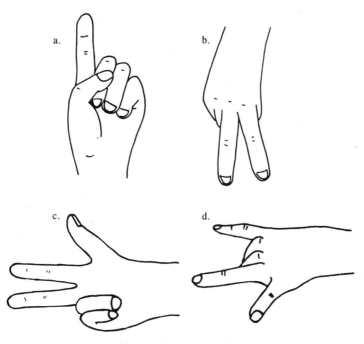

*Figure 1.* **Examples of CLASS handshapes. Represented are noun categories for (a) HUMAN, (b) PEOPLE, (c) VEHICLE, and (d) AIRPLANE.**

shapes represent the figure and ground nominals (see, verbs of motion and location, Supalla, 1978, 1982, 1985).[2] In these predicates, the locative relationship between the two nominals is represented by the relative positioning of the figure and the ground handshapes in space. With this type of representation, the grid network (Supalla, 1982) or reference frame for spatial relationships can be schematically and iconically mapped out. Because many points in space can serve as referents, locative morphemes can be quite complex (see Gee and Kegl, 1982; Shepard-Kegl, 1985).

## HANDLE PREDICATES

HANDLE predicates have a handshape that is a replication of an actual hand holding an object. Basically, HANDLE handshapes are a discrete categorization of object referents that in reality vary along a continuous dimension, such as size and shape. Moreover, HANDLE handshapes have handshape-internal morphemes that vary with the size and depth of the object and are realized phonetically by the addition of fingers and changes in the shape of the palm. Figure 2 illustrates two groupings of HANDLE handshapes, those for round and flat objects.

Morphosyntactically, HANDLE predicates are transitive constructions with an object argument (verb-object). These verbs are agentive forms that represent the

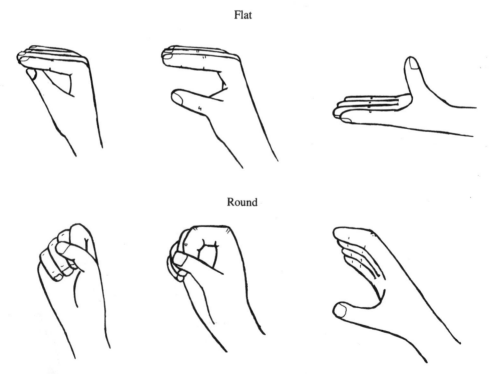

*Figure 2*. **Examples of HANDLE handshapes. Two groupings of handshape for shape—round and flat—are illustrated.**

handling and movement of a referent object (for example, "I gave her a soda," "He handed me a large box," "I played a guitar;" see Fischer and Gough, 1978; Kegl, 1985; McDonald, 1982; Shepard-Kegl, 1985). For some of these forms, this type of classifier is actually a subset of a larger group of verbs in ASL that has a theme specified (LOOK, ASK, HIT; see Padden, 1983). These predicates may combine with a prefix and/or suffix represented phonetically by movement in reference to a spatial index to indicate verb inflection. Most verbs can take a subject prefix and indirect object suffix (for example, GIVE, TOSS) while a few take an indirect object prefix and subject suffix (for example, TAKE): (Subject-) Verb-Object (-Indirect Object) or (Indirect Object-) Verb-Object (-Subject). For others, movement replicates, albeit in a schematicized sense, the actual movement or activity with the object (for example PLAY-GUITAR, CLIMB-A-ROPE, UNSCREW-JAR-LID). In the latter forms, the object is incorporated but not moved through space per se. For these HANDLE types, the predicate cannot be inflected for verb agreement although it may appear with null arguments.

## SASS PREDICATES

SASS predicates, or size and shape specifiers, are most typically inanimate predicate adjectives used to describe a nominal referent (for example "The pole is long and thin," or "The shirt is striped;" Klima and Bellugi, 1979). In a SASS construction, the handshape represents the visual-geometric features of the nominal referent by outlining its shape and dimensions. As with HANDLE handshapes, selection of a SASS handshape involves a discrete classification of the size and shape of the referent and handshape internal morphemes are required (Supalla, 1982). Figure 3 illustrates

Flat

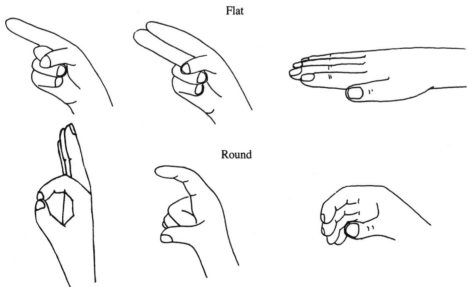

Round

*Figure 3.* **Examples of SASS predicates. Two groupings of handshape for shape—round and flat—are illustrated.**

two groupings of handshape for shape, round and flat. An increase in dimension is realized by the addition of fingers, which have morphemic status.

In order to establish a more complex secondary reference object or location in ASL, a signer may initially describe the ground using adjectival SASS constructions and then show the relationship another object has with the ground. In these forms, SASS predicates are similar to CLASS predicates; both are used to represent spatial relationships in an iconically motivated manner.

Summarized in example 1 is the morphosyntactic structure of a single sign in each classifier predicate category. Arguments in parentheses are optional; a morpheme may or may not be incorporated.

> (1)  CLASS:      (Location-) Subject-Verb (-Location)
>       HANDLE:     (Subject-) Verb-Object (-Indirect Object)
>       SASS:       Verb:Adjective (-Location)

## ACQUISITION OF CLASSIFIERS

Previous investigations have examined the acquisition of classifier morphemes in both spoken languages, such as Thai (Gandour et al., 1984) and Japanese (Matsumoto, 1984), and in ASL (Kantor, 1980; Supalla, 1982). These studies focus on the child's ability to select an appropriate classifier morpheme, which is a reflection of the child's semantic-categorization skills. For example, in ASL, both Kantor and Supalla show that by the age of five or six, children can appropriately select prototypical CLASS handshapes for common nouns.[3] However, both Supalla and Kantor remark that children appear to incorporate classifiers inconsistently; classifiers that seem to have been acquired are not used in certain syntactic environments, notably environments that seem more complex. This would indicate that the structural factors in ASL classifiers affect acquisition. Similarly, at these ages Thai and Japanese children are still substituting incorrect classifier morphemes. These errors occur in Japanese and Thai even though classifiers in these languages do not vary in their morphosyntactic structure, which is always of the form noun + classifier. These developmental differences reveal that semantic factors, not only structural ones, are relevant to the acquisition of classifiers.

For ASL, there is some preliminary research that shows that the ability to produce morphemes other than the handshape may not parallel the ability to produce a correct classifier handshape. Newport (1982; see also, Newport and Meier, 1985) reports on the acquisition of the movement roots in CLASS predicates.[4] Her results indicate that children omit morphemes in complex movement roots, particularly at younger ages. Her subject at the age range 4;7 to 5;1 continued to omit morphemes in 35 percent of predicates that required complex movement stems. Clearly, children are not producing adultlike forms at this age.

In general, this prolonged developmental timetable has been attributed to the multimorphemic nature of classifiers. This is not surprising: morphological complexity has been found to affect stages of acquisition in spoken languages (Berman, 1981, 1982; MacWhinney, 1978, 1985; Johnston and Slobin, 1979; Slobin, 1982). However, this explanation does not address the issue of what types of morphemes pose difficulty during acquisition.

The current project was designed to examine factors influencing the acquisition of multimorphemic predicates in ASL.

## METHOD

### Subjects

Subjects were twenty-four severely to profoundly deaf children (thirteen female), ranging in age from 4;5 to 9;0 years. All subjects were enrolled in programs located within a substantial deaf community. In addition, all subjects had two deaf parents, had been enrolled only in programs using manual communication, and were said to use ASL by parents and/or school administrators. All parents had been signing since at least five years of age and sixteen subjects had at least one deaf grandparent. For purposes of analysis, subjects were divided into three groups of eight (mean group ages were 5;3, 6;6, and 8;1 years, respectively).

### Stimuli

Six types of predicates were selected as targets to be elicited from subjects in this study. Target predicates exemplified all three types of productive predicates in ASL: HANDLE, SASS, and CLASS forms. In selecting these target stimuli, handshapes were counterbalanced for a range of referent objects for each predicate type (see table 1). For CLASS forms, the handshape represented two distinct groups: people or vehicles. For HANDLE and SASS predicates, the handshape represented round- or flat-shaped objects for three different depths and sizes.

In addition to the handshape morphemes, each predicate included morphemes that represent space syntactically. For HANDLE predicates, syntactic space is pro-

***Table 1.* Handshape Morphemes Selected for Each Predicate Category**

| HANDLE | |
|---|---|
| ROUND | FLAT |
| STRING (X#-) | THIN.FLAT.OBJECT (F#-) |
| THIN.CYLINDER (S-hollow)[a] | NARROW.FLAT.OBJECT (C-) |
| THICK.CYLINDER (C) | LARGE.FLAT.OBJECT (B.- ) |

| SASS | |
|---|---|
| ROUND | FLAT |
| FLAT.ROUND.OBJECT (F) | LINE (1) |
| THIN.CYLINDER (S-hollow)[a] | NARROW.STRIP (G real) |
| LARGE.CYLINDER (C) | FLAT.BROAD.SURFACE (B) |

| CLASS | |
|---|---|
| PEOPLE (V) | VEHICLE (3) |

*Note.* Phonological handshape specifications are given in parentheses using the written system proposed by McIntire, Newkirk, Hutchins, and Poizner (1987).
[a]The handshape (S-hollow) is the handshape used in some versions of TELESCOPE.

nominal and verbs can be inflected to represent subject, object, and indirect object relations. For both CLASS and some SASS predicates, syntactic space is commonly used to communicate spatial relationships. For other SASS forms, space represents the physical dimensions of the referent object (for example, length, width).

Each predicate type was elicited in two different levels of predicate complexity, Simple and Difficult. Although both Simple and Difficult predicates are multimorphemic, those at the Difficult level were constructed so they were morphologically more complex than those at the Simple level. Morphological complexity was increased in the Difficult predicates by including at least some morphemes that are acquired later than those selected as targets in the Simple predicates, as determined by previous studies in acquisition (Gandour et al., 1984; Kantor, 1980; Lillo-Martin, Bellugi, Struxness, and O'Grady, 1985; Supalla, 1982).

For Difficult CLASS predicates, the spatial relationships between the figure and ground were those that have been found to be acquired later by children crosslinguistically (Johnston and Slobin, 1979; Schick, 1986). In addition, the figure and ground handshapes differed for these predicates whereas for Simple CLASS predicates, the two handshapes were either identical or the ground handshape was an unmarked B handshape. Difficult HANDLE predicates required second- or thirdperson inflection, rather than first person, or serial verbs (for example, "He handed the cotton candy to her," and "She took the firewood and carried it to father"). Difficult SASS predicates involved using the SASS predicate as part of a complex spatial relationship rather than as a simple predicate adjective as was the case for Simple SASS predicates.

### Elicitation Activities

Target predicates were elicited in a set of games designed to make specific classifier predicates the most appropriate responses for the situation. In these games, the examiner also took turns, creating a naturalistic, communicative environment. Furthermore, the examiner's productions were similar in grammatical structure to the target structures. This provided models that made it more likely that the child would use similar structures. All target predicates were reviewed with a deaf native signer to assure their grammaticality. A sample activity is given in figure 4.

Twelve predicate combinations of predicate type (CLASS, SASS, or HANDLE) and complexity (Simple or Difficult) were used. For each combination, six predicates were elicited in two games occurring in two separate sessions. Order of presentation of the games was counterbalanced across subjects. Activity order within each session was randomized. Altogether, each child produced 72 predicates yielding a total of 1,728 predicates across subjects.

### Procedure

All testing was done individually by the author, a hearing native signer of ASL. Sessions were videotaped and predicate morphemes were later scored for accuracy of handshape and location morphemes.[5]

To assess reliability in the morphological coding, 13 percent of the games were randomly selected (225 of 1,728 predicates) and were independently scored by a deaf ASL signer. Item-by-item percentages of agreement between the author and the

Material: Two lotto boards (similar to Bingo) with pictures and a deck of cards to match the pictures on boards. Three pictures on child's board are targets. The other six pictures are foils.

Procedure: Examiner passes out three cards to both players. Examiner goes first and requests a picture to fill a square on her lotto board. If the child does not have it, the examiner draws from the rigged deck. Examiner and child alternate turns until one board is completely filled (the child always wins).

| | |
|---|---|
| Examiner turn 1: | Two clocks are on a shelf. |
| Child turn 1: | A bus is next to a red car. |
| Examiner turn 2: | A monkey sits between two trees. |
| Child turn 2: | A truck is parked behind a car. |
| Examiner turn 3: | An elephant stands near a light pole. |
| Child turn 3: | A blue van is next to a car. |

*Figure 4.* **Game to elicit classifier predicate in various spatial relationships.**

independent scorer were calculated for each morpheme across predicate type and predicate type across all morphemes.[6] Values ranged from 90 to 96 percent correct.

## RESULTS

Scores for the accuracy of handshape and location morphemes were analyzed separately using analyses of variance (ANOVA). Among subjects, main effects were age, subject (nested within age), and order of presentation of games. The repeated-measures (that is, within-subjects) factors were predicate type and difficulty level (nested within predicate type). Because some individual scores were greater than 90 percent correct, arcsine transforms were used.

Results of these ANOVAs are shown in tables 2 and 3. Figures 5 and 6 display mean scores across subjects within age groups. Because the ANOVAs failed to demonstrate any effect of order of presentation of games, scores were also pooled across order.

*Effect of subject.* Results indicated that subject variation was significant for the production of both handshape morphemes and location morphemes. In addition, a significant interaction was found for predicate type X subject for handshape morphemes.

*Table 2.* **Summary of Significant Effects in Analyses of Variance of Handshape Morphemes**

| Independent variable | Degrees of freedom | Error term | F | p |
|---|---|---|---|---|
| Subject | 21,63 | model | 4.0 | <.0001 |
| Complexity | 3,63 | CS(A) | 10.78 | <.0001 |
| Verb type | 2,42 | VS(A) | 32.53 | <.0001 |
| Subj × Verb | 42,63 | model | 1.59 | <.05 |

*Table 3.* **Summary of Significant Effects in Analyses of Variance of Location Morphemes**

| Independent variable | Degrees of freedom | Error term | F | *p* |
|---|---|---|---|---|
| Subject | 21,63 | model | .160 | <.0001 |
| Age | 2,21 | S(A) | 9.05 | <.0001 |
| Complexity | 3,63 | CS(A) | 38.96 | <.0001 |
| Verb type | 2,42 | VS(A) | 13.74 | <.0001 |

*Effect of age.* Significant differences among the three age groups were observed for location morphemes. There were no significant age-related differences for handshape morphemes.

*Effect of complexity.* For both dependent variables, handshape and location, the effect of complexity was significant: Simple predicates were produced more accurately than Difficult predicates.

*Effect of verb type.* Significant differences were observed for both dependent variables, handshape and location. As shown in figure 5, CLASS predicates elicited more correct productions than SASS predicates. Handshape was produced the least accurately for HANDLE forms. Newman-Keul t-tests, comparing scores at each level

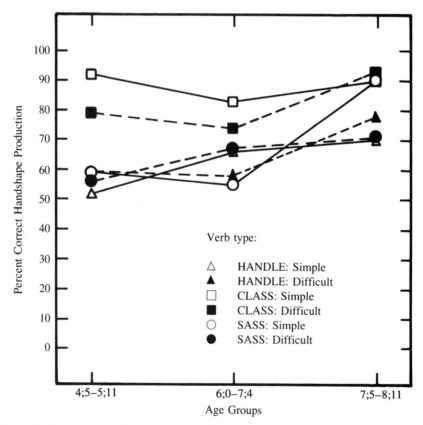

*Figure 5.* **Percent correct for production of handshape morpheme(s) as a function of age, predicate type, and level of complexity.**

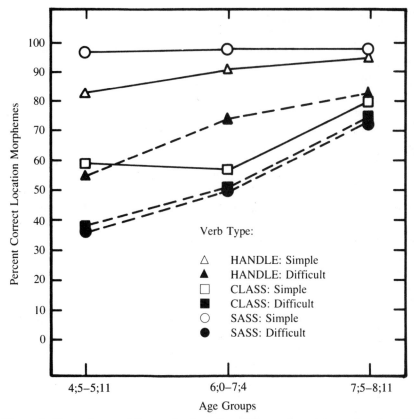

**Figure 6.** Percent correct for production of spatial morpheme(s) as a function of age, predicate type, and level of complexity.

of complexity for each verb type, showed that these differences were significant; all Newman-Keul tests used an alpha level of .05.

As shown in figure 6, Simple SASS predicates elicited nearly perfect use of space. Collapsing level of complexity, HANDLE predicates elicited correct use of these morphemes significantly more often than SASS predicates, which in turn elicited location morphemes more accurately than CLASS predicates. Results for Difficult SASS and Difficult CLASS were nearly identical. Newman-Keul t-tests revealed that HANDLE predicates elicited the most accurate production of location morphemes. SASS predicates elicited more correct location morphemes than CLASS predicates, which were the least accurate across all age groups.

## DISCUSSION

### *Development of the Use of Handshape Morphemes*

The results show that for handshape acquisition, CLASS handshapes are produced correctly at an earlier age than SASS or HANDLE handshapes. This early acquisition is likely a consequence of two factors. First, paradigms or matrices used to represent

CLASS handshapes do not require multiple dimensions. As characterized by Pinker (1984), the fewer dimensions in the paradigm the child must "discover," the quicker the child is able to learn the paradigm (see also Slobin, 1985b). Second, CLASS handshapes have no handshape-internal morphemes; there are no modifications in the CLASS handshape that correspond to changes in physical dimension in the object referent such as size, depth, and shape. In comparison, the selection of HANDLE and SASS handshapes requires consideration of several dimensions realized as fusional morphemes. In short, HANDLE and SASS paradigms require more features as well as changes in the surface form of the handshape.

Parallels to these differences in acquisition can be found in spoken languages that have classifier morphemes. For children learning Japanese and Thai, both classifier languages, classifier categories reflecting superordinate classification (for example, vehicles and animacy) are mastered earlier than classifiers for categories based on visual-geometric features (Gandour et al., 1984; Matsumoto, 1984). These differences in development exist despite the fact that, in both Thai and Japanese, all classifiers are syllabic and syntactically invariant. A plausible explanation for the differences in acquisition is the nature of the categorization and the complexity of the paradigms needed to represent them.

However, paradigm structure cannot explain why SASS handshapes were produced more accurately than HANDLE handshapes. For both of these types of handshapes, the paradigms are structurally similar. For some referent objects, the handshapes are homonymous. However, it appears that children who can correctly use shape, size, and depth for handshape selection in one verb type cannot necessarily transfer these features to other verb types.

A conceivable source for the difference between SASS and HANDLE handshape production lies in the morphosyntactic structure of HANDLE predicates. Although it is necessary to code the visual-geometric characteristics of the object referent in HANDLE classifiers, their morphosyntactic structure is not adjectival. The essential nature of HANDLE predicates involves the action associated with the object, the object's transfer through space, and the agentive nature of the predicate. The underlying morphosyntactic structure is V-O, with the object being incorporated into the verb via the information represented by the handshape. Unlike SASS predicates, which are adjectival predicates, the adjectival information represented by the HANDLE handshape is secondary and supplementary to what happens with the object. The handshape rarely supplies contrastive information not available from context. It is likely that, in part, the SASS handshapes are produced more accurately because the morphosyntactic nature of SASS predicates is consistent with the fact that they categorize according to physical characteristics and are a main source of adjectival information in ASL.

These differences also illustrate the fact that surface representation is not the only consideration of developmental difficulty. These data would indicate that semantic relevance to the predicate also influences relative acquisitional timetables. As expressed by Bybee, "the relevance of the morphological notion to the stem determines how cognitively distinguishable or discrete the resulting concept is" (1985, 208). Furthermore, Bybee hypothesizes that there exists a relevance principle that states that the more a concept has to do with the content of the verb, the closer it will occur to the verb stem. We see the effects of this principle in the acquisition of handshape in HANDLE and SASS forms. The handshape morpheme(s) in these forms are tightly bound to the predicate; without the handshape, there can be no sign construction. However, for the HANDLE handshapes, the type of information conveyed in the handshape is less relevant to the overall content of the verb, thus it appears less accessible to the language learner.

The differences in ability to produce SASS and HANDLE handshapes indicate that the creation of a paradigm based on visual-geometric features does not necessarily generalize to other similar paradigms. When the nature of the contrasts in SASS forms are "discovered" by the child, corresponding advances are not made for HANDLE handshapes.

### Development of the Use of Locative Morphemes

Unlike the results for the use of correct handshape, HANDLE predicates elicit the most accurate use of locative morphemes. Recall that for HANDLE predicates, syntactic space is used for verb inflection, which represents grammatical relations in ASL. It appears that the use of a locus for verb agreement is an easier task than using a locus to represent spatial relationships, as needed in CLASS and Difficult SASS structures. In contrast, CLASS predicates and Difficult SASS predicates produce prolonged developmental timetables for acquisition of syntactic space. These differences cannot be attributed to paradigm structure, as is the case with handshape acquisition. The morphosyntactic structure underlying syntactic space probably contributes to this differential acquisition. This is most likely the result of three factors.

First, the acquisition of the linguistic representation of spatial relationships in spoken and signed languages appears to reflect underlying cognitive complexity. As noted by Johnston and Slobin (1979), cognitive representation is the pacesetter for the development of the ability to represent spatial relationships linguistically (see also Johnston, 1984, 1985; Piaget and Inhelder, 1956; Washington and Naremore, 1978; Windmiller, 1976). Despite the nature of spatial representation in ASL, with its iconic substructure, deaf children proceed in a manner very similar to their hearing peers (Bellugi, 1988; Schick, 1986). The fact that results for ASL parallel those of spoken languages underscores this relationship between cognition and language form.

Second, it is likely that verb agreement and locative relationships in ASL are organized differently in the linguistic system. Although both systems are represented phonetically using syntactic space, the formal nature of these systems might be completely different. Verb agreement in many ways is subcategorization information. Verbs in ASL are notoriously idiosyncratic in their ability to inflect or in the type of inflection they receive. Some verbs take both subject and object agreement, and others take only subject agreement or only object agreement (Fischer and Gough, 1978; Kegl, 1988; Lillo-Martin, 1986; Padden, 1983). These types of differences are best considered as distinctions in thematic structure, which is specified in the subcategorization features for a particular verb. In contrast, it is possible that the use of syntactic space for locative relationships is best considered adjunct information. In these constructions, the presence of the locative information is a function of propositional content rather than the syntactic structure of a given verb. In general, children appear to be sensitive to special requirements of specific lexical items. They begin to create these subcategorizations from a very early stage of development, and major errors in subcategorization are conspicuously absent (Maratsos and Chalkley, 1981; Rispoli, 1987; Slobin, 1985b).

This distinction between verb agreement as subcategorization information and spatial relationships as adjunct information is supported by the fact that, in general, verb agreement is acquired early across languages (Bybee, 1985; Pinker, 1984; Slobin, 1985b). As Slobin (1985b) explains this phenomenon, verb agreement is a notion that is high on a "universal hierarchy," thus less evidence is needed to trigger its application in development (p. 1223).

Third, HANDLE forms are agentive, transitive predicates. In terms of acquisition, research has shown that transitive verbs appear earlier in children's lexicons than intransitive verbs (Huttenlocher, Smiley, and Charney, 1983; Schieffelin, 1985; Schwartz, 1988). Slobin concludes that "linguistic transitivity appears among the first notions marked by grammatical morphemes in languages as diverse as Hungarian, Polish, Hebrew, Turkish, and Kaluli" (1985b, 1,174). As noted by Slobin, a basic child grammar enables the child to give linguistic expression to certain prototypical scenes such as a canonical manipulative activity in which a scene is described from an agentive perspective. Certainly children seem to be aware of a transitive-intransitive distinction at the earliest stages of syntactic acquisition (Rispoli, 1987). Similarly, the earliest morphological markers are on verbs that are more prototypically transitive (for example, on "give," "take," "hit," but not "say" and "see"; Slobin, 1985b). Many linguists have proposed that transitivity is a universal core notion marked by grammars (for example, Hopper and Thompson, 1980; Lakoff and Johnson, 1980; Pinker, 1984).

### Implications

The results of this investigation indicate that the acquisition of handshape morphemes is not significantly related to age for children older than four and a half. This lack of age-related development suggests that handshape is an inadequate parameter to use as a benchmark of linguistic maturity. These results clarify conflicting observations from two independent studies: Kantor (1980) observes that children as old as eight years still produce classifier forms that are distinctly not adult level, but Supalla (1982) concludes that by age five and a half, his oldest subject was producing correct handshapes most of the time. The current results suggest that handshape use, for the most part, nears adult behavior at an earlier age than the use of spatial morphemes. Even at older ages, children continue to learn how to use space syntactically. These results are consistent with previous research, which has shown prolonged developmental timetables for some aspects of pronominal referencing (Lillo-Martin et al., 1985; Loew, 1984) and spatial representation (Schick, 1986). These data suggest that the key to characterizing and assessing ASL acquisition lies in the nature of the use of syntactic space.

Previous researchers have concluded that children learning ASL do not simply map an iconic use of space onto a linguistic system. As argued by Meier (1982), iconicity has little effect on the acquisition of a morphological system despite the potential for such an analysis. Not only does the current study add support to this conclusion, but it underscores the pervasive nature of the child's strategy. The system of verb agreement is only partially iconic; the idiosyncratic nature of subsets of verbs and its relationship with the underlying thematic structure might sufficiently obscure any iconic motivations for a young language learner. The linguistic expression of spatial relationships is more clearly and consistently iconic, yet children doggedly pursue a morphological analysis rather than capitalize on the iconic substructure. Furthermore, even when children appear to have developed the ability to incorporate syntactic space in their verb agreement, they do not necessarily incorporate linguistic space into all other predicate structures, such as spatial relationships.

Applying the notions of semantic bootstrapping (Pinker, 1984) to ASL, we are left with the notion that ASL learners use semantic meaning to discover the formal nature of grammar, but not so much that they discover that much of the classifier system is iconically motivated. This transparency of mapping does not appear to assist the child in developing meaning to form mapping. This means that a language learner, who has an innate propensity for semantics and formal structure, does not seem to look for formal structure in meaning itself. This could imply that children are not just looking for meaning in their language but are searching for structured organization. That is, the realization that the entire organization has meaning in its own right is a structural property and is not apparent to the language learner in any simple sense. It could also mean that iconicity itself is not perspicuous or transparent as much as it is metaphorical. Perhaps iconicity represents a higher order of linguistic organization, and as such, is more similar to notions that are metaphorical rather than structural. Given that some researchers have speculated that children come up with iconically motivated solutions to syntactic structures (see Slobin, 1985a), it remains unclear why some forms of iconicity appear to facilitate acquisition of language in children and others obscure the task.

## NOTES

This research was part of a dissertation completed under the direction of Ronnie B. Wilbur (advisor), Jackson T. Gandour, Laurence B. Leonard, and Richard G. Schwartz. Their help is gratefully acknowledged. This work was supported in part by a grant from the National Science Foundation, NSF BNS-8317572 to Ronnie B. Wilbur and a David Ross Fellowship from Purdue University. The superb ASL skills of Barbara Tubbs Gantt and David Geeslin strengthened this project. The generous participation of California State Schools for the Deaf, Fremont and Riverside, and the Kendall Demonstration Elementary School, Gallaudet University, is gratefully acknowledged.

1. The term "CLASS" is used to distinguish the group from predicates that have been termed classifiers in previous literature. CLASS is used to avoid confusion because HANDLEs and SASSes are also classifiers.
2. As described by Talmy (1975, 1985), a "basic motion event consists of one object (the 'Figure') moving or located with respect to another object (the reference-object or 'Ground')" (1985, 61). In ASL, the figure is usually represented on the signer's dominant hand, frequently the right hand. The ground is represented on the nondominant or left hand (compare "Central Object" and "Secondary Object" in Supalla, 1982).
3. Current terminology.
4. Newport's analysis was done on same data set as Supalla (1982); three deaf children of deaf parents, ages 2.4 to 5.1 years. The movement root, as analyzed by Newport and Supalla includes morphemes considered as locative morphemes in the current typology.
5. The accuracy of movement (MOV) morphemes was also scored, but the results of this analysis will not be reported in this paper.
6. Reliability was determined as a percentage of agreement: the number of agreements divided by the number of agreements and disagreements, multiplied by 100.

# REFERENCES

Allan, K. (1977). Classifiers. *Language* 53:285–311.

Baker, M. (1988). *Incorporation: A theory of grammatical function changing*. Chicago, IL: University of Chicago Press.

Bellugi, U. (1988). The acquisition of a spatial language. In *The development of language and language researchers*, edited by F. Kessel, 153–85. Hillsdale, NJ: Lawrence Erlbaum Associates.

Berman, R. (1981). Language development and language knowledge: Evidence from the acquisition of Hebrew morphophonology. *Journal of Child Language* 8:265–82.

———. (1982). Verb-pattern alternation: The interface of morphology, syntax, and semantics in Hebrew child language. *Journal of Child Language* 9:169–91.

Bybee, J. (1985). *Morphology: A study of the relation between meaning and form*. Philadelphia: John Benjamins Publishing Co.

Denny, J. P. 1982. Semantics of the Inuktitut (Eskimo) spatial deictics. *International Journal of American Linguistics* 48:359–84.

Fischer, S., and Gough, B. (1978). Verbs in American Sign Language. *Sign Language Studies* 18:17–48.

Gandour, J., Petty, S., Dardarananda, R., Dechongkit, S., and Mukngoen, S. (1984). The acquisition of numeral classifiers in Thai. *Linguistics* 22:455–79.

Gee, J., and Kegl, J. (1982). Semantic perspicuity and the locative hypothesis: Implications for acquisition. *Journal of Education* 164:185–289.

Hopper, P., and Thompson, S. (1980). Transitivity. *Language* 56:251–99.

Huttenlocher, J., Smiley, P., and Charney, R. (1983). Emergence of action-categories in the child: Evidence from verb meanings. *Psychological Review* 90:72–93.

Johnston, J. (1984). Acquisition of locative meanings: Behind and in front of. *Journal of Child Language* 11:407–22.

———. (1985). Cognitive prerequisites: The evidence from children learning English. In *The crosslinguistic study of language acquisition*, vol. 2, *Theoretical issues*, edited by D. Slobin, 961–1004. Hillsdale, NJ: Lawrence Erlbaum Associates.

———, and Slobin, D. (1979). The development of locative expressions in English, Italian, Serbo-Croatian, and Turkish. *Journal of Child Language* 16:531–47.

Kantor, R. (1980). The acquisition of classifiers in American Sign Language. *Sign Language Studies* 28:193–208.

Kegl, J. (1985). Causative marking and the construal of agency in ASL. *Chicago Linguistic Society* 21/2:120–37.

———. (1988). Predicate argument structure and verb-class organization in the ASL lexicon. In this proceedings.

Klima, E., and Bellugi, U. (1979). *The signs of language*. Cambridge, MA: Harvard University Press.

Lakoff, G., and Johnson, M. (1980). *Metaphors we live by*. Chicago, IL: University of Chicago Press.

Lillo-Martin, D. (1986). Two kinds of null arguments in American Sign Language. *Natural Language and Linguistic Theory* 4:415–44.

———, Bellugi, U., Struxness, L., and O'Grady, M. (1985). The acquisition of spatially organized syntax. *Papers and Reports on Child Language Development* 24:70–80.

Loew, R. (1984). Roles and references in American Sign Language: A developmental perspective. Ph.D. diss., University of Minnesota.

MacWhinney, B. (1978). The acquisition of morphophonology. *Monographs of the Society for Research in Child Development*, 43, Whole no. 1.

———. (1985). Hungarian language acquisition as an exemplification of a general model of grammatical development. In *The crosslinguistic study of language acquisition*, vol. 2, *Theoretical issues*, edited by D. Slobin, 1069–1155. Hillsdale, NJ: Lawrence Erlbaum Associates.

Mandel, M. (1977). Iconic devices in American Sign Language. In *On the other hand: New perspectives in American Sign Language*, edited by L. Friedman, 57–107. New York: Academic Press.

Maratsos, M., and Chalkley, M. (1981). The internal language of children's syntax: The ontogenesis and representation of syntactic categories. In *Children's language*, vol. 2, edited by K. Nelson, 127–214. New York: Gardner Press.

Matsumoto, Y. (1984). The child's acquisition of Japanese numeral classifiers. Paper presented at the International Congress for the Study of Child Language, 11 July, at University of Texas, Austin.

McDonald, B. (1982). Aspects of the American Sign Language predicate system. Ph.D. diss., State University of New York, Buffalo.

McIntire, M., Newkirk, D., Hutchins, S., and Poizner, H. (1987). Hands and faces: A preliminary inventory for written ASL. *Sign Language Studies* 56:197–241.

Meier, R. (1982). Icons, analogues, and morphemes: The acquisition of verb agreement in American Sign Language. Ph.D. diss., University of California, San Diego.

Newport, E. (1982). Task specificity in language learning? Evidence from speech perception and American Sign Language. In *Language acquisition: The state of the art*, edited by E. Wanner and L. Gleitman, 450–86. New York: Cambridge University Press.

———, and Meier, R. (1985). The acquisition of American Sign Language. In *The crosslinguistic study of language acquisition*, vol. 1, *The data*, edited by D. Slobin, 881–938. Hillsdale, NJ: Lawrence Erlbaum Associates.

Padden, C. (1983). Interaction of morphology and syntax in American Sign Language. Ph.D. diss., University of California, San Diego.

Piaget, J., and Inhelder, B. (1956). *The child's conception of space*. New York: Norton.

Pinker, S. (1984). *Language learnability and language development*. Cambridge, MA: Harvard University Press.

Rispoli, M. (1987). The acquisition of the transitive and intransitive action verb categories in Japanese. *First Language* 7:183–200.

Schick, B. (1986). Groping for orientation: The representation of space and form in child ASL. Paper presented at the Boston University Child Language Conference, 17–19 October, Boston.

———. (1987). The acquisition of classifier predicates in American Sign Language. Ph.D. diss., Purdue University. West Lafayette, Indiana.

———. (in press). Classifier predicates in American Sign Language. *International Journal of Sign Linguistics*.

Schieffelin, B. (1985). The acquisition of Kaluli. In *The crosslinguistic study of language acquisition* vol. 1, *The data*, edited by D. Slobin, 525–93. Hillsdale, NJ: Lawrence Erlbaum Associates.

Schwartz, R. (1988). Early action word acquisition in normal and language-impaired children. *Applied Psycholinguistics* 9:111–22.

Shepard-Kegl, J. (1985). Locative relations in American Sign Language: Word formation, syntax and discourse. Ph.D. diss., MIT.

Slobin, D. (1982). Universal and particular in the acquisition of language. In *Language acquisition: The state of the art*, edited by E. Wanner and L. R. Gleitman, 128–70. New York: Cambridge University Press.

———. (1985a). The child as a linguistic icon-maker. In *Iconicity in syntax*, edited by J. Haiman, 221–48. Amsterdam: John Benjamins Publishing Co.

———. (1985b). Crosslinguistic evidence for the language-making capacity. In *The crosslinguistic study of language acquisition*, vol. 2, *Theoretical issues*, edited by D. Slobin, 1157–1249. Hillsdale, NJ: Lawrence Erlbaum Associates.

Supalla, T. (1978). Morphology of verbs of motion and location in American Sign Language. In *National symposium on sign language research and teaching*, edited by F. Caccamise and D. Hicks. Silver Spring, MD: National Association of the Deaf.

———. (1982). Structure and acquisition of verbs of motion and location in American Sign Language. Ph.D. diss., University of California, San Diego.

————. (1986). The classifier system in American Sign Language. In *Noun classification and categorization*, edited by C. Craig, 181–214. Philadelphia: John Benjamins Publishing Co.

Talmy, L. (1975). Semantics and syntax of motion. In *Syntax and semantics*, vol. 4, edited by J. Kimball, 181–238. New York: Academic Press.

————. (1985). Lexicalization patterns: Semantic structure in lexical forms. In *Language typology and syntactic description*, vol. 3, *Grammatical categories and the lexicon*, edited by T. Shopen, 57–149. New York: Cambridge University Press.

Washington, D., and Naremore, R. (1978). Children's use of spatial prepositions in two and three dimensional space. *Journal of Speech and Hearing Research* 21:151–65.

Wilbur, R. (1987). *American Sign Language: Linguistic and applied dimensions*. Boston: College-Hill Press.

————, Klima, E., and Bellugi, E. (1983). Roots: The search for the origins of signs in ASL. *Chicago Linguistic Society* 19:314–36.

Windmiller, M. (1976). A child's conception of space as a prerequisite to his understanding of spatial locatives. *Genetic Psychology Monographs* 94:227–48.

# Index

An *f* following a page number indicates a figure; a *t* following a page number indicates tabular material.